OPEN DOORS

THE WORLD BANK GROUP

THE INTERNATIONAL MONETARY FUND

THE BROOKINGS INSTITUTION

This book is based on a conference entitled Open Doors: Foreign Participation in Financial Systems in Developing Countries, held on April 19–21, 2001, in New York City. The conference was jointly sponsored by the World Bank Group, the International Monetary Fund, and the Brookings Institution.

The previous volumes in this series, Financial Markets and Development: The Crisis in Emerging Markets *and* Managing Financial and Corporate Distress: Lessons from Asia, *published in 1999 and 2000, are available from the Brookings Institution Press.*

ROBERT E. LITAN
PAUL MASSON
MICHAEL POMERLEANO
Editors

OPEN DOORS

Foreign Participation
in Financial Systems
in Developing Countries

BROOKINGS INSTITUTION PRESS
Washington, D.C.

ABOUT BROOKINGS

The Brookings Institution is a private nonprofit organization devoted to research, education, and publication on important issues of domestic and foreign policy. Its principal purpose is to bring knowledge to bear on current and emerging policy problems. The Institution maintains a position of neutrality on issues of public policy. Interpretations or conclusions in Brookings publications should be understood to be solely those of the authors.

Copyright © 2001

THE BROOKINGS INSTITUTION

1775 Massachusetts Avenue, N.W., Washington, D.C. 20036
www.brookings.edu

Library of Congress Cataloging-in-Publication data

Open doors : foreign participation in financial systems in developing countries /
Robert E. Litan, Paul Masson, and Michael Pomerleano, editors.
    p. cm.
Based on a conference held on Apr. 19–21, 2001, in New York City.
    Includes bibliographical references and index.
    ISBN 0-8157-0245-0 (pbk. : alk. paper)
    1. Financial services industry—Developing countries—Congresses.
I. Litan, Robert E., 1950– II. Masson, Paul. III. Pomerleano, Michael.
    HG195 .O64 2001
    332.1'09172'4—dc21   2001004821

9 8 7 6 5 4 3 2 1

The paper used in this publication meets minimum requirements of the
American National Standard for Information Sciences—Permanence of Paper for
Printed Library Materials, ANSI Z39.48-1992.

M/L

Typeset in Adobe Garamond

Composition by Oakland Street Publishing
Arlington, Virginia

Printed by R. R. Donnelley and Sons
Harrisonburg, Virginia

Contents

v

PART THREE
What Foreign Institutions Do in Emerging Markets: Sector Report

PART FOUR
Policies toward Financial Sector FDI

PART FIVE
Moving into the Future:
Potential for Financial Sector E-Commerce

ROBERT E. LITAN
PAUL MASSON
MICHAEL POMERLEANO

1

BK Title: *Introduction*

NIA

One of the more noteworthy financial developments in developing countries of the past decade is the enormous growth of foreign direct investment (FDI): from $36 billion annually in 1991 to $173 billion in 1997, according to the World Bank's 2001 *Global Development Finance* report. Although the growth in FDI flows cooled off somewhat after the Asian, Russian, and Brazilian financial crises of 1997–98, in 2000 they still stood at an estimated $178 billion, not only higher than before these crises but well above the level at the beginning of the decade.

Given the importance of finance to economic growth, it is natural to ask how important FDI has become in that particular sector in emerging market countries, what benefits and costs have been associated with it, and what changes in policy toward foreign financial firms would be in the economic interests of developing countries in the years ahead. Another important issue facing these countries is how not to be left behind by the coming wave of e-finance that some say will revolutionize financial sectors in both advanced and developing countries.

These were the questions posed at the third annual conference on emerging markets finance conducted by the World Bank, the International Monetary Fund (IMF), and the Brookings Institution on April 19–21, 2001, in New York and attended by 170 financial experts and policymakers from around the world. This volume brings together the papers presented at the conference and provides a summary of two panel discussions: one by representatives of various large foreign financial institutions with operations in emerging markets, the other by experts in the burgeoning field of e-finance.

Among other things, the following chapters confirm the rising presence of foreign firms in financial sectors in key parts of the developing world, although Asia and Africa still lag significantly behind other emerging markets in this respect. In a number of countries, the foreign presence has increased from less than 10 percent to 50 percent or more within the past decade. The chapters also document the important benefits foreign firms bring to the markets they enter: added investment; cutting-edge technologies and managerial practices (especially risk management); and, because they tend to be more diversified than local institutions, more financial stability. At the same time, the globalization of finance raises new policy issues that must be addressed, most prominently the coordination of regulation and supervision across national borders.

On balance, however, foreign financial institutions provide net benefits to the countries in which they invest. For this reason alone, it is in the interest of countries that now restrict foreign entry in some form to drop those limitations, whether unilaterally or through multilateral negotiations. A crucial issue is how best to sequence that liberalization. What are the regulatory practices that need to be put in place? Should domestic financial institutions be made solvent first? This has been a particularly difficult problem in many economies that were formerly centrally planned, where state-owned banks held a large portfolio of nonperforming loans. Although conference participants did not settle the sequencing issues, several of their comments generated an animated discussion of the topic. Many argued that waiting until domestic institutions' problems were settled before opening up was a recipe for endless delay.

How Important Is Financial Sector FDI?

As Donald Mathieson and Jorge Roldos of the IMF point out in chapter 2, entry by foreign firms in the financial sectors of emerging markets increased significantly during the 1990s, especially in banking. In the Czech Republic, Hungary, and Poland, foreign ownership of banks (including banks that were at least 40 percent owned) rose from an average of 14 percent in 1994 to 57 percent in 1999. A similar trend occurred in Latin America, where by the end of the decade foreign banks accounted for 40 percent or more of the banking systems of Argentina, Chile, and Venezuela. Foreign bank penetration remains far lower in Africa and Asia, although even in Asia, it increased markedly during this period (from 1.3 percent to 13.2 percent).

What accounts for these increases? Banks in source countries, mainly in the developed world, have pushed outward into emerging markets by and large in search of higher profits. There is another reason: foreign banks have followed corporate customers that have opened foreign operations. This, in fact, was the reason Deutsche Bank was founded in the nineteenth century, with its original four offices in Shanghai, Yokohama, London, and Bremen. But banks cannot expand abroad unless destination countries let them in. Over time, many emerging market governments have taken this course. Since the early 1990s, Mathieson and Roldós report, attitudes toward foreign banks and other financial firms have experienced a sea change in much of the developing world arising out of periodic financial crises, or in the case of Eastern Europe, because new governments learned that formerly state-owned banks were in effect bankrupt. Foreign banks have been welcomed to help reduce the costs of resolving these financial problems.

For the most part, foreign banks have helped increase the competitiveness and efficiency of the domestic banks in the markets they have entered. The results are reflected in lower operating costs and smaller margins between interest rates on loans and deposits, not just among the foreign banks but among domestic banks as well. Mathieson and Roldos do not believe the verdict is as clear, at least not yet, as to whether foreign banks have contributed to more stability. In certain cases, foreign banks have pulled out in times of trouble, and in others they have remained. Nor do the authors find unequivocal evidence that foreign banks have reduced market volatility or increased the availability of credit to local borrowers.

Nonetheless, there is some evidence to suggest that most retail foreign banks have not pulled back from emerging markets hit by financial crisis. Where they have done so, it has been due more to problems in their home countries (especially Japan). The latest proposed Basel capital standards—which, if adopted, are scheduled to become effective in 2005—may encourage foreign banks to pull back from emerging countries in the future, however. This is because the proposed standards rely heavily on ratings agencies to determine how much capital international banks must maintain for various types of loans. In the aftermath of financial crises in particular countries, ratings agencies tend to lower their ratings on all emerging market debt simultaneously, and this could curtail bank lending in these markets across the board.

Foreign banks have not been the only financial firms to wade into emerging markets in recent years. In chapter 4, Harold Skipper of Georgia State University documents a similar, although less extensive, trend among foreign insurers. Insurance, Skipper explains, is important to economic development because it spreads the cost of risk, promotes economic stability for both families and firms, and mobilizes savings. Nonetheless, insurance in emerging markets remains less well developed than banking, especially in property-casualty lines, although life insurance is significant and rapidly growing in Southeast Asia, South Africa, and other selected countries where savings rates are high and public pension systems are weak or nonexistent. In several Asian countries, foreign insurers now account for about half of the life market, and a bit less of property-casualty, despite various noninstitutional and cultural barriers to foreign firms. Like foreign banks, Skipper reports, foreign insurers tend to have stimulated improvements in productivity in the markets they have entered. Moreover, the importance of internationalizing insurance risks is illustrated by the sinking of the forty-story Petrobras oil platform in Brazil in 2001, a facility that produces 6 percent of the country's entire national oil output. No one country's market can provide cover for such loss exposures.

Still, many emerging markets maintain some restrictions against foreign insurers, with only four countries having committed to "full liberalization" under the General Agreement on Trade in Services (GATS) implemented as part of the Uruguay Round trade agreement of 1995.

What Do Foreign Financial Institutions Do in Emerging Markets?

It is important in designing policy regarding the entry of foreign financial institutions to understand what lines of business they tend to emphasize. Michael Pomerleano of the World Bank and George Vojta of the Financial Services Forum examine the behavior of the largest multinational or global banks in chapter 3. These institutions are capable of offering cutting-edge wholesale and retail services, generally at lower cost than purely domestic banks. Allowing such institutions to enter a market brings much greater competitive pressure on local banks to consolidate and reach a scale at which they can effectively compete.

At the same time, as Thomas Fischer of Deutsche Bank also confirms later in this volume, global banks tend to concentrate on the largest corporate customers that have the greatest need for their sophisticated services (including foreign exchange and risk management, derivatives trading, underwriting of securities, and cross-border mergers and acquisitions). Although local banks worry that the global banks will run them out of the business of lending to individuals and small and medium-sized enterprises (SMEs), these concerns have proved to be unfounded. As a result, global banks tend to complement—and not substitute for—the banking services of the locally oriented institutions. Moreover, for countries that have experienced banking problems, foreign institutions help in restructuring, either through outright purchases or joint ventures and alliances.

There is a dichotomy in the operations of large foreign banks in emerging markets, however. Some large multinational banks—the local subsidiaries of Citibank, HSBC, and Standard Chartered—have developed strong and profitable local franchises with a wide range of services. Others, including JPMorgan-Chase and Deutsche Bank, are much more selective and in some cases are narrowing their activities in emerging markets, refocusing on investment banking and private banking activities.

Ranjit Singh (a member of the Securities Commission in Malaysia and chairman of an emerging markets securities market working group of the international organization of securities regulators, IOSCO), Attila Emam, and Kar Mei Tang present the results of a similar study of foreign entry into the securities business in chapter 5. They find that developing countries have become more welcoming of foreign firms in this business because they see the need to finance their nonfinancial enterprises and feel pressure to liberalize under the GATS. Singh and his colleagues also report the preliminary results of a survey of foreign firms operating in seventeen emerging markets, of which nine (including nearly all Asian countries in the sample) explicitly allow foreign majority ownership of domestic securities firms (and seven allow 100 percent ownership). The survey broadly revealed that foreign firms did not "run" from—and in some cases actually increased—their participation in local markets that had suffered financial crises. As for securities exchanges, in four of the seventeen markets at least one of the exchanges had been demutualized, a trend now evident among security exchanges in developed countries (as discussed by Benn Steil in chapter 11)—and another four are looking to do the same soon.

In chapter 6, Paul Masson summarizes the experiences of several financial institutions already involved in emerging markets. One such institution is the International Finance Corporation (IFC), which has made broad investments in private firms in emerging markets. Half of these are in domestic banks and the rest in private equity, venture funds, asset-based financing, and other related activities. In the IFC's view, financial institutions arise in response to the development of a middle class in emerging markets. The IFC has concentrated its investments in building secondary markets for mortgages to encourage home ownership, promote various savings vehicles (pension plans, insurance, and contractual savings systems), and facilitate retail banking, which, as Pomerleano and Vojta document in chapter 3, is still largely the province of domestic banks in these markets. Although Latin America is the IFC's largest region, the institution views Africa as a potentially large market, as liberalization and privatization proceed in that part of the world.

By contrast, Deutsche Bank's emerging markets strategy has historically concentrated on Asia. The bank located there in order to follow its corporate customers and plans to continue that function. Though it provides full banking services and has an extensive local presence, after the experience of the Asian crisis it no longer tries to compete with local banks in collateralized lending to smaller companies. Another global investment firm, Goldman Sachs, has found that technology makes it possible to avoid having to establish a major local presence in most emerging markets. Through New York or a limited local office, Goldman Sachs is able to offer global products for which it has a comparative advantage. The firm has become a leading underwriter of sovereign and corporate bonds issued from emerging markets, and non-U.S. activities now account for more than half of its revenues.

AIG, a global insurer founded in Shanghai, also has strong Asian roots. In addition to pursuing worldwide insurance activities, the company has recently sponsored more than twenty investment funds with assets in emerging markets. Unlike some other fund sponsors, AIG provides roughly 10 percent of the capital of each of the funds it sponsors, looking to exit (like the IFC) through initial public offerings and sales either to strategic buyers or to local managers. At AIG, a decision to invest depends on several aspects of the local environment: macroeconomic stability, a pro-market orientation, rule of law, and transparency of government bodies and regulations.

Regional Case Studies

Three chapters in this volume outline the experiences of countries and regions that have recently welcomed significant foreign investment in their financial sectors. The Czech Republic, as Donald Simonson of the University of New Mexico notes in chapter 7, privatized its formerly state-owned banks in the early 1990s but initially restricted share purchases by large foreign banks, hoping that Czech ownership would evolve. Emphasizing fairness toward its citizens, the government gave them vouchers, which maintained domestic ownership. Foreign interest was also deterred by the absence of effective legal support for creditors: weak laws and judicial administration. By the end of the decade, however, the main Czech banks were paralyzed by large holdings of nonperforming loans, so the government turned to foreign banks to mount a rescue and strengthened bank supervision by adopting international standards. Today, the Czech banking sector is significantly stronger and more competitive as a result.

In chapter 8, Jennifer Crystal, B. Gerald Dages, and Linda Goldberg of the Federal Reserve Bank of New York report similar positive results from the rapid increase in foreign ownership of banks in Latin America during the 1990s. For the most part, the team finds that local banks acquired by foreign owners became financially stronger in comparison with their domestic counterparts. Foreign banks in Argentina, Chile, and Colombia demonstrated higher and more stable average loan growth and higher risk-based capital ratios. Surprisingly, however, their profitability was only comparable to or weaker than that of domestic banks. This latter finding, coupled with the fact that foreign banks had higher loan loss provisions than domestic competitors during the period studied, suggests to the authors that foreign banks have not "cherry-picked" their loan customers but instead have taken more aggressive actions to deal with bad loans when they deteriorate. On average, the foreign institutions also did not "cut and run" when certain Latin American countries encountered financial difficulties during the decade. Because large-scale foreign ownership is a fairly recent phenomenon emerging in a rather inhospitable macroeconomic environment, however, the authors think it may take more time to gauge the true competitive dynamics of increased foreign ownership.

Chapter 9, by Nicholas Lardy of the Brookings Institution, focuses on China, where until recently foreign financial firms of all types have been subject to significant restrictions. Nonetheless, over 100 foreign banks with offices in China are poised to expand as China meets the conditions to which it agreed in order to become a member of the World Trade Organization (WTO). Some of these firms also may be in a position to help ease the cost of dealing with China's large problem of nonperforming loans now held by its state-owned banks (or transferred to asset management companies for resale). Still, Lardy expects that foreign bank expansion will be a slow undertaking in China for at least two reasons. One is that the government continues to limit the ratio of a foreign bank's domestic to foreign currency deposits. Even when this restriction is fully lifted, Lardy points out, there will be a shortage of creditworthy (by Western standards) domestic borrowers. Foreign insurance companies are also likely to enter China fairly slowly because, unlike banks, which expect to have all ownership restrictions eventually lifted as part of China's planned accession to the WTO, foreign insurers will continue to be limited to no more than a majority ownership interest. Even tighter restrictions will continue in the securities and fund management industries. Thus foreign financial institutions are unlikely to take a major role in the near future in the necessary process of modernizing China's financial sector.

Future Policies toward Financial Sector FDI

Like several other contributors, Edward Graham of the Institute for International Economics argues in chapter 10 that allowing foreign firms freely into financial activities appears to have overwhelming economic benefits. More controversially, Graham claims that this should happen even in countries experiencing financial problems, despite fears that foreign institutions could then destroy weak domestic competitors. If these fears constitute a significant political constraint, Graham suggests that governments could condition foreign entry—during some transition period—on acquiring weak or insolvent domestic institutions. In addition, countries fearing domination by foreign firms from one particular country (where financial difficulties may cause them at some time to pull back from activities abroad) could seek to diversify source country owners to address this concern. But maintaining existing investment restrictions can only deepen the cost of resolving a financial crisis, while penalizing potentially creditworthy borrowers who might otherwise not be able to obtain loans from the existing troubled banks or other financial institutions. Of course, countries that have strong domestic financial systems but nonetheless continue to restrict foreign entry have no good economic excuse for doing so, in Graham's view.

Two other factors of great potential importance to developing countries, as Benn Steil of the Council of Foreign Relations notes in chapter 11, are the technological advances that would sharply reduce financial transactions costs and the development of liquid and efficient securities markets. These changes have led to radical declines in the need for exchange intermediaries and hence have led to the restructuring of securities exchanges in advanced countries. As a result, exchanges in advanced countries have tended to demutualize and to be incorporated instead. Steil argues that since the costs of introducing trading systems and central securities depositories have already been incurred abroad, developing countries should import these technologies rather than start from scratch.

Moreover, given the large cost savings made possible by electronic networks, Steil advises emerging markets to abandon the traditional mutual exchange model—one that relies on floor broker-members to complete transactions as intermediaries on behalf of others—and to move instead to the vastly cheaper, privately owned electronic networks to facilitate the trading of securities. The listing of securities, which should be a competitive business open to nonexchanges subject to perhaps minimum government standards, can and should be separated from the infrastructure of trading itself, which, given the extraordinary advances in information technology, can be contracted out (as can settlement of trades, which need not be tied to the systems used to execute the trades). Often, the best contractors will be foreign.

Steil also urges emerging market exchanges not to feel compelled to provide continuous trading. For lightly traded stocks where liquidity may be a problem, the solution lies in periodic call auctions in which bids are cumulated and prices are set several times a day. Indeed, Steil notes that the Warsaw Stock Exchange started out with one call auction *per week.*

Much of the progress toward liberalization of foreign restrictions in the past has been in the context of multilateral negotiations, where the relaxations are reciprocal. The most recent example is the Financial Services Agreement (FSA) concluded in December 1997 under the auspices of the GATS. In chapter 12, Pierre Sauvé of the Organization for Economic Cooperation and Development (OECD) and Karsten Steinfatt of the Organization of American States survey the prospects for further reciprocal liberalization in light of the backlash against the WTO triggered in Seattle in 1999.

On the bright side, the authors point out, financial communities in developed countries are still showing a strong interest in further progress. But they also caution that because the commitments toward liberalization of ownership and activity restrictions in the financial sector under the FSA have been in effect for only two years, it is far from clear how much appetite developing countries have for additional commitments so soon after the earlier round. Furthermore, the negotiating agenda in the financial sector is a complicated one, involving such new issues as the applicability of existing restrictions to Internet-based finance, as well as how those restrictions can be rationalized in the new world of finance, where traditional barriers between different lines of business (banking, insurance, and securities) are becoming less relevant elsewhere around the world. Sauvé and Steinfatt conclude that the best chance for further reciprocal liberalization would be a new broad round of WTO negotiations launched by OECD governments that would afford ample opportunities for trade-offs between liberalizations in financial and nonfinancial arenas. In the meantime, they view the gradual development of international standards for financial supervision as a useful way of locking in measures to maintain competition in financial markets.

However rapidly current restrictions on foreign direct investment may be removed, governments both in emerging markets and in developed economies that are home to many global financial institutions also face a new set of policy challenges associated with the increased globalization of finance. As Mathieson and Roldós note in chapter 2, it is essential to maintain and implement antitrust policies to prevent undue concentration of their financial systems, especially where foreign firms are successful in driving out local competition. All countries also need to improve cross-border coordination of financial supervision, regulation, and the sharing of confidential information. At the same time, say various contributors, regulators in emerging markets can benefit from the risk mitigation and other managerial skills that foreign financial institutions bring with them when they enter these markets. Graham adds that strengthening domestic supervision is especially important after a crisis if bank deposits have been legally or de facto protected against loss. Otherwise, such guarantees can lead to a significant "moral hazard" by encouraging imprudent lending behavior and thus may lay the groundwork for future crises.

The Role of Financial Sector E-Commerce

The e-commerce revolution sweeping across many developed countries is also making its presence felt in emerging market countries and others that are nearing developed-country status. Indeed, South Korea and Singapore are considerably ahead of much of the developed world in the percentage of the population online. Mobile telephones, which will be used more and more to access the Internet, also are rapidly penetrating parts of the developing world. Still, e-commerce in emerging markets is by and large far behind that of the developed world. Will this change?

Philip Turner of the Bank for International Settlements is optimistic that it will, although the change will be gradual in many emerging markets because their telecommunications infrastructure is typically weaker than in the developed world. As Turner observes in chapter 13, the Internet is more than just an evolutionary development; it promises a revolution. Furthermore, the Internet's impact on financial systems is very uncertain at this point, and the need for infrastructure support for online activities will be massive. What this means for the competitive position of local banks in developing countries is unclear. At the same time, e-finance undoubtedly will have a far-reaching effect on the financial systems in emerging market countries. Although it is also likely to increase operational risk in the financial sector, regulators must try to be flexible in responding to technological changes. It will be essential to monitor service providers and not just financial firms and to enhance international regulatory cooperation, since the Internet respects no national boundaries.

In chapter 14, four comments on Turner's chapter extend his analysis in several respects. Thomas Glaessner of the World Bank, for instance, calls on telecommunications authorities around the world to prevent their incumbent telephone monopolies from refusing interconnection with other providers and from charging excessive rates for doing so. Nonetheless, assuming these difficulties eventually are overcome, the substantial gains in efficiency promised by the Internet—banking transactions costs can be reduced by a factor of 100, which banks in some countries, such as Brazil, are exploiting—suggest its increased penetration is inevitable. But as this happens, policymakers in both the developed and developing world will face new challenges: most notably, they will have to learn how to monitor operational risks of institutions that use the Internet, both for the sake of their customers and of the system (since many institutions may be using the same software); they will have to decide which country's law applies when bank transactions falter; and they must protect financial systems from the increased involvement of nonfinancial firms in finance, which the Internet makes possible.

The development of e-finance will also hinge on other factors. Both Ed Horowitz and Ed Ritscher emphasize in their comments the importance of trust on the Internet, a challenge that may be met, at least in part, by public infrastructure technology that will facilitate the authentication of parties doing business on the Internet. Financial institutions face special challenges that argue further for international rules of authentication and certification, says Horowitz. Ritscher notes that the emergence of business-to-business exchanges and the growing interest of telecommunications companies in completing payments on the Web threaten to disenfranchise banks in particular. He nonetheless believes that banks and other financial institutions can preserve their profitability by developing new business models that take advantage of the low cost infrastructure of the Internet.

Robert Ledig highlights a potential thorn in the side of Internet commerce: emerging disputes over whose laws apply to e-commerce. Ledig points to a growing tendency among developed countries at least to assert extraterritorial jurisdiction, in effect, requiring web sites either to screen out material that might be offensive to residents of different countries, or at a minimum, to tailor disclosures that are specific to these countries. A proliferation of these jurisdictional requirements could impede the growth of global e-commerce.

The overall conclusion that can be drawn from the discussions in this volume is that developments in emerging financial markets are creating tremendous opportunities for domestic and foreign firms, on the one hand, and enormous challenges for regulators, on the other. Most of the contributors believe that relaxing restrictions and attracting foreign competitors in the financial field will increase efficiency and thus encourage growth. At the same time, the entry of foreign firms and the development of new technologies (such as e-finance) may increase the level of financial sector risk and make best-practice financial supervision all the more important.

PART I

How Important Is Financial Sector FDI and What Are Its Impacts?

DONALD J. MATHIESON
JORGE ROLDÓS

2

Foreign Banks in Emerging Markets

During the 1990s, the growing presence of foreign-owned financial institutions, especially in the banking system, was one of the most striking structural changes in the financial systems of many emerging markets. As noted by Barry Eichengreen and Michael Mussa, many emerging markets have been reducing barriers to trade in financial services since the early 1990s, but it was not until the second half of the 1990s that foreign financial institutions acquired a substantial presence there.[1]

The increase in foreign participation has led to a series of studies on the effects of foreign bank entry in domestic financial systems. Although the sharp rise in foreign bank participation in many emerging markets is clear evidence that the authorities in these countries have concluded that foreign bank entry will have an overall positive effect on the banking system, the effects on the efficiency and stability of the local banking systems have been much debated in many countries. A general finding of the empirical studies that have included mixed samples of mature and emerging markets or have focused on emerging markets is that foreign banks in emerging markets have been more efficient in both costs and profits than domestic

We would like to thank Silvia Iorgova for her efficient and dedicated efforts as a research assistant on this project.

1. Eichengreen and Mussa (1998).

banks—whereas the opposite is true for mature markets.[2] Moreover, significant foreign bank entry was associated with a reduction in the profitability and the overall expenses of domestic banks.

The evidence on the stability effects of foreign bank presence is more mixed, but an increasing body of evidence points to the fact that banks with a long-term commitment to emerging markets tend to provide a stable influence. Evidence from the Japanese and Asian banking crises indicates that banks sometimes choose to shrink host country operations more quickly than those at home when they have home country problems. However, recent case studies suggest that foreign banks in Argentina and Mexico have expanded operations even when they face problems in the host country. Furthermore, David E. Palmer notes that U.S. money center banks usually sustained the operations of their offshore branches and subsidiaries during the recent emerging market crises.[3]

In this chapter we study these—and other—issues related to the increased role of foreign banks for a large sample of emerging markets. We measure the increase in foreign participation in some key emerging market banking systems during the 1990s, using measures of foreign control of domestic entities as well as the more standard measures of foreign participation. We show that in Central Europe, for example, total bank assets controlled by foreign-owned banks rose from 8 percent in 1994 to 56 percent in 1999, while in some major Latin American countries, almost half of total bank assets are controlled by foreign institutions. We find that an index of banking crises helps explain to a large extent the increased foreign bank presence in emerging markets.[4]

We examine how the lending and deposit-taking activities of domestic and foreign banks respond to large domestic and external shocks and the degree to which foreign banks have been supported by parents during a crisis or difficulty. The final section addresses emerging policy issues, including effective cross-border prudential supervisory and regulatory policies for large complex banking organizations and the new instruments and derivative products they introduce, parental support offered to local establishments, banking concentration issues that can arise, and the effects of foreign entry on the level of systemic risk in the banking system.

---

2. See, for instance, Claessens, Demirgüc-Kunt, and Huizinga (1999).
3. Peek and Rosengren (2000). See Goldberg, Dages, and Kinney (2000) and Palmer (2000).
4. Based on the work of Kaminsky and Reinhart (1999) and Caprio and Klingebiel (1999).

Increase in Foreign Bank Entry to Emerging Markets

Foreign ownership in emerging markets banking systems has increased dramatically during the second half of the 1990s, and further increases are already occurring in many countries. However, trends across different regions diverge widely, with Central Europe showing much larger increases than Asia (table 2-1). The increased activities of foreign banks in emerging markets can be measured either in terms of foreign bank participation in domestic banking markets or in terms of how effectively foreign banks control banking activities. For example, while foreign banks might participate in a number of joint ventures as minority shareholders, the overall operations of the banks might be controlled by the local majority shareholders. Table 2-1, using publicly available balance sheet and ownership data, presents measures of participation and control by foreign banks in different regions.[5] Foreign participation is measured as the ratio of the sum across all banks of the assets of each bank multiplied by the percentage of equity held by foreigners to total bank assets. In contrast, table 2-1 presents two measures of the extent of bank assets under effective foreign control since corporate control may not be directly and exclusively related to the proportion of a bank's equity held by a particular owner.[6] While holding more than 50 percent of total equity typically ensures effective control of a bank, analysts have argued that hostile takeovers are unlikely to occur when the existing owners hold more than 40 percent of bank equity.[7] Foreign control is thus measured by the ratio of the sum of the total assets of those banks in which foreigners own more than either 40 or 50 percent of total equity to total bank assets.[8]

5. The data are from Fitch IBCA's Bank Scope database. There are three major advantages of using this database. First, coverage is comprehensive, with banks included accounting for about 90 percent of the assets of banks in each country; second, the agency makes an effort to adjust individual bank accounts for differences in reporting and accounting standards and puts the accounts into a standardized global format (see Claessens, Demirgüç-Kunt, and Huizinga, 1999); and, third, it allows for the use of individual bank data (usually unavailable from official sources) to analyze several definitions of ownership and performance ratios for domestic and foreign banks. The main drawback is that the activities of some foreign branches are not captured, which leads to an underestimation of the level of foreign participation, especially in countries where entry through branches is the main modality—such as the Asian countries. Whenever such underestimation is important, this is indicated in the text.

6. See, for instance, Hellwig (1999); Crama and others (1999).

7. See García Cantera (1999).

8. The measures of foreign participation and foreign control would be identical if all banks were fully (that is, 100 percent) owned by either domestic or foreign investors. In some instances, our measures of foreign control can exceed the measure of foreign participation. This can occur because all the assets of a "controlled" bank are regarded as foreign-owned, whereas our participation measure counts as foreign-owned assets only the product of banks' assets and the proportion of equity held by foreigners.

Table 2-1. *Foreign Bank Ownership in Selected Emerging Markets*[a]

	December 1994				December 1999			
Region	Total bank assets (billions of US dollars)	Foreign participation (percent)	Foreign control[b] (50 percent) (percent)	Foreign control[c] (40 percent) (percent)	Total bank assets[d] (billions of US dollars)	Foreign participation (percent)	Foreign control[b] (50 percent) (percent)	Foreign control[d] (40 percent) (percent)
Central Europe								
Czech Republic	46.6	7.1	8.3	8.3	63.4	47.3	49.3	50.7
Hungary	26.8	38.8	23.8	31.7	32.6	59.5	56.6	80.4
Poland	39.4	5.2	2.3	2.6	91.1	36.3	52.8	52.8
Total	112.8	14.0	9.9	11.9	187.1	44.0	52.3	56.9
Turkey	52.0	3.2	3.7	3.9	156.2	1.6	1.7	1.7
Latin America								
Argentina	73.2	17.2	16.5	16.5	157.0	41.7	48.6	48.6
Brazil	486.9	12.4	12.2	12.6	732.3	18.2	16.8	17.7
Chile	41.4	23.0	17.6	20.0	112.3	48.4	53.6	53.6
Colombia	28.3	5.5	5.4	6.2	45.3	16.2	17.8	17.8
Mexico	210.2	0.9	0.9	0.9	204.5	18.6	18.8	18.8
Peru	12.3	10.7	2.9	2.9	26.3	33.2	33.4	33.4
Venezuela	16.4	9.8	10.4	10.4	24.7	34.7	41.9	43.9
Total	868.6	10.2	9.7	10.0	1302.4	24.2	25.0	25.5
Total excluding Brazil and Mexico	171.5	15.5	13.3	14.1	365.6	39.5	44.8	44.9
Asia								
Korea	601.1	7.9	0.8	0.7	642.4	11.2	4.3	16.2
Malaysia	148.1	8.5	6.8	5.7	220.6	14.4	11.5	11.5
Thailand	192.8	1.4	0.5	0.0	198.8	6.0	5.6	5.6
Total	942.0	6.7	1.7	1.3	1061.8	10.9	6.0	13.2

Source: Authors' estimates based on data from Fitch IBCA's BankScope database.

a. Both ownership and balance sheet data for 1994 are as of December 1994; ownership data for 1999 reflect changes up to December 1999, while balance sheet data are the most recent available data in Fitch IBCA's BankScope.

b. Ratio of assets of bank where foreigners own more than 50 percent of total equity to total bank assets.

c. Same as footnote b but at 40 percent level

d. For Central Europe and Asia available balance sheet data are in most cases for December 1998.

Central Europe

Foreign participation in Central Europe increased considerably in the second half of the 1990s, and by the end of the decade the share of banking assets under foreign control had reached more than 50 percent (table 2-1). After the banking crises of the first half of the decade, the privatization of state-owned banks increased foreign participation substantially. Initially, most of the sales were of medium-sized banks, but more recently the large state-owned saving and foreign trade banks have been sold (or are in the process of being sold). Hungary took the lead in the privatization process, and by end-1999 foreign participation in the banking system was about 60 percent of total assets. Poland's privatization process accelerated in 1999–2000 and, with the sale of Bank Pekao in mid-1999, the share of bank assets under foreign control rose to 53 percent. The Czech Republic began to privatize state-owned banks in 1998, and by early 2000 three of the four large state-owned banks had been sold. As a result, foreign institutions controlled 46 percent of total banking assets by end-1999, and that share increased to more than 60 percent with the sale of the second largest bank in March. With the privatization of the final large state-owned bank in 2001, foreign ownership will rise to about 90 percent of bank assets.

Latin America

Although foreign banks have been present in Latin America for many decades, a quantitative jump in foreign participation took place in the second half of the 1990s with the acquisition program initiated by the leading Spanish financial institutions. Indeed, the presence of foreign banks is important not just because of the size of their market share but also because leading institutions in almost every country are controlled by foreign institutions.

Foreign banks had a relatively large presence in Argentina and Chile by end-1994 (table 2-1), but the share of assets under foreign control increased to 50 percent following a series of mergers and acquisitions in 1996–97. In the larger markets of Brazil and Mexico, foreign participation has traditionally been lower, but assets under foreign control reached 18 percent by end-1999. However, the sale of the third-largest Mexican bank in May 2000 and of the second largest in June 2000 has brought the share of assets under foreign control to about 40 percent. Brazil is the only banking market in Latin America where foreigners are unlikely to have a dominant position, owing to a large share of bank assets under government control and the existence of three large, well-capitalized, and well-managed private banks. The entry of two large European banks in 1997–98 nevertheless changed the banking landscape and increased competition, and further foreign acquisitions are possible with the forthcoming privatization of several state banks.

Asia

Foreign banks have played a smaller role in most Asian financial systems than in Central Europe or Latin America, reflecting in part official policies that have limited entry, especially into local retail banking markets. Restrictions have typically involved limitations on the number of foreign banks that could enter the market and the number of branches they could establish within the market. After the crisis, several countries have liberalized entry norms for foreign banks, except for Malaysia. However, foreign bank participation in Malaysia is 23 percent of total commercial bank assets, one of the highest in the region.[9]

The speed and scope of the foreign influx in Korea and Thailand have been lower than originally expected by most analysts.[10] The sale of Korea First Bank to Newbridge Capital accounts for the increase in foreign control in Korea (table 2-1), while the increase in foreign participation also captures the increasing (minority) stakes in several banks.[11] Foreign bank participation in Thailand has been traditionally low, though the involvement of foreign banks has been larger than the figures in table 2-1 suggest, owing to the banks operating through the Bangkok International Bank Facility (BIBF).[12] After the crisis, four banks were sold to foreign institutions, increasing the share under foreign control from 0.5 percent at end-1994 to 4.5 percent at end-1999 (table 2-1). However, the share of assets

9. This figure refers to commercial banks only; the figures in table 2-1 are lower because they include finance companies and merchant banks that are majority owned by Malaysian interests.

10. The increase in foreign participation since the beginning of the financial crisis has been around 9 percent of total assets in both Korea and Thailand (including the recent sale of Bangkok Metropolitan Bank).

11. Foreign banks have been allowed to open branches in Korea since 1967. There were fifty-two foreign bank branches in September 1997, and their market share was just 2 percent of total financial system assets. See Baliño and Ubide (1999).

12. The BIBF scheme was established in 1993 to develop Bangkok as a regional financial center. Besides offshore lending, the BIBF was also allowed to lend locally in foreign currencies, and the rapid growth of this lending in 1994–97 contributed to the financial crisis. See IMF (1998a). Even though this type of lending has been substantially curtailed since 1998, the numbers in table 2-1 appear to underestimate foreign bank participation in Thailand.

under foreign control could rise with the privatization of the other intervened banks.

Factors Increasing the Role of Foreign Banks

The increase in foreign ownership of banks in emerging markets is one facet of the ongoing consolidation of banking systems in both mature and emerging markets. As noted by David Folkerts-Landau and Bankim Chadha and by Celina M. Vansetti, Philip Guarco, and Gregory W. Bauer, the globalization of the financial services industry has resulted in banks facing competition from a variety of nonbank sources of credit and financial services (particularly securities markets) that has put pressure on interest rate margins and profits, which in turn has eroded the "franchise" value of banks.[13] Moreover, banking is inherently an information-, communication-, and computation-intensive industry, and the cost of undertaking these activities domestically and across borders has declined dramatically in recent decades. These developments have created economies of scale (especially in back office operations) and scope (particularly with regard to the development of over-the-counter [OTC] derivative products). To capture these economies of scale and scope, banks have competed intensively to capture market share. The intense competitive pressures that have arisen during this process have resulted in a decline in the profitability of traditional banking activities and have driven the major banks to diversify geographically and also to enter into other financial activities.[14] A more liberal regulatory environment has made it possible to exploit complementarities among areas of banking, securities, and risk management, which has led to the emergence of new products (especially OTC derivative instruments) and improvements in the distribution of these new financial products and services.[15] For instance, telephone and electronic banking have been widely used by foreign banks to gain market penetration in European markets and more recently in emerging markets, especially in Asia.

The intense competitive pressures faced by large international and regional banks in mature markets have provided these banks with strong

13. Folkerts-Landau and Chadha (1999); Vansetti, Guarco, and Bauer (2000). The franchise value of a banking license reflects the discounted value of the net profits that bank would be expected to earn over time.

14. See Canals (1997).

15. Typical complementarities involve trade credit and the provision of hedging products, or the cross-selling of deposits, mutual funds, and insurance.

Box 2-1. *BBVA and BSCH: The Expansion of Spanish Banks to Latin America*

Since the mid-1990s, the two largest Spanish banks, Banco Santander Central Hispano (BSCH) and Banco Bilbao Vizcaya Argentaria (BBVA), have become the largest foreign institutions in retail banking in Latin America.[1] Together they have spent about U.S.$13 billion to purchase control of some thirty major banks in more than ten countries, accounting for some U.S.$153 billion in assets (almost 10 percent of the region's banking assets—or about 7½ percent of regional GDP). They have also expanded into the pension fund business, where they control around 45 percent of the region's industry.

Both banks had a small presence in the region in the 1970s and 1980s, but they started their current cross-border expansion in the early 1990s.[2] Both institutions bought relatively large stakes in large banks, aiming at competing in the lower- and middle-income mass retail markets. While BSCH has generally bought majority stakes in its acquisitions and has put its brand name on them, BBVA tended to buy minority stakes—provided the investment was large enough to render management control—and kept the local bank brand name in most instances. More recently, both have continued to acquire remaining minority holdings in their own subsidiaries to consolidate control of their operations.

Analysts have characterized the expansion of the Spanish banks as a case of "oligopolistic reaction," one in which a firm matches the location choices of a rival in a pattern of move-countermove or action-reaction. The pattern may begin with one firm (BSCH) making the first move and the other (BBVA) following the leader, but in this case leapfrogs of leadership have occurred so that at some point one can no longer unambiguously describe one firm or the other as the overall leader. Following a series of acquisitions that have put them among the three largest private banks in Latin America (see the table below), the banks have now focused their rivalry in the largest (and least foreign-controlled) markets of Brazil and Mexico.[3] Moreover, in early May 2000, BBVA and BSCH announced capital- raising programs representing around 7 percent of existing capital to finance acquisitions in Latin America and the Euro area and finance e-business ventures.

incentives to use the comparative advantages derived from the development of new financial products and services to enter both offshore and local emerging markets.[16] Only a few financial institutions have the management capabilities to conduct global commercial banking operations, but several others are establishing a significant regional presence.[17] The need to overcome the disadvantage of local knowledge makes location and

16. Williams (1997) surveys theories and evidence on multinational banking.
17. Foreign banks have adopted a variety of institutional arrangements to enter emerging markets, including representative offices, branches, subsidiaries, and joint ventures.

Bank Assets in Latin America, End of 1999
Billions of U.S. dollars

BSCH (Spain)	85.4
BBVA (Spain)	68.1
Bradesco (Brazil)	44.6
Banamex (Mexico)	30.6
Bank Boston (United States)	30.0

Source: BSCH.

The Spanish banks have already transferred significant financial expertise to Latin America, but their establishment of a regional banking network is still far from complete. Some obvious parent contributions have been the introduction of new products—such as lottery-linked deposit accounts and fast-approval mortgages—information and risk management systems. However, although the banks are already working on the integration of their common software and hardware platforms, analysts believe that it will still take some time before a full integration into a regional network becomes operative. Moreover, there are limits to the activities that local banks can share with their parent, and differences in local banking regulations also limit the development of regional networks.[4]

1. In January 1999 Banco Santander and Banco Central Hispano merged to form BSCH, the largest Spanish bank by end-1999 assets; in January 2000, Banco Bilbao Vizcaya and Argentaria merged to form BBVA, the second largest bank.

2. See Guillén and Tschoegel (1999) for a thorough analysis of the expansion of the Spanish banks into Latin America.

3. See IMF (2000). BSCH and BBVA have become the two largest private banks in the region following the recent merger of BBVA-Mexico with Bancomer.

4. See García Cantera (1999).

cultural factors (including language) important determinants of the willingness to enter emerging markets. This has led to the emergence of "regional evolvers"—that is, banks that focus their activities on a certain region, such as the Spanish banks in Latin America, the Austrian, Belgian, Dutch, and German banks in Central Europe, and, to a lesser extent, the Australian and Japanese banks in Asia.[18] The large Spanish banks redefined their international expansion strategy after the Asian crisis, pulling out of

18. A couple of Singaporean banks also have regional ambitions, especially Development Bank of Singapore, which has made acquisitions in Thailand, Hong Kong SAR, and the Philippines.

that region and focusing on becoming large regional banks in Latin America and Western Europe (box 2-1).

Removal of Barriers to Foreign Entry

Although there are strong incentives for foreign banks to expand abroad, they have until recently faced substantial barriers to entry in most emerging markets. While most countries establish licensing requirements applicable to both domestically and foreign-owned banks, foreign banks have typically faced stricter limits on the availability of banking licenses, restrictions on the number of branches, controls on permissible activities, and restrictions on foreign ownership of individual banks and total bank assets.[19] For instance, in many Asian countries up until the recent crisis, foreign banks were allowed only a single branch, and foreign bank licenses had been frozen for an extended period. Even in the financial centers of Singapore and Hong Kong SAR, where foreigners participate actively in wholesale banking and capital market activities, foreign retail banking has been restricted.

A greater openness to foreign trade and investment and the need to build up more efficient and stable financial systems in the aftermath of crises have been catalysts for the removal of barriers to entry of foreign institutions. As noted by Eichengreen and Mussa, many emerging markets have been reducing barriers to trade in financial services since the early 1990s, and allowing for the entry of foreign financial institutions has been just one facet of this more general liberalization. Nonetheless, by the mid-1990s, only a modest amount of foreign bank entry had occurred (table 2-1).[20] In part, this limited entry reflected concerns about the potential effects of foreign bank entry and political resistance by the domestic banking industry.

While significant changes in the restrictions on foreign bank entry have at times been motivated by a desire to improve competition and efficiency in the banking system, they have often been triggered by the need to help reduce the costs of restructuring and recapitalizing banks following a crisis, as well as a desire to build an institutional structure in the banking system that is more robust to future domestic and external shocks.[21] The experi-

---

19. While we focus on legal and regulatory barriers to entry, fixed costs and information asymmetries could also restrict entry into foreign markets. See Vives (1991), and Dell'Ariccia (1997).

20. Eichengreen and Mussa (1998).

21. The emergence of regional financial sector difficulties in the United States during the 1980s has

ence with banking system instability in many emerging markets since the 1970s has demonstrated the need to make domestic banking systems more robust.[22] Although the authorities in most emerging markets have moved to strengthen prudential supervision of their banking system, they have also recognized that relatively small banks holding internationally undiversified portfolios remain vulnerable to large shocks. To improve on this situation and often to help reduce the costs of recapitalizing and restructuring banks in a postcrisis period, the authorities in a growing number of emerging markets have begun to open their banking systems to foreign entry in an effort to improve banking system efficiency and to have banks that are part of organizations that hold globally diversified portfolios. However, some analysts have noted that, while internationalization of a banking system does yield institutions with more diversified portfolios, this may not necessarily yield a more stable source of credit for domestic borrowers, for two reasons. To the extent that foreign bank entry is accompanied by a reduction in barriers to capital outflows, banks may use funds raised in the domestic market to undertake external lending. As a result, domestic borrowers might not have the same access to domestic savings. Moreover, foreign banks may at times shift funds abruptly from one market to another as the perceived risk-adjusted returns in different markets change.

The relative importance of efficiency and stability considerations has differed across regions. In the transition economies of Central Europe, for instance, the need to build up institutions rather quickly—in an environment in which there were short histories of operation under market rules—combined with the cost of bank recapitalization programs, convinced the authorities that privatization to strategic foreign investors would be the best solution to their banking problems.[23] Similarly, the scale of banking problems in the mid-1990s in Mexico[24] and Venezuela, and to a lesser extent also in Brazil, created incentives to allow for more foreign bank entry to rebuild capital and bring in new financial expertise. In countries that had already allowed a significant foreign presence, such as Argentina and Chile, the financial turbulence of the second half of the 1990s contributed to a

---

also been a driving force behind the movement toward the removal of interstate banking restrictions. Gunther (1994).

22. Lindgren, García, and Sall (1996).

23. More recently, the need to comply with the requirements of membership in the Organization for Economic Cooperation and Development (OECD) and the prospects of EU accession have provided a further impetus to the removal of barriers to entry in the major transition economies.

24. In Mexico, the crisis accelerated a process of opening up the financial services industry in the context of the North American Free Trade Agreement (NAFTA).

process of mergers and acquisitions that substantially increased foreign participation in the local banking market.

To date, the increase in foreign ownership in Asia has been smaller than in Central Europe and Latin America, but market participants expect this situation to change soon. Analysts note several reasons for the relatively slow increase in foreign participation. First, there are still official concerns that foreign banks will "cut and run" during a crisis and are therefore not a stable source of funding for the local market. Second, family ownership and management structure have been perceived as an important obstacle to the resolution of the financial crises, in part because of an unwillingness to cede control to foreign investors.[25] Third, foreign bank entry was slowed by the fact that most international banks from Europe and the United States had to deal with their own balance sheet problems after the Russian crisis and the near failure of Long-Term Capital Management while the Japanese banks have been forced to focus on domestic problems.[26] Fourth, the level of bank intermediation is much higher than in Latin America; hence, prospects for growth are much less substantial—and lots of restructuring remains to be done. Finally, the franchise value of banks may be declining because corporate borrowers are turning to capital markets for funding, and the prospects of Internet banking have reduced the value of having a large branch network. However, market participants argue this situation will change sharply in the next few years as a result of greater openness to foreign bank entry (reflecting the need to recapitalize the banking systems in countries such as Indonesia, Korea, and Thailand and the desire to make financial centers such as Hong Kong SAR and Singapore more competitive and efficient) and the intense pressures for consolidation in local retail banking markets.

Although the above discussion indicates that a number of factors could potentially influence a bank's decision to enter a particular market or the authorities' willingness to allow such entry, discerning which factors were most important during the 1990s is an empirical issue. To examine the relative importance of different factors, we utilized data on 1,135 banks from fifteen countries for the period from 1991 to 1999.[27]

At the country level, we examined the determinants of the scale of foreign bank participation and the two alternative measures of foreign bank

---

25. See Fitch IBCA (1999a).

26. See Irving and Kumar (1999).

27. The countries are Argentina, Brazil, Chile, Colombia, the Czech Republic, Hungary, Korea, Malaysia, Mexico, Peru, the Philippines, Poland, Thailand, Turkey, and Venezuela.

control presented in table 2-1. Our basic hypothesis is that a higher level of foreign participation (control) in any banking system would fundamentally reflect the desire of foreign banks to enter what they see as a profitable market and the desire of the local authorities to open their financial system to foreign competition to improve efficiency and stability, as well as to help resolve banking crises. We assume that the level of foreign participation and control is influenced by relative costs and returns earned by foreign and domestic banks in the local market, by the authorities' need to help deal with the costs of restructuring the banking system following a crisis, and by the state of macroeconomic conditions in the local economy. We ran three sets of panel regressions that use as the dependent variable either the level of foreign bank participation or one of the two measures of foreign bank control, respectively, in 1995 and 1999. As explanatory variables, we used information on returns, costs, crises, and macroeconomic conditions as averages for the periods 1991–94 and 1996–98.[28] The use of lagged average values for the explanatory variables helps minimize simultaneity problems. The relationship between these variables is:

$$(1) \quad F_i = \beta_0 + \beta_1(ROED - ROEF)$$
$$+ \beta_2(CID - CIF) + \beta_3(NPLD - NPLF)$$
$$+ \beta_4\, CRISIS$$
$$+ \beta_5\, INFL + \beta_6\, GDPCH + \text{regional dummies,}$$

where

F_i =   Measures of foreign control and participation ($F50$ = proportion of total bank assets held in banks where foreign owners hold more than 50 percent of the banks' equity) ($F40$ = proportion of total bank assets held in banks whose foreign owners hold more than 40 percent of the banks' equity) (FP = scale of foreign participation—proportion of bank system's assets owned by foreigners)

$ROED$ = Average rate of return on equity of banks owned by domestic residents in previous three years

$ROEF$ = Average rate of return on equity of banks owned by foreign residents in previous three years

CID =   Average ratio of operating costs to net income of banks owned by domestic residents in previous three years

CIF =   Average ratio of operating costs to net income of banks owned by foreign residents in previous three years

28. This means that each pooled data set had thirty observations for fifteen countries.

$NPLD$ = Average ratio of nonperforming loans to total assets of banks owned by domestic residents in previous three years

$NPLF$ = Average ratio of nonperforming loans to total assets of banks owned by foreign residents in previous three years

$CRISIS$ = Existence of a banking crisis in the preceding three-year period

$INFL$ = Average rate of inflation in previous three years

$GDPCH$ = Average real rate of growth of GDP in previous three years.

This formulation assumes that foreign residents will tend to increase their participation or their control of local banks whenever domestically owned local banks have a higher rate of return on equity than do foreign-owned local banks (which makes the acquisition of local banks by foreigners more attractive [$ß_1 > 0$]); the ratio of operating cost to net income of domestically owned local banks exceeds that of foreign-owned local banks (which gives foreign-owned banks a cost advantage and allows them to expand their activities [$ß_2 > 0$]); the ratio of nonperforming loans to total assets in domestically owned local banks is higher than that in foreign-owned local banks (which implies that domestically owned local banks will face higher future provisioning charges and will be at a competitive disadvantage relative to foreign-owned local banks [$ß_3 > 0$]); if there has been a banking crisis in the past three years (which will make the authorities more inclined to allow foreign bank entry to help contain the fiscal costs associated with restructuring banks [$ß_4 > 0$]); and if there are improved macroeconomic conditions, particularly lower inflation [$ß_5 < 0$] and more rapid growth [$ß_6 > 0$].

Although this formulation captures some of the cost and return incentives for foreign banks to enter or expand their activities in emerging markets and the incentives that banking crises create for the authorities to allow greater foreign entry, it does not capture the effects of other key policy changes or stances that affect foreign bank entry. For example, policies toward foreign bank entry into emerging markets in Central Europe in late 1999 have been influenced by the fact that these countries are seeking entry into the European Union, and it is recognized that there will be a "single passport" for the entry of all European community banks once membership is attained. Moreover, the authorities in several Asian countries have generally limited entry of foreign banks in the past because of concerns that such banks are not a reliable source of funds during crises. We allow for some of these regional policy differences through the use of regional dummies.

Table 2-2. *Entry of Foreign Banks (Annual Data)*[a]

Coefficient	Dependent variable		
	Foreign participation	Foreign control (50 percent ownership)	Foreign control (40 percent ownership)
β_0	9.742	10.518	11.660
	(4.520)	(4.636)	(5.319)
β_1	0.396	0.527	0.485
	(0.163)	(0.167)	(0.191)
β_2	0.170	0.169	0.178
	(0.112)	(0.115)	(0.132)
β_3	0.871	1.061	1.016
	(0.502)	(0.515)	(0.590)
β_4	9.160	11.125	9.932
	(4.099)	(4.205)	(4.824)
β_5	−0.006	−0.009	−0.009
	(0.004)	(0.004)	(0.005)
β_6	1.589	1.448	1.444
	(0.726)	(0.744)	(0.854)
β_7 (Asia)[b]	−10.417	−15.104	−14.864
	(4.949)	(5.076)	(5.82)
β_8 (Central Europe)[c]	24.086	22.998	36.889
	(6.406)	(6.571)	(7.538)
R[b]	.721	.746	.768
$\bar{R}$[b]	.609	.644	.676

a. Standard errors in parentheses.

b. Equal to one for each Asian country in both 1994 and 1999; zero otherwise.

c. Equal to one for each Central European country in 1999; zero otherwise.

The estimation results for the pooled annual data are presented in table 2-2. In comparing these results, certain variables seem to have had a significant effect on the degree of foreign bank participation and the extent of foreign bank control. For the cost and return variables, the rate of return on equity differential is significant (at the 5 percent level) in all three equations. Not surprisingly, this suggests that foreign banks increase their participation in and control of banks that earn relatively high rates of return on equity. Furthermore, a relatively high level of nonperforming loans relative to total bank assets for domestic banks seems to have had a more significant positive impact on foreign control than foreign participation. This finding could mean that foreign banks would not want to merely participate, for example, in the form of a joint venture with local banks that are in a difficult position but would acquire the institution and use what they regard as their better risk management and debt resolution skills to restructure a newly acquired bank. In contrast, the operating cost to net income differential does not appear to significantly influence participation or control.

The results also suggest that a banking crisis and improved macroeconomic conditions are likely to lead to greater foreign participation and control. A banking crisis during the previous three-year period raised both foreign participation and control by about 10 percentage points. This suggests that countries experiencing a banking crisis regularly turn to foreign banks to help rebuild and restructure the domestic banking system. A higher rate of growth of GDP also significantly increased foreign participation and control. In contrast, the level of foreign control seems to have been more adversely affected by high inflation than does the degree of participation (although the significance is relatively low in all three regressions). Finally, the regional dummies are highly significant, confirming the differential attitude toward foreign bank entry in Asia and Central Europe.

Effects of Foreign Bank Entry

The sharp rise in foreign bank participation in many emerging markets is clear evidence that the authorities in these countries have concluded that foreign bank entry will have an overall positive effect on the efficiency and stability of the banking system. Nonetheless, effects on the efficiency and stability of the local banking systems have been much debated in many countries.

Arguments about Efficiency and Stability

Allowing foreign banks to enter is typically viewed as having the most beneficial effects when such entry occurs in the context of a more general liberalization of trade and production of financial services.[29] It is argued that a general liberalization of trade in financial services induces countries to produce and exchange financial services on the basis of comparative advantage. Allowing foreign bank entry as part of this liberalization process is seen as

---

29. The arguments about the effects of foreign bank entry are discussed in Berger and others (2000); Claessens, Demirgüc-Kunt, and Huizinga (1999); Claessens and Glaessner (1999); Barajas, Steiner, and Salazar (1999); Clarke and others (1999); Denizer (1999); Kiraly (1999); Laeven (1999); and Tamirisa and others (2000).

improving the efficiency and the stability of the banking system. It is argued that foreign banks will help improve the quality, pricing, and availability of financial services, directly as providers of such enhanced services and indirectly through competition with domestic banks, which will encourage the latter to introduce similar improvements. These new financial products can offer better opportunities for portfolio diversification and intertemporal trade. A transfer of technology occurs if the authorities allow high-quality international banks with solid reputations to enter and permit the immigration of skilled banking personnel. Since these banks will also hire local bankers with a better knowledge of the local economy, these local bankers will assimilate the practices and technology of the international banks, which they retain when they move back to domestic banks. Foreign banks are also often seen as improving the allocation of credit since they have more sophisticated systems for evaluating and pricing credit risks. Similarly, it is often argued that foreign banks can better assess and price the risks connected with various derivative products because of their experience with the use of these products in international financial markets.

Others see foreign banks as making much less of a contribution to an efficient allocation of credit. One concern is that foreign banks "cherry-pick" the most profitable domestic markets and customers, leaving domestic banks to serve the other (more risky) customers and thereby increase the overall riskiness of domestic banks' portfolios. Under this cherry-picking strategy, foreign banks are viewed as focusing their lending activities on wealthy individuals and the most creditworthy corporates. It has also been argued that it may be difficult for foreign banks to transfer some of the credit risk evaluation methods used in mature markets. While some analysts have claimed that foreign banks have a comparative advantage in evaluating the credit risks in retail and consumer lending markets because of their use of statistical credit scoring methods, others have noted that such credit scoring methods may face informational constraints in emerging markets.[30] Moreover, reliance on credit scoring methods is seen as reducing lending to small firms, as this type of lending usually requires "soft" information (that is, information that is not easily quantifiable and is generally obtained through a long-term relationship with the client) as opposed to hard, statistical information.[31] As a result, some have argued that this pattern of lending encourages the development of oligopolistic and monopolistic

---

30. See Garber and Weisbrod (1994).
31. See Belaisch and others (2000).

industrial structures, especially in economies with relatively small domestic markets.

It has also been suggested that foreign banks can provide a more stable source of credit and can make the banking system more robust to shocks. This greater stability is said to exist because the branches and subsidiaries of large international banks can draw on their parent for additional funding and capital when needed. In turn, the parent may be able to provide such funding because it will typically hold a more internationally diversified portfolio than domestic banks, which means that its income stream will be less correlated with purely domestic shocks.[32] Moreover, large international banks are likely to have better access to global financial markets than domestic banks.

It has also been argued that the entry of foreign banks improves the overall stability of the domestic banking system. The entry of sound foreign banks is seen as implicitly allowing a country to import strong prudential supervision for at least part of the financial system. This would be especially true for foreign branches of international banks since they are supervised on a consolidated basis with the parent under the terms of the Basel Concordat. While a local subsidiary of an international bank is technically a stand-alone entity with its own capital, it is argued that the reputational effects of allowing a subsidiary to fail will lead the parent to closely monitor the subsidiary's activities. Moreover, when the subsidiary is part of a holding company or a universal bank, then the subsidiary may also be supervised on a consolidated basis by the parent's supervisory authority. Foreign banks, which engage in new and more sophisticated activities and provide new products, may also lead the domestic supervisory authorities to upgrade the quality and size of their staff in order to better supervise the activities of both domestic and foreign banks. The branches and subsidiaries of major international banks are also likely to have disclosure, accounting, and reporting requirements that are closely aligned with international best practices. To the extent that local banks emulate these practices so as to be perceived as being as strong as the foreign banks, the overall quality of information about the state of the banking system would be improved. It has also been suggested that the presence of foreign banks during a crisis can

32. Similar issues have been discussed in the context of the removal of interstate banking restrictions in the United States. The lack of geographical diversification of U.S. banks until the removal of interstate restrictions has been noted as a source of financial instability, especially when compared with unrestricted Canadian banks. See Williamson (1989). However, opponents to the removal of such restrictions argued that interstate banks would siphon funds from local areas and deprive local customers of credit. See Jackson and Eisenbeis (1997) for evidence against this claim.

add to the stability of the banking system by allowing domestic residents "to do their capital flight at home." In essence, if domestic residents have doubts about the stability of domestic banks during a crisis period, they can shift their deposits to foreign banks located in the country rather than abroad, which should help stabilize the overall stock of deposits. Finally, some have argued that foreign banks may allow for indirect access to the lender-of-last-resort facilities of the mature markets through their parent.

Others have argued, however, that foreign bank entry can worsen banking system stability. If domestic banks are relatively inefficient and have weak capital positions, for example, they may either respond to increased foreign competition by undertaking higher-risk activities in an attempt to earn the returns needed to rebuild their capital positions or they will be forced into bankruptcy. Moreover, as already noted, this problem may be intensified if foreign banks tend to cherry-pick the most creditworthy domestic markets and customers. Experience during the early stages of financial liberalizations (with or without foreign bank entry) in many countries suggests that this is not an unwarranted concern. In many cases, this weakened financial position of domestic banks has reflected the fact that such institutions entered the liberalization period holding loans carrying fixed interest rates (that had been subject to interest rate ceilings in the preliberalization period) and had to compete with other institutions that were free to set higher lending rates and offer higher deposit interest rates. As the profit and capital positions of the disadvantaged institutions deteriorated, some undertook high-return but high-risk activities, especially in situations in which their deposit liabilities were subject to deposit insurance guarantees.

Apart from the impact of foreign bank entry on the stability of domestic banks, there have also been concerns about the behavior of foreign banks during crisis periods. Indeed, in Asia one of the most frequently cited reasons for limited foreign bank entry is the perception that foreign banks have "cut and run" during recent crises, especially in the period following the 1997 crisis. While it is evident that cross-border lending to emerging markets has often fallen sharply in the 1990s in postcrisis periods, there is the question of whether foreign banks with a local presence are more likely to maintain their exposures to domestic borrowers than are foreign banks that only engage in cross-border lending.

A final concern often voiced about the entry of foreign banks is linked to whether they will be adequately supervised. As noted earlier, it has been argued that the entry of foreign banks is a means of importing strong prudential supervision for at least part of the banking system and possibly stimulating improvement in the quality of the staff and practices of domestic supervising. In contrast, some observers argue that the complex cross-border financial transactions undertaken by international banks may be difficult to supervise by either the host or the home country supervisors. They cite the examples of Bank of Credit and Commerce International (BCCI) and Peregrine Investments, which they see as having "fallen between the cracks" in terms of appropriate supervision.

Empirical Evidence on Efficiency Effects

One of the striking results of recent studies of the effects of foreign bank entry on banking system efficiency is the differing results for mature and emerging markets. In examining the experience of France, Germany, Spain, the United Kingdom, and the United States, for example, Allen Berger and others analyzed cost and profit efficiency for foreign and domestic banks using annual data for 1993–98.[33] In these mature markets, they found that foreign banks were less efficient in either costs or profits, on average, than domestic banks. However, some banking organizations—particularly from the United States—were found to consistently operate at or above the efficiency levels of domestic banks. They argued that this latter result meant that the home field advantages (arising from local knowledge and proximity to the local market) of domestic banks were offset by the global advantages (which reflect the superior risk management practices, superior product mix, or more diversified portfolios) enjoyed by some foreign banks.

In contrast, virtually all empirical studies that have included either mixed samples of mature and emerging markets or have focused on emerging markets have concluded that foreign banks have been more efficient in both costs and profits. For example, Stijn Claessens, Asli Demirgüc-Kunt, and Harry Huizinga examined the behavior of banks in eighty mature and emerging markets in the period from 1988 to 1995 to investigate how net interest rate margins (between lending and deposit rates), overhead expenses, taxes paid, and profitability differed between foreign and domestic banks.[34] Foreign banks were found to have higher interest rate margins, profitability, and tax payments than domestic banks in emerging markets, while the opposite was true in mature markets. Moreover, significant foreign bank entry was associated with a reduction in both the profitability and

33. Berger and others (2000).
34. Claessens, Demirgüc-Kunt, and Huizinga (1999).

overall expenses of domestic banks. The efficiency effects of foreign banks on emerging markets banking systems also appeared to occur as soon as there was entry and did not depend on gaining a substantial market share.[35]

On a more regional level, performance indicators for a sample of emerging markets in the more recent period 1996–98 (table 2-3) seem to confirm that foreign banks operating in these markets are relatively more efficient than domestic banks. In Central Europe, foreign banks have on average higher returns on average equity, and lower cost-to-income and problem loan ratios, than domestic banks. A similar picture seems to emerge for Latin America, especially considering the countries that experienced foreign entry early in the sample period (Argentina, Colombia, Peru, and Venezuela). Interestingly, Chile shows indicators that are to some extent more in line with the evidence on mature markets, namely, more profitable local banks. Two factors explain this difference relative to Chile's peer group. First, following a severe banking crisis in the early 1980s, Chile developed one of the strongest and best regulated emerging markets banking systems, and several domestic banks substantially improved their operating efficiency following more than a decade of stable growth while facing foreign competition. Second, the largest foreign banks merged with other local banks in 1996–97, and their performance was initially damaged by the nonrecurring merger-related expenses. In the Asian countries, performance indicators of foreign banks are worse than those of domestically owned banks, because ownership changes are very recent and previously weak banks were taken over by foreigners.

Qualitative studies that assess the response of the successful local incumbents provide further evidence on the beneficial effects of foreign competition. For example, Daniel Abut held discussions with the senior management of four Latin American banks that were widely regarded as competing successfully with foreign banks.[36] It was argued that local banks had to overcome a number of relative disadvantages to compete effectively with foreign banks, including limited access to capital, a lack of geographical diversification in the lending portfolios and sources of funds, lack of experience with multiple markets, delays in and higher costs of implementing new products and services, and limited capacity to afford sizable investments in computer systems and other technologies. These relative

35. Studies of the experiences of Argentina (Clarke and others, 1999), Colombia (Barajas, Steiner, and Salazar, 1999), Turkey (Denizer, 1999), and eight Asian economies (Claessens and Glaessner, 1999) also report results that support these conclusions.

36. Abut (1999). These banks were Banco Galicia (Argentina), Bradesco (Brazil), Banacci (Mexico), and Credicorp (Peru).

Table 2-3. *Bank Performance Indicators in Selected*
Emerging Markets (1996–98)

	Return on equity		Cost-to-income ratio		Problem loans/ total loans	
	Foreign[a] banks	Domestic banks	Foreign banks	Domestic banks	Foreign banks	Domestic banks
Central Europe						
Czech Republic	14.4	–1.6	70.9	40.5	18.8	28.5
Hungary	16.1	–26.0	62.4	113.0	10.6	15.1
Poland	24.1	–0.1	50.9	59.9	11.1	9.2
Total	19.3	–5.0	59.9	62.1	13.7	17.1
Turkey	68.3	29.8	39.0	48.2	6.1	4.1
Latin America						
Argentina	5.8	–0.7	73.4	76.9	5.7	17.3
Brazil	10.4	5.2	73.3	68.8	7.5	7.6
Chile	10.9	14.9	59.8	64.4	1.9	1.5
Colombia	2.7	1.7	70.6	69.1	5.4	6.8
Mexico	–14.3	–2.1	112.3	78.5	4.1	8.7
Peru	14.9	10.8	64.8	80.5	6.0	13.2
Venezuela	40.6	38.2	56.3	64.6	3.9	4.1
Total	6.3	4.7	77.9	71.2	6.1	8.5
Total excluding Brazil and Mexico	9.9	7.5	67.5	71.9	4.5	10.4
Asia						
Korea	–44.2	–20.0	53.7	69.2	15.1	8.6
Malaysia	16.4	7.8	34.7	42.6	6.8	8.4
Thailand	–66.1	–20.2	128.9	72.0	46.2	36.5
Total	–35.7	–14.3	63.8	64.2	19.2	13.8

Source: IMF staff estimates based on data from Fitch IBCA's BankScope Database.

a. Foreign banks are those where foreign institutions own more than 50 percent of total equity (see table 2-1).

disadvantages had been overcome by development of new sources of international funding (such as by securitization of foreign-currency-denominated receivables); the use of international consultants to assess the effectiveness of new products and services that had been developed in different markets; selective associations with foreign and local companies to develop new products; and the formation of alliances with other local banks to develop systems and products jointly in order to obtain economies of scale.[37] Moreover, the successful local banks were viewed as building a strong and stable management team that adopted a proactive rather than a reactive strategy for confronting the competition from foreign banks.

There are no broad-based studies on whether foreign banks ration credit to small firms to a larger extent than domestic banks, but a recent study on the Argentine banking industry does find evidence supporting that hypothesis. Allen Berger, Leora F. Klapper, and Gregory F. Udell show that small businesses tend to receive less credit from large banks and foreign banks, and that this effect is magnified for small firms with loan repayment delinquencies.[38] The authors argue that foreign-owned institutions may have difficulty extending relationship loans to opaque small firms.

Why is there such a sharp contrast between the effects of foreign bank entry for mature and emerging markets? The contrasting results mostly reflect differences in initial conditions. All of the recent studies of mature markets cover periods in which the banking system regulations and controls have long since been liberalized, and banks faced competition not only from other banks but also from a variety of nonbank sources of credit (especially capital markets). Such competition had already put intense pressures on net interest rate margins and forced banks to merge or adopt new technologies to help reduce overhead costs. While foreign bank entry could intensify these competitive pressures, the scale of such an increase would typically be marginal. In contrast, the studies of the effect of such entry on emerging markets have typically focused on periods when the banking systems have only recently been liberalized or were coming out of crisis periods. In either situation, the banks were just emerging from periods in which there had often been extensive restriction on new entry (from new domestic or foreign banks) into the banking system, nonmarket determination of key interest rates (because of either official interest rate ceilings or oligopolistic determination of the interest rate structure by bankers' associations), and limited competition from nonbank sources of credit. Although such an environment increased the franchise value of banks and allowed relatively inefficient banks to survive, these created strong profit opportunities for new banks (whether foreign or domestic) that could operate with more efficient cost structures and offer more market-related interest rates. In this

37. It was also noted that local banks have a number of advantages when competing with foreign banks. These local banks had dominant size and market share in the local market, superior knowledge of the domestic market and its companies, reputation and brand-name recognition, and the ability to react and respond more quickly to unexpected events.

38. Berger, Klapper, and Udell (2001).

situation, the entry of foreign banks could have a major impact on banking system efficiency, directly because of their own operations and indirectly because they forced other banks to become more efficient if they wished to survive.

Empirical Evidence on Stability Effects

Whatever the effects of foreign bank entry on banking system efficiency, equally important for many emerging markets is whether such banks are likely to contribute to banking system stability and to be a stable source of credit, especially in crisis periods. There are two related issues: whether the presence of foreign banks makes systemic banking crises more or less likely to occur, and whether foreign banks have a tendency to "cut and run" during a crisis.

There are surprisingly few studies of the relationship between foreign bank entry and systemic banking crises. However, Ross Levine has recently attempted to analyze the impact of foreign bank presence on the probability that a banking crisis will occur. Levine's empirical study builds on the earlier work of Asli Demirgüc-Kunt and Enrica Detragiache, which used a multivariate logit model to relate the probability that a banking crisis would occur during a particular period to a series of macroeconomic and banking system indicators by adding a measure of the number of foreign banks relative to the total number of banks.[39] The foreign bank share variable was found to have a negative and statistically significant coefficient, which led Levine to conclude, after controlling for the effects of other factors that are likely to produce banking crises, that greater foreign bank participation was a stabilizing factor.

The stability of foreign bank lending has also been examined by contrasting the behavior of cross-border and local lending by foreign banks during crisis periods.[40] For example, substantial declines occurred in both cross-border and local lending by foreign banks to Asian borrowers during the recent crises (table 2-4). While cross-border claims declined for all nationalities of banks, the largest declines in lending occurred for Japanese banks. Analysts attribute this sharper decline to the difficulties faced by Japanese banks in their home markets, particularly the need to deal with

39. Levine (1999); Demirgüc-Kunt and Detragiache (1998).
40. Cross-border claims are those booked outside the foreign counterparty's home country, usually at the lender's head office. Local claims on the foreign counterparty are those booked in the local office of the reporting bank, that is, offices located in the country of the counterparty.

domestic nonperforming loans and to rebuild capital. Moreover, the cut-back in local lending by foreign banks was only slightly higher (a 40 percent decline) than that for domestic banks (a 35 percent decline).

There is some evidence from the Asian crisis that foreign banks' behavior toward emerging markets is related not just to the inherent risks of their counterparts but also to their long-term commitment to a particular emerging market. For example, Palmer noted that U.S. money center banks generally sustained the operations of their offshore branches and subsidiaries during the recent emerging market crises. While cross-border claims in Asia decreased 36 percent between June 1997 and June 1999, local claims declined just 6 percent (in Korea, local claims rose 19 percent). In addition, U.S. banks' claims on Latin American countries increased during that period. Palmer argued that the disparity between movements in cross-border and local claims meant that U.S. banks that had developed local franchises in the region saw good prospects beyond the crises, while the extent of franchise development (and the associated commitment) was much less prevalent for institutions primarily involved in cross-border lending.[41]

Since much of the increase in foreign banks' entry has occurred only in the latter part of the 1990s, only limited evidence exists on how foreign banks behaved in other crisis periods. In Brazil, for example, cross-border exposures of BIS-reporting banks decreased in the aftermath of the Russia and LTCM crises. During 1996–98, local lending by foreign banks declined while lending by domestic banks increased (table 2-4). Foreign lines of credit to Argentina did increase during December 1994 to May 1995, even though some foreign banks with branches in the country did cut off credit lines to their branch operations at the height of the Tequila crisis in February 1995.[42] Joe Peek and Eric S. Rosengren studied several measures of foreign bank penetrations—including both lending by subsidiaries and offshore lending—and found that for most Latin American countries foreign bank penetration rises after a crisis explodes. Moreover, Linda Goldberg, Gerard Dages, and Daniel Kinney examined the lending behavior of foreign and domestic banks in Argentina and Mexico in the period surrounding the 1994–95 Mexican crisis and concluded that foreign banks exhibited stronger loan growth compared with all domestic-owned banks, with lower associated volatility, and thereby contributed to greater stability in overall financial system credit.[43] Furthermore, they found strong sim-

41. Palmer (2000).
42. See IMF (1996).
43. Peek and Rosengren (2000); Goldberg, Dages, and Kinney (2000).

Table 2-4. *Cross-Border and Foreign Bank Lending in Selected Emerging Markets*
Billions of U.S. dollars

	Total			Cross-Border Claims of BIS Banks 1996–99								Total Lending by Domestic and Foreign Banks 1996–98			
				European banks		North American banks		Japanese banks		Other banks		Foreign banks		Domestic banks	
	1996	1998	June 1999	1996	1998	1996	1998	1996	1998	1996	1998	1996	1998	1996	1998
Central Europe															
Czech Republic	9.6	12.2	9.9	7.5	10.3	0.0	0.6	1.1	0.6	1.0	0.8	18.4	18.8	12.6	11.2
Hungary	11.7	16.1	14.5	9.0	13.9	0.8	0.7	1.1	0.8	0.8	0.7	5.9	7.8	3.8	3.1
Poland	7.6	14.5	17.2	5.6	10.6	1.0	1.9	0.1	0.3	0.9	1.7	13.0	21.0	13.7	11.7
Total	28.9	42.8	41.7	22.1	34.8	1.7	3.1	2.3	1.6	2.7	3.3	37.3	47.5	30.1	26.0
Turkey	22.6	35.7	34.1	11.8	19.5	2.4	4.7	2.0	2.0	6.4	9.5	0.80	1.2	36.4	46.5
Latin America															
Argentina	44.8	61.5	66.7	23.8	40.3	14.6	14.2	1.8	2.0	4.6	5.0	22.5	30.2	35.8	41.1
Brazil	67.9	73.3	62.3	30.0	43.2	20.6	14.1	5.2	4.2	12.2	11.8	32.8	29.1	209.7	217.5
Chile	15.2	22.2	23.5	7.6	13.9	4.9	5.2	0.8	1.2	1.8	1.9	18.0	23.9	28.9	30.9
Colombia	16.8	17.1	15.8	9.4	9.8	4.5	4.4	1.3	1.5	1.5	1.3	5.4	5.4	24.5	21.6
Mexico	60.1	65.0	63.8	25.1	31.1	20.3	21.4	5.4	4.7	9.4	7.8	12.9	13.3	107.2	98.9
Peru	8.0	10.6	10.9	4.1	7.0	1.5	2.4	0.2	0.1	2.1	1.1	5.5	7.3	5.7	8.2
Venezuela	11.1	12.5	13.2	6.0	7.3	3.2	3.7	0.5	0.4	1.4	1.1	2.8	3.9	5.2	8.0
Total	223.9	262.2	256.2	106.0	152.6	69.6	65.5	15.1	14.1	33.1	30.0	100.0	113.2	417.0	426.1
Asia															
Hong Kong SAR	207.0	131.4	120.9	86.0	74.6	12.1	7.3	87.5	38.7	21.5	10.8	...	...	...	...
Korea	100.0	65.3	63.5	33.8	26.2	10.7	7.8	24.3	16.9	31.1	14.4	29.5	12.3	446.9	287.6
Malaysia	22.2	20.8	18.6	9.2	10.6	2.5	1.3	8.2	6.6	2.3	2.3	15.0	13.5	158.7	112.2
Singapore	189.2	125.1	112.6	102.8	75.2	8.8	5.7	58.8	29.5	18.9	14.7	...	...	...	...
Thailand	70.1	40.7	34.7	19.1	14.1	6.2	1.9	37.5	22.4	7.3	2.3	13.1	8.5	210.3	129.2
India	16.9	19.3	22.6	7.8	8.9	1.7	2.0	3.5	3.0	3.8	5.5	...	...	...	...
Total	605.5	402.7	372.9	258.8	209.5	42.0	26.0	219.9	117.1	84.9	50.1	57.6	34.3	815.9	529.0

Source: BIS, Consolidated International Banking Statistics; and staff estimates based on Fitch IBCA's BankScope.

ilarities in the portfolio composition of lending and the volatility of lending by private foreign and domestic banks in Argentina, while the same was true in Mexico for banks with low levels of problem loans. Overall, they argued that bank health, and not ownership, was the critical element in the growth and volatility of bank credit.

In a more recent study of the Asian experience, Luc Laeven considered the behavior of foreign and domestic banks in East Asia (Indonesia, Korea, Malaysia, the Philippines, and Thailand) in 1992–96 to identify how ownership structure determined vulnerability to domestic and external shocks.[44] In examining the profitability and risk-taking activities of banks, he found that foreign-owned banks took relatively limited risks and showed an increase in efficiency relative to other banks. Family-owned and company-owned banks were also found to hold the most risky portfolios. Moreover, banks that required restructuring after the crisis of 1997 occurred were mostly family owned or company owned and almost never foreign owned.

It is often argued that local operations of foreign banks are likely to have recourse to additional capital from their head offices in times of financial stress. However, this proposition is largely untested, with only a few clear examples to support it. In Hungary, for example, when the brokerage subsidiaries of foreign banks suffered large losses in the aftermath of the Russian crisis, head offices quickly injected capital.[45] However, relative to the size of local operations, the recapitalizations required were small. In another example of foreign support, Portugal's Banco Espírito Santo injected more capital into its Brazilian subsidiary Banco Boavista Interatlantico, after the latter had to make good on the losses sustained by its mutual funds after the real's devaluation of January 1999. Similarly, Credit Commercial de France injected capital into its Brazilian subsidiary (CCF do Brasil) in 1998 to absorb losses derived from the financial markets turbulence of October 1997.[46] However, there are also plenty of examples of foreign banks that withdrew from emerging markets after having failed to establish a profitable presence. Market participants suggest foreign banks will likely examine whether or not to inject capital on a case-by-case basis, trading off future value (including international effects on reputation) against cost. Minority shareholders are viewed as less likely to make capital injections during periods of financial stress.

44. Laeven (1999).
45. See IMF (1999).
46. See Fitch IBCA (1999b).

Box 2-2. *Argentina: Foreign Banks and the Resilience of the Deposit Base*
When the Tequila crisis hit Argentina in early 1995, it went hand in hand with massive
deposit withdrawals from the banking system. Deposits declined by about 15 percent,
and there was a (relative) shift of deposits to foreign banks. No such phenomenon was
observed in the three subsequent financial crises. Deposits remained flat or even
increased during financial market turbulence in the Asian, Russian, and Brazilian crises,
though pressures were felt in interest rates, and there was a slight shift from peso to dol-
lar-denominated deposits (see figure).

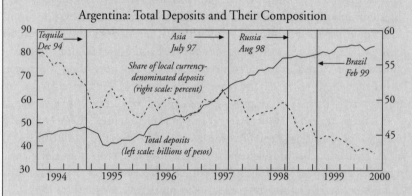

Argentina: Total Deposits and Their Composition

There are several interpretations of this recent stability. First, the central bank is
viewed as having gained substantial credibility by having proven its ability to manage a
crisis within the limits imposed by the currency board (including by lowering reserve
requirements and availing itself of the provision in the Convertibility Law allowing the

Apart from the stability of foreign bank lending, whether foreign banks
can contribute to the stability of the domestic deposit base is also a concern.
Foreign banks can contribute to the stability of the domestic financial system, for example, if depositors, rather than engaging in capital flight, shift
their funds to foreign institutions that are perceived as sounder than the local
banks. Flight to quality was widespread during the Asian financial crises, as
depositors shifted funds from finance companies and small banks toward
large banks, especially foreign banks. The market share of deposits in foreign
banks tripled in Korea and Indonesia between January 1997 and July 1998,
while in Thailand it increased from 2 percent of total deposits to 5 percent
in the period December 1996 to December 1997.[47] The crisis that began
with the failure of a large bank in Argentina in March 1980 led to runs on

47. See Domac and Ferri (1999).

extension of credit to banks in an emergency). The negotiation in late 1996 of a stand-by repurchase facility with international banks added to the ability of the currency board system to create emergency liquidity. This led to greater stability of deposits in the ensuing emerging market crises.

Second, observers have pointed to improved confidence in the banking sector. Given the limited lender-of-last-resort functions under the currency board arrangements, reforms undertaken in 1991–94 had already emphasized improving liquidity and capitalization as well as transparency at the level of individual banks.[1] The second generation of reforms in the wake of the Tequila crisis focused on consolidating and deepening these reforms, including through the introduction of a remunerated liquidity requirement and the development of a so-called BASIC system of banking oversight, which emphasizes the monitoring and discipline imposed by the market (including through increased transparency in reporting and the mandatory use of credit ratings).[2] These measures were accompanied by the development of a privately funded limited deposit insurance for small depositors in April 1995, enhancing confidence in the system.

Third, analysts have mentioned the growing presence of foreign banks (foreign banks are currently part owners in all of the ten largest private banks) as another source of stability of the deposit base. Indeed, in each of the contagious currency crisis episodes, there was flight to quality, from small banks to large and foreign banks, in part based on the perception that the latter would be supported by their parent institutions. This flight to quality contributed to the ongoing consolidation and the increasing share of foreign ownership in the banking system.

1. See Dziobek, Hobbs, and Marston (2000).
2. See IMF (1998a, p. 161).

three other banks, with foreign banks among the beneficiaries of the flight to quality.[48] Similarly, concerns about the ability of Argentine banks to meet depositor demands following the Mexican crisis of 1995 led depositors to shift their funds to foreign banks;[49] however, during more recent crises, deposits remained remarkably stable (box 2-2). More recently, rumors of financial difficulties at Postabank—the second largest retail bank in Hungary—led to a run by depositors that benefited in part foreign institutions.[50]

In sum, the evidence supports the conclusion that the competitive pressures created by foreign bank entry have led to improvements in banking system efficiency through lower operating costs and smaller margins between lending and deposit interest rates. As yet only limited evidence

48. See Baliño (1991).
49. See IMF (1995).
50. See OECD (1999).

exists as to whether a greater foreign bank presence contributes to a more stable banking system and less volatility in the availability of credit.

Policy Issues

The growing presence of foreign banks has raised several complex policy issues, especially in relation to cross-border supervision and regulation, banking system concentration, and systemic risks and official safety nets.

Cross-Border Supervision and Regulation

The growing presence of foreign banks in many emerging markets, and the expansion of emerging markets banks to offshore markets, has increased the complexity of the tasks facing supervisory authorities, especially in emerging markets. Banking supervisors have long been aware of the potential problems associated with cross-border banking activities, and a series of principles and best practices has evolved to establish effective prudential supervision of these activities.[51] The key objective of the supervisors of internationally active banks has remained that of ensuring that no activity of these banks escapes effective supervision and that coordinated remedial action can be undertaken when necessary. Nonetheless, the collapse of institutions such as BCCI in 1991 and Peregrine Investments in 1998 has illustrated how a constantly evolving set of institutional structures and legal arrangements could potentially be used to escape effective prudential supervision.[52]

Moreover, the recent experience of the Bank of New York has demonstrated how readily cross-border banking linkages can be used for fraud and money laundering. Indeed, one of the ongoing concerns of bank analysts and supervisory authorities is that the increasing complexity of cross-border banking activities and institutional arrangements will allow some activities to "fall between the cracks."

Many issues have become more and more important to emerging markets banking supervisors as the presence of foreign banks has expanded. The first concern is how to monitor the local establishments of large interna-

51. See BIS (1996) and IMF (1998b).

52. Peregrine had grown to become Asia's largest investment bank outside Japan before its collapse in January 1998. It was not registered or regulated as an investment bank but was in fact structured as a group with some two hundred subsidiaries, of which many were special purpose vehicles registered offshore. See IMF (1998a).

tional and regional banks. As foreign banks become an important source of financial services, supervisors need to be aware of the financial positions of not only the local branches and subsidiaries of major international and regional banks but also the parent bank. Indeed, difficulties at the parent bank could raise questions about the survivability of the local affiliate, even if its position is fundamentally sound. Second, one of the key strategies employed by major international banks to gain market share when they enter an emerging market is to offer a variety of new financial products, including OTC derivative products. While these new derivative products can allow for better hedging of a variety of risks, experience has shown that they can be readily used to evade prudential regulations. As a result, emerging markets' supervisors will need to upgrade their ability to analyze the growing use of these instruments. A third issue is understanding when and to what extent parent banking organizations will support their local operations in times of difficulty or crisis. Finally, the expansion of large banks into emerging markets can raise issues about their concentration in the local banking industry, especially if this result creates banks that are regarded as "too big to fail."

Large, Complex Banking Organizations

The ongoing consolidation of the global bank industry has created a set of large international and regional banks that engage in a broad range of complex on- and off-balance-sheet transactions, and their total assets are multiples of the GDPs of most emerging markets. These institutions are typically the parents of the foreign branches and subsidiaries established in most emerging markets. Understanding and supervising the exposure of these large international organizations has led to special measures by mature markets supervisors and requires a financial expertise that may be lacking in many emerging markets. For instance, supervisors in the United States have selected a small subset of large, complex banking organizations (LCBOs), and have established teams of examiners—assisted by specialists in payments systems, risk management, information technology, financial engineering, and modeling—that are dedicated to monitor each one of these LCBOs.[53] Since difficulties at one of these parent organizations could quickly create doubts about the viability of its local branches and subsidiaries, the stability of emerging markets financial systems has become more dependent on the quality of prudential supervision in the mature

53. See Meyer (1999).

markets. Nonetheless, emerging markets supervisors will still need to develop the expertise to monitor new activities and instruments that are likely to be used by the local establishments of LCBOs. The need to acquire such expertise has been demonstrated by the importance of derivative products in recent balance of payments crises.

Derivative Products and Prudential Supervision

As noted earlier, one of the strategies employed by major international banks when they enter an emerging market is to offer a variety of new products, including OTC derivative products. These new derivative products can be a source of considerable benefit since they increase the ability to separate and market risks and thereby allow for better hedging of a variety of risks that were previously undiversifiable. However, as noted by Peter M. Garber, these instruments can also be used to take on excessive risks, especially in weak financial systems with obsolete accounting systems, slow reporting systems, and unprepared supervisors.[54] Moreover, derivatives can affect balance of payments dynamics during a crisis and can be used to evade prudential regulation and capital or exchange controls.

The use of OTC derivative products has influenced balance of payments dynamics in several emerging markets, for example, in the balance of payments crises of the 1990s in countries such as Mexico, Korea, Brazil, and Russia.[55] A strategy used by some Korean banks in 1996–97 was to acquire structured notes that involved taking leveraged positions on currencies. In some cases, banks bought notes tied to movements in the Indonesian rupiah.[56] Korean banks that were attempting to rebuild capital positions were attracted to such notes by the seemingly high returns in a stable rupiah exchange rate environment. When the rupiah depreciated sharply, Korean banks took a double hit: they saw the U.S. dollar value of the capital of the structured note decline, and they had to deliver U.S. dollars to meet margin requirements or to wind up their repurchase agreements. Such pressures intensified during December 1997 and contributed to the sudden drain of official reserves. While most of these notes were obtained through offshore transactions, a local presence by a foreign bank providing such instruments would only facilitate the marketing process.

54. Garber (2000).

55. See Garber (2000) for a detailed discussion of the types of instruments that were used.

56. The note would pay a high coupon, but the principal repayment would depend on the U.S. dollar-rupiah exchange rate—if the rupiah depreciated, the principal repayment and interest coupon would be reduced. These positions were often leveraged by having the foreign seller of the notes enter into a repurchase agreement with the buyer with a 20 percent margin requirement.

Structured notes, equity swaps, credit derivatives, and other derivative instruments can also be used to evade the intent, if not the letter, of prudential regulations such as those designed to limit net foreign currency exposures, limits on large exposures to single borrowers, and reserve and liquidity requirements against domestic and foreign currency liabilities. At times, this will involve booking the principal as a foreign currency asset (such as U.S. dollars) but structuring the financing of and ultimate return on the instrument so that it becomes a foreign currency liability.[57]

It is evident from the experience of the 1990s that the supervisory authorities in emerging markets will need to upgrade their capacity to acquire information on and to analyze the implications of the growing use of derivative products by domestic and foreign banks operating in their markets. This will be especially true when new foreign banks are attempting to establish their position in the local markets through the marketing of these instruments and when some domestic banks are still in a weakened financial position.

Parental Support

A key consideration influencing the decisions of the authorities to allow foreign banks to enter and local residents to place deposit in these banks is the extent of support that these banks are likely to receive from their parents. There are legal and reputational issues involved in determining the support that is likely to be forthcoming during difficult periods. From a narrow legal perspective, a bank subsidiary is a stand-alone entity with its own dedicated capital, and the parent's formal obligation to support its subsidiary is generally limited to the amount of invested capital. However, the relationship between a bank and its subsidiary can be broader as a result of statutes (U.S. law, for example, requires banks to guarantee their subsidiaries' capital) or from contractual provisions between a bank and its subsidiary (that may be imposed by the regulatory authorities as a condition for issuing a license to a subsidiary). In contrast, a branch has no independent legal personality distinct from that of its parent, and claims on the branch constitute claims on the parent.[58] Even apart from the legal requirements, a parent bank would typically have an incentive to support local branches and subsidiaries because of the reputational effects associated with allowing their

---

57. Garber (2000) describes in detail the so-called Tesobono swap, which allowed Mexican banks to essentially convert a reported U.S. dollar asset into an obligation to deliver U.S. dollar payments if the Mexican peso depreciated relative to the U.S. dollar.

58. See IMF (1998b, p. 51).

failure and collapse. Indeed, the failure of a large branch or subsidiary in one country could call into question the parent's support for its establishments in other countries or even the strength of a parent's financial position.

Several factors are likely to influence the likelihood and extent of a parent bank's support for its foreign establishments. One key factor is the financial position of the parent bank. A parent bank under profit pressure and with a weak capital position may have little capacity to raise the funds needed to recapitalize a large troubled foreign entity. Another important factor is how committed the parent bank is to developing a sustained presence in the local market. As noted earlier, some foreign banks enter a market primarily to service customers from their home market who have set up operations in the local market. Should those customers fail or leave the market, these banks would be less inclined to maintain a local presence. Another issue is how much the difficulties encountered by the local establishment have arisen as a result of its own actions (such as having inadequate controls against fraud) or occur because of events beyond its control (such as the imposition of capital controls or the expropriation of its assets). While the parent bank will typically have a strong incentive to remedy problems created by weak internal controls, it may have a much smaller incentive to support its local establishment if *force majeure* events prevent the local entity from making payments.

It is evident from recent episodes of "ring fencing" of the obligations of the local branches of some major international banks in Asia that there are clear limits on the extent of parental support for these local operations. The ring-fencing banks argue that the imposition of controls on capital outflows by Malaysia led to internal reviews of what similar controls in other countries might do to the ability of their branches to make payments on foreign-exchange-related transactions. They found that under some agreements, such as the master International Swaps and Derivatives Association (ISDA) netting agreements for derivative products, the parent would be responsible for completing the transaction if its onshore branch could not make payment. In their view, the parent was therefore implicitly providing its counterparts with insurance against sovereign events such as the imposition of capital controls. To correct this situation, they inserted the ring-fencing clauses into their confirmation documentation to spell out the conditions under which the parent would not be responsible for the payments of the onshore branch and to make the pricing of these transactions more transparent.

Other banks have argued that ring fencing is not just a pricing issue but has broader systemic implications because it will alter how much support parent banks will offer their onshore branches and subsidiaries during crises. These bankers made two points. First, the recent ring-fencing clauses were quietly inserted into the confirmation sheets without any prior announcement, and this could be done in the documentation governing other cross-border products. Second, the ring-fencing clauses change not only the credit risks associated with these contracts but also the jurisdiction in which they can be enforced. While the master ISDA agreements are enforceable in mature market courts (typically in the United States or the United Kingdom), the ring-fencing clauses mean that any claims on a ring-fenced branch would most likely have to be litigated in the local courts.

While this ring-fencing activity applies to derivative products contracts and was initiated by the banks, other obligations of branches are in some cases ring-fenced by law. For example, under the Federal Reserve Act and also New York banking law, all deposit liabilities of the foreign branches of U.S. banks are already ring-fenced if the local authorities take actions that prevent the local branch from making payment (such as the imposition of capital controls).[59] This policy was apparently motivated by earlier experiences when the branches of some U.S. banks were unable to make payments on maturing deposits owing to the imposition of capital controls or expropriation (in Cuba and Vietnam).

Banking System Concentration

The expansion of large foreign banks (often with global balance sheets several times local GDP) into emerging markets has prompted concerns about concentration in the local banking markets. The entry of such institutions can affect concentration directly and indirectly. In some cases, large foreign banks have acquired a significant share of local bank assets by purchasing a local state bank that was being privatized or by acquisition of a large private bank that was in need of recapitalization. The entry of such banks would in turn create pressures on local banks to merge to remain competitive by capturing economies of scale in back office operations and by being viewed by depositors as offering the same safety and soundness as large for-

59. The relevant Federal Reserve statute states "a member bank shall not be required to pay any deposit made at a foreign branch of the bank if the bank cannot repay the deposit due to: (1) an act of war, insurrection or civil strife; or (2) an action by a foreign government or instrumentality (whether de jure or de facto) in the country in which the bank is located unless the member bank expressly agreed in writing to repay the deposit under those circumstances."

eign banks. Moreover, in some countries, such as Chile, the concentration issue arose when the parents of two local foreign banks merged.[60]

There are concerns that such concentration could create monopoly power that would reduce banking system efficiency and the availability of credit, open up new avenues for the transmission of disturbances from mature to emerging markets, and increase the risk that these institutions will become too big to fail locally. It has been argued that a high degree of concentration will adversely affect output and growth by yielding higher interest rate spreads (with higher loan rates and lower deposit rates) and a lower stock of credit than in a less concentrated, more competitive system. However, theoretical views on the effects of such concentration on growth and output conflict, and the limited empirical evidence available yields conflicting results.[61] In any event, the recent experiences of Chile and Mexico suggest that emerging markets should equip themselves with antitrust laws appropriate to deal with the complex issues involved in the definition and resolution of anticompetitive cases in the financial sector.

Even if there is ambiguity about the effects of banking system concentration on economic performance, it is evident that a highly concentrated system could face a too-big-to-fail dilemma. In this situation, the failure of a single large bank could seriously disrupt the local payments system and money markets. Moreover, when the largest banks consist of foreign banks, then a high degree of concentration can open up a new channel for the transmission of shocks in the sense that difficulties for the parent bank can create immediate uncertainties about its local branches and subsidiaries. The share of total assets held by some of the international banks in Central Europe and Latin America is around the 15–25 percent level, suggesting fairly large exposures in relatively volatile regions. That some of these banks have a large presence in individual banking markets highlights the potential for "reverse contagion."[62]

60. The merger of Banco Santander with Banco Central Hispano resulted in the merger of their respective subsidiaries, Banco Santander Chile and Banco Santiago, the two largest banks in the country with a combined market share of about 28 percent of total deposits.

61. For example, Levine (2000) found no statistical relationship between banking system concentration and any negative outcomes for financial sector development, banking system fragility, or growth. In contrast, Cetorelli and Gambera (1999) found that, while banking system concentration helps those industries heavily dependent on external financing, the overall effect on output was negative.

62. See IMF (2000).

Systemic Risk, Official Safety Nets, and Cross-Border Banking

Systemic risk associated with cross-border banking can arise if either liquidity or solvency problems of banks in one country create similar problems for financial institutions elsewhere in the international financial system. As noted by Allen Berger and others, the contagion effects associated with such problems can be transferred across different financial systems through failures to settle in payments systems, panic runs that follow the revelation of institutional problems, or falling prices, liquidity problems, or markets failing to clear when large volumes are traded under crisis conditions.[63] Besides creating problems for the implementation of monetary policy, such contagion will also impose the costs arising from the bankruptcy and financial distress of institutions affected by the contagion.

Systemic risk can conceptually decrease or increase as a result of a growing foreign presence in the banking system. As noted earlier, foreign bank entry is likely to lead to consolidation in the banking system directly (if foreign banks acquire local banks) and indirectly (as competitive pressures lead local banks to merge). This consolidation may help reduce systemic risks if it creates a smaller set of larger institutions that are more efficient and can be monitored more readily by prudential supervisors and market participants. The large foreign banks would also be part of institutions that have business activities diversified across national borders and can potentially be a source of support for their local bank. Systemic risks, however, arise because the failure of larger institutions can be more severe. Furthermore, a weakened parent bank could quickly drain funds from a local bank to support its own position.

Cross-border banking activities can affect the cost of maintaining an official safety net under the financial system in several ways. If governments are more likely to protect large banks because they are "too big to fail," then the mergers stimulated by foreign bank entry could increase the implicit costs associated with maintaining the official safety net. To contain these costs, there will be a need to strengthen prudential supervision of such institutions or eventually to limit mergers that increase systemic risks sharply. Moreover, the entry of foreign banks and associated local mergers could bring into the official safety net institutions that normally receive only limited access to the safety net. In many emerging markets, banks are not stand-alone institutions but are rather a part of holding company groups. Even when banks are of a relatively modest size, the existence of these

63. Berger and others (2000).

groups raises issues about what level of consolidation should occur when one is evaluating bank capital adequacy. The key issues are that the holding company can potentially transfer capital and asset and liability positions among its various entities if they are not treated on a consolidated basis and that there will not be arm's-length transactions among the various members of the group. As the banks owned by the groups become too large to fail, concern arises that support provided to the bank during a crisis will directly or indirectly assist the rest of the group. In many respects, these potential problems can only be minimized by consolidation at the group level.

References

Abut, Daniel. 1999. "The Independent Local Bank in Latin America." Goldman Sachs (November).

Baliño, Tomás. 1991. "The Argentine Banking Crisis of 1980." In "Banking Crises: Cases and Issues," edited by V. Sundararajan and Tomás Baliño, 58–112. Washington: International Monetary Fund.

Baliño, Tomás, and Angel Ubide. 1999. "The Korean Financial Crisis of 1997—A Strategy of Financial Sector Reform." Working Paper 99-28. Washington: International Monetary Fund (March).

Bank for International Settlements (BIS). 1996. *Report on International Developments in Banking Supervision: Report Number 10.* Basle (June).

———. 2000. *Consolidated International Banking Statistics* (May).

Barajas, Adolfo, Roberto Steiner, and Natalia Salazar. 1999. "Foreign Investment in Colombia's Financial Sector." Working Paper 99-150. Washington: International Monetary Fund (November).

Belaisch, Agnes, Laura Kodres, Joaquim Levy, and Angel Ubide. 2000. "Euro Area Banking at the Cross-Roads." Unpublished. Washington: International Monetary Fund (May).

Berger, Allen, Robert De Young, Hesna Geney, and Gregory F. Udell. 2000. *Globalization of Financial Institutions: Evidence from Cross-Border Banking Performance.* Brookings; also published as Federal Reserve Bank of Chicago Working Paper WP-99-25, December 1999.

Berger, Allen, Leora F. Klapper, and Gregory F. Udell. 2001. "The Ability of Banks to Lend to Informationally Opaque Small Businesses." Washington: World Bank (Mimeo).

Canals, Jordi. 1997. *Universal Banking: International Comparisons and Theoretical Perspectives.* Oxford: Oxford University Press.

Caprio, Gerard, and Daniela Klingebiel. 1999. "Episodes of Systemic and Borderline Financial Crises." Mimeo. Washington: World Bank.

Cetorelli, Nicola, and Michele Gambera. 1999. "Banking Market Structure, Financial Dependence and Growth: International Evidence from Industry Data." Federal Reserve Bank of Chicago Working Paper WP-99-8 (March).

Claessens, Stijn, Asli Demirgüç-Kunt, and Harry Huizinga. 1999. "How Does Foreign Presence Affect Domestic Banking Markets?" Unpublished. Washington: World Bank (August).

Claessens, Stijn, and Thomas Glaessner. 1999. "Internationalization of Financial Services in Asia." Unpublished. Washington: World Bank (April).

Clarke, George, Robert Cull, Laura D'Amato, and Andrea Molinari. 1999. "The Effect of Foreign Entry on Argentina's Domestic Banking Sector." Unpublished. Washington: World Bank (April).

Crama, Y., L. Leruth, L. Renneboog, and J. P. Urbain. 1999. "Corporate Governance Structures, Control and Performance in European Markets: A Tale of Two Systems." Working Paper 9997. Center for Economic Research (October).

Dell'Ariccia, Giovanni. 1997. "Cross-Border Banking Liberalization with Asymmetric Information." Unpublished. Washington: International Monetary Fund.

Demirgüc-Kunt, Asli, and Enrica Detragiache. 1998. "The Determinants of Banking Crises in Developing and Developed Countries." *Staff Papers* 45 (March): 81–109. Washington: International Monetary Fund.

Denizer, Cevdet. 1999. "Foreign Entry in Turkey's Banking System, 1980-1997." Paper prepared for WTO-World Bank Conference on Liberalization and Internationalization of Financial Services, Geneva (May).

Domac, Ilker, and Giovanni Ferri. 1999. "The Credit Crunch in East Asia: Evidence from Field Findings on Bank Behavior and Policy Issues." Paper prepared for workshop on Credit Crunch in East Asia: What Do We Know? What Do We Need to Know? Washington: World Bank.

Dziobek, Claudia, J. Kim Hobbs, and David Marston. 2000. "Toward a Framework for Systemic Liquidity Policy." Working Paper 00-34. Washington: International Monetary Fund (March).

Eichengreen, Barry, and Michael Mussa. 1998. *Capital Account Liberalization—Theoretical and Practical Aspects.* Occasional Paper 172. Washington: International Monetary Fund.

Fitch IBCA. 1999a. "Thailand: Slow Progress on Restructuring Thailand's Banks." *Thailand* (March).

———. 1999b. "Selective Brazilian Banks: 1998 Results" (April).

———. 2000. "Internet Banking: Separating the Myths from Reality" (May).

Folkerts-Landau, David, and Bankim Chadha. 1999. "The Evolving Role of Banks in International Capital Flows." In *International Capital Flows*, edited by Martin Feldstein, 191–234. University of Chicago Press.

Garber, Peter M. 2000. "What You See vs. What You Get: Derivatives in International Capital Flows." Paper prepared for "Emerging Markets in the New Financial System: Managing Financial and Corporate Distress." World Bank-Brookings-IMF Financial Markets and Development Conference, New Jersey.

Garber, Peter M., and Steven R. Weisbrod. 1994. "Opening the Financial Services Market in Mexico." In *The Mexico-U.S. Free Trade Agreement*, edited by Peter Garber. MIT Press.

García Cantera, José. 1999. "Foreign Financial Institutions in Latin America." New York, Salomon Smith Barney (October).

Goldberg, Linda., B. Gerard Dages, and Daniel Kinney. 2000. "Foreign and Domestic Bank Participation in Emerging Markets: Lessons from Argentina and Mexico." Unpublished. New York: Federal Reserve Bank of New York (March).

Guillén, Mauro, and Adrian Tshoegel. 1999. "At Last the Internationalization of Retail Banking? The Case of the Spanish Banks in Latin America." Unpublished. University of Pennsylvania, Wharton (September).

Gunther, Jeffery W. 1994. "Regional Capital Imbalances and the Removal of Interstate Banking Restrictions." *Economic Letters* 44: 439–42.

Heinkel, Robert L., and Maurice D. Levy. 1992. "The Structure of International Banking." *Journal of International Money and Finance* 11 (June): 251–72.

Hellwig, Martin. 1999. "On the Economics and Politics of Corporate Finance and Corporate Control." Unpublished. Manheim, Germany: University of Mannheim.

International Monetary Fund. 1995. *International Capital Markets: Developments, Prospects, and Key Policy Issues.* World Economic and Financial Surveys. Washington (September).

———. 1996. *International Capital Markets: Developments, Prospects, and Key Policy Issues.* World Economic and Financial Surveys. Washington (September).

———. 1998a. *International Capital Markets: Developments, Prospects, and Key Policy Issues.* World Economic and Financial Surveys. Washington (September).

———. 1998b. *Toward a Framework for Financial Stability.* World Economic and Financial Surveys. Washington (January).

———. 1999. *International Capital Markets: Developments, Prospects, and Key Policy Issues.* World Economic and Financial Surveys. Washington (September).

———. 2000. *International Capital Markets: Developments, Prospects, and Key Policy Issues.* World Economic and Financial Surveys. Washington (September).

Irving, Keith, and Girish Kumar. 1999. "Asia-Pacific Banks: Progress and Issues in Bank Restructuring." Merrill Lynch (February).

Jackson, William E. III, and Robert A. Eisenbeis. 1997. "Geographic Integration of Bank Deposit Markets and Restrictions on Interstate Banking: A Cointegration Approach." *Journal of Economics and Business* 49: 335–46.

Kaminsky, Graciela, and Carmen Reinhart. 1999. "The Twin Crises: The Causes of Banking and Balance-of-Payments Problems." *American Economic Review* 89 (June): 473–500.

Kiraly, J., and others. 1999. "Experience with Internationalization of FSP. Case Study: Hungary." Unpublished. Budapest (April).

Laeven, Luc. 1999. "Impact of Ownership Structure on Bank Performance in East Asia." Unpublished. Washington: World Bank (September).

Levine, Ross. 1999. "Foreign Bank Entry and Capital Control Liberalization: Effects on Growth and Stability." Unpublished. University of Minnesota (October).

———. 2000. "Bank Concentration: Chile and International Comparisons." Working Paper 62. Santiago: Central Bank of Chile (January).

Lindgren, Carl-Johan, Gillian García, and Matthew I. Saal. 1996. *Bank Soundness and Macroeconomic Policy.* Washington: International Monetary Fund.

Meyer, Laurence. 1999. "Implications of Recent Global Financial Crises for Bank Supervision and Regulation." Chicago: Federal Reserve Bank of Chicago (October).

OECD. 1999. *Economic Survey: Hungary.* Paris: Organization for Economic Cooperation and Development.

Palmer, David E. 2000. "U.S. Bank Exposure to Emerging-Market Countries during Recent Financial Crises." *Federal Reserve Bulletin.* U.S. Board of Governors of the Federal Reserve Board (February).

Peek, Joe, and Eric S. Rosengren. 2000. "The Role of Foreign Banks in Latin America." Boston: Federal Reserve Bank of Boston (Mimeo).

Tamirisa, Natalia, and others. 2000. "Trade Policy in Financial Services." Working Paper 00-31. Washington: International Monetary Fund (February).

Vansetti, M. Celina, Philip Guarco, and Gregory W. Bauer. 2000. "The 'Fall' of Bancomer and the Future of Indigenous Mega-Banks in Latin America." Moody's Investor Service, *Global Credit Research* (April).

Vives, Xavier. 1991. *Banking Competition and European Integration.* Cambridge: Cambridge University Press.

Williams, Barry. 1997. "Positive Theories of Multinational Banking." *Journal of Economic Surveys* 11 (March): 71–100.

Williamson, Stephen D. 1989. "Restrictions on Financial Intermediaries and Implications for Aggregate Fluctuations: Canada and the United States, 1870–1913." In *NBER Macroeconomics Annual 1989*, edited by Olivier Blanchard and Stanley Fischer, 303–40. MIT Press.

II

*What Foreign
Institutions Do in
Emerging Markets:
Overview*

MICHAEL POMERLEANO
GEORGE J. VOJTA

3

Foreign Banks in Emerging Markets: An Institutional Study

Asia, L. America F23 G21 016 L25

This paper provides an institutional analysis of the role of foreign and domestic banks in the context of a globalizing banking industry. The discussion explores the range of products and services offered by foreign financial institutions and the complementarity of these offerings with the capacity of domestic banks. We highlight differences in foreign bank strategies, products, services, management processes, and management information systems, both within the foreign bank group and relative to domestic banks.

Foreign banks historically had limited operations in emerging markets, with very few exceptions. In most countries, they operated under restrictive regulations, such as prohibitions or limitations on opening new branches. Foreign ownership of domestic banks increased dramatically in the 1990s, however, partially in response to liberalized regulations and, importantly, partially through equity investments in banks in need of restructuring. As a result, foreign banks garnered a substantial share of banking assets in many countries.

The degree of foreign participation is very much a regional story. In Latin America, acquisitions in the financial services sector occurred at a hectic pace over the past few years. Several sizable and important foreign banks,

We are grateful to Colleen Mascenik for excellent research assistance and to Marcos Brujis, Jeffrey Carmichael, Luigi Passamonti, and William Shaw for helpful comments.

in particular, increased their presence, including Spain's Banco Santander and Banco Bilbao Vizcaya, the United Kingdom's HSBC, and the Netherlands' ABN AMRO. Chile has the highest share of foreign control in the banking system (54 percent), followed by Argentina (49 percent). In Mexico, the share of assets under foreign control rose from 19 percent at the end of 1999 to around 40 percent in 2000. Venezuela currently has about 40 percent, as well. The need to restructure domestic banks and changes implemented under NAFTA combined to create these opportunities for foreign investors.

In Central Europe, the share of total bank assets controlled by foreign banks rose from less than 10 percent in 1994 to more than 50 percent in 1999.[1] Hungary has the highest level of foreign ownership (57 percent of banking assets), while Poland has the second-highest level (53 percent); in both cases, the increase is largely the result of restructuring.

Only in Asia is the presence of foreign banks relatively low, ranging from a 2.1 percent loan market share in China and 3.1 percent deposit market share in Taiwan to a 32.8 percent deposit market share in Hong Kong. Several countries fall in the middle of this range: foreign banks have an 8.6 percent deposit market share in Thailand, 9.7 percent in Korea, 10 percent in both the Philippines and Singapore, and 22.8 percent in Malaysia.[2] However, the regional situation is bound to change. A large share of bank assets is still under government control in the aftermath of the crisis, and governments will eventually have to reprivatize domestic banks. In addition, as part of its entry into the World Trade Organization, China agreed to open its domestic corporate banking market to foreign financial institutions in two years and its domestic retail banking market in five years.

The issue of foreign bank presence in emerging markets has a long history. Traditional arguments in favor of encouraging the participation of foreign banks in the banking systems of emerging markets maintain that foreign bank presence is effective for introducing best practices, improving credit analysis and other processes (as well as the allocative efficiency of investment), fostering greater competition, and accelerating the pace of banking reform. On the other hand, policymakers in emerging economies face difficult questions in determining how rapidly to open their financial sectors to foreign competition. They must confront nationalistic perceptions that the banking system is an inherent part of sovereignty, fears that domestic groups will lose access to financial services, and concerns that the

1. IMF (2000).
2. Goldman Sachs (1999).

country could lose control over the course of development if the domestic banking system were taken over by global banks.

New factors have emerged, however, that are stimulating the participation of foreign banks in emerging market banking systems. These factors derive from current trends in banking. The industry is consolidating on a global basis, and the global economy is increasingly interconnected in real and financial terms—the crises of the 1990s notwithstanding. A small number of very large banking institutions of global scope are coming to dominate the competitive arena for cross-border activities. Domestic banks in emerging (and many other) markets do not have the resources or the desire to build competitive global networks; they must therefore create alliances with the global banks to provide global services to their customers in many areas.

Another important trend, which was arrested by the financial crises of the 1990s, is the development of local capital markets, often fueled by pension reform. The development of local markets requires importing foreign expertise, in the form of branches, joint ventures, and other forms of collaboration. The reemergence of this phenomenon following the crises of the 1990s is in an early stage. It is strengthened, however, by the reality that the global financial system supports a movement to achieve universal acceptance of global best practices. Consequently, standards in certain key policy areas must be recognized.[3] Compliance with these standards requires linkages between domestic banks and foreign sources of expertise. A final factor, namely, increased foreign direct participation in domestic banks, relates to the restructuring of the domestic banking systems, often through privatization, as a result of the transition to market economies under way in many countries, the problem of asset impairment in banks following the crises of the 1990s, and the need to bring management and regulation of domestic banking up to world-class standards.

The paper takes a clinical approach to analyzing the role of foreign banks in emerging markets in the above context. We first prepared a questionnaire that highlights key aspects of banks' operations, which we used to guide us and our interlocutors during the interviews with foreign and domestic

3. Following the recent financial crises, the international community has emphasized the need for specific measures to strengthen the architecture of the international financial system. The development and implementation of standards and codes in a number of areas—including data dissemination, fiscal, monetary and financial policy transparency, banking regulation and supervision, securities and insurance regulation, accounting, auditing, bankruptcy and corporate governance—have become central elements of these efforts.

banks. The list of interviews and the questionnaire are presented in appendix 3A.

The analysis is presented in seven principal sections. The following section provides a general overview of the strategies pursued by foreign and domestic banks. The paper then describes the corporate products and services of foreign and domestic banks. Subsequent sections explore services to small and medium-sized enterprise; consumer products and services; lending policies, practices, procedures, internal controls, and management information systems; and the differences in personnel policies with respect to recruitment, incentive pay, training resources, and promotions. The final section derives policy implications from the analysis.

Strategies in Emerging Markets

In this section, we describe the strategies followed by key foreign and domestic banks in emerging markets. Some foreign banks are developing profitable local franchises that target the top end of the market in consumer and commercial banking, while others focus on investment banking, private banking, and operating services. Foreign banks offer innovative products and services, and they are putting increasing pressure on domestic banks.

The strategy of domestic banks is characterized by three patterns. First, domestic banks are adopting the technologies and services associated with foreign banks. Second, they are refocusing their role in the corporate sector to provide distribution and investment capabilities in international financing and local corporate services. Third, they are allocating resources to the retail sector and to small and medium-sized enterprises (SMEs) in order to enhance products and upgrade the technology and infrastructure necessary to attract customers.

Foreign Banks

The form of foreign bank participation is determined first by the motivations that drive the bank to enter an emerging market. Many are present in an emerging market only to serve multinational firms that are headquartered in the banks' home market and have a presence in the emerging market. Japanese and Korean banks, for example, have usually entered emerging markets on the heels of a home-based customer they serve. These banks offer little or no service to multinational corporations or local customers in the country, and they do not offer banking services or market presence comparable to domestic banks. In the Philippines, foreign banks from Japan, Korea, and Thailand do not interact either with a domestic clientele or with most multinationals; rather, they serve specific firms from their home market and have little effect on the domestic economy beyond this role.

The globalization of economies and foreign direct investment have expanded cross-border asset holdings and international trade. In response, some foreign banks have increased cross-border operations to support multinational clients with which they have global relationships. Banks such as ABN AMRO and Deutsche Bank have entered emerging markets to expand their services to major multinational corporations and large domestic corporations. Others have entered emerging markets to serve corporate and retail clients and are becoming part of the fabric of domestic banking. Citibank, HSBC, and Standard Chartered are banks in this category.

Foreign bank entry can take one of two forms: entry via a branch or subsidiary and entry via the purchase of an existing franchise. Banks such as Citibank, J.P. Morgan Chase, and Deutsche Bank follow the first strategy and grow organically in the new market, while ABN AMRO, Commerzbank, HSBC, and Banco Santander tend to purchase existing franchises. Both strategies have advantages and disadvantages. Organic growth takes time and involves risks related to unfamiliarity with local market conditions. The acquisition of a minority or majority interest requires internal restructuring (shedding excessive staff) and the transfer of staff and operational processes from the foreign bank to the acquired bank. Table 3-1 summarizes the strategies and products of key foreign banks in emerging markets; appendix 3B presents this information in more detail and for more banks.

Domestic Banks

The strategies pursued by domestic banks reflect their local advantages in the corporate, retail, and SME sectors and the competitive pressures posed by foreign banks. The penetration of foreign banks has generated technology and process transfers into the domestic market. Their presence pushes domestic banks to upgrade their services and encourages bank customers to demand better products and services (see table 3-2 for a summary of strategies and products and appendix 3C for a more detailed discussion). Domes-

Table 3-1. *Strategies and Products of Key Foreign Banks in Emerging Markets*

Bank	Region	Emerging market strategy	Important products and services
Citibank	Global presence	Become a full-service domestic bank targeting the high end of the market, typically through internal growth	Full range of retail and corporate services
Banco Santander Central Hispano (BSCH)	Focused expansion in Latin America	Create a regional platform through the acquisition of disparate local holdings; Santander is becoming one of the leading regional banks in Latin America	Retail banking operations, asset management, and wholesale banking
HSBC Holdings	Global reach; subsidiaries operating in Hong Kong, Southeast Asia, and Latin America	Become one of the leading global banks through the acquisition of franchises and internal growth	Retail and commercial banking, greater focus on private banking through the acquisition of Republic Bank and expansion of retail operations
J. P. Morgan Chase Manhattan Bank	Asia, Latin America	Cut back on existing consumer banking business and refocus on corporate services in select markets	Investment banking, treasury sales, private banking, equity and fixed income underwriting, proprietary trading, investment management and operating services
Standard Chartered	Extensive network in the emerging markets of Asia, Africa, and Latin America	Position itself as a leading emerging market bank through acquisitions and internal growth	Corporate and consumer banking

Table 3-2. *Strategies and Products of Key Domestic Banks in Emerging Markets*

Bank	Region	Emerging market strategy	Important products and services
Banacci	Mexico	Combine large-scale financial intermediation and payment transactions; balance business and retail banking	Deposit and lending products, credit cards, asset management services
Banco Galicia	Argentina	Capitalize on technological efficiency by expanding the network of ATMs, point-of-sale terminals, and twenty-four-hour banking	Collateralized lending, credit card services, individual deposit accounts
Bangkok Bank	Thailand	Compete across a broad range of products by upgrading products and services and employing more sophisticated and automated sales techniques	Corporate banking, retail banking, credit cards, personal services, investment products
Bradesco	Brazil	Maintain brand recognition by continuing to invest in automation; improve the quality of products and services; and restructure the branch network	Commercial, rural, and housing lending, consumer credit, savings, domestic investment banking, leasing, brokerage, insurance, and pension funds
State Bank of India	India	Respond to the changing needs of retail and corporate business by introducing new products and services, upgrading internal systems, focusing on retail lending, and computerizing its branch network	Retail banking, including credit cards, ATMs, and Internet banking

tic banks increasingly adopt the products, services, credit measurement, compensation, and management methods used by foreign banks. Beyond these immediate transfers within the banking sector, the domestic market is exposed to a much broader transfer of related services, such as marketing, public relations, accounting, and law, which leads to increased sophistication of financial and other services in the host country.

A second pattern in domestic banks' strategies is the relative contraction of exposure to wholesale lending to prime clients—an area in which the demonstrated superiority of foreign banks is difficult and costly to challenge. Instead, domestic banks increasingly focus on providing international and local services to corporate clients. Domestic resources have also migrated toward retail and SME services. This pattern is especially evident in banks such as Bangkok Bank and the State Bank of India.

Domestic banks are not affected by foreign banks in the same way in all regions. For example, the entry of foreign banks poses a threat to domestic franchises throughout Latin America, but as yet not in Asia.

Corporate Banking Products and Services

This section describes the wholesale products provided by foreign banks, with an emphasis on products and services that have not been successfully offered by domestic banks. In particular, foreign banks have a competitive advantage in products that require a global platform, such as foreign exchange operations, derivatives trading operations, cross-border underwriting, mergers and acquisitions, trade finance, multiple-currency cash management, global custody, and investment services. Domestic banks, in turn, have a competitive advantage in products that require local capabilities, particularly funding and know-how. The discussion is summarized in table 3-3.

Lending

Lending products consist of working capital and term loans, syndicated loans, project finance, trade finance, and equipment finance. Each is described below.

WORKING CAPITAL AND TERM LOANS. Foreign banks offer working capital loans, overdrafts, term loans (including real estate loans and other secured debt), backstops, and revolvers. Domestic banks, however, have a

Table 3-3. *Products, Services, and the Respective Competitive Advantages of Foreign and Domestic Banks*

Product	Description	Competitive advantage
	Corporate banking	
Lending		
Working capital and term loans	Working capital loans, overdrafts, term loans (including real estate loans and other secured debt), backstops, and revolvers	For bread-and-butter working capital and overdraft lending, domestic banks have a distinct advantage owing to their access to domestic currency and broad franchise base. Although foreign banks have better underwriting skills, they do not tend to show a competitive advantage in this area.
Syndicated loans	Loans to help borrowers meet substantial financing needs that exceed capital adequacy of an individual bank	Foreign banks have superior credit underwriting skills and strong relationships with a base of diversified investors to place the debt. These are complemented by credible trust and agency capacity. Domestic banks' roles in distributing and investment in financings has grown into comanager roles.
Project finance	Financing for large needs like infrastructure	Foreign banks possess corporate finance structuring skills and global placement experience.
Trade finance	Financing for international trade transactions	Foreign banks can apply an integrated global platform and fully integrated global electronic reporting across functional processes and geographic areas.
Equipment finance	Finance for equipment lease programs, vendor programs, secured franchise financing, and dealer financing	Foreign banks were innovators in this field and have experience.
Capital markets		
Global custody clearing and settlement	Trade settlement and related custody functions—safekeeping, registration, income collection, corporate actions, confirmations, and appropriate reporting	Foreign banks can offer multiple-currency cash and securities statements, multiple-market coverage, and a global product. Domestic banks are important local partners in these businesses.
Depository receipts (ADRs, GDRs)	Securities that represent shares of non-U.S. firms and that trade in the United States and other financial markets	Foreign banks offer a range of depository receipt services, including knowledge of the legal and regulatory issues in the United States and custodian arrangements (ability to provide transfer and registration services, account management, and corporate action services).
Securitization	A range of products from asset-backed and mortgage-backed securities to securitization of future revenues	Foreign banks employ a broad base of skills and global experience, as well as placement reach.
Global and domestic equity and bond underwriting	Underwriting of sovereign and corporate global and domestic equity and bonds	Foreign banks have market knowledge and global distribution strength using domestic bank relationships. Experience enables them to execute complex financing in multiple currencies and to distribute securities globally. The integration of underwriting, sales, trading, and research offers a competitive advantage. Domestic banks have important complementary roles in distribution and investments.

Table 3-3. *Continued*

Product	Description	Competitive advantage
Private equity investments	Investment in private equity, venture capital	Most foreign banks have proprietary subsidiaries in the private equity market, with equity and expertise.
Agency and trust services	Trustee and agency-related appointments for various debt products, in addition to escrow, project finance, tenders and exchanges, and other specialized agency services	Foreign banks command a greater degree of confidence from issuers because of their experience and full range of support across currencies.
Treasury operations		
Foreign exchange	Foreign exchange services	Global infrastructure, skills, and strong technical platforms are foreign banks' strengths.
Risk management products	Structured risk management products—swaps, options, floors, caps, collars, and credit derivatives—for managing foreign exchange, interest rate, and credit risk	Foreign banks pioneered derivatives, such as interest rate swaps and options. The combination of skills, expertise, access to counterparties, and a global risk management platform are competitive advantages.
Cash management services	Centralized foreign exchange and interest rate risk management to control working capital surpluses and deficits	Foreign banks have automated global platforms and processes that capture and deliver updated comprehensive information regarding customer cash positions.
Financial advisory services		
Mergers and acquisitions (M&As)	Traditional M&As, takeover defense, strategic restructurings, international M&A regulations, tax-advantaged structures, leveraged transactions, and special committee assignments	Foreign banks benefit from ability and experience in all these fields.

Small and medium-sized enterprises (SMEs)

SME lending	Loans for small and medium-sized businesses	Domestic banks benefit from broad franchise networks, brand-name recognition, local knowledge, cultural preferences, and sometimes regulatory preferences, while foreign banks are often barred from entering this market by the high costs of establishing a network and other risks.

Consumer banking

Traditional products		
Home mortgages	Loans for home or other real estate purchases	Although foreign banks have a reputation for easy application procedures, longer-term loans, and competitive rates, domestic banks have an equally strong advantage stemming from brand-name recognition outside of cities, widespread geographic franchise networks, local knowledge, and cultural preferences.
Personal loans	Loans for immediate or well-planned needs	Advantages to domestic banks include access to local markets and consumer familiarity, as well as access to domestic currency. Although foreign banks enjoy a base of global capital and superior credit analysis processes and tools, they tend not to hold competitive advantages in this area.

Table 3-3. *Continued*

Product	Description	Competitive advantage
Credit cards	Many credit card products	Advantages to foreign banks come from large information technology platforms, global networks, superior data management, credit evaluation procedures, and research and development investments. Domestic banks are an important source of customers.
Asset management	Personal asset management	Capacity and expertise benefit foreign banks.
Private banking	Services that meet the needs of high-net-worth clients	Foreign banks offer one-stop shopping in virtually any market in the world.
Innovative products and services		
E-finance	Banking services offered via the Internet	Foreign banks appear to be using e-finance to complement existing services. Many domestic banks are also developing e-finance capabilities, often in conjuction with Internet firms.
New products and services	Products and services introduced by foreign banks in local markets	Foreign banks have skills and technology to offer a broader range of services involving greater risks, multiple currencies, and greater technological demands than their domestic counterparts.

distinct advantage in this field, which is partly attributable to their ability to access local funding through the mobilization of domestic deposits via a branch network. Regulatory impediments are another consideration for foreign banks. In some countries, foreign banks lack access to local currency funding, which inhibits their domestic lending.[4] In Korea, for instance, foreign banks can only fund themselves in the call market through the sole authorized broker, and they have to pay higher rates than domestic banks. Some banks, such as Citibank, have succeeded in building up a base of retail funding, such that their margins are wider. Limited capital and legal lending limits are additional factors in countries in which foreign banks operate as locally incorporated subsidiaries.

Outside the bread-and-butter working capital and overdraft lending, foreign banks generally accrue greater advantages through other types of lending and additional products and services. In these areas, foreign banks leverage three distinct advantages: their global platform; skills and experience; and access to global capital. In Asia, for example, Greenwich Associates ranked the world's top financial providers and quantified the

4. See U.S. Department of the Treasury, "National Treatment Study 1998" (www.ustreas.gov/nts). The National Treatment Study is a quadrennial report required by the Financial Reports Act of 1988.

Figure 3-1. *Quality of Relationship between Top Corporate Banks and Major Firms in Asia*[a]

Bank's importance to firm (percent)[b]

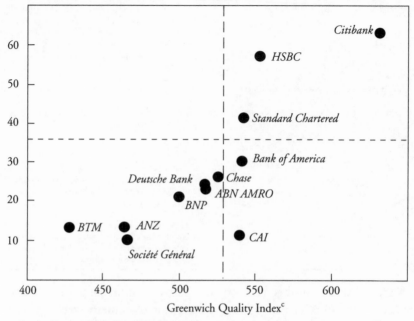

Source: Greenwich Associates (2000a, 2000c).

a. ANZ: Australia and New Zealand Banking Group; BTM: Bank of Tokyo-Mitsubishi.

b. Proportion of respondents who ranked bank as important to their firm.

c. The Greenwhich Quality Index is calculated using a normalized composite of all qualitative evaluations, with scores ranging from 0 (lowest) to 1,000 (highest).

relationship management of banks offering services to a large number of companies in the region.[5] The survey targeted banks that are headquartered outside of Asia (to capture trends in cross-border business) and that provide services in all eight countries covered, namely, Hong Kong, India, Korea, Malaysia, the Philippines, Singapore, Taiwan, and Thailand. Figure 3-1 shows how the 325 corporate financial officers included in the survey rank the relationship management of banks in terms of the importance to the company and the overall quality of service. The upper-right quadrant shows that three of these banks—Citibank, HSBC, and Standard Chartered—are seen as important to at least 40 percent of the major companies in Asia today and that all of them receive above-average ratings on quality of service by the companies that use them frequently.

5. Greenwich Associates (2000a, 2000b).

Figure 3-2. *Quality of Relationship between Top Corporate Banks and Major Firms in Latin America*

Bank's importance to firm (percent)[a]

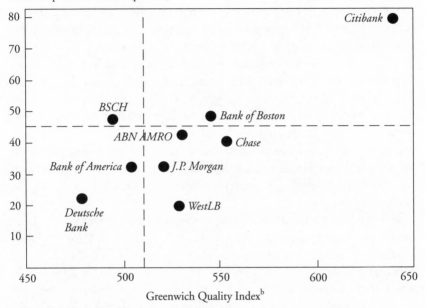

Greenwich Quality Index[b]

Source: Greenwich Associates (2000b, 2000d).

a. Proportion of respondents who ranked bank as important to their firm.

b. The Greenwhich Quality Index is calculated using a normalized composite of all qualitative evaluations, with scores ranging from 0 (lowest) to 1,000 (highest).

In a similar study, corporate financial officers ranked the relationship management of major money center banks in Latin America (see figure 3-2).[6] Four of these banks—Citibank, Bank of Boston, ABN AMRO, and BSCH—are seen as important to 40 percent or more of the major companies in Latin America today; the first three of these also are rated favorably for quality of service.

SYNDICATED LOANS. Syndicated loans help borrowers meet financing needs that exceed the capital adequacy of an individual bank by enabling them to reach investors through syndicated debt offerings. Foreign banks have a competitive advantage in loan syndication as a result of their credit underwriting skills and their ability to reach a base of diversified investors that includes domestic banks, foreign banks, loan funds, insurance companies, investment banks, and finance companies. They use syndication teams to bring specialized

6. Greenwich Associates (2000c, 2000d).

industry knowledge to the structure of transactions. Domestic banks, in turn, play an increasing role in the distribution and investment of this type of financing, and they are beginning to achieve comanager mandates.

PROJECT FINANCE. As emerging economies grow, so does their need to build and finance infrastructure, such as power plants, telecommunications networks, toll roads, and airports. Foreign banks possess corporate finance structuring skills, including financial advice, loans, bonds, export credit, and multilateral agency financing, as well as local currency financing, foreign exchange, and cash management. Their global experience facilitates the mobilization of debt and equity in large cross-border transactions.

TRADE FINANCE. Foreign banks offer a range of financing techniques, and they simplify the complexities of international trade transactions. For instance, structured trade finance improves political and credit risk through the use of export credit agencies, multilateral agencies, bilateral agencies, and commercial insurers.

Foreign banks have distinct competitive advantages in this area. They provide an integrated global approach to trade settlement, credit risk mitigation, and information services, and the integration of their global systems benefits customers. Multinational companies have reengineered the way in which they manage their international trade in order to streamline processing activities and gain maximum efficiency and control. Foreign banks can respond to the needs of an automated, fully integrated environment by offering corporations integrated global electronic reporting across functional processes and geographic areas. Finally, the recent crises in emerging markets created an enormous advantage for foreign banks over domestic banks. During the crises, documentary credits issued by domestic banks had to be scrutinized by foreign banks for counterparty risk and, in many instances, had to be endorsed or confirmed by the head offices of first-tier foreign banks prior to being accepted by beneficiaries.

EQUIPMENT FINANCE. The range of leasing and equipment finance transactions includes equipment lease programs, vendor programs, secured franchise financing, and dealer financing, as well as leasing programs for ships and railcars. Foreign banks, such as Citibank, were industry innovators in introducing leasing programs, and as such they bring decades of experience in structuring leasing and equipment finance transactions. Leasing reduces the need for working capital. Furthermore, it is an ideal financing instrument in markets that lack collateral and foreclosure laws and in which corporations lack access to finance.

Capital Markets

Capital markets include global custody clearing and settlement, depository receipts, securitization, global and domestic equity and bond underwriting, private equity, and agency and trust services.

GLOBAL CUSTODY CLEARING AND SETTLEMENT. Trade settlement and related custody services encompass a range of activities, including safe-keeping, registration (where applicable), income collection, corporate actions, confirmations, and appropriate reporting. Multinational banks that offer the services required for the efficient settlement of such trades are the basis of the global clearing process. The capacity of foreign banks to provide efficient multiple-currency cash and securities statements to international broker-dealers makes them a favorite of leading investment firms. Mutual funds and investment managers favor handling the receipt, delivery, safekeeping, and related cash and foreign exchange through global banks. The services of a global bank include multiple-market coverage, collateral management, and trading capabilities. By offering a global product, they reduce both operating and capital costs for their broker-dealer clients.

Foreign banks engage in safekeeping, settlement, income collection, information reporting, and associated custodial services, which enable institutional investors to access both established and emerging markets worldwide. The advantages of foreign banks include their global reach and their ability to offer a full menu of clearing, custodial, and information reporting services. Global technological platforms provide institutional investors or their global custodians a timely consolidated report. For example, Citibank offers securities services in sixty-two markets and has a large proprietary branch network in fifty locations.

These services clearly benefit domestic markets. Foreign banks offer global institutional investors the comfort and confidence to invest in emerging markets. They therefore promote portfolio equity flows to emerging markets, which enhance the depth and liquidity of domestic capital markets.

DEPOSITORY RECEIPTS. Depository receipts, including American depository receipts (ADRs) and global depository receipts (GDRs), are securities traded in the United States and other major markets that represent shares of firms based outside the United States. They trade in the United States and other financial markets in a manner similar to that of ordinary shares of U.S. companies. Depository receipts enable companies in emerging markets to broaden their base of global shareholders and to raise capital through registered public offerings or private placements. Foreign banks issue depository receipts against deposits of underlying shares, and they also provide transfer and registration services, account management, and corporate action services. Their presence in both the United States and emerging markets enables them to offer a range of services, including acting as a liaison between the issuer, investment banks, the issuer's legal representative, and regulatory agencies during the development of the program.

SECURITIZATION. Securitization ranges from the issuing of asset-backed and mortgage-backed securities to the securitization of future revenues. Securitized structures offer companies a funding alternative by allowing them to turn assets with predictable cash flows into a distributable instrument. By removing assets from leveraged balance sheets, securitization activity reduces capital requirements.

GLOBAL AND DOMESTIC EQUITY AND BOND UNDERWRITING. Foreign banks have taken the lead in this fast-growing segment of the market, and they remain the top underwriters of sovereign and corporate global bonds and equity. J.P. Morgan and Standard Chartered, for example, offer primary underwriting and create secondary markets for debt in domestic bond markets. The competitive advantage of such banks derives from the support that they offer institutional investors by leveraging their sales and trading capabilities with high-quality research, technical expertise, risk management ability, and capital.

The benefits of foreign bank participation for the development of domestic debt markets are particularly evident in Latin America. Figure 3-3 illustrates the results of a Greenwich Associates survey ranking the fourteen leading nonregional banks operating as sellers in Latin American debt markets. More than 35 percent of the respondents give three banks—namely, Citibank, J.P. Morgan, and Chase—very high ratings for the quality of their debt market services.

The growth of developing countries' capital markets is supported by foreign financial intermediation expertise. The wave of pension reform seen in emerging markets, such as Chile and Poland, in the 1980s and 1990s generated large pools of capital, and the transition to funded pension plans and other contractual savings is leading to a virtuous cycle in domestic financial systems. The increased supply of capital raises the demand for shares, which in turn increases market capitalization and volume traded. The reduced reliance on foreign capital mitigates market volatility. Similarly, the increased pool of capital has attendant advantages for the demand

Figure 3-3. *Quality of Debt Market Services of Leading Banks in Latin America*[a]

Proportion of evaluators (percent)[b]

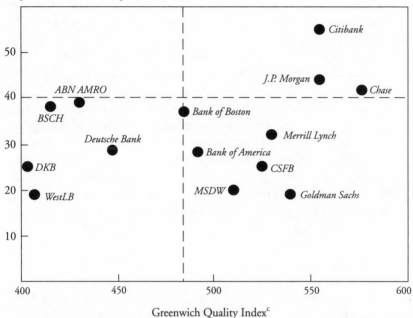

Greenwich Quality Index[c]

Source: Greenwich Associates (2000b, 2000d).

a. CSFB: Credit Suisse First Boston; BSCH: Banco Santander Central Hispano (BSCH); MSDW: Morgan Stanley Dean Witter.

b. Proportion of evaluators who ranked bank's service quality as above average.

c. The Greenwhich Quality Index is calculated using a normalized composite of all qualitative evaluations, with scores ranging from 0 (lowest) to 1,000 (highest).

for long-term bonds and loans. It reduces the pressure on banks to engage in excessive term transformation risks, reduces debtors' refinancing risks by lengthening the maturity of debts, and reduces enterprise vulnerability to interest rate and demand shocks by improving financial structure. The development of financial markets leads to improvements in regulations and transparency, and it fosters financial innovation, competition, and efficiency, together with improved corporate governance. The agents for the transformation of pension savings into financial instruments are foreign intermediaries, predominately banks. These banks serve both as underwriters in primary equity and bond markets and as market makers in secondary markets.

PRIVATE EQUITY INVESTMENTS. Most foreign banks have subsidiaries, such as Chase Private Equity, that are responsible for investing the bank's proprietary funds in the private equity market. They invest in venture capital situations through equity and quasi-equity instruments. These instruments and the banks' expertise stimulate the development of local small and medium-sized enterprises.

AGENCY AND TRUST SERVICES. Foreign banks provide trustee and agency-related appointments for various debt products, including commercial paper, medium-term notes, bonds, asset-backed securities, and mortgage-backed securities. They also initiate escrow, project finance, tenders and exchanges, and other specialized agency services. If the agency and trust functions need to be exercised, foreign banks can maximize the speed of payment for corporations, sovereigns, and financial institutions in both mature and emerging markets. Because multinational banks have experience and offer a full range of support across multiple currencies, they command a greater degree of confidence from issuers that are raising debt in regional and global markets and from investors in general.

Treasury Operations

Treasury operations consist of foreign exchange services, risk management products, and cash management services for corporations.

FOREIGN EXCHANGE SERVICES. Our personal conversations with foreign and domestic bankers confirm that foreign banks are the leading market makers and providers of foreign exchange services. For instance, three foreign banks dominate foreign exchange trading in Colombia. One reason for this leadership position is that foreign banks have the global infrastructure to provide a wide range of services. They also have the skills and technical platform to assist customers with risk assessment and risk management, based on their outreach and participation in global markets.

RISK MANAGEMENT PRODUCTS. Global corporations need to centralize the management of foreign exchange and interest rate risks to hedge exposure. Because foreign banks maintain global platforms and because they pioneered the development of derivatives such as interest rate swaps and options, they are better equipped than domestic banks to offer customers a full range of instruments for managing risk, including swaps, options, floors, caps, collars, and swaptions. Domestic banks are in the process of learning the technology, and they are thus becoming players in the markets.

Figure 3-4. *Quality of Cash Management Services of Leading Banks in Asia*

Proportion of evaluators (percent)[a]

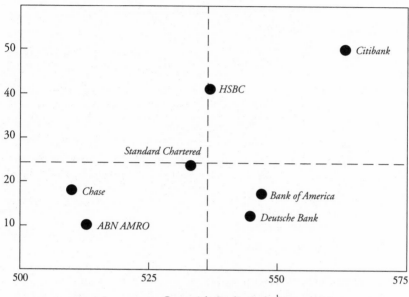

Greenwich Quality Index[b]

Source: Greenwich Associates (2000b, 2000d).

a. Proportion of evaluators who say they use the bank's cash management services frequently.

b. The Greenwhich Quality Index is calculated using a normalized composite of all qualitative evaluations, with scores ranging from 0 (lowest) to 1,000 (highest).

CASH MANAGEMENT SERVICES. Cash management services are designed to capture transactions and deliver comprehensive, timely information regarding the cash position of firms. These services consist of the management of liquidity for corporations and the management of payables and receivables. The global cash management that multinational firms need can be delivered only by the major international banks with access to the global payments system. These banks have global computer platforms and a nearly ubiquitous presence. In Asia, for example, Citibank and HSBC already dominate cash management services, and Citibank and ABN AMRO have developed global automated platforms and processes. Smaller banks simply cannot compete in this area. Figure 3-4, which shows how corporate financial officers in Asia rank banks in terms of their cash management and operations systems, indicates that two banks, namely, Citibank and HSBC, are used most frequently by at least 40 percent of the major companies in Asia and receive above average ratings for the quality of their service.

Financial Advisory Services

Many foreign banks are leading global advisors in mergers and acquisitions (M&A). The key players in this area include Deutsche Bank following the acquisition of Bankers Trust, Chase with the acquisition of J.P. Morgan, and Citigroup with the acquisition of Salomon Smith Barney's investment banking franchise. In addition to advising buyers and sellers in traditional M&A transactions, their experience includes takeover defense, strategic restructurings, command of international M&A regulations, tax-advantaged structures, leveraged transactions assignments, and special industry expertise.

Small and Medium-Sized Enterprise Services

While foreign banks enjoy significant, though not universal, competitive advantages in corporate lending, their ability to penetrate the small and medium-sized enterprise sector is limited. Credit scoring for SMEs is in its infancy, and foreign lenders applying traditional corporate banking approaches, namely, credit analysis based on cash flow standards and transparent financial statements, have been unable to develop effective methods for penetrating the small- and medium-scale lending to any significant degree. Moreover, foreign banks' experience with SME lending in emerging markets has been checkered; they remain constrained by the high transaction costs and credit risks associated with small loans. Significant barriers to entering this market include regulatory barriers, lack of cultural familiarity, the high costs of establishing a branch network, and poor profitability.

By contrast, domestic banks command this arena. Dickens and Keppler cite several sources of competitive advantage for domestic banks in the SME credit markets of developing countries.[7] First, domestic banks have an advantage in serving relatively small, geographically limited, often industry-specific market segments in which they are able to collect precise data. Second, domestic banks tend to be older and better established than foreign banks. They benefit from the time horizon of their credit information and the longevity of their relationships with local SMEs, and they hold a wealth

7. Dickens and Keppler (2001).

of data from which to draw accurate, local sample populations and make relatively precise calculations about creditworthiness. Third, domestic banks are better suited to carrying out due diligence on SME loans than are foreign banks. With more local personnel and greater geographic penetration, these banks can more effectively follow isolated, smaller clients in the provinces of their countries. Finally, to the extent that domestic banks collaborate through some kind of credit bureau, the effectiveness of credit managers is enhanced.

Domestic banks can realize increasing returns on their SME lending business if they successfully carry out further reform and innovation. They must upgrade their lending processes and improve their data mining techniques, for example, through credit scoring and the use of reliable information from credit bureaus. These methods promote faster credit decisionmaking and greater reliance on data and forecasting models, which represents a great advance over traditional, subjective evaluation. As domestic banks adopt technology innovation, they will boost their efficiency and profitability in this market.

Consumer Banking Products and Services

A number of foreign banks have entered the domestic consumer banking sector, taking household deposits directly in competition with domestic banks and extending credit via consumer loans and credit cards, appliance loans, car loans, and residential mortgage loans (see table 3-4 regarding Argentina and Mexico). In this section we describe the retail products provided by these foreign banks, including innovations in consumer finance. These innovations have strongly affected the local markets.

Traditional Consumer Banking Products

Consumer banking encompasses a range of services for the retail banking market. These include mortgages, personal loans, credit cards, asset management, and private banking. Foreign banks with operations in emerging markets are increasingly participating in each of these areas, although domestic banks are bound to maintain a strong presence.

MORTGAGES. Customers use mortgage financing to purchase a new house or apartment. In many markets, foreign banks have introduced mortgages with higher financing (up to 80 percent) and longer maturities than

Table 3-4. *Composition of Bank Loans in Argentina and Mexico, by Type of Bank Ownership*

Percent

Type of bank ownership	Type of loan		
	Personal	Mortgage	Commercial, government, and other[a]
Argentina			
State-owned banks			
1994	5.2	32.1	62.7
1997	5.8	32.2	62.0
1999	5.9	35.1	59.0
Private domestic banks			
1994	13.2	9.4	77.4
1997	10.4	13.2	76.4
1999	6.1	15.0	78.9
Foreign-owned banks			
1994	14.1	11.0	74.8
1997	13.3	11.7	75.0
1999	5.5	14.7	79.8
Mexico			
Private domestic banks			
1992	12.0	16.0	72.0
1995	5.6	22.4	72.0
1998	3.3	14.3	82.4
Foreign-owned banks			
1992	0.3	2.0	97.7
1995	6.9	0.3	92.8
1998	1.9	4.5	93.6

Source: Dages, Goldberg, and Kinney (2000).

a. In Mexico, commercial, government, and interbank.

those offered by domestic banks. Local banks have traditionally provided housing loans based on collateral value for periods of two to three years, whereas foreign banks, such as Citibank in Korea, offer more sophisticated, complex mortgage options with maturities of two to fifteen years. Because foreign banks use derivatives to hedge interest rate risks, combined with sophisticated credit analysis techniques to hedge more accurately, they have been able to reduce transaction costs and improve the terms on which mortgages are made. In addition, foreign banks have gained a reputation for relatively simple application procedures and professional personal service.

Domestic banks, however, claim an equally strong competitive advantage deriving from their extensive local franchise networks, brand recognition, long history of client relationships, and knowledge of local markets. Cultural and regulatory preferences also play in favor of domestic banks.

PERSONAL LOANS. Domestic banks enjoy competitive advantages in personal loans for many of the same reasons listed above for the home mortgage market. Broad franchise networks, access to domestic currency, and local knowledge are assets to domestic banks; these same factors often pose barriers to entry for foreign banks. Although foreign banks have introduced personal loans for both immediate and well-planned needs, with flexible terms and payments tailored to customers' needs, they do not claim a competitive advantage in this market.

CREDIT CARDS. Foreign banks dominate the credit card market. In Thailand, for example, Citibank wrestled market share from Thai Farmers in the span of just a few years. The success of foreign banks is partly attributable to their experience with data mining and marketing, as well as research and development for the information technology platform. Another advantage is that their credit cards offer access to a worldwide network of automated teller machines (ATMs) and are accepted by merchants worldwide.

Local markets have adapted to the influx of global credit cards through initiatives to develop parallel domestic cards and to issue cards jointly with major credit card companies, such as Visa and MasterCard.

ASSET MANAGEMENT. Asset management represents a large potential business for foreign banks, including, for instance, BBVA and BSCH in Latin America. The recent acquisition of investment management firms (for example, Chase's acquisition of Jardine Fleming and Citibank's acquisition of Salomon Smith Barney) has further strengthened the capacity and expertise of foreign banks in asset management. Asset management in emerging markets has the potential to provide a valuable product to retail customers, as well.

PRIVATE BANKING. Private banking is dedicated to meeting the needs of clients with a high net worth. It encompasses investment advisory services on a discretionary or directed basis across a wide range of asset classes, including money market funds, equities, private equity, and alternative investments such as real estate and commodities. Global banks have an advantage because they offer access to virtually any market in the world, together with global trade execution, settlement, and custody. Although private banking was controversial in the past (given its association with capital flight), the market has matured and is now less vulnerable to crises.

Innovative Products and Services

In addition to pursuing market share in the traditional areas of consumer banking, foreign banks have introduced a number of important innovations in the sector and had strong effects on the activities of domestic banks.

E-FINANCE PRODUCTS. The long-term potential of Internet finance is compelling. The market still features considerable uncertainty, however, regarding the platforms for delivering services to both retail and corporate customers, and the strategies of major banks are still evolving. Banks such as HSBC and Citibank appear to be pursuing a strategy in which e-finance complements existing services, rather than positioning it as a head-on substitute. Despite the lack of infrastructure and the presence of legal and regulatory obstacles in developing countries, there is little doubt that the low penetration of financial services and rapidly growing Internet usage combine to make e-finance a very attractive future opportunity for both foreign and domestic banks. Size and scale are important in securing access to resources, and they are critical for attaining adequate levels of profitability in a reasonable time frame. Network effects and first-mover advantages appear to give incumbent banks a competitive advantage in e-finance in East Asia and Latin America. However, all financial institutions recognize the existence of a synergy among various client segments, different geographic markets, and alternative products and businesses, which makes a strong case for investing in e-finance.

Another noteworthy pattern is clearly evident in Latin America. The biggest domestic players, namely, Bradesco, Banacci, and Unibanco, do not appear to be adopting and expanding electronic financial services in direct response to competition from foreign banks. Rather, these winning banks have been first-movers in the e-finance field, adopting information technology to capture market share. The demographics of Latin America—specifically Mexico, Brazil, Argentina, and Chile—indicate that strong markets for e-finance will develop: with 500 million people, 34 percent of whom are under the age of fifteen and 20 percent of whom control almost 80 percent of the region's gross domestic product, Latin America offers a ready market for e-finance.

The key domestic bank players in Latin American e-finance have entered strategic partnerships with foreign (often U.S.) Internet and financial services firms. For example, Banacci in Mexico has forged alliances with such preeminent Internet firms as Commerce One, the Dutch insurance giant Aegon, MCI WorldCom, and Andersen Consulting; each endeavor aims to forward one facet of Banacci's overall strategy. Patagon.com took a similarly aggressive approach to mining foreign technologies and foreign capital. As Wenceslao Casares describes his firm's strategy, "The first thing we did was research what had already been tested and tried in the United States."

The current winners of e-finance in Latin America have a unique set of competitive advantages. Their foremost strength has been the first-mover advantage, followed by size and scale, which have been vital to securing access to resources and attaining profit levels.

PRODUCTS AND SERVICES INTRODUCED BY FOREIGN BANKS. Foreign banks have skills and global information technology that enable them to offer a broader menu of services and deal with complex financial structures that involve greater risks, multiple currencies, and greater technological demands than their domestic counterparts (see the list of products in appendix 3D). In retail services, foreign banks are poised to introduce a wide selection of asset management, credit services, and bank card products in emerging markets. They leverage highly advanced and efficient processes of credit evaluation (many foreign banks possess proprietary credit-scoring methodologies), superior information technology networks, and experienced marketing experts drawn from branded consumer products worldwide. Foreign banks also reap positive network effects from their global physical infrastructure, which encompasses ATMs, international calling centers, international data collection centers, and multiple clearinghouses, and from their human organizational structure, including standardized processes and credit scoring methods, to a greater extent than smaller, localized domestic banks.

Foreign banks likewise offer a broad range of corporate services, such as structured finance, investment banking, treasury services, and trade services. This menu reflects foreign banks' superior access to global skills, technology, and international capital. In this area, human resources and institutional skill building, complemented by a global presence and global technological platform, are the key competitive advantages of foreign banks. Their ongoing investment in training, their commitment to innovations in process, and their merit-based organization allow most foreign banks to tackle complex transactions and to manage the risks of corporate finance efficiently. The individual products and services that foreign banks offer in individual countries are a matter of managerial judgment, reflecting the unique characteristics and risks in each market. The tendency of foreign banks to focus on top-tier local corporations, however, creates a divide between larger companies that have access to world-class financial services and disadvantaged smaller companies that cannot tap into this range of products.

THE EFFECTS OF FOREIGN COMPETITION ON DOMESTIC BANKS. In most emerging markets, domestic banks have traditionally relied heavily on interest income from working capital, from overdraft loans to very large corporations (so-called name lending) and priority sector borrowers (that is, directed credit with government guarantees), and from large government securities portfolios. Greater foreign competition has now forced domestic banks to introduce new products and practices. Domestic banks are upgrading their systems of internal control—management information systems and credit monitoring—to respond to the banking needs of retail and business customers. They are focusing more on retail lending, including housing loans, car loans, and consumer durable loans, and they are launching credit cards, a field that has long been dominated by foreign banks. They are also investing in the computerization of branches. Finally, domestic banks are expanding and networking their ATM systems so that they can offer banking services anywhere, anytime. Domestic banks are also considering Internet banking, but it is still in its infancy in most markets. All of these changes benefit the financial marketplace.

Similarly, many domestic banks are reorganizing their operations in the business segments to offer their major corporate clients a single interface in the form of a relationship officer. Domestic banks are forming corporate accounts groups to address the needs of major clients and to cross-sell the full range of their products and services. There is growing recognition of the potential of small- and medium-sized enterprises and therefore greater emphasis on lending to the trade and services sectors. Finally, domestic banks are exploring new fee-generating services and are adding cash management services to their mix of products.

Processes

The lending policies, procedures, internal controls, and practices of domestic and foreign banks in emerging markets exhibit marked differences. This section addresses issues related to banking processes: loan portfolio management, asset-liability management, and management information services. We also examine how domestic firms have responded to the challenges of foreign competition.

Loan Portfolio Management

The credit underwriting process differs greatly between domestic and foreign banks. Cash-flow-based lending has only recently taken root in emerging markets. Traditionally, domestic banks relied extensively on collateral in lending decisions. This approach is explained, in part, by the lack of readily available, reliable financial information. Even under these circumstances, however, close monitoring of the collateral's existence, value, and marketability is critical. Many domestic banks do not have sound processes for supervising credit. The lack of documentation for loans has resulted in several systemic crisis situations: in Mexico, for example, the Asset Management Company (AMC) was not able to dispose of collateral as a result of inadequate supporting collateral documentation. Foreign banks, in contrast, place significant emphasis on the financial strength, profitability, and cash flow of the core business for repayment of commercial loans. Their monitoring approach relies on continuous surveillance of the business's financial condition and the profitability of the borrowing clients. Other standard practices include information requirements, such as collateral-inspection and documentation, and loan covenants requiring the business to maintain financial soundness and to submit periodic financial statements.

Domestic banks need to upgrade their policies and procedures for managing and controlling loan portfolios. Appropriate loan management starts with an adequate set of policies and procedures articulated by senior management and communicated to the organization. The objectives are to ensure sound credit underwriting standards, control and manage risk, evaluate new business opportunities, and identify, administer, and collect problem loans.

Loan policies establish what information the borrower will have to supply during the application process, what information the borrower will have to submit while the credit remains outstanding (foreign banks rely on cash flow analysis), and which bank personnel are responsible for obtaining the information. In addition, loan policies specify who is responsible for reviewing the adequacy of loan documentation and for citing and correcting documentation exceptions. Loan policies are supplemented by loan procedures. Whereas the institution's credit policies provide credit risk diversification and concentration limits, which may define concentrations to a single or related borrower, the procedures provide for heightened monitoring to address deterioration in the quality of credit. An effective internal loan review function complements the policies and procedures and detects weaknesses in the various levels of an institution's system of credit approval and monitoring. An effective, independent internal loan review ensures consistent application of the credit-grading system, identifies loans with potential or well-defined credit weaknesses, and ensures the development and implementation of an appropriate action plan to minimize credit losses. The internal loan review function is independent and provides senior management and the board of directors with objective, timely assessments of credit quality.

Asset-Liability Management

Asset-liability management is at the core of sound risk management. It is the process of managing the spread between interest earned and interest paid, while ensuring adequate liquidity. Asset-liability management has two components: liquidity management and interest rate risk management. In response to the broadening range of funding instruments and lending products, as well as the volatility of interest and exchange rates, banks currently emphasize asset-liability management and techniques. They need an analytical framework for understanding the mix of customers, the nature of assets and liabilities, and developments in the financial markets. Highly technical models and risk management techniques that measure value at risk have been developed in recent years; one example is Riskmetrics from J.P. Morgan. Domestic banks lag behind foreign banks in implementing asset-liability management practices. Even though domestic banks are adopting these practices, they still rely largely on arithmetic gap analysis.[8] Foreign banks use more sophisticated techniques such as present-value basis points, which more accurately account for the time value of money. Moreover, the asset and liability committees of foreign banks appear to be more effective in guiding each bank's liquidity, capital structure, and funding and in setting limits across banks. The framework of asset-liability management has to be complemented with a technological platform that supports an effective information system for capturing the data necessary for the analysis. In this area, the main differences between foreign and domestic banks appear to be in the analysis and interpretation of asset and liability information.

8. Gap analysis uses maturity buckets to determine a bank's sensitivity to interest rate fluctuations and its ability to meet funding requirements.

Management Information Systems

The use of sophisticated information technology that provides management with accurate, informative, and timely data is critical to modern banking. It enables an institution to monitor its risks and overall performance and allows senior management and the board of directors to make timely decisions. Foreign banks tend to have a distinct advantage in information technology, in that they have considerable economies of scale in implementing such systems. Given the high costs of developing, running, and maintaining a sophisticated information technology system, together with the risks of rapid obsolescence, this competitive dimension favors foreign banks that can spread the costs of development over a larger base of customers. Several of the largest foreign banks in Asia have regional operational centers that serve a large customer base and are highly cost effective. For example, Standard Chartered is consolidating its Asian back-office operations in two processing centers: back-office processing and customer support in India and Malaysia are being centralized in two global hubs to provide support for the bank's retail and wholesale businesses and to cut about 20 percent of staff.

Most foreign banks already have state-of-the-art systems that can be imported quickly and cheaply into the domestic market. For example, Citibank's rapid penetration of the credit card market in Thailand is attributed to its superior technological platform. Domestic banks usually have to develop or purchase the technology and know-how. The challenge of implementing adequate management information systems in emerging markets should not be underestimated. Even large banks lack the resources and expertise to launch the massive investments needed to revamp their information systems; the challenges and limited success to date of the big state banks in China, India, and Indonesia suggest an extreme challenge to smaller and privately owned emerging market banks attempting to make the same investment.

Those financial institutions that lack adequate internal information systems and that decide to automate face the difficult choice of whether to build or buy—both risky propositions. Some have used external software platforms for certain banking applications. Others have centralized information systems in internal development centers for their affiliates.

Domestic Responses to Foreign Competition

Domestic banks are adopting the practices of foreign banks. For instance, the first credit manual used in the Philippines was that of Citibank. Chohung Bank in Seoul, Korea, is currently undertaking a major transformation of its internal systems, adopting a new asset-liability management system, and instituting a relationship management system. Key aspects of the process include tightening credit extension policy, improving the management of credit risk, and training credit experts, as well as introducing activity-based profit analysis, merit-based compensation packages, and integrated database management. Progressive foreign banks adopted these fundamentals of bank management twenty or thirty years ago.

Foreign banks contribute to the development of better processes in domestic banks. A notable transfer of technology from foreign banks has enhanced management processes and information systems in domestic banks. Beyond this, a more subtle process involves the transfer of auxiliary services that foreign banks bring with them to emerging markets in the form of research analysts, accountants, lawyers, marketers, consultants, and appraisers, all of whom enhance the quality of foreign banks' services.

The development of the financial services sector in developing countries lags behind that of the economy and the financial sector. For instance, in South Korea, services account for 45.5 percent of real gross domestic product (GDP), while the respective share in the United States is 74.1 percent. The penetration of foreign banks increasingly exposes domestic banks in emerging markets to auxiliary services; as these banks recognize the utility of such services, they gradually integrate them into the domestic markets. Foreign banks insist on periodic audited financial statements, which fosters the development of local accounting firms. Similarly, the use of law firms to perfect collateral nurtures the development of the legal profession. The increasing sophistication of both banks and auxiliary services are mutually supporting processes that ultimately benefit the quality of services for all customers.

With regard to technology transfers, generalizations do not apply—the learning curve varies from country to country and from bank to bank. The time lag between foreign import and domestic adoption of financial management process and technologies seems to be a function of the competitive pressures exerted by foreign banks on domestic banks, which stimulates them to develop countrywide competitiveness.

Human Resources

Ultimately, a banking organization is only as good as its employees, and therein lies the most important competitive advantage for foreign banks. In all banks, the lines of business have to be managed and staffed by personnel whose knowledge, experience, and expertise are adequate for supporting the organization's activities.

The personnel policies and practices associated with the recruitment, promotion, training, and compensation of employees generally differ between domestic and foreign banks.[9] Foreign banks dedicate considerable effort to ensuring that the depth of staff resources is adequate for managing the institution's activities, and they select employees whose ethical values, integrity, and competence are consistent with the culture and operating style of the individual bank. Foreign organizations rely on detailed job descriptions, carefully planned recruiting, appropriate training, periodic performance reviews, and salaries, bonuses, and options that are globally competitive and that recognize performance.

The story is vastly different among domestic banks. In some countries, such as Korea and Japan, uniform, age-based salaries and promotions and career-long employment in a particular bank are the norm. Domestic banks in these countries do not reward initiative, performance, or the taking of calculated risks.

Recruitment and Staffing

State banks are the norm in the majority of developing countries. More than 40 percent of the world's population still lives in countries in which the bulk of bank assets are in majority-owned state banks.[10] Public sector banks are hampered by a set of values that all public sector entities share. The public sector culture is simply not adapted to a dynamic and entrepreneurial operating environment. Consequently, state banks have considerable difficulty keeping step with a private sector culture that emphasizes customer service and innovation.

---

9. This generalization should be qualified to recognize the diversity of personnel policies in various countries and in different banks. Clearly, some domestic banks in emerging markets have been more successful in maintaining high-quality human resources than others.

10. Caprio (2001).

Domestic banks often face constraints in their staffing practices. In some countries, bank unions oppose job cuts aimed at restructuring the work force to achieve greater productivity.

Foreign banks have several competitive advantages in the recruitment of staff for emerging markets. They can select and dispatch the most qualified persons for particular international assignments. Furthermore, the smaller number of employees per office makes foreign banks more flexible in adjusting staffing requirements. Foreign banks can also capitalize on certain cultural biases, such as gender-biased hiring, to select talented women or members of other underrepresented groups from the pool of underutilized skills.

Promotions

Foreign banks foster merit-based systems for promotions, whereas domestic banks in many cultures base promotions on seniority. Countries in which state banks and family-funded banks predominate have opaque systems of promotion that rely on personal relationships with superiors and owners.

Finally, foreign banks offer employees a highly rewarding and empowering working environment through exposure to overseas assignments and the skills gained in job rotations. The process creates a cadre of seasoned managers with a broad perspective.

Training

Foreign banks tend to emphasize intensive professional training. For instance, Citibank offers Asian staff extensive training at its own Asia Pacific Banking Institute in Manila. The institute provides training in credit and treasury operations through programs lasting as long as six months. Similarly, J.P. Morgan allocates an estimated 15 percent of staff time to training: J.P. Morgan Chase in Bangkok has two local professional staffs rotating in overseas assignments at all times, gaining exposure to complex financial products.

Compensation

Foreign banks pay salaries and benefits similar to those paid by global money-center competitors for the same-caliber personnel. Their employment compensation packages are thus considerably higher than those paid by domestic banks. Because of rigid employment policies and the role of unions, domestic state banks cannot offer competitive salaries and consequently cannot obtain the most qualified people.

One of the ways in which global banks are able to attract the best domestic and international talent is by incorporating stock option plans in their compensation and benefits packages.[11] The ability to offer a global currency—a stock listed on the New York or London stock exchange—clearly gives foreign banks a competitive advantage.

Conclusions

The evidence presented in this paper confirms that domestic policymakers should welcome foreign banks. The current trend in banking is the consolidation of global financial services in the hands of about twenty very large global players. These institutions can afford the greatest range of products and services, make the largest investments, manage the most information, and rationalize costs and risks most efficiently. They offer an unsurpassed level of corporate and retail financial services, as well as better credit underwriting and diversification of credit risks supported by a large global capital base. They can also organize people and information more efficiently than domestic banks. Emerging markets countries that promote the entrance of foreign banks into their markets tend to enjoy healthier corporate and individual sectors as a result. On the domestic side, the increasing value added offered by foreign banks creates pressures for further consolidation of domestic banks to reach economies of scale. The role of domestic financial institutions will not be eliminated. Domestic banks will assume increasing roles in the distribution of corporate financing. They will continue to provide the local component of services to the corporate sector. As foreign banks increase their presence in the corporate market, domestic banks will increase their focus and competence in the local retail and SME markets. The role of domestic banks thus remains a very important one.

The evidence also suggests that domestic banks will increasingly capitalize on their local knowledge and relationships in the retail and SME markets. Very few foreign banks are likely to penetrate these domestic mar-

11. A recent KPMG International Human Resources Survey of more than 300 Fortune 1000 companies showed that 88 percent of companies offered stock option plans (www.kpmgihrsurvey.com/login.asp).

kets to a meaningful degree. On the negative side, this trend toward a two-tiered segmentation of banking services in emerging markets could result in competitive disadvantages for small and medium-sized enterprises, whose growth prospects may be constrained by the service capacity of domestic banks. This issue certainly requires domestic banks to improve their capacity to serve SMEs by using new credit scoring techniques.[12]

The presence of foreign banks is not a zero-sum game, but rather deepens domestic financial markets. Foreign banks complement the range of wholesale and retail products and services offered by domestic banks, which continue to have very positive roles in all market segments.

Foreign banks have demonstrated superiority in certain products that require global platforms. These include foreign exchange and derivatives-trading operations, global underwriting of bonds and equities, cross-border M&A, trade finance, multiple-currency cash management, global custody, and investment management services.

In addition to competitive product advantages, foreign banks have competitive advantages in terms of management processes and the quality of support. Foreign banks hire competitively, tap pools of specialized and seasoned skills, invest heavily in training and development of human capital, and offer salaries and bonuses that are globally competitive. Consequently, they are able to attract and maintain the most capable work force. Foreign banks also enjoy a greater degree of staffing flexibility compared to their domestic competitors in emerging markets, because the number of staff per office is smaller and because the banks' worldwide presence allows them to dispatch specialists from one location to another to meet precise knowledge or managerial needs.

The operations of foreign banks in emerging markets exhibit a clear dichotomy. At least three banks—the local subsidiaries of Citibank, HSBC, and Standard Chartered—have developed strong and profitable local franchises targeting the top end of the market in consumer and commercial business. They are known for innovative and high-quality retail services, credit cards, and mortgage and personal lending for individuals. Other money-center banks, such as J.P. Morgan Chase and Deutsche Bank, are narrowing and even contracting their activities in emerging markets. These banks are limiting their credit exposure and refocusing on investment banking and private banking activities. They offer some trade finance, but they mostly focus on advanced treasury and capital market products, cross-border underwriting, mergers and acquisitions, and operating services for

12. Dickens and Keppler (2001).

business customers. They continue to take market and operating risk in these markets.

Finally, foreign banks play a large role in developing local financial markets. They will increase their equity participation in domestic banks in need of restructuring, enter into alliances and joint ventures to market global services to domestic customers, and bring expertise to the local markets.

Appendix 3A: International Banking Questionnaire

Much of the paper is based on a series of interviews that we conducted in January 2001 at the following banks and other institutions: in Bangkok, Thailand, the Bangkok Bank Public Company Ltd., the Bank of Thailand, Chase Manhattan Bank, the Ministry of Finance, and the Securities and Exchange Commission; in Hong Kong, Bank of America, Goldman Sachs, and Citibank; in Manila, Philippines, Bankers Trust-Deutsche Bank and Central Bank of the Philippines; and in Seoul, Korea, Bank of America, Chohung Bank, Deutsche Bank, Hanvit Credit Information Corporation, and J.P. Morgan Chase Bank.

We prepared the following questionnaire to serve as the basis for the interviews. The use of this questionnaire allowed us to compare domestic and foreign banks; to measure and quantify the differences; and to assess the impact of these differences on the competitive landscape of the banking sector in the country. Topics include strategy, products and services, processes, human resources, and management information systems.

Strategy

How would you describe your bank's strategic positioning in the country—wholesale or retail? That is, what market segment(s) does your bank target in this country?

In which areas do you consider your bank to hold a natural competitive advantage vis-à-vis domestic banks in this market? Vis-à-vis other foreign banks?

Has the entrance of major multinational banks into this market had an impact on domestic banks?

Since your bank's initial entry in this market, what—if any—transformation have you witnessed in the domestic product offerings of domestic competitors?

How has your clientele, or their needs, changed since your bank's arrival?

Has your own bank undergone repositioning or transformation since coming to this market?

Products and Services

Which product offerings are most undersupplied by domestic banks?

What products and services has your bank targeted? How was your bank able to exploit the weaknesses of domestic banks in these offerings?

Has your bank succeeded in changing the depth and breadth of the market—that is, in raising the benchmark—in any of these offerings? If so, in which offerings has your bank made the most dramatic changes?

Please describe your impression of the differences that existed between your bank's menu of products and services and the menu of competing domestic banks when your bank first entered this market.

Please describe your impression of the differences that exist now.

Processes

Please describe any meaningful differences that you perceive in lending policies, practices, procedures, and internal controls in your bank versus the domestic banks.

How does your bank's asset-liability management process compare to that of domestic competitors?

Is your bank making significant investments in e-finance? Are domestic banks investing in the area as well?

In which aspects of technology and processes does your bank excel beyond the industry standard in this market?

How—if at all—have the processes of competitor banks changed in response?

Human Resources

In which human resource areas does your bank stand out from its domestic competitors?

How have your bank's human resource policies affected its strategic position?

In which, if any, of the human resource areas have you seen the domestic banking sector respond to the competition from foreign banks? In which areas has the domestic banking sector failed to respond?

Management Information Systems

How would you describe your bank's investment and capacity in information systems and technology as compared to that of domestic banks?

Describe any meaningful differences that you perceive between the management information systems processes of your bank versus those of its domestic competitors.

How have these differences changed since your bank's arrival?

Appendix 3B: Strategies and Products of Selected Foreign Banks in Emerging Markets

ABN AMRO. ABN AMRO has a history of cautious expansion in developing countries. It has a number of operations in the Asia-Pacific region and is also present in Latin America and the Caribbean. At the end of 1998, ABN AMRO developed what it calls a third home market, with the acquisition of Banco Real, one of Brazil's strongest banks and the fourth-largest privately owned bank.

Bank of America. Bank of America has a well-known brand and franchise. It is scaling down its consumer banking businesses in Asia, however, with recent sales of operations in Thailand.

Banco Bilbao Vizcaya Argentaria (BBVA). BBVA has a strong market position in Spain and a diversified retail and wholesale franchise. Like other Spanish banks, BBVA has exhausted the benefits of consolidation and is now under pressure from rising domestic competition, which is constraining lending margins. The corporation responded with a growth strategy, both at home and abroad. Its ambitions are to play a leading role in Southern Europe and Latin America. BBVA is the second major financial group in Latin America, with total investments amounting to $7 billion, equivalent to 39 percent of its regulatory capital. BBVA holds an average of 9 percent of market share in the region. In September 2000, 35 percent of BBVA's net interest income plus fees and commissions were generated in the region—a share that is equal to domestic retail banking activities. Therefore, concerns remain about the new banking group's exposure in Latin America, considering the size of its aggregate investments.

Among BBVA's strengths is its position as a leading pension fund franchise in Latin America. However, there are risks associated with BBVA's expansionary strategy in Latin America's volatile environment. BBVA also faces the challenges of developing a coherent management group in the region and implementing strong credit and risk cultures across different countries. BBVA has implemented a single information technology platform in the region, ahead of other banks.

Citibank. Citibank is committed to global consumer and private banking businesses as well as to commercial operations abroad. It has a strong presence in developing countries. Citibank and HSBC (and, to a lesser extent, Standard Chartered) stand out among foreign banks for the extent of their network of retail banks in developing countries. These banks have targeted overseas consumer banking as a high-growth area. Citibank has improved liquidity in recent years by expanding its base of foreign deposits. Consumer banking remains one of Citicorp's most important core businesses, reflecting the bank's recent efforts to emphasize lower-risk personal lines, such as residential mortgages and credit cards, over corporate lending. Consumer and private banking for high-net-worth individuals in emerging markets is an important driver of earnings. In many developing countries, Citibank has developed strong and profitable local franchises in both consumer and commercial business. In commercial banking, it is particularly strong in multiple-currency cash management, trade finance, advanced treasury and capital markets products for business customers, high-end retail services, credit cards, and mortgages or personal loans for individuals. With the integration of Salomon Smith Barney's investment banking resources, increased emphasis is being placed on investment banking services. The bank enjoys a competitive advantage in two respects. In contrast to most foreign banks, it benefits from a long-standing presence and brand recognition in developing countries, and in many it nearly holds the status of a domestic bank.

Commerzbank. Banks like Commerzbank and ABN AMRO have adopted a different strategy for emerging markets. In Korea Commerzbank has taken a minority position in Korea Exchange Bank. All indications are that it has revamped the bank's credit culture and traditional approach to credit risk management and has improved the risk-based pricing techniques. It is restructuring the corporate classification systems, and it has adopted statistical techniques for all personal and small business lending. A central credit risk function reviews the operation of its grading system and monitors industry concentrations and provisioning policies.

Deutsche Bank. Deutsche Bank's global strategy is underpinned by its universal banking charter. As a universal bank, Deutsche Bank offers a full spectrum of banking, securities, investment, and insurance products to a broad base of clients, including retail customers, small, medium-sized, and large commercial institutions, and public law institutions. In light of the challenges it faces in the highly fragmented German retail banking market—reflected in lower net interest margins and a slower buildup of income from fees and commissions—Deutsche Bank has focused on an ambitious international diversification strategy in Europe and elsewhere that emphasizes investment banking. The acquisition of Bankers Trust extends the scope of Deutsche Bank's commitment to investment banking; it also makes Deutsche Bank one of the few foreign banks to have a solid base in the United States and thus offers synergistic opportunities. Deutsche Bank is now one of the top four providers of global custody in the world and stands to benefit from economies of scale through the acquisition of Bankers Trust and consolidation in the industry overall.

Deutsche Bank is one of only a handful of banks that can achieve a longer-term position in investment banking. The acquisition of Morgan Grenfell in the early 1990s enhanced its capabilities in merchant and investment banking. The acquisition of Bankers Trust reflects a continuing emphasis on investment banking.

HSBC Holdings. HSBC Holdings ranks as one of the world's largest banking and financial services franchises, with consolidated assets of $580 billion as of June 2000. HSBC is committed to a one-brand approach. The operational focus is on retail and commercial banking, based on the acquisition of strong regional franchises and internal growth. HSBC has built a balanced portfolio of commercial and retail banking assets in both mature and emerging markets and has subsidiaries in Europe, Hong Kong, Southeast Asia, North America, and Latin America. Its market strategy is to focus on private banking (for example, with the acquisition of Republic Bank) and to expand its retail operations. Part of this strategy is the recent $1 billion joint venture by HSBC and Merrill Lynch to develop an e-business platform to attract investors in the $300,000 to $1 million range and offer them global investment opportunities. A long-standing policy has been to reduce its cross-border exposure, a policy that runs counter to that of virtually every other foreign competitor. HSBC's approach to taking market risk is relatively cautious, and investment banking is expected to remain below 10 percent of operations. Trading operations are largely customer driven, and proprietary activities are limited.

ING. ING recently reduced its exposure to emerging markets owing to concerns about volatility. By mid-2000, loans to emerging markets had fallen to 5.1 percent of total lending, from a peak of about 9 percent. ING expects that lending in emerging markets will continue declining as a percent of the total and that the risk profile of this lending will improve as countries such as Poland and the Czech Republic become more stable risks.[13] Of the bank's total exposure to emerging markets, Asian countries account for a little less than 50 percent, with Europe and Latin America splitting the remainder evenly. ING's decision to begin shedding parts of Barings reflects its willingness to sell investments that are not sufficiently profitable.

J.P. Morgan Chase. Chase is cutting back on its existing consumer banking businesses in Asia. Similarly, J.P. Morgan has reduced the economic risk of its credit portfolio by roughly 50 percent in the past two years and has made a significant change in the direction of the firm. J.P. Morgan Chase will continue to extend credit in emerging markets, but only as part of a comprehensive package of financial solutions and not in isolation.

J.P. Morgan has become a leading over-the-counter derivatives franchise, combining this with strong risk management capacity. It also has invested heavily to expand its investment banking capabilities. J.P. Morgan is targeting the market of investment firms such as Morgan Stanley Dean Witter, Goldman Sachs, Merrill Lynch, and Salomon Smith Barney. Since its merger with Chase, the combined firm is focusing on five business lines: investment banking, treasury sales, private banking, equity services, and proprietary trading. It is also building the group's global custody capabilities and expanding its mergers and acquisitions and initial public offering businesses.

Banco Santander Central Hispano (BSCH). The product of a merger between Banco Santander and Banco Central Hispanoamericano, BSCH enjoys a balanced business profile. It has an impressive combined market share and a strong competitive position across all business segments. Like other Spanish banks, BSCH is under increasing pressure from domestic competition, and it is focused on expansion in Latin America, where it has a broad-based presence. The merger diluted the weight of the group's Latin American investments: before the merger, Banco Central Hispanoamericano's involvement in the region was more limited than Banco Santander's. Aggregate investments remain sizable and are growing, however. More recent investments in the area include the $750 million bid to buy out minority shareholders of its Argentine subsidiary, Banco Río, and the $1 billion purchase of Brazil's Banco Meridional. At year-end 1999, retail banking operations, asset management, and wholesale banking activities in Latin America contributed 30 percent of BSCH assets. Moreover, Latin

13. Moody's Investors Service (2000).

America contributes close to 50 percent of the group's preprovision income. The rest of the group's international activities are largely focused on the wholesale market. BSCH considers that it has achieved the right retail presence in Latin America, but it remains interested in acquiring pension and fund management companies—a business sector in which BBVA holds a leading position with one-third of the market. Opportunistic acquisitions cannot be ruled out, however, in certain geographical markets where the group's franchise is more limited. Although BSCH's leading franchise in Latin America is a clear strength, the bank faces challenges in creating a coherent management group, implementing stronger credit and risk cultures, and modernizing antiquated and inefficient processes across countries.

Standard Chartered. Standard Chartered is continuing to position itself as a leading bank in emerging markets. Headquartered in London, almost all of Standard Chartered's activities take place across an extensive network in Asia, Africa, and Latin America. Standard Chartered has a diverse portfolio of franchises in emerging market countries, but it is one of the longest operating foreign banks in the Asia-Pacific region, which accounts for two-thirds of the bank's assets. The bank sees itself as a leading player in both corporate and consumer banking. Operations center around three classes of business: consumer banking, corporate and institutional banking, and treasury services. Standard Chartered's recent strategy has been to lower its risk profile by booking lower-risk assets, such as consumer loans and credit cards. The fee-based businesses that the bank has sought to develop in recent years include trade finance and cash management, while corporate lending has been cut significantly. The bank also has shifted toward fee-based activities and away from proprietary position taking. Lending is now performed extensively in trade financing and (in Hong Kong) residential mortgages. As part of this strategy, Standard Chartered has established special agreements with Westpac, First Chicago, NatWest, and Fleet Financial Services, helping them to expand their services into the Asia-Pacific region.

Appendix 3C: Strategies and Products of Representative Domestic Banks in Emerging Markets

Banacci. Banamex-ACCIVAL has a market share of 25 percent of all corporate and consumer lending in Mexico. It accounts for 27 percent of Mexico's core banking deposits and 33 percent of the country's credit card billings. Banacci balances its business between business and retail banking, and it serves 8 million customers with deposit and lending products, credit cards, and asset management services. According to the bank's president and chief executive officer, Manuel Medina Mora, the core of Banacci's business lies in its combination of large-scale financial intermediation and payment transactions—Banacci accounts for about one-third of Mexico's payment system, linking businesses and consumers.

Banco Galicia. The largest private sector bank in Argentina, Banco Galicia has been a leader in consumer banking since the 1960s. With an asset base of approximately $11 billion, 219 branches, and 5,300 employees, Banco Galicia has a strongly established domestic base; it is considered second only to Citibank in terms of brand recognition. Banco Galicia has a strong retail banking franchise and holds about 850,000 deposit accounts. It places strong emphasis on collateralized lending, with mortgages accounting for half of the total consumer loan portfolio. Consumer lending is currently monitored by a generalized credit and behavioral scoring system and a centralized approval system put in place during the recession of 1995. Credit card services and deposit accounts, most of which are individual accounts, have grown substantially. Galicia is gearing up to capitalize on technological efficiency by expanding its network of automated teller machines, point-of-service terminals, and twenty-four-hour banking centers. It does not lend to small businesses.

Bangkok Bank. Bangkok Bank has a dominant franchise in Thailand's commercial and retail markets. The bank's principal strength is the breadth of its current customer base. For example, it has 11 million customer accounts and already operates 1,000 ATMs, a dominant position that it is virtually certain to retain. It aims to compete across a broad range of products, including corporate banking, retail, credit cards, personal services, and investment products. The bank plans to invest in all of these areas. It has recognized that the greatest opportunity for profit is in retail business, an area that was previously neglected by most Asian banks. To maintain profitable customers, it plans to introduce upgraded products and services, together with more sophisticated and automated sales techniques involving customer profiling and data mining.

Bradesco. As Brazil's largest bank, Bradesco considers its name to be synonymous with retail banking. Bradesco's activities include commercial lending, rural lending, housing lending, savings products, and investment banking, as well as leasing, brokerage, credit card management, insurance, pension funds, and a special savings company. The bank maintains more than 1,900 full branches and 6,300 banking facilities; it holds 5.5 million checking accounts and 14.5 million savings accounts. With $43 billion in total assets and a market capitalization of about $10 billion, Bradesco reaches across Brazil. The bank recently undertook a massive investment program in automation, reducing the work force from 150,000 employees in 1986 to 90,000 employees in 1991 and to 50,000 in 1997. Management also emphasizes improvements in the quality and variety of products and services, and it is focused on substantial restructuring of the branch network. Areas that have experienced particularly strong growth include consumer credit, with credit card products and services growing 25 percent in 1997; Bradesco Seguros, one of the largest insurance groups in Brazil, with 20 percent revenue growth; and Bradesco Previdencia e Seguros, the largest private pension fund company in Brazil.

Malayan Banking. Malayan Banking, Malaysia's largest bank, has a 30 percent market share and an outstanding local franchise. The quality of the assets of the domestic banking system remains under pressure from the effects of the financial crisis and the lack of effective local corporate restructuring in Malaysia. Like other banks, it remains heavily exposed, directly or through collateral, to property and financial companies and to stock market volatility. It will face much tougher competition over the longer term, as local financial markets undergo further deregulation. The government's involvement remains a handicap: the bank is 51.5 percent owned by the government-controlled Permodalan Nasional Berhad and two of its unit trusts.

State Bank of India (SBI). SBI is undertaking a number of initiatives in an attempt to respond to the changing banking needs of retail customers and businesses. It is introducing new products and services and upgrading its internal systems. In retail banking it is focusing on retail lending, including housing loans, car loans, and consumer durable loans. SBI has launched a credit card in conjunction with General Electric and hopes to capture a 5 percent market share by the end of fiscal 2001. Foreign banks currently dominate the credit card market. SBI also sought to computerize 2,117 branches by March 2000, covering about 70 percent of the bank's business. Likewise, SBI intends to expand the number of ATMs from about 108 at present to 1,000 by the end of fiscal 2002; steps are being taken to network them. SBI intends to launch Internet banking by the end of fiscal 2001.

In the corporate sector, SBI is emphasizing lending to the trade and services sectors (as opposed to industry), in recognition of their contribution to India's economic activity. The bank has also set up a corporate accounts group, offering a full range of products and services and serving as a single interface for the bank's top 100–200 corporate clients. Finally, SBI recently introduced several new business products, including cash management services.

Appendix 3D: Range of Banking Products, by Region

The following table highlights the range of banking products offered by banks with international operations, using Eastern Europe as a representative sample. The information was compiled on the basis of reports published on the banks' websites.

Table 3D-1. *Range of Banking Products Offered by Foreign Banks in Eastern Europe*

	Type of product		
Country and bank	Consumer	Electronic	Business and corporate
Czech Republic			
ABN AMRO	No operations	No operations	No operations
Citibank	None	Internet banking, e-commerce services	Cash management, loans and leasing, treasury services, corporate finance, lending products, custody services
Credit Suisse Group	Asset management	None	Mutual funds, institutional client services (insurance, government, corporate, pensions, money market, fixed-income, equities)
Hungary			
ABN AMRO	No operations	No operations	No operations
Citibank	Checking, investment, credit cards, loans, bank cards	Electronic banking	Cash management, CitiService, trade services, treasury services, investment products, transaction banking, financing
Credit Suisse Group	No operations	No operations	No operations
Poland			
ABN AMRO	None	Correspondent banking	Cash management, commercial lending, custody, structured finance, trade services, treasury services, securities and bonds, leasing, asset management
Citibank	Checking, savings, investment, credit cards, loans, insurance	CitiPhone	None
Credit Suisse Group	No operations	No operations	No operations
Romania			
ABN AMRO	None	Electronic banking	Cash management, loans, trade services, treasury services, structured finance, equity, debt structuring, corporate banking, custody services, current and deposit accounts
Citibank	Cash management, payment and collections	None	Cash management, treasury services, financing, trade services, syndicated loans, custody services, training, current accounts
Credit Suisse Group	No operations	No operations	No operations

References

Caprio, Gerard. 2001. *Finance for Growth: Policy Choices in a Volatile World.* Oxford University Press and World Bank.

Dages, B. Gerard, Linda Goldberg, and Daniel Kinney. 2000. "Foreign and Domestic Bank Participation in Emerging Markets: Lessons from Mexico and Argentina." Federal Reserve Bank of New York *Economic Policy Review* 6(3): 17–36.

Demirguc-Kunt, Asli, Stijn Claessens, and Harry Huizinga. 2001. "How Does Foreign Entry Affect Domestic Banking Markets?" *Journal of Banking and Finance* 25(5).

Dickens, Mark, and Bob Keppler. 2001. "Summary on Credit Application Scoring." Paper prepared for the Global Conference on Profiting from Small Business Lending. World Bank, April 2–3, Washington.

Goldman Sachs. 1999. "The Prize: WTO and the Opening of China's Banking Market to Foreign Banks." Goldman Sachs Investment Research (December 14).

Greenwich Associates. 2000a. "Banking the World's Top Financial Providers." *Asian Corporate Finance,* 1–4. Report to research partners (May).

———. 2000b. "Banking the World's Top Financial Providers." *Latin American Corporate Finance,* 1–4. Report to research partners (May).

———. 2000c. "Market Penetration and Tier Position." *Asian Corporate Finance,* 1–2. Report to research partners (May).

———. 2000d. "Market Penetration and Tier Position." *Latin American Corporate Finance,* 1–2. Report to research partners (May).

Moody's Investors Service. 2000. *Analyses of Various Banks and Bank Groups, 1999–2000.* Global Credit Research.

HAROLD D. SKIPPER JR.

4

Liberalization of Insurance Markets: Issues and Concerns

(Asia, L. America,
CééC)

G22616 F23
G28 P34

This paper addresses several issues relevant to liberal insurance markets. After offering some definitions, I provide an overview of insurance both worldwide and by region and then explore how insurance aids economic development. Next, I discuss the role of foreign insurers, with particular emphasis on the concerns that historically have been expressed about their role in the insurance markets of emerging economies. Most of these concerns are unfounded, and foreign insurers should be expected to play an important role in market evolution and development.

I then set out the role and importance of government policy in insurance. Government intervention in insurance markets is essential, but it should be carefully targeted to minimize undue interference. This discourse might appear academic to some readers, but it clarifies the circumstances under which government should and should not intervene in insurance markets.

The Language of Insurance

Insurance is both a risk-shifting and risk-sharing device. For a consideration (the premium), an individual or organization (the insured) is guaranteed to be reimbursed by the insuring organization (the insurer) if a covered event occurs. The scheme functions because the insurer insures a sufficient quantity of similar exposures such that its overall claims experience is reasonably predictable. Generally, the greater the number of insured parties, the more predictable is the insurer's experience, given the law of large numbers.

This comfortably predictable situation might not materialize if the insured events have a catastrophic potential, that is, if losses are correlated. Also, unforeseen changes can drastically alter insurers' pricing assumptions: life and health insurers did not anticipate the additional claims resulting from the AIDS epidemic, for example, and liability insurers still do not know how much they will have to pay for pollution claims—losses they never intended to cover. In spite of these and a host of other possible operational glitches, the world's insurers and reinsurers are largely profitable, stable financial institutions.

Insurance can be classified in many ways. The framework used here is based on four distinctions: social versus private insurance; life versus nonlife insurance; retail versus corporate insurance; and direct insurance versus reinsurance.

Social versus Private Insurance

Governments have determined that certain types or minimum levels of insurance coverage are public goods and that this coverage should therefore be provided by the government, as opposed to the private sector. Most countries have extensive government-administered social security schemes that provide survivor, retirement, disability, and unemployment benefits. Health insurance and benefits for job-related accidents and illnesses, in turn, are typically provided by the government or the private sector or some combination of the two.

Social insurance may be distinguished from private insurance through its emphasis on social equity (that is, income redistribution) rather than on individual actuarial equity (in which premiums reflect the expected value of losses). Furthermore, participation in social insurance schemes is compulsory, and financing relies on government-mandated premiums (taxes).

Life versus Nonlife Insurance

The insurance business differentiates between companies that sell insurance on the person, known as life insurance (or personal insurance in many markets), and companies that sell insurance to protect property, called nonlife insurance (or property/casualty insurance or general insurance). The latter includes insurance to cover property losses, such as damage to or destruction of homes, automobiles, businesses, and aircraft; liability losses, including payments for professional negligence, product defects, and negligent automobile operation; and, in some countries, workers' compensation and health care. Life insurance benefits include payments on a person's death (usually called life insurance or assurance); payments for living a certain period, such as endowments, annuities, and pensions; disability insurance; and medical coverage for injury or disease (health insurance). In many markets, health insurance is classified as nonlife insurance.

Firms in the life and nonlife sectors of the insurance industry perceive themselves quite differently, with some justification. Many countries prohibit a single corporation from selling both types of insurance, although joint production via holding companies and affiliates typically is permitted.

Retail versus Corporate Insurance

Insurance purchased by individuals, including homeowners insurance, automobile insurance, and individual life insurance, is often called retail insurance. Retail nonlife insurance is classified as personal lines insurance. In the European Union (EU), such nonlife insurance (as well as that for small businesses) is defined as insurance for mass risks.

Insurance purchased by businesses and other organizations is called corporate insurance. Examples include product liability, business interruption, automobile insurance, and group life insurance. Corporate nonlife insurance is classified as commercial lines insurance. In the EU, such insurance (except for small businesses) is defined as insurance for large risks. In some markets, insurance purchased by commercial organizations, especially manufacturing firms, is termed industrial insurance. Government oversight is more stringent in the retail than in the corporate insurance market because of greater information asymmetry in retail lines.

Direct Insurance versus Reinsurance

Insurance sold to the public and to noninsurance commercial and industrial enterprises is classified as direct insurance. Insurers selling such insurance—both life and nonlife products and both retail and corporate lines—are called direct writing (or primary) insurers and the attendant premiums are direct premiums.

Insurance purchased by direct writing insurers to hedge their own portfolios is classed as reinsurance and is sold by reinsurers; some is also sold by
the reinsurance departments of direct writing companies. Reinsurance is
wholesale insurance. Direct writing companies purchase reinsurance to
avoid undue concentrations of potential loss, increase their underwriting
capacity, stabilize overall financial results, and take advantage of the reinsurer's special expertise.

Almost all insurers worldwide purchase reinsurance. Reinsurers themselves purchase reinsurance (that is, they retrocede business to other reinsurers and the reinsurance departments of direct writing companies).
Dozens of insurers and reinsurers typically "have a line" on insurance policies with high limits.

Reinsurance typically involves large exposure to loss, often with a catastrophic loss potential. The reinsurer must therefore be skillful at underwriting and pricing. Because the direct writing company ordinarily is a
knowledgeable buyer and the reinsurer a knowledgeable seller, government
intervention in this transaction has historically been nonexistent or minimal. Reinsurance is probably the most international segment of the insurance business.

The Importance of Insurance Worldwide

Insurance markets vary enormously in size and structure.[1] The size of a
given country's insurance market depends greatly on the size of its economy,
with innumerable environmental influences also shaping its structure. The
most commonly accepted measure of insurance market size is gross direct
premiums.[2] Globally, gross direct premiums totaled more than U.S.$2.324
trillion in 1999, after experiencing a real average annual growth rate of
about 4.0 percent over the preceding ten years. Developing countries in
south and east Asia, eastern Europe, and Latin America saw particularly
strong market expansion in the 1990s, although the Asian economic crisis
hindered growth in that region toward the end of the decade. Insurance premium growth in emerging markets was roughly double that of the advanced
economies throughout the 1980s and 1990s, although advanced economies
continue to dominate premium writings worldwide.

1. This discussion draws, in part, on Skipper (1998, chaps. 1, 3, and 4; forthcoming).
2. All international insurance premium data are from Swiss Re (2000b).

Life versus Nonlife Insurance

The life sector accounts for 60.8 percent of world direct premiums, while the nonlife sector generates the remaining 39.2 percent.[3] Considerable regional diversity exists in the balance between the life and nonlife sectors. Africa, for instance, demonstrates a high proportion of life business because of the large South African insurance market: four-fifths of all African premiums written are for life insurance products, with more than 90 percent of this proportion being life premiums. Asia has a similarly high propensity to save via life insurance. Conversely, the adverse effects of past high inflation rates and political instability have historically depressed life premium growth in Latin America, although the situation has changed dramatically for several countries in recent years. Life premiums are relatively less important in Central and Eastern Europe because realistic growth began only during the 1990s, after fundamental reform. Generally speaking, the more developed is a country's capital market, the less important is the life sector relative to other savings and investment media, particularly the securities markets.

Distribution of Premiums

North America was the world's largest insurance market in 1999, accounting for 36 percent of total direct premiums written. Western Europe followed with a 32.1 percent share. Asia's share was 26.7 percent, after having fallen both absolutely and relatively because of the economic crises in the region. Japan, in particular, experienced difficulties that affected the insurance market. In addition, year-to-year results for Asia are distorted because of currency fluctuations. The small shares accounted for by Latin America (1.5%), Africa (1.1%), and Central and Eastern Europe (0.7%) reflect comparatively low levels of economic development among many countries in these regions, together with past or present economic and political difficulties.

The world's ten largest national markets are shown in figure 4-1. The United States is by far the largest, followed by Japan. The United Kingdom, Germany, and France are closely bunched thereafter. Note the relatively high share of life business in Japan, the United Kingdom, France, and Korea. The high share for the two Asian countries is attributable to a high propensity to save, favorable tax treatment, and less developed capital markets.

---

3. The data source follows the Organization for Economic Cooperation and Development (OECD) in including health and accident premiums in the nonlife category.

Figure 4-1. *Ten Largest Insurance Markets, 1999*

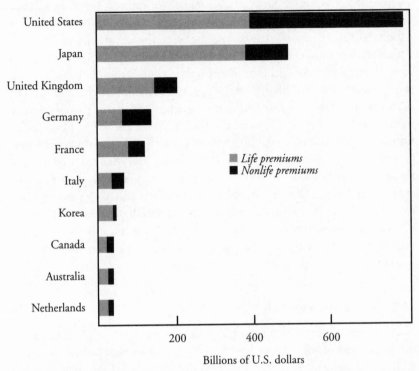

Source: Swiss Re (2000b).

The Structure of Insurance Markets

National insurance markets have evolved to suit each country's particular environment. The interaction of supply and demand forces determines market structure. Price and innumerable economic, social, and cultural factors influence the demand for insurance. At the national level, studies consistently find that insurance demand is strongly related to national income.[4] Higher income countries purchase more life and nonlife insurance than do lower income countries. When incomes are low, individuals have little disposable income with which to purchase insurance and fewer assets that justify insurance protection. Economic development increases incomes and assets, together with the demand to protect them and the money to pay premiums. At the same time, informal insurance arrangements, such as the

4. See Skipper (1998, chap. 4) for a summary of the studies on insurance demand and supply.

extended family, become increasingly less able to offer sufficient security as families shrink in size, become more geographically dispersed, and grow more dependent on employment income. Informal arrangements give way to formalized economic security mechanisms, such as social insurance programs, employer provided security, and individually purchased private insurance. Nonetheless, informal insurance arrangements remain important sources of economic security in all countries.

Two measures are traditionally used to show the relative importance of insurance within national economies. First, insurance density indicates the average annual per capita premium within a country. Values are usually converted from national currency to U.S. dollars. Currency fluctuations can therefore affect comparisons, which can lead to distortions over time. Second, insurance penetration is the ratio of yearly direct premiums written to gross domestic product (GDP). This measure provides a rough estimate of the relative importance of insurance within national economies, and it is unaffected by currency fluctuations. It does not give a complete picture, however, as it ignores differences in insurance price levels, national product mixes, and other market variations.

The income elasticity of insurance premiums indicates the relative change in insurance premiums written for a given change in national income. An income elasticity of 1.2, for example, implies that a 10 percent increase in per capita income will give rise to a 12 percent increase in premiums written. If countries are assumed to follow an essentially common development path, then the income elasticity of insurance premiums can be estimated to be not less than 1.0. Figure 4-2 shows income elasticities for selected countries. Studies suggest that the elasticity itself varies with level of income.[5] For the least developed countries, the income elasticity is fairly low, at around 1.0. Income elasticity increases in middle-income countries, reaching 2.0 and higher. In economically advanced economies, elasticity seems to flatten out again to around 1.0. Income elasticities are frequently 2.0 and higher for life insurance and 1.5 for nonlife insurance. These high elasticities occur in countries with a per capita income of about U.S.$10,000 for nonlife insurance and about U.S.$15,000 for life insurance. Elasticities are about 1.0 at income levels less than U.S.$300 and greater than U.S.$30,000. Of course, individual country results vary from these averages as a result of factors other than GDP, such as culture, demographics, government policy, and inflation.

5. Enz (2000).

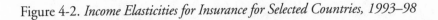

Figure 4-2. *Income Elasticities for Insurance for Selected Countries, 1993–98*

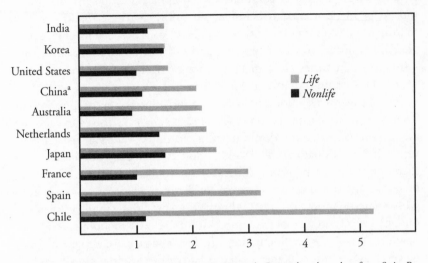

Source: Calculated by Georgia State University Research Center, based on data from Swiss Re, *Sigma*, various issues.
a. Data for China are from 1987 to 1998.

These measures of the insurance market provide a context for an examination of the insurance markets of emerging countries. With regard to insurance density, Swiss per capita expenditure is easily the world's highest at $4,643, followed by Japan ($3,909), the United Kingdom ($3,244), the United States ($2,921), and Ireland ($2,455). The average for member countries of the Organization for Economic Cooperation and Development (OECD) in 1999 was $1,951, while the average for the European Union was $1,806. In addition to such differences in total expenditures, countries exhibit substantial variation in the ratio of expenditures for life versus nonlife insurance.

Insurance penetration, in turn, was highest in South Africa (16.5 percent in 1999), followed by the United Kingdom (13.4 percent) and Switzerland (12.8 percent). Japan and Korea also display high degrees of penetration (11.1 and 11.3, respectively). The high overall penetration in these countries is driven by high life insurance penetration. This partially reflects favorable tax treatment for life insurance as a savings instrument and, for South Africa and South Korea, relatively less developed financial markets (that is, fewer savings options). The OECD ratio was 8.6 percent, and the European Union average was 8.0 percent.

The differences in the relative importance of insurance internationally stem from many factors, including taxation, religion, economic development, and culture. The role of the government as a source of personal economic security also greatly influences the role of the private sector.

The International Dimensions of Insurance

With the increasing internationalization of business comes a corresponding internationalization of financial services. Additionally, the size and concentration of many purely domestic loss exposures require a mustering of international insurance capacity. One has but to recall the March 20, 2001, sinking of the forty-story Petrobras oil platform—the world's largest—off the coast of Brazil. The rig accounted for 6 percent of Brazil's entire national daily oil output. The platform was insured internationally, although I understand that the risk manager for Petrobras had just recently failed to renew business interruption coverage on the platform. No single country's market can provide coverage for such large loss exposures, such that an international spread is essential if these risks are to be insured.

Reinsurance is particularly important in this regard. The large reinsurance companies, such as Munich Re (Germany), Swiss Re (Switzerland), General Cologne Re (the United States), and SCOR (France), conduct substantial international operations and thereby augment national insurance capacity. Reinsurance is generally one of the most international insurance lines.

Perhaps fewer than a dozen direct-writing insurers are truly international. Firms that are capable of servicing their customers worldwide include the American International Group, Aetna, and Chubb in the United States; the Royal and Sun Alliance and CGNU in the United Kingdom; AXA in France; Zurich in Switzerland; Allianz in Germany; ING in the Netherlands; and Generali in Italy. Dozens of other insurers, particularly many life insurers, have important foreign operations or seek to initiate such operations. For many, international expansion offers an effective means of achieving additional growth, given that domestic markets such as the United States may be saturated.

The success of foreign insurance firms in a specific market depends on the market's structure. Foreign firms traditionally have been most successful in the more complex insurance lines, such as commercial insurance and marine, aviation, and transport (MAT) insurance and reinsurance. Their large size, geographic spread of risk, in-depth knowledge of complex risks, and management efficiency enable them to compete successfully with local firms in these areas. They have also used their pricing, marketing, and management expertise to gain an important share of particular retail market segments, although domestic firms generally dominate the less complex retail lines as a result of the high information and distribution costs associated with mass risks as well as historically restrictive regulation.

Finally, in some markets, foreign firms have encountered government impediments to entry or impediments stemming from certain market structures that have made it difficult or even impossible to establish business. Regulatory transparency has presented a particular problem for firms seeking entry into certain insurance markets. Consistent with a cultural tradition of allowing their officials considerable latitude, some countries feature insurance laws and regulations that are written very generally, with interpretation and the details of implementation left to administrative personnel. As a result, a foreign insurer may not be able to know in advance the specific nature of entry requirements or whether it will be treated according to the same standards as domestic firms. The absence of detailed written standards can also hinder foreign insurers' ability to question or challenge arbitrary or unreasonable actions of the regulator. Numerous countries have recently undertaken steps to render their regulation more transparent and to ensure more open, competitive markets than have characterized their markets in the past.

Overview of Emerging Insurance Markets by Region

This section explores the structure and current developments of insurance markets in several emerging economies.[6] The analysis considers developing countries from Asia, Latin America, Central and Eastern Europe, and, to a lesser extent, Africa.

Recent Insurance Market Developments

Insurance markets in emerging Asia enjoyed rapid growth in the decade before the economic crisis of 1997–98. Figure 4-3 shows individual country growth rates for most of the 1990s. While the economic crisis significantly weakened regional economies and undermined the financial position of regional insurers, it also accelerated the process of insurance liberalization

6. Much of this section is drawn from Swiss Re (2000a).

Figure 4-3. *Real Premium Growth Rates for Selected Asian Insurance Markets, 1990–98*

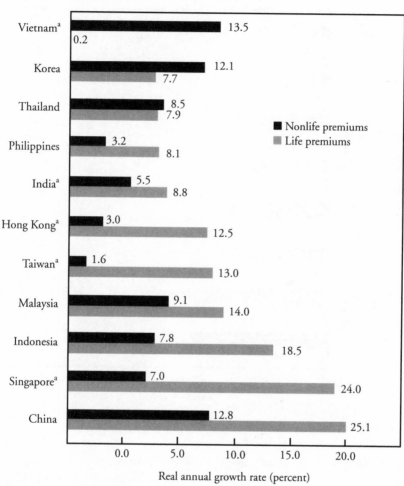

Real annual growth rate (percent)

Source: Swiss Re (2000b).
a. Data are from 1990 to 1997.

and deregulation. The prospects for insurance in emerging Asia are therefore promising as the economies resume robust growth.

With the exception of South Korea and Malaysia, penetration of the nonlife insurance market in emerging Asia is generally below the global average for countries with comparable per capita incomes. This reflects the underinsurance of industrial and natural catastrophe risks against a back-

Figure 4-4. *Insurance Penetration Ratios for Selected Asian Insurance Markets, 1999*[a]

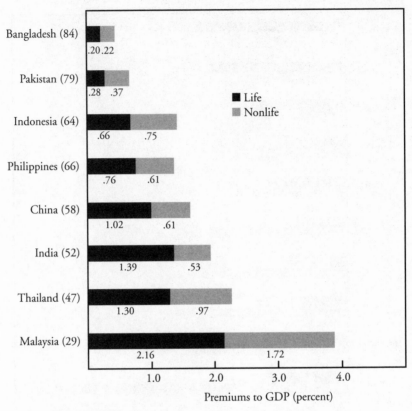

Source: Swiss Re (2000b).
a. Numbers in parentheses indicate world rank out of eighty-four countries.

ground of a relatively weak corporate risk management culture. The higher penetration level in South Korea and, to a lesser extent, Malaysia could be partly due to the inclusion of savings-type policies in nonlife business.

In sharp contrast to nonlife insurance, emerging Asia's life insurance markets are generally highly developed. This mainly reflects the lack of public sector retirement schemes, which forces individuals to look after their own retirement needs. The emergence of a substantial middle class over the last decade accelerated the trend. The nascent stage of development of emerging Asia's financial intermediation capability, in the face of a high level of household savings, further encourages the ownership of life policies.

Figure 4-5. *Real Premium Growth Rates for Selected Latin American Insurance Markets, 1990–98*

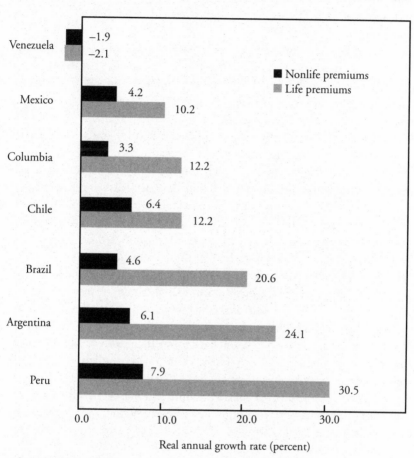

Real annual growth rate (percent)

Source: Swiss Re (2000b).

The region's huge population, a disproportionate number of elderly people, a tradition of frugality, and the lack of state-sponsored pension schemes all point to the prospects of sustained growth in life insurance business in the near future. Figure 4-4 offers insurance penetration figures for several Asian insurance markets.

In Latin America, economic reforms under way beginning in the early 1990s have created new business opportunities for domestic and foreign insurers. The stabilization of the economic environment, the privatization of state-owned companies, the partial privatization of public pensions, and, in some countries, the privatization of the health and occupational accident insurance sectors have all fueled demand for private insurance. Growth has been three times as high as in the industrialized countries, albeit starting from a very low level.

The region's economic development has not been without setbacks, as evidenced by the Mexican crisis of the mid-1990s and the consequences of the Asian crisis in the late 1990s. Between 1990 and 1998, premium income in the nonlife sector increased by a real annual 4.6 percent, on average, in the region's six biggest economies, whereas it stagnated in the second half of the decade because of fierce competition and an overcapacity in the global reinsurance market. Life insurance premiums rose by more than 13 percent annually since the beginning of the 1990s. Venezuela was the only country not to benefit from these developments: insufficient economic reform and a serious financial crisis shrank insurance volume, especially life insurance. Figure 4-5 gives growth rates for the countries studied.

Insurance penetration in both the life and nonlife sectors is markedly below that of industrialized countries. With the exception of Mexico, which has a poorly developed nonlife sector despite its high vulnerability to natural catastrophes, insurance penetration in the region corresponds to the average for other countries with similarly low per capita incomes. Life insurance is still underdeveloped across the entire region (with the sole exception of Chile), although this is likely to change over the next five to ten years in response to the social security reforms being introduced throughout the region. This proved to be the case in Chile, where such reforms were introduced in the early 1980s. At the same time, regional demand for a wider spectrum of financial services and more complete pension products can be expected to increase. Figure 4-6 offers insurance penetration ratios for selected Latin American markets.

In central and eastern Europe, the political changes that have taken place since the end of the 1980s have led to deregulation and liberalization in the insurance sector. Entry barriers to foreign providers were lowered over a relatively short period of time, and regulatory conditions in several markets are now converging toward European Union standards. The abolition of state monopolies and the entry of foreign and local companies into the market sharpened competition for insurance customers.

The region comprises twenty-seven countries and is quite diverse in terms of economic strength, population size, and maturity of insurance

Figure 4-6. *Insurance Penetration Ratios for Selected Latin American Insurance Markets, 1999*[a]

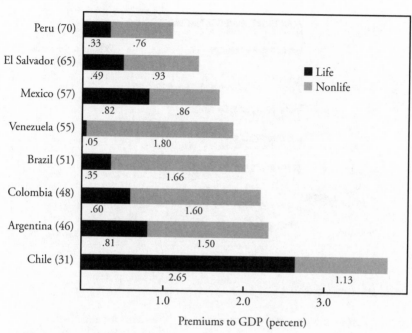

Premiums to GDP (percent)

Source: Swiss Re (2000b).

a. Numbers in parentheses indicate world rank out of eighty-four countries.

markets.[7] The ten candidates for membership in the European Union include five countries in central eastern Europe (namely, the Czech Republic, Hungary, Poland, Slovakia, and Slovenia), the Baltic states (Estonia, Latvia, and Lithuania), Bulgaria, and Romania.

Growth rates in the life insurance industry were quite volatile in the 1990s. Russia's life insurance market was especially unpredictable, owing to changes in tax regulations. In the Baltic states, real premium volume declined sharply between 1993 and 1996; the sector then started to grow again, reaching its 1993 level in 1999. The five central eastern European countries enjoyed relatively constant high growth rates.

The nonlife business is generally more developed than the life sector in central and eastern Europe. The star performance came from the Baltic

7. This section draws from Swiss Re (2001).

Figure 4-7. *Real Premium Growth Rates for Selected Central and Eastern European Insurance Markets, 1993–99*

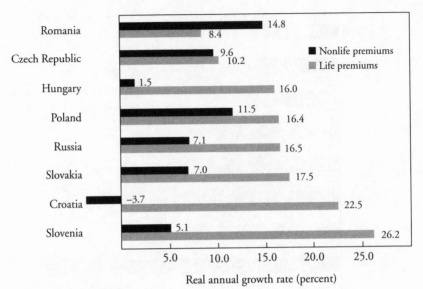

Real annual growth rate (percent)

Source: Swiss Re (2000b).

states, with average growth in excess of 21.5 percent a year. Trends in the five central eastern European countries and the Commonwealth of Independent States (CIS) were similar, with average growth rates of 8.4 percent and 7.4 percent, respectively. Only southeastern Europe and the CIS countries suffered a brief decline in real premium volume in 1994 and again in 1998, as a result of political and economic crises. Figure 4-7 displays growth rates for several countries, while figure 4-8 presents insurance penetration ratios for the same countries.

With regard to Africa, insurance penetration in South Africa is the highest in the world. The South African life insurance market is ranked twelfth in the world based on premium volume. Real life premium growth averaged 10 percent a year between 1990 and 1998. The nonlife insurance premium real growth rate averaged about 4.1 percent over the same time period.

For 1999, the real growth in insurance premiums throughout all of Africa was generally positive, with significant differences between the life and nonlife business.[8] Premiums in the life sector increased by 8.2 percent throughout the region, whereas they fell in the nonlife sector by 1.9 percent.

8. This discussion draws from Swiss Re (2000b).

Figure 4-8. *Insurance Penetration Ratios for Selected Central and Eastern European Insurance Markets, 1999*[a]

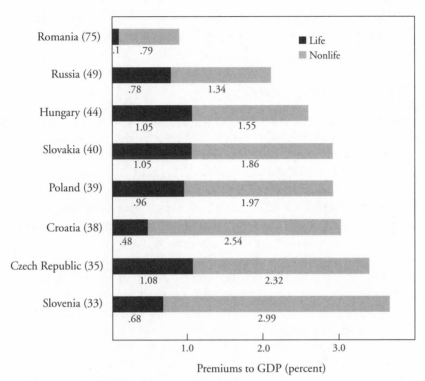

Premiums to GDP (percent)

Source: Swiss Re (2000b).
a. Numbers in parentheses indicate world rank out of eighty-four countries.

South Africa accounted for more than one-half of the region's nonlife premiums. Interim figures indicate a 2 percent real decline in premiums in South Africa in 1999, which translates into a 7 percent decline in dollars given the devaluation of the rand. This fall was due mainly to strong competition in this market. In other countries, too, such as Libya and Mauritius, premiums fell in real terms in 1999. Premiums increased in Algeria, Egypt, Kenya, Morocco, and Tunisia.

Developments in the life sector for Africa as a whole were determined almost exclusively by South Africa, which was responsible for some 95 percent of the region's life premium volume. This share has remained constant over recent years. Interim figures indicate a strong increase in pure savings products in South Africa. This led to life premium growth for the country of almost 8 percent in real terms. Although the real growth rates of some countries are far above those of South Africa—most notably Morocco (18.8 percent) and Egypt (17.7 percent)—these markets are relatively small. Their strong growth is balanced out to some extent by falling premium volumes in other countries of the region, such as Algeria (7 percent) and Libya (17.4 percent).

The Competitive Environment

I now provide a quick assessment of the competitive environment of the major regions examined. The main focus here is market concentration.[9]

Significant diversity exists in market concentration among emerging Asia's life and nonlife insurance markets. The recently opened Chinese market is dominated by a state insurer that alone accounts for more than three-quarters of total premiums. The Indian insurance market was partially opened to competition in 2000, including foreign minority-owned joint ventures. The state-owned insurers thus still account for the totality of both the life and nonlife insurance business in that market. A handful of large insurers also claim the bulk of nonlife business in South Korea. This reflects the historically closed nature of the Korean market and the ability of these insurers to leverage their group affiliation with the leading Korean conglomerates, or *chaebols*. In comparison, the nonlife markets in Southeast Asia are more fragmented: the top five insurers generally account for 30–40 percent of the market. A business culture based on relations and the lack of dominant state insurers have led to a market characterized by a large number of small insurers.

The life insurance market in emerging Asia is highly concentrated. Where foreign insurers are denied entry, a handful of state or major domestic life operators dominates with overwhelming market shares. For example, PICC Life in China alone accounted for 70 percent of the market in 1998, while the largest five life insurers in Korea claimed a market share of 79 percent. Where foreign entry has historically been allowed, a few foreign insurers have been able to secure substantial market share through their superior capacity in branding, pricing, and servicing. The American International Group (AIG), for example, accounted for 47 percent of Thailand's life insurance market in 1998.

The insurance markets of Latin America are currently opening to foreign insurers as part of the process of general economic reform, while product

9. This section draws heavily from Swiss Re (2000a).

and pricing regulations are being lifted and solvency controls introduced. At the same time, consolidation has set in. The financial and economic crises of the mid-nineties accelerated the trend in several countries. In Argentina, more than sixty insurers have gone into liquidation since the market opened in 1992. Despite frenetic merger and acquisition activity, the number of insurers increased in most of the other Latin American countries as a result of new start-ups.

Market concentration increased in the first half of the 1990s and then followed a downward trend. The life area is generally more concentrated than the nonlife area, although this varies greatly from country to country. The Argentine nonlife market continues to be fragmented despite the increasing consolidation, for example, whereas Mexico stands out for its strong concentration. Mexico's biggest company now holds a 35 percent market share after taking over two of its major competitors over the last ten years.

In Central and Eastern Europe, the cornerstones of insurance reform have been the abolition of state insurance monopolies, the opening of the market to foreign insurers, and the establishment of an effective supervisory framework. INSIG in Albania was the last comprehensive state monopoly in the region; it was privatized in 1999, and now there is open competition for customers in every market. The former state monopolies have continuously lost market share in the face of competition, particularly to new subsidiaries of financially strong foreign insurance groups. Almost without exception, however, they are still market leaders in both life and nonlife business.

The market shares of the leading companies are generally smaller in nonlife insurance than in the life business, which reflects the significantly larger number of companies in the nonlife sector. In Russia and to some extent in the Baltic States, the number of registered insurers has fallen sharply in recent years because of high capital requirements and industry mergers.

The Importance of Foreign Insurers

This final section in the regional discussion sets out the importance of foreign insurers in different markets.[10] The figures showing the market shares of insurers with foreign ownership in each market include firms with minority as well as majority foreign shareholdings; foreign presence is thus overstated in some markets, particularly in Latin America and in Poland.

10. This section draws heavily from Swiss Re (2000a).

The Asian financial turmoil accelerated the pace of insurance market deregulation and liberalization in that region. Governments throughout the region have realized the benefits of market opening and competition, and they continue to dismantle entry barriers and ease rules on foreign ownership. The weakened financial status of some domestic insurers has encouraged mergers and acquisitions with foreign partners.

Generally speaking, Southeast Asian markets are the most open to foreign participation. The Philippines, for example, has been home to a number of major foreign insurers for years. In contrast, India and China only recently opened their market to foreign participation, and substantial restrictions apply in both cases. This different level of acceptance is aptly manifested in the market share of foreign insurers in these countries' life and nonlife sectors (see figure 4-9).

Where the institutional setting is not overly hostile, foreign insurers have generally been able to establish a visible market presence. Their ability to provide a wide range of solutions supported by creative initiatives and professional underwriting secured high market shares in the 1990s. Hurdles remain, however. A business culture based on relations complicates commercial lines expansion, and various noninstitutional barriers impede foreign participation. To a certain extent, these factors were less prohibitive to the distribution of life than nonlife insurance products.

Latin American markets currently place few major restrictions on the stakes held by foreign insurers or on the formation of subsidiaries in the region. Of all the emerging markets under examination, the market share of insurers with foreign ownership is highest in Latin America. Nonlife market shares range from 30 percent in Brazil to more than 70 percent in Chile, while life insurance market shares range from just under 30 percent in Colombia to more than 80 percent in Argentina.

The importance of foreign investors more than doubled in the 1990s in all the Latin American markets considered here. The greatest number of foreign insurers is in Argentina and Mexico: a total of twenty-five foreign life insurers hold an 80 percent market share in Argentina; Mexico has a similar number of foreign insurers but with a lower market share. Figure 4-10 shows foreign insurers' market shares for selected Latin American markets.

Foreign insurers in Latin America normally have a higher market share in the life and health insurance business than in the nonlife business. The number of foreign investors is also greater in this segment. This result is due in part to the growing demand for new products related to the privatization of social security systems. In this respect, foreign insurers can capitalize on

Figure 4-9. *Foreign Participation in Selected Asian Insurance Markets, 1998*[a]

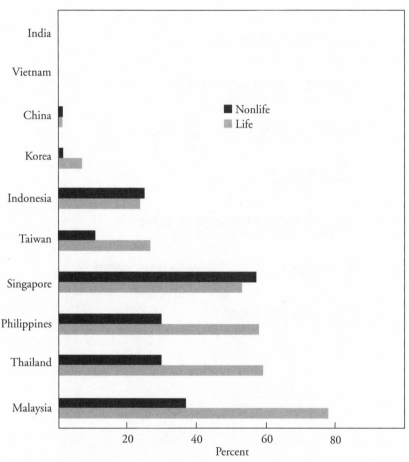

Source: Swiss Re (2000a).
a. Figures adjusted for mergers and acquisitions through March 2000.

their experience in other countries. Their reputation as solid, financially sound companies represents a not-to-be-underestimated advantage in a region that was plagued by high inflation and political instability in the past. This instability explains why growth of life insurance has historically been weak. Few citizens trust in local financial intermediaries, and even today many consumers would rather entrust their money to a company with a global, proven brand name than to a local insurer.

Figure 4-10. *Foreign Participation in Selected Latin American Insurance Markets, 1998*[a]

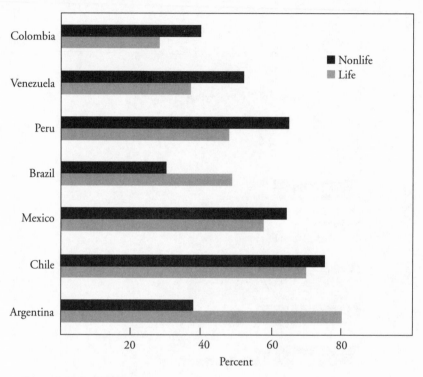

Source: Swiss Re (2000a).
a. Figures adjusted for mergers and acquisitions through March 2000.

Throughout central and eastern Europe, in turn, foreign insurance companies are now allowed to establish a local presence. Russia still restricts the proportion of foreign shareholdings and imposes limitations on the conduct of the nonlife business. Barriers to foreign establishment have gradually been dismantled in other countries, particularly those seeking admission to the European Union.

The market shares of foreign insurers are highest in Poland, Lithuania, Estonia, and Hungary (see figure 4-11). The market share of foreign insurers is much smaller in countries in which the former state monopoly retains a dominant market position and is still owned mainly by the government; this is particularly the case in nonlife insurance. In the latter half of the 1990s, however, foreign insurers markedly expanded their presence in both

Figure 4-11. *Foreign Participation in Selected Central and Eastern European Insurance Markets, 1999*

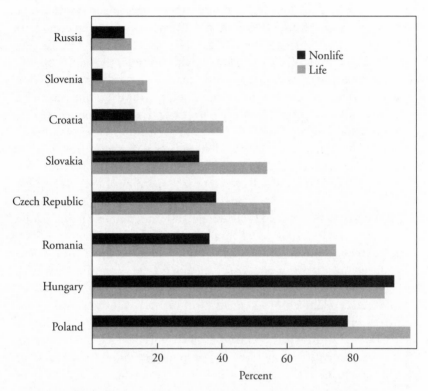

Source: Swiss Re (2000a).

life and nonlife insurance in most countries of central and eastern Europe. This general trend is likely to continue given existing plans to sell former state monopolies as well as local banks.

In Africa, very little information is available on individual markets, with the exception of South Africa. With regard to the South African life insurance market, foreign insurers essentially have no presence. Most chose not to enter or withdrew in the face of poor results and small market shares. The large size and dominance of existing life insurers make it extremely difficult to secure an adequate market share. Foreign-owned insurers account for about a third of the South African nonlife market, although this share is likely to decline as some global insurers seem poised to withdraw.

Emerging Market Insurance Commitments under the
General Agreement on Trade in Services

To gain better insight into regional insurance markets, it is instructive to
briefly examine the insurance commitments made by emerging economies
under the General Agreement on Trade in Services (GATS). This analysis
draws from the work of Aaditya Mattoo, who examines the nature of market access commitments in direct insurance for 105 developing and transition economies.[11] Mattoo divides developing countries and transition
economies into four geographical regions: Africa (forty-one countries), Asia
and the Pacific (twenty-five countries), eastern Europe (seven countries),
and Latin America, including the Caribbean (thirty-two countries). Neither
China nor Russia is yet a member of GATS. About one-half of the countries in the study group, which account for 95 percent of the GDP of less
developed member countries, made commitments on direct insurance services. In both numerical and GDP-weighted terms, country participation
was highest in eastern Europe, where all World Trade Organization (WTO)
members made commitments. Participation was lowest in Africa, where
only thirteen of the forty-one WTO members made commitments. The
participating countries account for four-fifths of African members' GDP. In
Latin America, eighteen of the thirty-two member countries made commitments in insurance; these eighteen countries account for 97 percent of
the region's GDP. In Asia, seventeen of the twenty-five member countries
made commitments in insurance; they account for 95 percent of GDP of
member countries in the region.

Participating countries demonstrate significant differences in the extent
of binding commitments and the restrictiveness of scheduled limitations.
Full liberalization across the three major modes of supply is rare. Of the
fifty-two countries making commitments in direct insurance, only four
small countries committed to full liberalization. Egypt and South Africa are
the only two developing countries to guarantee an absence of restrictions
on either of the two cross-border modes.

In each of the regions examined by Mattoo, commercial presence was
clearly the mode through which members preferred to guarantee access to
domestic markets for direct insurance services; this was also the preferred
mode among OECD countries. As many as nineteen countries, accounting
for almost 25 percent of participants' GDP, guaranteed the absence of
restrictions on commercial presence (other than restrictions on legal form).

11. Mattoo (1998).

Mattoo observes that of the participant countries, eastern Europe potentially represents the most liberal regional market for foreign investment in direct insurance. Next in degree of openness is Africa, where seven of the 13 countries making commitments imposed no restrictions on commercial presence, other than on legal form. Nigeria and South Africa are included among the seven. Egypt, Gabon, and Mauritius apply economic needs tests or discretionary procedures in allowing new entry, while Morocco includes a reciprocity condition in its schedule. Egypt, Ghana, and Kenya (in life insurance) impose equity limitations, but Ghana and Kenya already allow majority foreign ownership. Egypt limits foreign equity to 51 percent for life insurance and 49 percent for nonlife insurance, although the latter is scheduled to be raised to 51 percent in 2003.

The number of countries that guarantee fully open markets for foreign investors is higher in Asia and the Pacific (seven out of seventeen) than in Latin America (three of eighteen). Several relatively large Asian markets—including Hong Kong, Indonesia, Israel, and Turkey, which together account for 32 percent of Asian participants' GDP—have no significant restrictions on the establishment of foreign commercial presence. In Latin America, the same can be said only for Guyana, Panama, and Paraguay, which account for just 1 percent of Latin American participants' GDP. Mattoo highlights an important difference in the nature of the restrictions in place in the two regions: the Latin American group seems primarily reluctant to guarantee free entry, whereas the Asian group seems reluctant to assure full foreign ownership. Eleven Latin American members (including Argentina, Brazil, and Chile) do not assure fully liberal entry conditions. Cuba and Mexico impose only equity limitations for entry, while the Dominican Republic and Honduras do not assure liberal entry and also impose equity limitations. In the Asian group, entry limitations are accompanied by restrictions on foreign equity in eight cases, including India, Malaysia, Philippines, and Thailand. Korea imposes equity limitations only, whereas Qatar imposes limitations on entry only. Mattoo observes that the contrast between the regions may be less stark than it appears because the discretion that Latin American countries retain for imposing conditions on new entry could also apply to foreign equity participation.

Most emerging markets bound the status quo, as did OECD countries. A few countries bound at less than the status quo, including Korea, Malaysia, and Mexico. Some, such as Brazil, Egypt, and most transition economies, effectively bound at greater than the status quo, inscribing future liberalization commitments as additional commitments. A few countries' commitments were particularly disappointing. As just mentioned, three large economies bound at less than status quo, with Korea and Mexico failing to bind the level of their OECD commitments. Some commentators believe that these failures were due more to the rush of final negotiations than to a lack of commitment to liberalization on the part of these two countries. Malaysia's offers were among the most disappointing given the level of development of the economy and the insurance market. It did not grandfather access of existing insurance firms, did not provide for majority ownership for new entrants, and guaranteed little new market access. Another major disappointment was India's failure to make any liberalization commitments in insurance, which reflected the country's inability at the time to achieve national insurance reform.

Insurance and Economic Development

Insurance is important for economic development.[12] Because insurance companies are financial intermediaries, they perform the same types of functions and provide similar generic benefits to a national economy as do other financial intermediaries. At the same time, their role in individual and corporate risk management means that their contributions to economic development do not precisely overlap those of other financial intermediaries. Nations that hinder their insurance markets through unnecessarily restrictive market-access requirements and regulation limit the contributions that insurance can make to development.

How Insurance Aids Economic Development

The more developed and efficient a country's financial market, the greater will be its contribution to economic prosperity. Governments should therefore foster competition among financial service providers, while ensuring that the market is financially sound.

It is wrong to view insurers as simple pass-through mechanisms for diversifying risk, through which the unfortunate few who suffer losses are indemnified from the funds collected from many insured parties. Laudable though that function is, it masks other fundamental contributions that insurance makes to prosperity. Countries that harness these contributions improve the economic opportunities of their citizens and businesses. Insurance provides

12. This section draws partially from Skipper (1997).

seven categories of services that collectively constitute the mechanisms by which insurance contributes to economic growth.

INSURANCE CAN PROMOTE FINANCIAL STABILITY. Insurance helps stabilize the financial situation of individuals, families, and organizations. It accomplishes this task by indemnifying those who suffer loss or harm. Without insurance, individuals and families could become financially destitute and forced to seek assistance from relatives, friends, or the government. Businesses that incur significant uninsured losses may suffer major financial reverses or even fail. Such an event not only causes a loss in the value of the owners' stake in the business, but it also terminates the firm's future contribution to the economy. Employees lose jobs, suppliers lose business, customers lose the opportunity to buy from the firm, and government loses tax revenues. The stability provided by insurance encourages individuals and firms to create wealth with the assurance that their resources can be protected.

INSURANCE CAN SUBSTITUTE FOR AND COMPLEMENT GOVERN-MENT SECURITY PROGRAMS. Insurance, especially life insurance, can substitute for government security programs. Private insurance also complements public security programs. It can thus relieve pressure on social welfare systems, reserving government resources for essential social security and other worthwhile purposes and allowing individuals to tailor their security programs to their own preferences. Studies confirm that greater private expenditures on life insurance are associated with a reduction in government expenditures on social insurance programs. This substitution role is especially important given the growing financial challenges faced by national social insurance systems.

INSURANCE CAN FACILITATE TRADE AND COMMERCE. Insurance underpins much of the world's trade, commerce, and entrepreneurial activity. Many products and services are produced and sold only if adequate insurance is available, such that insurance coverage is a condition for engaging in certain activities. Because of the high risk of failure among new businesses, venture capitalists often make funds available only if tangible assets and the entrepreneurs' lives are adequately insured. Entrepreneurs are more likely to create and expand their business ventures if they can secure adequate insurance protection.

Modern economies are built on specialization and its inherent productivity improvements. Greater trade and commercial specialization demand, in turn, greater financial specialization and flexibility. Without a wide insurance product choice and constant service and pricing innovations, insurance inadequacies could stifle both trade and commerce. It is in these ways that insurance serves as a lubricant of commerce.

INSURANCE CAN HELP MOBILIZE SAVINGS. Countries that save more tend to grow faster than countries that save less.[13] Insurers play an important role in channeling savings into domestic investment. They enhance financial system efficiency in three ways. First, insurers reduce the transaction costs associated with bringing together savers and borrowers. Thousands of individuals each pay relatively small premiums, and insurers then invest these amassed funds as loans to businesses and other ventures. This intermediation eliminates the need for direct lending and investing by individual policyholders, which would be time consuming and costly. It is more efficient for insurers to acquire the information necessary to make sound investments than for individuals to acquire the same information. The efficiencies and higher returns achieved by insurers are passed on to policyholders as lower premiums.

Second, insurers create liquidity. Insurers make long-term loans and other investments using the funds entrusted to them by their customers. Policyholders, however, have immediate access to loss payments and savings, while borrowers need not repay their loans immediately. If all individuals instead undertook equivalent direct lending, the proportion of their personal wealth held in long-term, illiquid assets would be unacceptably high. Insurers and other financial intermediaries thus reduce the illiquidity inherent in direct lending.

Third, insurers facilitate economies of scale in investment. Many investment projects are quite large, especially in relation to the available financial capital in many emerging markets. Such large projects often enjoy economies of scale, promote specialization, and stimulate technological innovations, and they can therefore be very important for economic development. By amassing large sums from thousands of small premium payers, insurers can meet the financing needs of such large projects, which enlarges the set of feasible investment projects in the national economy and encourages economic efficiency. For example, insurers in the United States provide financing for fully one-third of all corporate debt.

A well-developed financial system will have a myriad of financial institutions and instruments. Other things being equal, the greater the variety

13. This finding does not suggest that every country with a high savings rate will have a high growth rate. Countries whose financial systems are inefficient are relatively unlikely to achieve high growth rates even with high savings rates. Conversely, countries with efficient financial markets can achieve impressive economic growth even with modest savings rates.

of financial institutions and products, the more efficient is the system and the greater is its contribution to economic development. Contractual savings institutions, such as life insurers and private pension funds, can be especially important financial intermediaries in emerging markets. Whereas commercial banks often specialize in collecting short-term deposits and extending short-term credit, contractual saving institutions usually take a longer-term view. Their longer-term liabilities and stable cash flows are ideal sources of long-term finance for government and business.

INSURANCE CAN FACILITATE MORE EFFICIENT RISK MANAGEMENT. Financial systems and intermediaries price risk and provide for risk transformation, pooling, and reduction. If a nation's financial system provides these various risk management services, then saving and investment will be stimulated and resources will be allocated more efficiently.

A competitive market's success depends on pricing. The pricing of risk is fundamental to all financial intermediaries; it is no less important to their resource allocation than to any other supplier of goods or services. Insurers price risk at two levels. First, they evaluate the loss potential of businesses, persons, and property for which they might provide insurance. The greater the expected loss potential, the higher the price. By pricing loss potential, insurers cause insureds to quantify the consequences of their risk-causing and risk-reducing activities and thus to deal with risk rationally. When projects are judged too risky for insurance at any price, investors are put on notice and should rationally expect returns commensurate with the risk. When governments interfere with accurate insurance pricing, their actions can distort the allocation of insurance and, therefore, other resources.

Second, insurers evaluate the creditworthiness of those to whom they extend loans and the likely business success of those in whom they invest. These investment activities contribute to informing business owners, potential investors, customers, creditors, employees, and other stakeholders about the firm's overall risk characteristics and thereby help them to make informed decisions.

With regard to risk transformation, insurance allows businesses and individuals to transform their risk exposures to better suit their own needs. Many property, liability, loss-of-income, and other risk exposures can be transferred to an insurer for a price; in the process, the risk profile of the insured changes. Moreover, life insurers tailor contracts to the needs of different clients, which helps individuals and businesses transform the characteristics of their savings to reflect the liquidity, security, and other risk profile desired.

Risk pooling and reduction, in turn, lie at the heart of insurance. As with risk pricing, they occur on two levels. First, because insurers aggregate many individual risk exposures, they can make reasonably accurate estimates as to the pool's overall losses. The larger the number of insured parties, the more stable and predictable is the insurer's experience. This leads to a reduction in volatility and permits insurers to charge smaller risk premiums for uncertainty and to maintain more stable premiums. Second, insurers benefit from pooling through their investment activities. They diversify their investment portfolios by providing funds to a broad range of enterprises and individuals. The default of a few borrowers is therefore likely to be offset by the many sound investments in the portfolio. The more stable and predictable an insurer's investment experience, the less it can charge for loans.

INSURANCE CAN ENCOURAGE LOSS MITIGATION. Insurance companies have economic incentives to help the insured prevent and reduce losses. Moreover, their detailed knowledge about loss-causing events, activities, and processes affords them a competitive advantage over many other firms in loss assessment and control. If pricing or availability is tied to loss experience and risky behavior, the insured has economic incentives to control losses.

Insurers support many loss control activities and programs, including fire prevention; occupational health and safety activities; industrial loss prevention; and reduction in automobile property damage, theft, and injury. These programs and activities reduce losses to businesses and individuals and complement good risk management. Society as a whole benefits from the reduction of such losses.

INSURANCE CAN FOSTER CAPITAL ALLOCATION EFFICIENCY. Insurers gather substantial information for evaluating firms, projects, and managers, both in the process of deciding whether and at what price to issue insurance and in their role as lenders and investors. Individual savers and investors may not have the time, resources, or ability to undertake this information gathering and processing, such that insurers have an advantage in this regard. Their access to these data sources improves their ability to allocate financial capital and risk-bearing capacity. Insurers will choose to insure and finance the soundest and most efficient firms, projects, and managers.

Insurers maintain a continuing interest in the firms, projects, and managers to whom they provide financial capital and risk-bearing capacity. They monitor business activities and encourage managers and entrepreneurs to act in the best interests of their various stakeholders, such as customers, stockholders and creditors. By doing so, insurers tangibly signal the market's approval of promising, well-managed firms, and they foster a more efficient allocation of a country's scarce financial capital and risk-bearing capacity. National financial systems that impose minimum constraints on insurers' abilities to gather and evaluate information will thus facilitate a more efficient allocation of capital and stronger economic growth than will systems that restrict insurers' activities in this area.

Empirical Evidence on the Role of Insurance in Development

The above benefits of insurance in economic development are logical extensions of the role that economists expect financial intermediaries to play in society. A recent doctoral dissertation at Georgia State University establishes this importance in a way that no one has done before by investigating the mechanisms through which insurance and banking jointly stimulate economic growth.[14] Early economists considered that economic growth was driven mainly by labor and capital inputs. These two factors alone left much of economic growth unexplained, however, so economists added technology to their equations. The addition increased the explanatory power of the equations, but troubling gaps remained. Webb's doctoral research considers whether adding banking and insurance to existing economic growth models might further explain economic growth.

He shows that nonlife insurance, life insurance, and banking are all significant factors in explaining national productivity gains. The results indicate that the exogenous components of banking, life insurance, and nonlife insurance are important predictors of economic productivity. He also finds evidence of synergies among financial intermediaries. Each sector fuels economic growth independently, but collectively they provide an impetus for growth that is greater than the sum of their component contributions. Webb's research provides tangible support for what has to date been largely reasoned economic suppositions.

The Appropriate Role of Foreign Insurers

Concern persists that a liberal insurance market may carry unacceptable risks and drawbacks. One such concern relates to the appropriate role of foreigners in the provision of financial services generally and of insurance in

14. Webb (2000).

particular.[15] The arguments in favor of increased participation of foreign insurers are that countries could realize one or more of the following benefits: improvements in customer service and value; increased domestic savings; transfers of technological and managerial know-how; additional external financial capital; improvements in the quality of insurance regulation; and beneficial domestic spillovers, including the creation of high quality jobs, quality-enhancing backward and forward linkages, and reductions in societal loss. In an earlier study, I examine each of these points in detail and conclude that each is potentially relevant.[16]

Policymakers have expressed numerous reservations about the involvement of foreign insurers in their domestic markets, however. My 1997 study classifies such reservations around seven common themes, five of which have little or no justification or can be addressed more adequately and with less welfare loss through alternative means. The validity and importance of a sixth theme cannot be established a priori, while the seventh reservation does warrant policymaker concern. The seven classes of reservations are analyzed below, beginning with the five that either lack factual justification or are better addressed through more efficient alternatives.

First, policymakers often express concern that foreign insurers might dominate the domestic market and thereby precipitate adverse microeconomic effects, such as reducing consumer choice and value, or macroeconomic outcomes, including the failure to contribute adequately to economic development. If a market offers great potential and if domestic insurers are inadequate and unsophisticated, market liberalization could lead to foreign domination. No rational basis exists, however, to support the belief that this would harm either the nation's consumers and businesses or the national economy. On the contrary, the fact that the market offered great potential, was unsophisticated, and had an inadequate capacity suggests that the status quo was stifling microeconomic and macroeconomic improvements.

The second common reservation is that foreign insurers might market insurance selectively, choosing to insure only the best risks. This is sometimes called cherry picking. The presumption is that such practices lead to adverse microeconomic or macroeconomic effects; otherwise they would not be objectionable on economic grounds. This reservation may be expressed as a concern that foreign insurers will market insurance only to

15. This section draws from Skipper (1997).
16. Skipper (1997).

the most profitable segments, including multinational corporations and the commercial sector, while ignoring the retail market and other market segments that the government believes ought to be served. However, governmental efforts to discourage selective marketing can be harmful. Specialization and market segmentation lead to improvements in insurer efficiency, as suggested earlier. Market segmentation practices may, in fact, lead both national and foreign insurers to ignore certain market segments. If they do and if these underserved segments are judged critical, policymakers would be wise to follow this three-part analysis:

—Inquire why government believes the segment ought to receive more attention from private insurers than it does at present. Is the motivation political or economic? Bear in mind that segments deemed highly profitable (unprofitable) in the short run, will tend to be less (more) profitable in the long run, as well.

—Inquire whether repressive regulation (such as price suppression) or adverse tax policy is at fault.

—Finally, if it is determined that the segment should receive greater attention from the private sector, consider using subsidies or other, less distorting, positive means of encouraging private insurers to serve the neglected sector.

The third class of reservations is that foreign insurers might fail to make lasting contributions to the local economy. There is no reasonable factual basis to support this belief, however. Indeed, the opposite seems the more supportable contention.

The fourth class of arguments for limiting the market access of foreign insurers is that the domestic market is already well served by locally owned insurers or by reinsurers. Again, no reasonable factual basis can be established to support this belief. If the market is, in fact, already well served by local insurers, then newly permitted insurers would fail to achieve acceptable market share and would be forced to withdraw. The market ordinarily makes such decisions more efficiently and effectively than the government.

The fifth reservation is that the national industry should remain locally owned for strategic reasons, such as national security, or for promoting economic diversification. To the extent that these goals are valid and are not driven by special interests, they are better accomplished through means that are less market distorting than imposing limits on the participation of foreign insurers.

The sixth class of reservations is that foreign insurers may provoke a greater foreign exchange outflow. The validity of this concern cannot be ascertained a priori. In the short term, of course, foreign exchange would flow into the country as foreigners establish local firms. If the net insurance-related foreign exchange flow turns negative in the long term, the overall foreign-exchange effect will not necessarily be negative. A more competitive insurance market allows national businesses and consumers to buy lower-priced, better-valued insurance. Since insurance is a cost of doing business for local firms, lower-cost insurance should translate into more competitive products and services, which could potentially enhance international trade and foreign exchange inflows. More importantly, any foreign exchange loss will likely prove of minor importance to the national economy in comparison with the opportunity cost associated with exchange or other restrictions that would hinder the orderly development of national insurance corporations.

The final reservation relates to the belief that full market liberalization should await regulatory reforms so as to minimize the chances of micro- or macroeconomic disruptions. This concern is valid in certain situations, particularly with regard to adequate prudential supervision, the regulation of competition, and market conduct oversight. Reasonable insurance laws and regulation and their appropriate enforcement are essential. They should exist prior to full market liberalization to avoid abuse by the unscrupulous.

The study concludes that opening insurance markets to appropriate foreign insurers is likely to aid economic development, enhance overall social welfare, and carry few unresolvable negative possibilities. Countries that maintain unjustifiable barriers to market access and that fail to extend national treatment to foreign-owned insurers do their citizens, businesses, and national economies a disservice.

The Role and Importance of Government Policy in Insurance

Liberalization cannot be separated from regulation. I use the terms *liberalization* and *deregulation* to mean the process by which government takes actions to move toward liberal markets. Liberalization refers to the process of allowing greater market access; deregulation encompasses the process of lessening unnecessarily restrictive government regulation. A liberal insurance market is one in which the market, subject only to economically justifiable government restrictions, determines who should be allowed to sell insurance, what products should be sold, how products should be sold, and the prices at which products should be sold. Liberal insurance markets are competitive and thus generally offer businesses and individuals greater choice and better value than alternative approaches. Consequently, they enhance societal welfare.

Numerous governments have undertaken liberalization efforts. Some seem tentative, however, verbally endorsing competitive markets while retaining elements of restrictive regulatory systems. Thus many governments continue to deny their citizens and businesses access to low-priced, high-quality insurance policies and services. These actions suggest either that regulation exists more to protect established private interests than to further the overall national interest or that policymakers remain skeptical that competitive markets will deliver the benefits to the national economy suggested above. I analyze both issues below.[17]

Different Regulatory Approaches Reflect Different Interests

Government intervention into insurance markets takes many forms, some direct and some indirect. Its stated purposes are always noble—to protect consumers, to offer products not offered by the private market, to raise revenue to support worthwhile social objectives, or to ensure orderly, well-functioning markets. In reality, regulation does not always serve noble purposes.

Various factors influence regulatory policies and behavior, including market problems that regulators aim to rectify, ideology, special interests, and regulatory resources. Other factors sometimes distort regulation. Private interests or special interest groups often exert undue influence on regulation to serve their own interests at the expense of consumers and the overall welfare. For example, established interests might support government action that bars entry and diminishes competition from new insurers, both national and foreign. The resulting restrictions might be cloaked in the guise of protecting the consumer, protecting the national interest, or protecting domestic jobs, but consumers and the national economy are harmed by such restrictions. Special interest groups typically are better informed, financed, and organized than consumers, so their views often predominate. Additionally, the economic justification for liberal insurance markets—while proved to be sound—cannot be explained simply, whereas those opposing liberal markets can tout simplistic slogans that are superficially appealing.

17. This section draws partially from Skipper and Klein (2000).

Regulation that is unduly influenced by such special interests is characterized by restrictions on entry of new national and especially foreign insurers, the suppression of price, product, and distribution competition, and the control of interindustry competition from firms selling similar or complementary products. The result is that both individual and commercial consumers are penalized through high prices, lack of product innovation, and poor product choice. Unfortunately, private interests sometimes take precedent over the greater national good, with great harm to the overall national interest. Citizens and businesses must work with dedicated government representatives and use publicity effectively to expose such abuses of the public trust, and they must support measures that uncover and thwart such abuses. Transparency in all relevant government decisions and processes provides the strongest, most effective means of preventing and detecting abuse.

Competition Enhances Choice and Value

Some policymakers seem skeptical about the benefits of competition. While the case for liberal insurance markets may seem clear to those schooled in economics, others can easily become confused by an array of conflicting claims. In a market-oriented economy, the objective for the insurance industry is the same as that for other industries: namely, an efficient allocation of society's scarce resources. Society further desires an economic system that leads to continuous innovation and improvement. These objectives are most likely to be achieved through liberal markets.

Competition not only leads to economic efficiency, but also provides an automatic mechanism for fulfilling consumer needs and wants and creating a wide variety of choices. Competition also compels insurers to improve their products and services. A perfectly competitive market requires no government direction or oversight to accomplish these desirable social goals. Although perfect competition is an ideal that is not realized in practice, it provides a useful construct against which to compare actual market functioning. The closer a market is to this competitive ideal, the more efficiently it functions. Indeed, a market that is workably competitive functions well and provides most of the benefits of perfect competition. Workably competitive markets generally have low entry and exit barriers, numerous buyers and sellers, good information, governmental transparency, and the absence of artificial restrictions on competition. The markets for numerous products satisfy these conditions to such a degree that little government intervention is required for the market to function well. However, rather substantial government intervention is usually necessary for an insurance market to be workably competitive, because of imperfections that exist in such markets.

Scant empirical evidence is available on the practical effects of insurance liberalization and deregulation in emerging markets. A recent doctoral dissertation provides a key contribution in this regard by examining the effects of insurance market liberalization and deregulation in Korea, the Philippines, Taiwan, and Thailand on the efficiency of life insurance providers.[18] All four countries undertook some degree of market opening during the study period, while Korea and the Philippines implemented modest deregulation, as well. In neither instance were the deregulation efforts substantial, but the two markets contrast with those of Taiwan and Thailand, which undertook virtually no deregulation during the study period. Boonyasai finds that liberalization and deregulation of the Korean and Philippine life insurance industries stimulated increases and improvements in productivity and created more competitive markets, as firms achieved considerable cost savings and adjusted their scale of operations. Merely allowing greater market access without dismantling restrictive regulatory regimes, as occurred in Taiwan and Thailand, did little to increase or improve productivity.

The study's findings are thus consistent with the view that market access is a necessary, but not sufficient, condition for fostering contestable markets. Furthermore, in a restrictive regulatory environment, welfare gains will be minimal if deregulation does not closely follow market opening. Boonyasai's rigorous research speaks eloquently in favor of liberal insurance markets.

The Importance of Property Rights

In general, countries that allow their citizens and businesses a broad degree of economic freedom are those with relatively high incomes and high economic growth rates. Gwartney and Lawson study the relation between economic freedom and economic growth rates in the 1990s.[19] They find that countries ranked in the highest quintile of economic freedom enjoyed a real per capita GDP growth rate of 2.3 percent on average. The rate falls to 1.6 percent for the second quintile, 0.3 percent for the third quintile, 0.8 per-

---

18. Boonyasai (1999). Thitivadee Boonyasai is now a professor at Chulalongkron University in Thailand.

19. Gwartney and Lawson (2000).

cent for the fourth quintile, and a striking –1.3 percent for the bottom quintile.

Economic freedom depends on private property rights, including the right to own and alienate real and personal property, the right to contract, and the right to be compensated for damage resulting from the tortuous conduct of others. Government's responsibility is to establish a system to protect property rights and resolve related disputes (for example, through a court system). Without a well-defined system of private property rights and a means to enforce these rights, markets do not function well. Markets are, after all, simply means of exchanging property rights.

A recent World Bank study confirms that openness, which is an important dimension of economic freedom, spurs economic growth.[20] The authors find that openness has no discernible negative effect on a nation's income distribution. Thus, the poor benefit proportionately as much as the rich from economic growth. They also statistically verify that strong property rights promote economic growth.

Similarly, private insurance will not flourish unless individuals' ownership interests in property are well defined, are protected by the state, and can be freely used and exchanged. National insurance penetration is strongly related to economic freedom. The ratio of premiums to GDP is highest in countries ranked in the top quintile of economic freedom, at 6.76 percent. It falls steadily and consistently through the quintiles, to 5.38 percent in the second quintile, 3.55 percent in the third quintile, 2.67 percent in the fourth quintile, and 1.54 percent in the bottom quintile.[21]

Certain government action (or inaction) diminishes the value of such ownership interests, as in the case of a failure to set up an independently functioning judiciary or to establish mechanisms that allow clear title to property.[22] If I do not have clear title to the land on which my factory is located, I will be less inclined to make major additional investments and less likely to purchase insurance, and financial institutions will be less likely to loan me money using the property as security. Some government actions diminish property value. These include the failure to control inflation, which diminishes the value of savings; the imposition of high income tax rates, which diminish the value of earnings; the application of substantial trade restrictions, which diminish purchasing power; and poor design of fis-

20. Dollar and Kraay (2000).

21. See Swiss Re (1999); and Gwartney and Lawson (2000).

22. Hernando de Soto (2000) argues that clearly defined property rights generate positive externalities essential for economic growth and that failure to record these rights hinders the development of modern economic systems.

cal policy, which leads to currency devaluation and thus diminishes purchasing power.

Private property rights, however, are restrictive by nature. Without some restraints, their full exercise interferes with the efficient functioning of markets. The monopoly prohibitions that are common worldwide are restraints on private property rights. Prohibitions on insider trading legitimately restrict one's use of private information. Property rights are not unlimited.

Insurance Regulation Should Rectify Market Imperfections

Government's role in crafting insurance regulation should be limited to rectifying imperfections that can cause significant harm. A procompetitive approach, therefore, would employ governmental regulation of insurance only with respect to matters that meet three conditions: an actual or potential market imperfection exists; the market imperfection causes or can reasonably be believed to cause meaningful consumer or public harm; and government action can ameliorate the harm. All existing and proposed insurance regulations should be tested against these three conditions. Some existing and proposed regulations will meet all three conditions. Others will not and should be abandoned or modified.

Insurance markets in all countries, but especially in emerging economies, contain no shortage of situations in which government intervention is justified. Consumers in emerging markets are generally less able to protect themselves against harm than are consumers in developed markets because they are usually less informed about insurance matters. Regulators in emerging markets could therefore be expected to take a more activist approach to regulation, for example, by encouraging publicity about insurance and insurance companies, by increasing their oversight of policy contract language, by vigorously enforcing laws prohibiting misleading advertising and other market conduct, and by diligently enforcing laws that prohibit anticompetitive behavior.

On the other hand, regulators in emerging markets must be vigilant against inappropriately imposing supervision. If any one of the above three conditions is not met, no government intervention is warranted. Thus no government intervention is justified with respect to any insurer operation that does not cause demonstrable or reasonably expected harm. If some aspect of insurer operations might adversely affect some individuals, no intervention is warranted if the intervention would be ineffectual or might actually exacerbate the problem. Just as there are imperfections in markets, so too are there imperfections in government regulation. Recognizing those circumstances and not imposing regulation can be more difficult than carrying out the positive regulatory functions.

The likelihood of consumer abuse resulting from market imperfections will vary from country to country. Countries with a long history of competitive insurance markets will have already resolved many of the complex issues concerning appropriate government intervention. Countries moving from monopolistic or other restrictive regimes, on the other hand, must exercise a certain degree of caution to ensure that abusive practices do not undermine confidence in an embryonic, competitive insurance market. The building of consumer trust is essential for the insurance market.

Justifiable government intervention should be minimally intrusive and as efficient as possible. For example, one way to minimize consumer harm occasioned by insurer insolvencies is to allow insurers to collude to set prices so high that even the most inefficiently operated insurer is guaranteed a profit and, therefore, survival. Such an approach, however, results in high-priced insurance and excessive profits for insurers, all at the expense of consumers and businesses and, therefore, to the detriment of the national interest. The superior approach is to allow price competition while establishing reasonable capital standards and closely monitoring insurer financial condition. This approach yields lower-priced insurance—which benefits the national economy—and minimizes the possibility of consumer harm that would otherwise arise from excessive insurer financial risk and insolvencies.

The Path toward Competitive, Solvent Insurance Markets

In the context of today's globally competitive financial services industry, each government should reassess the nature and specific features of its intervention in the domestic insurance market to determine whether every aspect is essential and is accomplishing key goals at minimum market disruption in light of the country's economic, political, and social situation. Insurance regulation should seek to ensure that quality, reasonably-priced products are available from reliable insurers. A well-structured competitive market will facilitate this objective. Hence, an important role of government is to promote fair competition to achieve these goals, while protecting buyers from misleading, collusive, and other anti-competitive practices.

Insurance markets in developing countries face important challenges. Too often, the relevant laws and regulations are inadequate for supporting a competitive market. Assistance in this regard is available from several intergovernmental and governmental organizations. More difficult to resolve is the problem of ensuring sound enforcement of laws and regulation, which requires adequate funding and staffing. These matters can only be resolved over time, but given the importance of insurance for economic development, they deserve priority.

Developing countries' insurance markets also often lack the managerial, technical (especially actuarial), and marketing skills found in more developed markets. Foreign insurers are excellent sources of such skills. One well-known international insurer asserts that it has provided more training to insurance markets in developing countries than has any insurance training institute. Even so, national training institutes—supported by self-interested private organizations—will prove essential for most markets. Advanced education in risk management, actuarial science, marketing, management, accounting, finance, and economics at national and foreign universities will help cement the long-term success of national insurance markets.

Insurance product development lags behind in many developing countries. This may stem from a lack of actuarial or marketing talent, but it often reflects an immature capital market. For example, the successful creation of long-duration life insurance, pension, and other retirement products demands appropriate investment outlets for insurer funds, which should ideally be placed in long-term corporate and government securities with competitive yields. If a country's financial market lacks such securities, authorities should consider allowing the foreign investment of insurer reserve funds. Other techniques, such as product design, can also address such shortcomings.

An important dimension of product development relates to pricing. Too often, the pricing schemes used in developing countries are based on systems used and abandoned decades earlier by former colonial powers. There is no reason why insurance pricing in emerging markets should not be almost as sophisticated as that in developed markets. Again, foreign insurers are a good source for the diffusion of contemporary pricing techniques and practices. Their presence will ensure beneficial spillovers of such information to domestic insurers over time. Information on contemporary techniques and practices is also readily available through numerous other sources, such as textbooks, academics, universities, actuarial societies, and consultants.

Arguably, the most important governmental role in insurance in any market is to see that insurers are reliable. To promote the twin goals of establishing a competitive and solvent insurance market, insurance regulation should be adequate, impartial, minimally intrusive, and transparent. A set of principles for regulatory reform is summarized and briefly discussed in the appendix. Application of these principles should help move a national insurance market toward the competitive ideal. They are not an argument for eliminating regulation. In fact, procompetitive regulation requires a greater—not lesser—emphasis on competition law, prudential matters, and market conduct. As market liberalization generates increased competition, domestic insurers will face new pressures to push the limits of solvency, to resort to unfair competition (and to lobby for restraining competition), and to mislead consumers. Regulatory institutions must respond by reinforcing regulation in these areas.

The Future Role of Government

Governments should take careful note of the economic consequences of their regulatory and tax decisions. The mobility of people, ideas, information, and financial capital seem to be driving regulation and taxation toward convergence. Markets, other governments, and businesses value consistency in government policy. Inconsistency hobbles the competitiveness of national firms and markets. As governments acknowledge their growing inability fully to control national economic activities, they will likely recognize the need for greater cross-national regulatory and tax cooperation.

Liberalization and deregulation permit a deeper integration of financial services, which calls for increased integration of financial services regulation. At the same time, regulation should be enhanced in selected areas, especially solvency, competition law, and market conduct. Governments will also have to evolve new standards for dealing with innovative alternatives in risk financing.

A nation's tax system should not be the basis for allocating international risk-bearing capacity, as is presently the case. Tax and regulatory arbitrage is a problem that a liberalized international financial services market should eventually resolve.

New forms of protectionism must be addressed in the twenty-first century. Behind-the-border measures that impede true equality of competitive opportunity for foreign entrants and that hinder liberalization efforts should become central issues in the international trade agenda and, ultimately, in the next round of multilateral services negotiations. An effective means of addressing these issues would be to embed regulatory principles (such as those set out in the appendix) into the General Agreement on Trade in Services. These principles could then serve as the basis against which national governments and trading partners assess regulation.

Establishing liberalized markets and reasoned regulation that efficiently addresses market imperfections will allow insurance to play an even larger role in individual, business, and national economic security and prosperity.

Appendix: Insurance Regulatory Principles

This appendix sets out general principles around which insurance regulation should be crafted if it is to support a competitive and solvent market.[23] The four most basic requirements are that insurance regulation be adequate, impartial, minimally intrusive, and transparent.

Regulation Should Be Adequate

Regulation should be sufficient to rectify meaningful market failures and thereby protect the public. Several principles of adequacy follow.

COMPETITION LAW. To establish an adequate system of regulation, government must have the necessary laws and regulations in place to create the framework for a competitive market. The first principle, therefore, is that government should enact and enforce laws that provide an effective framework for competitive insurance markets.

Competition law is a vitally important component of competitive markets. Competition law regulates the nature of competition in the marketplace rather than controlling individual competitors. It becomes increasingly important as markets move from restrictive to liberal regulatory approaches, since some firms will try to engage in anticompetitive practices. The law should give regulators clear, strong authority to prevent or punish collective behavior that undermines competition, such as collusive price setting and market sharing arrangements.

PRUDENTIAL REGULATION. Insurance laws and regulations should address all relevant aspects of insurer operations, from creation to liquidation. The most essential component relates to prudential regulation and supervision, which gives rise to the second principle related to the adequacy of regulation: government should enact and enforce laws that estab-

---

23. This appendix draws from Skipper and Klein (2000).

lish reasonable solvency standards and regulation as the primary means of protecting the public.

The more competitive a market, the more important is prudential regulation and accompanying supervision. The insurance regulator in a deregulated market faces more complex and difficult issues than his or her counterpart in a strictly regulated market. Indeed, prudential regulation and supervision can be deceptively simple in a market in which all insurers charge the same or similar prices, such that the least efficient insurer can enjoy reasonable profitability. Insolvencies in such markets are diminished by overcharging.

Not all insolvencies can or should be prevented. In a competitive market, some insolvencies are inevitable. Government's delicate task is to minimize consumer harm occasioned by such difficulties, without signaling to other insurers that mismanagement or other unsound business practices will be tolerated. This requires rigorous but fair enforcement of well-crafted prudential regulation.

Prudential regulation and supervision should focus on preventing insurers from incurring excessive levels of financial risk and on intervening in a timely fashion when an insurer's financial condition becomes hazardous. This can be accomplished by reasonable minimum financial standards and effective monitoring of insurers' financial conditions. Such a strategy should include frequent informal consultations with insurer executives to keep regulators well informed about potentially adverse developments and enable them to steer insurers away from actions that threaten their policyholders' interests.

Resolving the problems of financial difficulties for existing insurers should be a priority. Thus the third principle points to the creation of appropriate and consistent ways of dealing with insurers that incur financial difficulties: as a part of reasonable solvency regulation, government should establish, make public, and enforce appropriate, consistent rules and procedures for identifying and dealing with financially troubled insurers.

Insurance regulation should establish proper incentives for efficient and safe insurer operation and institute safeguards to keep the number of insolvencies to an acceptable minimum. A marketplace with no insurer failures is likely to be one in which insurance is expensive and consumer choice limited.

Government's responsibility is to establish rules and procedures for identifying and dealing with financially troubled insurers. A key element in the identification process is the establishment of appropriate accounting, reporting, and auditing standards and requirements. Government would be wise to borrow freely from international best practices.

The rules and procedures for dealing with troubled insurers should be sufficient for addressing the particular difficulty of each case and should be applied consistently across all competitors. The rules and procedures should be made public, and any changes should be subject to transparent regulatory processes (see below).

REGULATORY EFFECTIVENESS. The next step to ensure adequate regulation in a competitive market involves creating an independent regulatory agency with sufficient resources to enforce laws and regulations efficiently, effectively, and impartially. The fourth principle is thus that government should establish an insurance regulatory agency that operates in society's interest and has sufficient resources to efficiently, effectively, and impartially enforce the nation's insurance laws and regulations.

If the agency is to function in society's interest, as opposed to private interests, it should operate without undue influence from the insurance industry and other special interests. It is insufficient that the regulatory body be established as an agency of the government. The means by which industry input is secured must be transparent, impartial, and consistent. Rules may be necessary to limit undue influence over regulatory decisions, such as not allowing former heads of the regulatory agency to lobby the agency for a certain period of time after vacating the office. Due process and transparency are critical for ensuring that the regulator deals at arm's length with the regulated (see below).

The regulatory body must be provided sufficient financial and other resources, including information technology, to carry out its regulatory function. A critical and related issue is the quality and integrity of supervisory personnel. Regulation in competitive markets is more complex and difficult than regulation in restrictive markets. Consequently, highly skilled, competent, and technical employees are required for effective regulation in a competitive market.

Regulatory efficiency means that responsibilities are carried out expeditiously, with prudent use of the agency's resources. Regulatory effectiveness means that responsibilities are carried out in ways that genuinely ameliorate the identified market failure, using approaches that are minimally intrusive (see below). Regulatory impartiality means that responsibilities are carried out with fairness to all market participants and without favoritism (see below).

GRADUAL LIBERALIZATION. Observers correctly note that in many transition market economies, regulatory oversight of the insurance industry may not be sufficiently attuned to protecting consumers in a liberalized, competitive market. These countries may need to enhance prudential, competition, and market-conduct regulation and supervision as they liberalize their insurance markets and undertake regulatory reform. The shift from a restrictive to a competitive market does not take place overnight, however, which leads to the fifth principle: Government should develop and implement procompetitive insurance regulation in a way and at a pace that ensures adequate protection of the public, that proceeds without undue delay, and that is subject to a reasonable implementation timetable.

The entry of new insurers into formerly restrictive markets should not be allowed to disrupt the stability of the national insurance industry or to overwhelm government's ability to protect consumers. On the other hand, concerns for consumer protection are often asserted as a justification for unreasonable delays in liberalizing and deregulating the market. Policymakers should recognize that entrenched interests will always urge slowness in reform. Yet the road to reform should be traveled at the maximum possible safe speed, not the minimum. Reform should also follow a reasoned, carefully crafted route, which means that an implementation timetable, with clear deadlines, is essential.

Regulation Should Be Impartial

The principle of impartiality is fundamental for a competitive market. Impartially means that government should accord no competitor or group of competitors more favorable treatment than that extended to other competitors or groups of competitors. Thus the sixth procompetitive regulatory principle is that government should ensure that insurance regulation and enforcement are applied with consistency and impartiality among competitors, irrespective of nationality.

Historically, the fair trade principle of national treatment has been the standard for impartiality, and it continues to be a reasonable test of impartiality in minimally intrusive regulatory regimes. It is intended to ensure equality of competitive opportunity for foreign entrants. The national treatment standard is insufficient to ensure effective market access under certain circumstances, however. Foreign insurers encounter considerable obstacles in some markets. Some countries have different deposit or capital requirements for foreign insurers than for national ones, for instance. Some countries, such as India, limit foreign ownership of national insurers. Many countries assess higher taxes on foreign than on national insurers. Some countries deny or restrict foreign insurer membership in local trade associations, thus denying them equivalent access to national statistics, research, and lobbying.

Other government actions that can distort the competitive balance include exchange controls, deposit and lending rate ceilings, privileged access to credit, and unnecessarily strict controls with respect to investments and business powers. Such strict regulation affords established firms a competitive advantage over new entrants.

Regulation Should Be Minimally Intrusive

Without question, the insurance industry should be subject to meaningful regulation, as discussed above. At the same time, however, regulation must allow markets to function at optimum efficiency. Accomplishing this goal requires that regulation be carefully crafted.

THE LIMITS OF REGULATION. As noted above, all insurance regulation should be based on the goal of rectifying meaningful market imperfection—that is, of protecting the public interest. A government will have multiple alternatives for rectifying each imperfection that it identifies. All of the methods might be adequate for the purpose, but some will prove less disruptive to the competitive market than others. In selecting among the many alternatives, the government should select those that accomplish the purpose at minimal disruption to the smooth functioning of the country's insurance market; in trade terms, government should select among those that are the least trade restrictive (that is, that meet a necessity test). The seventh important procompetitive regulatory principle, then, is that insurance regulation should be limited to actions that provide meaningful protection and are minimally intrusive.

Government should thus avoid any regulatory intervention with respect to transactions and matters that have little or no possibility of harming the public. Moreover, in selecting among alternative regulatory approaches to address problems that involve the possibility of meaningful public harm, authorities should always opt for those approaches that solve the problem with minimal interference in or imposition on insurance transactions. This is the principle embedded in the GATS Article VI requirement that measures should be no more burdensome than necessary to ensure the quality of the service.

Insurers should be allowed to offer an array of insurance products at prices that they deem appropriate, without being subject to severe restrictions or a cumbersome pre-approval process, unless meaningful consumer harm could result from their actions. Market forces usually prevent insurers from sustaining prices above a competitive level. Insurers that charge inadequate prices or incur excessive financial risk can be removed from the market. Similarly, products that do not serve consumer needs will not succeed. Regulators should move decisively against insurers that attempt to defraud consumers or treat them unfairly. The threat of timely regulatory enforcement and appropriate penalties will help to discourage insurers and intermediaries from engaging in abusive practices. This approach conserves regulatory resources by directing them toward the small number of insurers and intermediaries that treat consumers unfairly, without subjecting all market participants to unnecessary constraints or burdensome oversight.

An important element of the minimally intrusive principle is that government can increase corporate accountability without being directly responsible for the details of oversight. Requiring audits and certification by independent actuaries and accountants can both relieve government of these tasks and create positive incentives for insurers. Placing more responsibility on management and boards of directors can have similar effects. The importance of fit and proper standards for key management grows with increased market competition.

The standard of minimal intrusion does not imply a laissez-faire policy or an absence of regulatory oversight. Rather, it implies that regulation should be confined to interventions that are truly needed and that can meaningfully benefit consumers. Effective regulatory monitoring can help alert regulators to problems that require action on a timely basis.

In determining appropriate regulatory restrictions, policymakers and regulators must consider the frequency and severity of market abuses and problems. It is not possible to prevent consumers from ever making poor choices. Regulatory policies should focus on areas in which there is a pattern of abuse or practices harmful to consumers, reflecting fundamental gaps in consumers' abilities to protect themselves.

DISTRIBUTION AND PRODUCT REGULATION. Restrictive markets usually adopt the philosophy that insurers may do only that which is expressly authorized. Regulation in such cases tends to rely on an ex ante system of detailed oversight and approval. This type of regulation can ensure a stable market, but such markets are rarely innovative, they typically offer high-priced insurance, and they provide comparatively limited consumer choice and value. Thus the eighth principle is that the government should subject the market only to that regulatory oversight that is essential for protecting the public, and it should allow the market to determine what financial services products should be developed and sold, the methods by which they will be sold, and the prices at which they will be sold.

Deregulation connotes a lessening of national regulation with the goal of retaining only that which is adequate and minimally intrusive. The most critical first step along the path toward reasoned deregulation is to adopt the philosophy that insurers should have the flexibility to respond to consumer needs in ways that they deem appropriate, subject, of course, to regulatory oversight to prevent insolvency and to minimize misleading or abusive practices. Market forces will encourage insurers to develop and sell products on terms that are in the best interest of consumers.

This philosophy encompasses greater reliance on an ex post system of oversight whenever it is most efficient. Ex ante regulation will remain appropriate for some areas, such as insurer licensing and solvency oversight, because certain market failures are best addressed by imposing minimum standards and prohibiting activities that could harm consumers. These include situations in which lack of information and unequal bargaining power between consumers and insurers can lead to abuses that can and should be prevented by regulators.

Although many countries have shifted toward the philosophy of ex post regulation, remnants of earlier, more restrictive systems persist, if not strictly de jure then at least de facto. The product approval process in many countries is at best sluggish and at worst erratic, arbitrary, and opaque. The benefits of competition are blunted when regulation is slow, unpredictable, or inconsistent.

Prior approval and other restrictive approval mechanisms tend to retard price adjustments and product innovation. Such actions should be unnecessary in a competitively structured market. Government requirements that certain lines of insurance subsidize other lines distort the market and lead to perverse, unexpected outcomes. A better approach is to allow full-cost pricing and then create a less distorting economic subsidy for specific insurance buyers if deemed necessary.

A competitive insurance market will have numerous channels for insurance distribution. New products and services require channels attuned to the buyer's needs and wishes. Brokers and other marketing intermediaries can help insurance buyers make better informed decisions. Government-imposed limitations on distribution channels that could serve the market more efficiently are inconsistent with a market-driven regulatory philosophy. They are examples of governmentally created barriers to entry.

DISCLOSURE AND CONSUMER INFORMATION. When a government moves from a restrictive regulatory system to increased reliance on competition, some consumer protection functions shift from the government to consumers themselves. Government should clearly communicate to consumers that such a fundamental shift has taken place. Insurance buyers will need to become more active in evaluating insurers and their products so that they can make good purchase decisions and protect their own interests. This generates the ninth principle: government should ensure that insurance customers have access to sufficient information for making informed, independent judgments as to an insurer's financial condition and the benefits and value of its products.

This principle directly addresses the information asymmetry problems that insurance buyers face. Regulation may be necessary to compel insurers to make certain disclosures in connection with their sales efforts. In other instances, the government itself may prove to be the most efficient and effective source of unbiased information. This approach will require additional governmental efforts to facilitate informed and prudent customer choices.

Rating agencies and other independent information sources can greatly assist customers by providing unbiased information. Unfortunately, some governments discourage or prohibit entry of rating agencies and other independent financial service information firms. Such actions hinder competition and undermine the national interest by denying local businesses and citizens information on which to base their decisions regarding the purchase and maintenance of insurance and other financial service products.

The Regulatory Process Should Be Transparent

Transparency in the regulatory process is fundamental for ensuring a competitive market. Two of the most important procompetitive regulatory principles are therefore aimed at promoting transparency. The tenth principle is that government should make existing insurance laws and regulations easily available to the public, including consumers, businesses, insurers, and other financial services providers.

The fair trade principle of transparency, as embedded in GATS Article III, requires that regulatory and other legal requirements regarding market access and national operation should be clearly and fully set out and easily available. Transparency problems are too common in insurance markets. Many governments' laws and regulations are incompletely formulated and not readily available. Foreign firms, in particular, encounter transparency problems in countries that grant their insurance regulatory authorities broad discretionary powers, as the foreign insurer may have no clear understanding of the market access or operational requirements. Due process standards are unclear or nonexistent in many countries, especially those that historically have been relatively closed. In such instances, foreign (and national) insurers may not fully understand either their rights to appeal regulatory decisions or the process by which an appeal is undertaken.

The second dimension of transparency applies to proposed laws and regulations. All interested parties should have the opportunity to learn about and to comment on proposed regulations, and the system should incorporate methods for challenging regulatory decisions. The final principle is thus that in crafting proposed insurance laws and regulations, government should make the proposals easily available to the public, including to consumers, businesses, insurers, and other financial service providers; invite comment on the proposals; allow sufficient time for interested parties to provide comment; provide justifications for decisions to accept and reject comments; and establish and communicate a fair process by which decisions considered arbitrary or unjust can be challenged.

Although many markets have made impressive gains in transparency, others continue to draw international criticism. Close relations between government and established insurers are inconsistent with the ideal of transparency. Transparency implies that regulators keep all insurers at arm's length, so that some insurers do not gain an unfair advantage through privileged associations with regulators.

References

Boonyasai, Thitivadee. 1999. *The Effect of Liberalization and Deregulation on Life Insurer Efficiency.* Ph.D. dissertation, Georgia State University.

de Soto, Hernando. 2000. *The Mystery of Capital: Why Capitalism Succeeds in the West and Fails Everywhere Else.* Basic Books.

Dollar, David, and Aart Kraay. 2000. "Growth *Is* Good for the Poor." Working Paper. World Bank (March).

Enz, Rudolf. 2000. "The S-Curve Relation between Per-Capita Income and Insurance Penetration." *Geneva Papers on Risk and Insurance: Issues and Practice* 25: 396–406.

Gwartney, James, and Robert Lawson. 2000. *Economic Freedom of the World: 2000 Annual Report.* Vancouver: Fraser Institute.

Mattoo, Aaditya. 1998. "Financial Services and the WTO: Liberalization in the Developing and Transition Economies." Unpublished paper. World Trade Organization.

Skipper, Harold D., Jr. 1997. *Foreign Insurers in Emerging Markets: Issues and Concerns.* Washington: International Insurance Foundation.

———. 1998. *International Risk and Insurance: An Environmental-Managerial Approach.* Boston: Irwin/McGraw-Hill.

———. Forthcoming. "Insurance in the General Agreement on Trade in Services: Successes and Prospects." Washington: American Enterprise Institute for Public Policy Research (AEI).

Skipper, Harold D., Jr., and Robert W. Klein. 2000. "Insurance Regulatory Reform in the Public Interest: The Path towards Competitive, Solvent Markets." *Geneva Papers on Risk and Insurance: Issues and Practice* 25: 482–504.

Swiss Re. 1999. "World Insurance in 1997: Booming Life Business but Stagnating Non-Life Business." *Sigma* 1999(3).

———. 2000a. "Emerging Markets: The Insurance Industry in the Face of Globalisation." *Sigma* 2000(4).

———. 2000b. "World Insurance in 1999: Soaring Life Insurance Business." *Sigma* 2000(9).

———. 2001. "Insurance Industry in Central and Eastern Europe—Current Trends and Progress of Preparations for EU Membership." *Sigma* 2001(1).

Webb, Ian P. 2000. *The Effect of Banking and Insurance on the Growth of Capital and Output.* Ph.D. dissertation, Georgia State University.

RANJIT AJIT SINGH
ATTILA EMAM
KAR MEI TANG

5

Foreign Participation in Emerging Securities Industries

G21 G12 G15
(LDCs, CEEC)
F23 O16

In recent years, developing countries have come under increasing pressure from both domestic and global sources to allow for greater foreign participation in their financial services sectors. Amid such pressures, the challenge for policymakers lies in being able to extract the full value that globalization has to offer, while minimizing the possible risks and costs associated with greater openness. This potential value is widely regarded as being significant, and policy in many countries has therefore focused on maximizing the benefits of allowing greater foreign involvement in financial services, rather than on resisting liberalization altogether.[1] Hence issues such as the degree, speed, and sequence of opening up the financial services sector are matters of particular interest to policymakers.

Within the context of the securities industry, greater foreign involvement might be expected to bring several potential benefits. For instance, the presence of foreign market intermediaries, through their global reach and worldwide client base, can allow better access to foreign capital by facilitating capital inflows into local industries and asset markets. Asset markets

The authors are grateful to the survey respondents and others who provided comments and feedback on the issues raised in this chapter. We are also grateful for the research assistance provided by Wong Kah Teck.

1. We use the term "liberalization" to refer to the opening up of domestic markets to foreign competition, and "deregulation" to denote the removal of restrictions to allow for greater competition among domestic incumbents.

where domestic liquidity is insufficient to achieve critical mass and industries where economies of scale and scope remain unexploited are two areas that could stand to gain in this way. The entry of foreign players can also raise the efficiency of the securities industry by introducing greater competition. In addition, entry opens up the possibility of skills and technology transfer, which can help develop more cost-efficient operations and processes, introduce higher-quality products and services, and promote greater innovation overall. Foreign participation might also arguably raise standards of regulatory compliance and risk management in the industry as a whole.

At the same time, liberalization raises a host of immediate and longer-term issues concerning the costs and risks of adjusting to a more open and competitive environment. It has been argued, for instance, that the growing ability of international market participants to shift capital relatively quickly across markets heightens the vulnerability of national markets to sharp capital-flow reversals. It has also been argued that the presence of foreign participants—many of whom are likely to be global players across a wide spectrum of market activities—can diminish the role of domestic market intermediaries, thus reducing the autonomy of the national financial system to parties that may not necessarily have a particular commitment to the local market over the longer term. Hence, a firmer stance toward foreign participation might be considered necessary to ensure minimal dislocation of economic activity and to maintain national interests.

With these issues still the subject of debate, poor knowledge of the impact that liberalization might have—not only on financial services but also on the functioning of the financial system in general—can hamper attempts at framing an appropriate policy response. We examine the experience of developing countries in liberalizing financial services with a view to shedding light on some of these issues. We address a number of questions of interest to policymakers and to domestic market participants. For instance, to what extent is foreign ownership actually permitted in the financial services sectors of developing countries? And how much does it differ from commitments framed within negotiated trade agreements? How are foreign-owned entities treated in comparison with locally owned entities? How much market penetration and market share do foreign-owned participants enjoy in comparison with domestic participants? What impact has liberalization had on the breadth and depth of the financial system? Are there significant regional or sectoral differences? Are there possible policy implications for developing countries to consider?

This chapter offers a unique perspective on these issues in two respects. First, it focuses on the securities industry, which has tended to receive relatively less attention than the banking and insurance industries in studies of financial services liberalization in developing countries.[2] A better understanding of the securities industry will, we believe, become increasingly important to developing countries in view of the global trend away from "balance-sheet intermediation" toward the greater use of "market-based intermediation" for financing and for allocating and managing risk. To this end, we also examine the extent and impact of liberalization on the different components of the securities industry, including broking services and investment management, among others.

Second, we make use of information obtained through direct feedback from securities regulators of developing-country jurisdictions themselves.[3] In many jurisdictions, regulators play a significant role in determining and enforcing policy on the liberalization of financial services. They are often closely involved with, if not responsible for, the design of liberalization policy, regulation of foreign participation, and the supervision and monitoring of foreign players in their conduct of financial activity. As a result, regulators are able to provide very accurate information on the specific policy framework that exists in their particular jurisdiction (including statistics on the extent of foreign participation and so on). More important, perhaps, many of them are also in a position to observe firsthand the impact that liberalization has had in their particular jurisdictions.

The discussion opens with a brief overview of the international and domestic factors that appear to be giving impetus to greater foreign participation in developing country securities industries. It then turns to a review of some recent research findings on financial services liberalization in the securities industries, and more generally financial services sectors, of developing countries, which is followed by a description of the survey-based approach adopted and some descriptive statistics about the sample set of countries used in the survey, and a detailed discussion of the survey findings. The chapter concludes with a discussion of further issues raised by our results and of possible policy implications for developing countries.

2. The securities industry in this context refers to that involved with the intermediation of equity, debt, and financial derivatives market activity. This includes broking, trading, and the management of collective investment schemes.

3. That is, a member of the Emerging Market Committee of the International Organization of Securities Commissions (IOSCO). For further details, see the section "Selected Experiences of Foreign Participation."

Drivers of Foreign Participation

Developing countries feel increasing pressure to liberalize and deregulate their securities industries owing to the gathering pace of international financial integration. Global developments in this direction include increased cross-border investment and a growing pool of international financial capital, the globalization of financial services amid rapid advances in communication and information technology, and formal commitments to international trade agreements. Pressure to liberalize the industry is also coming from the increasingly challenging national development priorities of individual countries, as well as, in some cases, the need for crisis-related financial reform.

INCREASED CROSS-BORDER INVESTMENT AND LARGER POOL OF FINANCIAL CAPITAL. With investors from industrial countries venturing beyond their own economies in search of higher yields and greater diversification opportunities, capital flows to developing countries have experienced rapid growth. During 1991–2000, cross-border capital market flows to developing countries increased by nearly 207 percent to an estimated US$236 billion, while foreign direct investment (FDI) rose by almost 395 percent, from US$36 billion in 1991 to an estimated US$178 billion in 2000.[4] The global pool of managed funds invested internationally has grown as well, as mutual, pension, and insurance funds, among other institutional investors, increasingly compete with more traditional financial intermediaries for a share of the world's financial savings. Since 1980, funds invested abroad have grown from around US$100 billion (or 5 percent of the total global pool of managed funds) to some US$4 trillion in 1995, amounting to a fifth of the total global pool of managed funds.[5]

GLOBALIZATION OF FINANCIAL SERVICES AND TECHNOLOGICAL ADVANCES. The financial services industry has changed considerably in the past two decades and has become increasingly global and competitive in nature. Deregulation in more developed jurisdictions, which has challenged traditional distinctions between various forms of financial intermediation such as commercial banking, investment banking, insurance, securities broking, and investment management, is bringing large, integrated, and internationally focused players into the arena. Increased competition, with its emphasis on cost-reduction and greater customer orientation, has driven financial market intermediaries to seek business

4. See World Bank (2001).
5. IMF (1998).

opportunities across different countries and market sectors. These trends have been accelerated by advances in information and communication technology, which in turn have made globally integrated operations more cost-effective. This has opened up new potential channels for intermediation and has created greater international linkages between markets.

INTERNATIONAL TRADE AGREEMENTS. Securities markets worldwide are increasingly expected to offer the necessary infrastructure for effective investment, capital raising, and risk management, commensurate with (for instance) their respective level of real economic integration, stage of market development, and developmental aspirations. To meet these challenges, many countries have committed themselves to liberalizing their financial services sector as a whole (which includes the various components of the securities industry).[6] The total number of World Trade Organization (WTO) members with commitments in financial services stood at 104 upon the entry into force of the Fifth Protocol in 1999. The new commitments in the protocol contained, among other things, significant improvements allowing commercial presence of foreign financial service suppliers by eliminating or relaxing limitations on foreign ownership of local financial institutions, limitations on the commercial presence (including branches, subsidiaries, agencies, and representative offices), and limitations on the expansion of existing operations. Improvements were made in all of the three major financial service sectors, namely, banking, securities, and insurance, including services such as asset management and provision and transfer of financial information.

Regional trade blocs have also created substantial leeway in terms of the liberalization of financial services. In the European Union, for instance, foreign financial institutions authorized in any EU member state may provide their services through cross-border sales within the Union without any additional authorization. There are generally no branching restrictions, and the Union is committed to providing national treatment to foreign financial services firms. Within the Association of Southeast Asian Nations (ASEAN), member states also entered into the ASEAN Framework Agreement on Services (AFAS) to develop commitments on services liberalization in December 1995. Following the first round of negotiations, completed in 1998, financial services were further liberalized in a number of subsectors. The current round of negotiations is scheduled to be completed by the

6. Written into the General Agreement on Trade in Services (GATS) is a commitment by WTO member governments to progressively liberalize trade in services. Article XIX commits to start a new round in 2000. These negotiations are now under way.

end of 2001. Many countries have announced the gradual liberalization of key securities industry segments (such as stock broking, derivatives broking, asset management, corporate finance services) in order to accelerate the development of their capital markets.[7]

NATIONAL DEVELOPMENT PRIORITIES AND REFORMS RELATED TO FINANCIAL CRISES. National development strategies have provided additional impetus to foreign participation in the securities industry. These have focused on a variety of objectives, such as projecting the financial system into regional or international financial centers, promoting certain economic sectors (for example, the information and communications technology sector) that are ancillary to the financial services industry, and improving savings mobilization within the economy by enhancing market intermediation services. Core aims in this regard have typically been to attract foreign capital, to enhance standards and skills, and to foster competition and innovation.

Financial crises have also led to greater foreign involvement in securities industries of some developing countries. For instance, defaults of some crisis-affected securities intermediaries in Asia led to foreign involvement in the resolution process.[8] Foreign participation has also increased with the implementation of national and internationally driven programs designed to deal with the problems of crisis countries. These have typically emphasized structural reforms of the financial sectors.[9] For instance, International Monetary Fund programs in Korea, Thailand, and Indonesia called for the substantial involvement of private funds—foreign as well as domestic—in the recapitalization and restructuring of financial institutions. In some cases, the laws and regulations regarding foreign ownership of financial institutions had to be modified.[10] While in all cases reforms mainly concentrated on the speedy resolution of nonperforming loans as well as banking and corporate sector restructuring, it was also recognized that securities

---

7. For instance, Singapore has announced that it will completely remove restrictions on the International Members class of stock exchange members and the cap on foreign ownership of stock exchange member companies within five years from 1998.

8. One such case involves the acquisition by France's Banque Nationale de Paris (BNP) of Peregrine Investment Holdings' stockbroking and corporate finance businesses in Hong Kong and China in early 1998. Peregrine was one of the largest independent investment banks in Asia before it went into liquidation in January 1998.

9. The central focus of these reforms was to reestablish the financial systems on sound footing, address existing weaknesses, and put in place conditions for sustainable resumption of activity.

10. In Indonesia, for example, legislation eliminating restrictions on foreign investment in banks was passed in October 1998.

industry reform was necessarily part and parcel of any attempt to carry out broad-based debt restructuring.[11]

As a result of these trends and developments, developing countries have felt increasing pressure to allow access to foreign participants. Domestic financing needs have added further pressure on them to tap this pool by facilitating capital inflows. The need to raise the global competitiveness of domestic securities industries is another factor in this regard. Securities institutions in developing countries are finding that a wider global network is becoming necessary to offer their clientele added value, especially where the lack of such a network and global expertise allows foreign competitors to charge locals a higher premium for their services.[12] These effects can be seen in figures for trade in services. Developing countries now account for a little over 20 percent of world output and about 30 percent of world trade in services (in U.S. dollars), of which financial services more than tripled between 1985 and 1995 and today total more than US$50 billion for the biggest trading countries.

Selected Experiences of Foreign Participation

Since the Financial Services Agreement went into force on March 1, 1999, the WTO has been covering virtually all forms of financial services, including services related to banking, insurance, and the securities market, as well as to financial information. Although significant progress appears to have been made in major areas of negotiations, many offers were short of substance. Financial systems of developing countries, in particular, are more or less closed in comparison with those of more developed economies.[13]

The true extent of liberalization is quite difficult to gauge. Several problems arise in assessing the level of commitments alone. In the case of the General Agreement on Trade in Services (GATS) commitments, for instance, the structure of national schedules has not always been uniform, especially where member countries have adopted their own classifications

11. In Korea, nonbank financial institutions (life insurance companies, investment trust companies, leasing companies, and securities companies) had an estimated 30 trillion won in nonperforming loans as of the end of March 1998, about 7 percent of those institutions' total assets and almost equal to NPLs in commercial banks.

12. Although the increasing use of the Internet and other forms of technology may eventually significantly weaken the case for physical barriers to entry, it is envisaged that in the near to medium term, at the minimum, having a commercial presence in the local market is still important. This is particularly pertinent in developing countries where the current Internet penetration still remains relatively low.

13. See, for instance, Financial Leaders Group (1997).

of financial services.[14] Nevertheless, recent findings by the WTO itself appear to confirm that more commitments in financial services have been made in comparison with other service sectors, with the exception of tourism.[15]

The same WTO study, however, finds substantial variation in the levels of commitments of different countries and of different industry subsectors. Moreover, the number of limitations on market access and on national treatment remains higher than in several other sectors.[16] These findings are broadly supported in an analysis of eight developing and more developed Asian countries that shows banking services tend to be more open to foreign entry than insurance or capital market services.[17] In addition, this study finds the treatment of the three categories of financial services to be significantly different across the countries examined.

Assessing the extent of liberalization is further complicated by the fact that actual practices may not necessarily correlate with commitments under the 1995 interim GATS Financial Services Agreement, especially among developing countries. Some studies have found that member countries with less developed financial sectors are more liberal in opening up than those with more developed financial sectors.[18] Interestingly, while commitments can fall short of as well as surpass current practices, many Asian countries tend to practice a degree of liberalization well beyond that to which they have committed.[19]

Unilateral measures to liberalize financial services are thought to be one reason that GATS commitments (which are based on multilateral negotiations) and current practices differ. These can be the result of a country's domestic financial deregulation agenda, crisis-related financial reform efforts, or simply a desire to project an international presence in the form of a regional or global financial center. Moreover, GATS commitments may be superseded by those made within the context of other international agreements, for instance, participation of a regional trade bloc or economic

14. See Qian (1999).
15. WTO (1997).
16. Unless stated otherwise in a member country's schedule of commitments, the *market access* provision under GATS Article XVI prohibits limitations on the number of suppliers, the total value of service transactions or assets, the total number of service operations, or on the total quantity of service output, the total number of people employed, restrictions or conditions on the type of legal entity or joint venture, and limitations on the participation of foreign capital. The *national treatment* provision under Article XVII is defined as treatment no less favorable than that accorded to similar domestic entities.
17. Claessens and Glaessner (1998).
18. Sorsa (1997).
19. See Claessens and Glaessner (1998).

union, or accession to a formal grouping of countries, such as the Organization for Economic Cooperation and Development.

Policymakers are also interested in knowing what impact the liberalization of financial services can have on the financial sector. Empirical evidence in this regard has only recently started to amass, and even then mainly in relation to the banking sector. Depending on the size of their businesses, many domestic banks appear to have improved operations and efficiency following liberalization, as has been the case in Australia.[20] In some countries, foreign bank entry has also driven down gross interest margins and operating expenses, depending on the size of banking activity.[21] More recent studies suggest that positive effects of banking services liberalization can start to occur at a relatively low level of foreign participation. This was the case in Colombia, where in spite of the low degree of foreign ownership in its banking sector (4 percent), an increase in foreign participation substantially reduced the cost of banking services provision.[22] This is corroborated by Argentina's experience, where the ratio of operational costs to assets declined from 1.3 percent in 1990 to 0.5 percent in April 1997, while the share of foreign banks' assets only increased from 15 percent to 22 percent.[23] There also appears to be anecdotal evidence that the presence of foreign banks has led to product innovation and a higher quality of existing services. Interestingly, however, foreign participation appears to achieve its impact more through the increased number of foreign players rather than expansion of the market share of incumbent foreign participants.

The liberalization of financial services can have a relatively stronger impact on less-developed financial sectors through increased competition and the influence of market forces on business strategies of financial sector intermediaries. Following the implementation of the European Union's Single Market Programme in 1992, jurisdictions that had embarked on somewhat less financial sector reform experienced lower costs of financing, a wider range of financial services, and new channels of delivery after liberalization.[24] In addition, financial sector intermediaries were able to realize further economies of scale and found greater opportunities to exploit economies of increased scope of services and products.

There does not appear to be significant evidence linking liberalization of financial services with greater economic instability or reduced market

20. See McFadden (1994).
21. Terell (1986).
22. Barajas (1996).
23. Arriazu (1997).
24. European Commission (1997), as quoted in Claessens and Glaessner (1998).

integrity. In the case of the Single Market Programme, systemic stability did not appear to have been threatened by banks' strategic responses to a more open market. Nor does there seem to be much evidence in other markets that foreign banks have lower commitment to the local market or of any adverse impact on monetary policy or capital flows as a result of a high degree of foreign participation in the banking sector. In New Zealand, for example, there has been no reduction in the effectiveness of monetary policy or increase in the volatility of capital outflows as a result of having foreign firms dominate the financial system.[25] While there are clearly a wide range of concerns over the possible less desirable ramifications of liberalization—particularly for developing markets where the management and sequencing of such liberalization requires careful thought before implementation—empirical studies have yet to explore these issues in depth, especially in the securities industry.[26] So far, banking seems to have received the most attention, possibly because the banking sector has tended to play a bigger role in the financial systems of many developing countries compared with other financial sectors.

Over the past decade, however, securities markets have begun to play an increasing role in spurring economic growth in many developing countries. They are being enhanced to meet growing financial needs, and the amounts being raised directly from markets is in many cases growing faster than funds acquired through banking intermediaries. Progress has been especially strong in the area of equity financing and trading, where the significance of foreign participation has been clearly recognized. Since the 1980s, many developing countries have taken measures to facilitate greater foreign investment in their equity markets.[27] Empirical evidence suggests that the economic impact of greater foreign participation in stock markets has generally been positive, for instance, in terms of growth in private investment.[28] Therefore, in looking to broaden and deepen their capital markets, many countries are being motivated to examine the scope for greater foreign involvement in their securities industries.

Issues of particular interest to policymakers in relation to the securities industry include the extent to which foreign ownership is actually allowed

25. Nicholl (1997).
26. From the broader perspective, some of these concerns are summed up by Stiglitz (2000), who argues for serious consideration of the implications of liberalization in general for developing countries' capital markets in particular, which typically face greater risks (such as less diversified economies and the possibly weaker presence of automatic safety nets).
27. See Kawakatsu and Morey (1999).
28. Henry (1999).

in other jurisdictions; the manner in which foreign participants are treated in comparison with domestic participants; the numbers of foreign participants in relation to domestic participants and the degree of market penetration enjoyed by foreign participants; the impact of liberalization on market breadth and depth, and on the operations of the securities industry and its participants; and the existence of any regional or sectoral differences. A better understanding of these issues will help in the framing of appropriate policy responses to liberalization in their own jurisdictions. To help elucidate these issues, we now turn to the experience of securities industry liberalization in a selection of developing countries.

Study Approach

We adopt a qualitative approach and focus on the extent to which liberalization has been adopted and its impact on the securities industry and on the performance of securities markets. Our purpose is to distinguish geographical differences in foreign participation and differences in foreign participation between securities markets segments. These segments constitute intermediation services (broking, investment management, corporate advisory services, underwriting, and research and advisory services, among others) and market institutions.[29] We do not look at capital account liberalization (that is, the removal of capital controls and other restrictions on currency convertibility), nor do we examine domestic financial deregulation (that is, the practice of allowing greater scope for market forces to work by eliminating direct controls on financial activity, removing barriers to participation across different services, reducing the role of government in the domestic financial system).

In order to gather information on the experience of foreign participation in the securities industries of developing countries, we obtained survey feedback directly from securities regulators from developing-country jurisdictions. Those surveyed were drawn from members of the Emerging Markets Committee (EMC) of the International Organization of Securities Commissions (IOSCO), a grouping of securities market regulators from around the world, and covered developing-country jurisdictions in Asia, Africa, Europe, and Latin America.[30] The EMC's objective is to promote the development and improve the efficiency of emerging securities and

29. This study specifically examines exchanges.

30. For more information on IOSCO, see the organization's Internet website, whose home page can be found at www.iosco.org.

Table 5-1. *List of Jurisdictions Sampled and Their Respective Capital Market Regulators*

Jurisdiction	Capital market regulator
Argentina	Comision Nacionale De Valores
Brazil	Comissao De Valores Mobiliarios
Chile	Superintendencia De Valores y Seguros
China	China Securities Regulatory Commission
Egypt	Capital Market Authority
Hungary	Hungarian Financial Supervisory Authority
India	Securities and Exchange Board of India
Indonesia	Indonesian Capital Market Supervisory Agency
Korea	Financial Supervisory Service
Lithuania	Lithuanian Securities Commission
Malaysia	Securities Commission
Mexico	Comision Nacional Bancaria y De Valores
Oman	Capital Market Authority
Singapore	Monetary Authority of Singapore
South Africa	Financial Services Board
Taiwan	Securities and Futures Commission
Thailand	Office of the Securities and Exchange Commission

futures markets by establishing principles and minimum standards, preparing training programs for the staff of members, and facilitating the exchange of information and transfer of technology and expertise. The regulatory agencies surveyed are significantly involved in the formulation of liberalization policy in their respective jurisdictions and play a major role in determining and enforcing policy on the liberalization of securities market services.

A total of seventeen jurisdictions were surveyed through a 102-point questionnaire, along with personal and telephone interviews with relevant officials of each regulatory agency (see table 5-1). In addition, data and qualitative information were obtained through independent research, literature reviews, and other sources. Survey questions regarding intermediation services broadly focused on

—Whether the jurisdictions allowed foreign participation in each of the services categories (brokering, investment management, advisory services, underwriting, and so on) and, if so, whether and to what extent majority foreign ownership is permitted.

Figure 5-1. *Average Annual Growth Rate of Real GDP and Gross Fixed Investment in Relation to GDP aross Sample Countries*

Percentage points

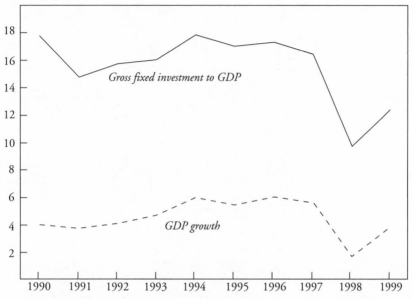

Source: World Bank, Securities Commission calculations.

—Whether current levels reflect those formally committed to in regional or international agreements, and what prompted the opening up of their markets. This was of particular interest because several respondents had experienced major financial crises in recent years.

—Whether there were differences in the treatment of foreign- and domestic-owned market intermediaries and what particular concerns, if any, lay behind the supervision of foreign-owned intermediaries.

—What the experience with foreign participation was like in general, especially in terms of the nature and extent of market penetration by foreign-owned market intermediaries and possible impact on market performance. Respondents were also asked to comment on their experience with foreign participation in relation to their market institutions.

Sample Jurisdictions

During the 1990s, the decade preceding the survey, the average growth rate for the jurisdictions sampled was about 4–6 percent, while gross fixed

Figure 5-2. *Average Annual Growth Rate in Financing*

Percentage points

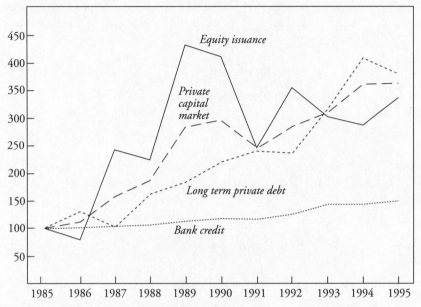

Source: World Bank, Securities Commission calculations.

investment amounted to some 14–16 percent of gross domestic product (GDP) (see figure 5-1).[31] Growth for the sample slipped to around 1.8 percent with the onset of financial crisis in several of the sample jurisdictions. In 1998 gross fixed investment as a proportion of GDP fell sharply to around 9.7 percent before recovering slightly along with real economic growth the next year.

Bank financing appears to have played a fairly significant role in many of these jurisdictions. Average private credit through the banking system for the sample grew from around 44 percent of GDP in the second half of the 1980s to over 65 percent by the mid-1990s. By contrast, the average amount of funds raised through the issuance of equity and private debt securities within the sample grew from around 1 percent of GDP to around 3.5 percent of GDP during the same period. Despite the dominance of the banking sector, capital market financing experienced significantly higher growth compared with bank financing. Between 1985 and 1995, the average value of equity and private debt securities issued in relation to GDP

31. Simple averages for the sample, subject to available data, are used throughout this subsection.

Figure 5-3. *Gross Private Capital Flows as a Percentage of GDP*[a]

Percentage points

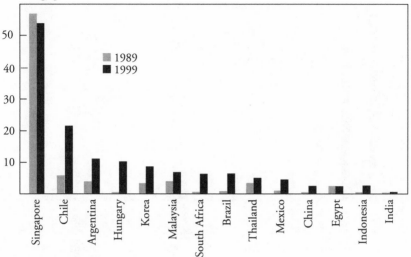

Source: World Bank.
a. In purchasing power parity terms.

across the sample countries grew by more than double the rate of bank credit (see figure 5-2). At the same time, sample countries became more open to capital flows in the form of both portfolio and direct investment (see figures 5-3 and 5-4).

For the majority of the sample, the relative size of the stock market remains below 50 percent of GDP (see figure 5-5). However, a few jurisdictions have seen the relative size of their markets grow far beyond those of the rest of the sample. In the case of Singapore, South Africa, and Malaysia, stock market capitalization as of 1999 amounted to over 150 percent of nominal GDP. Compared with the stock market, the private bond market remains relatively underdeveloped in many jurisdictions. As of 1997, the average value of outstanding private bonds (where data were available) amounted to about 9 percent of GDP.[32] By comparison, the proportion of bank credit as a proportion of GDP in 1999 amounted to more than 50 percent—and in many cases significantly more—across most of the jurisdictions in the sample (see figure 5-6).

Larger stock markets tend to be associated with greater liquidity within the sample, although the relationship is not consistent among markets (see

32. The date of the latest available data is 1997.

Figure 5-4. *Foreign Direct Investment as a Percentage of GDP*[a]

Percentage points

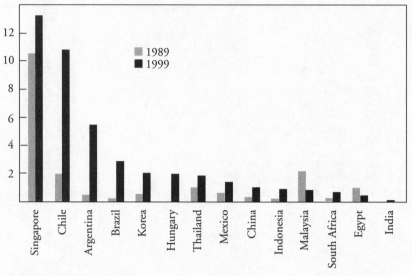

Source: World Bank.
a. In purchasing power parity terms.

figure 5-7). Similarly, larger stock markets also tend to be associated with larger banking sectors (measured by the relative value of deposit money in banks' assets to GDP), suggesting some complementarity in the development of bank and capital market sectors among sample jurisdictions (see figure 5-8).

Survey Findings

The survey findings are organized around the following points: extent of foreign ownership allowed, trends in foreign participation, regulatory treatment of foreign-owned entities, market presence and penetration by foreign participants, liberalization of market institutions, and general feedback on the impact of liberalization.

EXTENT OF FOREIGN OWNERSHIP OF INTERMEDIATION SERVICES ALLOWED. The majority of jurisdictions sampled (fifteen out of seventeen) allow some level of foreign ownership of firms that conduct broking, investment management, underwriting, and advisory and other securities-related activity. Of those, a total of fourteen jurisdictions confirmed that they allow

Figure 5-5. *Stock Market Capitalization to GDP (1999)*

Percentage points

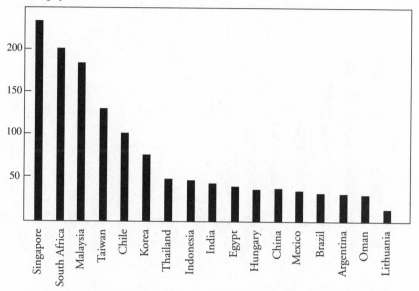

Sources: World Bank; Federation Internationale des Bourses de Valuers (FIBV); WEFA Group; Securities Commission calculations.

foreign majority ownership in one or more of the service categories. Twelve indicated that they permit 100 percent ownership in at least one category, either universally or on a case-by-case basis (see table 5-2 for a breakdown according to service category and degree of ownership allowed).[33] In some jurisdictions, foreign ownership is generally allowed up to 49 percent only, although greater holdings may be permitted either on a case-by-case basis or for a particular industry category.

No significant regional patterns emerged, and contrary to the suggestion of some earlier studies, nothing in the survey findings indicated that limits to foreign participation in Asia are any more stringent than in other regions: nearly all jurisdictions within the Asian subsample allow majority foreign ownership in at least one service category, with more than half of those permitting 100 percent ownership.[34] Some differentiation was observed among

33. One particular jurisdiction allows up to 99 percent foreign holdings as a result of certain legal provisions stipulating the need for there to be at least two shareholders, one of whom has to hold at least 1 percent of equity in the firm in question.

34. Claessens and Glaessner (1998, abstract), for instance, suggest that "most of Asia limits entry of foreign financial firms much more than otherwise comparable countries." However, it should be

Figure 5-6. *Proportion of Domestic Credit Provided by the Banking Sector as a Percentage of GDP (1999)*

Percentage points

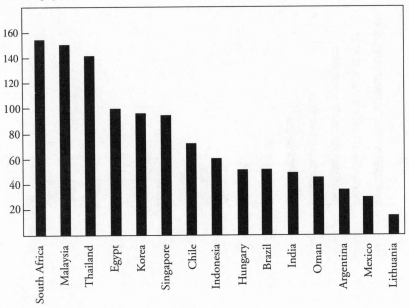

Source: World Bank.

service categories, although this was not widespread across the sample. Differentiation occurred mainly in relation to broking and investment management services within the Asian subsample.

TRENDS IN FOREIGN PARTICIPATION AND REASONS BEHIND FURTHER LIBERALIZATION. Many jurisdictions were liberalizing financial services in conjunction with broader plans to develop the financial sector further. Some also mentioned WTO negotiations as having spurred liberalization. In some cases, the role of foreign firms in supplying capital resources to domestic financial institutions appears to be a strong motivation for policymakers to promote greater financial integration of their financial services sectors.[35]

---

noted that their article was written before the 1997–98 financial crisis in East Asia and the conclusion of the WTO negotiations in 1997.

35. See Gavin and Hausmann (1996). This is consistent with the finding that foreign financial service providers in general do not necessarily allocate the majority of their loans to affiliates headquartered abroad, as they also tend to allocate a substantial share of their loans to local borrowers (Nolle and Seth, 1997).

Figure 5-7. *Scatter Plot of Stock Market Capitalization to GDP Ratio versus Stock Market Turnover Velocity (1999)*

Stock market turnover velocity

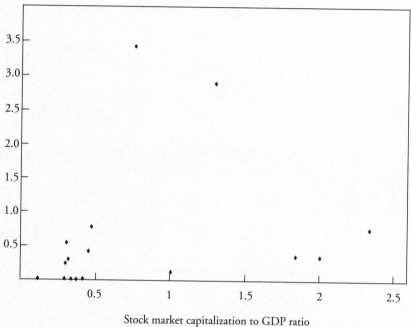

Stock market capitalization to GDP ratio

Source: World Bank, Federation Internationale des Bourses de Valuers (FIBV), Securities Commission calculations.

Of note is that jurisdictions that had experienced episodes of financial crisis within the last decade typically witnessed sustained or increased foreign participation following the resolution of the crisis. Those previously less open to foreign participation in the securities industry tended to reduce limits to foreign participation quite significantly after the crisis period. For instance, several crisis-affected jurisdictions said that post-crisis recapitalization of brokerages and other market intermediaries was a major consideration for liberalizing the market. Indeed, increased interest by foreigners in taking a strategic stake in the domestic securities industry—especially after the implementation of economic or financial reform efforts—was also reported to be a factor that prompted greater liberalization in some jurisdictions. A respondent from a crisis-affected jurisdiction noted that foreign partners of domestic brokerages continued to maintain a domestic presence throughout the period of the crisis and brought in further capital upon the

Figure 5-8. *Scatter Plot of Stock Market Capitalization to GDP Ratio versus Ratio of Deposit Money Banks' Assets to GDP (1997)*

Ratio of deposit money banks' assets to GDP

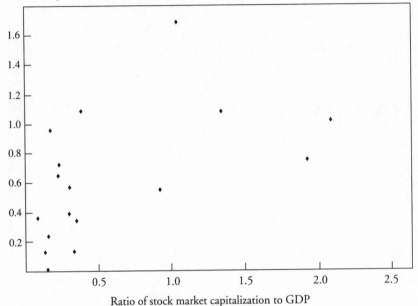

Ratio of stock market capitalization to GDP

Source: World Bank, Securities Commission calculations.

lifting of the crisis. However, it is not clear whether this experience applies throughout the sample.

REGULATORY TREATMENT OF FOREIGN-OWNED ENTITIES. On the whole, the survey found that there were no major differences between domestically owned and foreign-owned market intermediaries in terms of the scope of activities permitted and regulatory treatment accorded to them. Specific conditions imposed on foreign-owned entities typically involve residential and other administrative requirements. Otherwise, the key criterion for permission to operate in a particular jurisdiction across the relevant sample was typically cited as being the ability to maintain capital requirements and other prudential rules, rather than the ownership status of the entity. Again, very few geographical differences were noted, and survey respondents did not distinguish much across the different service categories in respect of treatment. It was noted that the increased presence of more sophisticated and integrated securities market intermediaries through

Table 5-2. *Limits to Foreign Ownership of Securities Markets Intermediaries in Sample Jurisdictions*[a]

Service category	0% to 50%	50% to 100%	100%	Foreign ownership permitted but details not available
Securities brokering	Malaysia, Mexico	India (75%), Indonesia (99%)	Argentina, Brazil, Chile, Egypt, Korea, Lithuania, Mexico, Singapore, South Africa, Taiwan, Thailand	Hungary
Investment management	Mexico, Thailand	Indonesia (99%), Malaysia (70%)	Argentina, Brazil, Chile, Egypt, India, Korea, Lithuania, Singapore, South Africa, Taiwan	Hungary
Other services, including advisory and underwriting activities	Malaysia, Thailand	India (75%), Indonesia (99%)	Argentina, Brazil, Chile, Egypt, Korea, Lithuania, South Africa, Taiwan	Hungary, Mexico

a. Respective jurisdictions may impose certain conditions, such as commercial presence, registration requirements, and exchange membership requirements on foreign-owned market intermediaries. In *Brazil,* both securities broking companies and investment banks may provide corporate advisory and underwriting services. However, presidential authorization is needed to establish a new bank or for a foreign bank to add further capital; but this can allow for up to 100 percent foreign equity capital. In *Indonesia,* the 99 percent limit stems from a legal provision requiring that registered companies have at least two shareholders, one of whom must own at least 1 percent of the firm's equity. In *Thailand,* foreign ownership greater than 49 percent requires approval of the Foreign Business Committee; for security broking companies, approval can be given for up to 100% foreign ownership. In *Mexico,* foreign ownership of investment management companies is limited to a minority stake, under Article 12 Bis LMV; however, there is no limit if the company is formed as a subsidiary of a foreign institution. *China* does not allow foreign ownership of securities brokers or investment management companies. *Oman* does not allow foreign ownership in its securities industry.

liberalization could—and often did—pose a significant challenge to effective regulation and supervision. Most foreign-owned firms, through their parents' global network of operations, had "many legs" to their activities and processes and were able to take on cross-border and cross-asset exposures to a degree that domestic firms were as yet unable to do.

MARKET PRESENCE AND PENETRATION BY FOREIGN PARTICIPANTS. The general feedback indicated that domestic market intermediaries were not significantly displaced following increased foreign participation. This finding is similar to the earlier experience of the EU Single Market Program

(SMP) where widespread foreign ownership of the local banking sector did not result in spite of an increase in cross-border mergers.[36] In many cases, local banks were able either to maintain the dominance they enjoyed prior to the entry of foreign competitors, or to secure lucrative niche markets over which they enjoyed a competitive advantage. This lends support to previous research that reports an increase in the scope of local financial firm post-liberalization, which has allowed them to maintain their pre-liberalization profitability.[37] In many of these cases, the sheer number of domestic intermediaries heavily outweighed that of foreign participants.

With regard to the broking industry, several jurisdictions with larger and relatively more active markets reported that domestic brokers outnumber those with foreign interests (in one case by around twenty to one), and continued to maintain a sizable share of business activity. In several cases, this involved a domination of the retail segment as well as some institutional business.[38] Feedback indicated that reasons for this include the ability to wage aggressive price competition as well as the ability to maintain strong long-standing relationships with corporate and retail clients. (Nevertheless, some respondents from smaller crisis-affected jurisdictions did report a sharp decline in domestic brokers' share of business following the onset of crisis.) In terms of the particular market share of foreign brokerage firms, brokers from the United States and European Union were said to focus mainly on institutional rather than on retail business activity, while Asian-owned brokerages were said to compete for retail business as well.

Less information on market presence and penetration was available for investment management services than for broking, although the overall message in this area was more consistent: foreign investment management firms were generally more successful than foreign brokerages in penetrating the domestic market within sample jurisdictions. The general response was that both foreign market intermediaries and host jurisdictions appear to recognize the value of foreign participation in the investment management industry. According to respondents, foreign entities are particularly interested in participating in the investment management industry, and several jurisdictions have taken specific measures to open up the industry. However, allowing greater foreign ownership did not appear to equate with liberal-

36. Gardner, Molyneux, and Moore (1997a, 1997b).

37. Claessens, Demirguc-Kunt, and Hunziga (1997).

38. Although it was noted that domestic brokers there were not necessarily being spared competitive pressures, their numbers were reported to have declined through consolidation from around 300 in the past to fewer than 200 today.

ization of investment management activity, as it tends to do for the broking industry. In several jurisdictions, certain conditions—such as restricting the investment universe to the domestic market or limiting the client base to nonresidents—still applied to the scope of activity of majority foreign-owned firms. Nevertheless, foreign investment management firms were said to have generally secured a substantial share of business within a number of jurisdictions and enjoy a fairly sizable presence compared with other service categories.

LIBERALIZATION OF MARKET INSTITUTIONS TO FOREIGN PARTICI-PATION. Jurisdictions that allow foreign-owned brokerages to operate also tend to allow them to become members of market institutions (such as exchanges and clearing organizations), subject of course to the availability of seats. In some cases, where new seats were not available foreign entities reportedly bought over incumbent domestic members in order to gain a seat on an exchange or clearinghouse.

The issue of foreign *ownership* of an exchange or other market institution (as opposed to exchange membership) did not typically apply to the majority of sample jurisdictions. Of the seventeen jurisdictions surveyed, only five maintain "corporatized" exchanges (one of which is listed), as a result of recent demutualization or having been established as a corporate body since inception. Among the rest, market institutions adopt a mutual structure, although four jurisdictions did express a strong interest in demutualizing their major market institutions in the near future.[39] Hence the little information available on foreign participation with regard to exchange ownership was varied: some jurisdictions restrict foreign ownership completely, whereas others impose strategic shareholding limits; one imposed no limits at all. One respondent whose jurisdiction was strongly contemplating exchange demutualization and listing suggested that shareholdings limits, were these to be imposed, would be based primarily on public interest (as opposed to national interest) considerations, and that there would probably be scope for limits to be increased or decreased on a case-by-case basis.

GENERAL FEEDBACK ON THE IMPACT OF LIBERALIZATION. Most respondents felt that liberalization had increased the level of competition in the securities industries of the jurisdictions sampled. Many also noted that foreign participation had brought greater innovation and had improved the standards of operations, regulatory compliance, and risk management.

39. This clearly reflects international trends. Of the fifty-two exchange members of the International Federation of Stock Exchanges (FIBV), fifteen are reported to have demutualized, fourteen have members' approval to demutualize, and a further fifteen are said to be actively contemplating demutualization.

Several noted that levels of compliance and standards of governance improved significantly, especially with the participation of foreign partners or shareholders. For instance, foreign-owned entities were said to maintain a higher quality of backroom processes and risk management. Others highlighted the better quality of research and services offered. Skills and technology transfer was also mentioned as one effect of liberalization, but the extent to which this occurred was unclear.

The participation of foreign market intermediaries was also thought to facilitate portfolio inflows, given that many of them focused primarily on foreign institutional clients. Some respondents argued that the move to liberalize the securities industry signaled a greater commitment to global financial integration and hence made their markets more attractive to foreign portfolio and direct investment, among other things. The pursuit of liberalization to facilitate recapitalization efforts in some crisis-affected jurisdictions has already been mentioned. Although one respondent did note an association between greater foreign participation and higher market liquidity, the general view among respondents was that liberalization of securities services had little direct impact on market activity and performance overall.

Issues and Implications

The first conclusion that can be drawn from the survey is that developing-country financial services sectors are more open to foreign participation than generally perceived, particularly those of countries with more developed capital markets. Moreover, in line with the findings of other studies, the actual level of openness in many of the sampled jurisdictions appears to be some way beyond that formally committed to under the GATS framework. Countries within the sample have opened up their securities industries by and large because they recognize the significance of global integration, are experiencing increasing global pressures, and are concerned about national development. Most of the recent advances in liberalization have been made through unilateral initiatives based on domestic considerations and needs, rather than through multilateral trade agreements and other international mechanisms.

When considered together, these findings raise some questions about views on using multilateral mechanisms to secure progressive financial services liberalization more widely. Such mechanisms are believed to have a number of distinct advantages: for example, they are said to tie the degree of current or future liberalization commitments, help shape macroeconomic and regulatory reforms, send appropriate policy signals to potential foreign investors, and encourage liberalization efforts globally.[40] However, financial systems of developing countries usually operate under a wide range of economic circumstances and are at different stages of development. Hence developing countries may consider a unilateral approach to be more flexible in relation to their particular needs and priorities, which may, under certain circumstances, reduce a conservative bias toward liberalization.

The survey also revealed that the experience with securities industry liberalization has on the whole been positive. In particular, fears of displacement of domestic firms have not, in general, been realized. Survey respondents also acknowledged certain positive externalities of liberalization, including a signal to the international community about the strength and competitiveness of the domestic securities industry, as well as the gains associated with greater global integration. At the same time, the precise factors that lay behind the experiences of different jurisdictions remain vague, although survey responses suggest that a great deal depends on whether domestic firms attained a critical mass of market share before liberalization, and whether they have certain competitive advantages in niche areas over foreign intermediaries. These issues would benefit from a closer examination of how the microeconomics of the securities industry affects the dynamics of liberalization.[41]

In addition, a number of survey respondents mentioned the importance of managing short-term adjustment costs and ensuring that such costs did not outweigh the benefits available from liberalization in the long run. Some respondents worried about the potential costs arising from unforeseen systemic risks before the establishment of sufficient regulatory capacity to monitor and supervise the increased (foreign) presence of more sophisticated and globally connected intermediaries.

In our view, an important step in liberalizing the securities industry would arguably be to formulate a framework that outlines a properly sequenced and managed process for maximizing the benefits of further opening up the market while minimizing the possible risks and costs within the context of their particular circumstances. An important element of such a framework is an explicit time frame for liberalization that enunciates

40. See WTO (1997).
41. See Lo (1996) for an example of work in the area of the industrial organization of securities industries.

an appropriate order of sequencing based on the degree of preparedness of the local industry and the needs of specific areas of priority. By implication, therefore, such a framework should focus on at least two immediate objectives: (a) the development of domestic capacity to face a more globally integrated environment; and (b) identification of where and what aspects of the industry ought to be opened up further.

Development of Domestic Capacity

Considering the market as a whole, the adoption of international best practices constitutes a fundamental element of stronger domestic capacity. Such practices relate to the accounting and financial reporting framework as well as other dimensions of the securities market, including market infrastructure (such as clearing and settlement processes), trading systems, and standards of governance. International best practices serve not only to raise the general quality of accounting standards, disclosure, and market processes within the local market, but also to help prepare domestic participants for the challenge of operating in a more international and globally integrated setting once foreign participation is further liberalized.

From the perspective of market intermediaries, building institutional capacity is a key priority, ahead of greater foreign participation in the local market. Intermediaries need to achieve and maintain strong market penetration and ensure a sufficiently diverse revenue base. A more cost-competitive environment will be achieved through the elimination of rigid fee and cost structures that hinder competition for services and products. Market intermediaries must be encouraged to pursue a high level of operational efficiency and to develop core strengths and skills, possibly through the involvement of foreign expertise. At the same time, they must adopt high prudential standards and levels of business conduct and an appreciation of the need to actively manage risks.

Greater regulatory capacity will be crucial in ensuring that core regulatory objectives continue to be met amid a more liberalized environment. Broadly speaking, the regulatory structure will have to be sufficiently flexible to ensure that market authorities are able to address a host of complex factors—especially in relation to standards of supervision, surveillance operations, and regulatory cooperation—across a much wider range of financial activity. More specifically, supervisory and monitoring capacity will need to be upgraded. This entails improving skills and better understanding the manner in which a more globally integrated environment operates. Just as important, however, is the need to have close cooperation and coordination among financial authorities—both at the international and the domestic level—to ensure that systemic issues are fully considered and acted upon if necessary.[42] Due consideration must also be given to macroeconomic issues, to ensure that the stance and priorities in relation to liberalization remain consistent with broader policies. In terms of sequencing, a careful assessment of timing can help policymakers identify areas of potential vulnerability and formulate additional safeguards to minimize the risk of economic dislocation.

Identifying Liberalization Parameters

As implied by conceptual studies of the potential benefits from liberalization, a first step in assessing the areas and extent of deregulation and liberalization should be to gauge the comparative advantage to be gained from allowing greater market access to foreign competition.[43] Policymakers might distinguish certain "parameters" to this end (figure 5-9).[44] For instance, liberalization may be necessary where foreign expertise is needed to upgrade efficiency and such expertise is not available locally. Greater foreign participation may also be needed to promote the development of core and value added segments in the securities industry. Where the industry is fragmented (whether in terms of capital, expertise, or global connections), industry consolidation and the formation of preliminary strategic alliances with appropriate foreign partners may be necessary in advance of increased foreign participation. At the same time, certain limitations to foreign participation may require earlier removal, especially in strategic and nascent sectors of the securities industry that need to develop critical mass. In addition, it may be worthwhile to consider further liberalization where the supply of local capital is insufficient to match the capital needs of local securities firms and when the nature of business requires global linkages and international exposure. In general, foreign participation must bring added value to the domestic industry, whether by bringing financial capital, nurturing local talent, or acting as a conduit for global clients and other businesses.

Clearly, the priority for each country must be to tailor its globalization policies to its own needs and circumstances. For instance, a country may

42. See IOSCO (1999). Available from the IOSCO website.

43. For a theoretical framework on how comparative advantage can be applied to the internationalization of services, see Hufbauer and Warren (1999).

44. These parameters can also assist in systematic reviews of the effectiveness of liberalization policies and processes and in the effective tracking of progress over time.

Figure 5-9. *Possible Parameters for Liberalization*

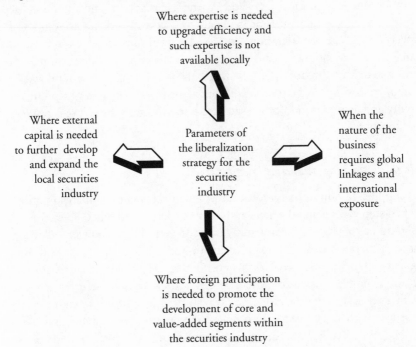

Where expertise is needed
to upgrade efficiency and
such expertise is not
available locally

Where external
capital is needed
to further develop
and expand the
local securities
industry

Parameters of
the liberalization
strategy for the
securities
industry

When the
nature of the
business
requires global
linkages and
international
exposure

Where foreign participation
is needed to promote the
development of core and
value-added segments within
the securities industry

deregulate its domestic financial system but still keep its financial markets closed to foreign competition, while another might regulate its domestic markets tightly but freely allow foreign financial firms to open local establishments and to compete with domestic firms within that system of regulation. The challenge for developing-country securities market authorities lies in the fact that global securities industries are indeed becoming more integrated. Whatever their overall policy aim, authorities must likewise be prepared to adopt a global perspective.

References

Arriazu, R. 1997. "Open Financial Systems in Argentina." Paper presented at Economic Development Institute workshop, "Internationalization of Financial Services." Singapore, August 8.

Barajas, A. 1996. "Interest Rates, Market Power, and Financial Taxation: An Application to Colombian Banks 1974–1988." Washington: International Monetary Fund. Mimeo.

Claessens, S, and T. Glaessner. 1998. "Internationalization of Financial Services in Asia." Washington: World Bank. Mimeo.

Claessens, S., A. Demirguc-Kunt, and H. Huizinga. 1997. "How Does Foreign Entry Affect the Domestic Banking Market?" Washington: World Bank, East Asia and Pacific Region, Development Research Group. July.

European Commission. 1997. "Credit Institutions and Banking." *Single Market Review* 11 (3).

Financial Leaders Group. 1997. *Barriers to Trade in Financial Services.* London: Barclays.

Gardner, E., P. Molyneux, and B. Moore. 1997a. "Impact of the Single Market Programme on the EU Banking." Paper presented at Economic Development Institute workshop, "Internationalization of Financial Services." Singapore, August 8.

————. 1977b. "Impact of the Single Market Programme on the EU Banking: Select Policy Experiences for Developing Countries." Institute of European Finance.

Gavin, M., and R. Hausmann. 1996. "Make or Buy? A Case for Deep Financial Integration." Inter-American Development Bank. Washington.

Henry, P. 1999. "Do Stock Market Liberalizations Cause Investment Booms?" *Journal of Financial Economics* 58 (January): 301–34

Hufbauer, G., and T. Warren. 1999. "The Globalization of Services: What Has Happened? What Are the Implications?" Washington and Canberra: Institute for International Economics and Australian National University. October.

International Monetary Fund (IMF). 1998. *International Capital Markets.* Washington.

International Organization of Securities Commissions (IOSCO), Emerging Markets Committee. 1999. "Causes, Effects and Regulatory Implications of Financial and Economic Turbulence in Markets." Basle.

Kawakatsu, H., and M. Morey. 1999. "Financial Liberalization and Stock Market Efficiency: An Empirical Examination of Nine Emerging Market Countries." *Journal of Multinational Financial Management* 9 (November): 353–71.

Lo, A. 1996. "The Industrial Organization and Regulation of the Securities Industry." National Bureau of Economic Research Conference Report. University of Chicago Press.

McFadden, C. 1994. "Foreign Banks in Australia." Washington: World Bank. Mimeo.

Nicholl, P. 1997. "New Zealand's Experience with Foreign Ownership in its Financial System." Paper presented at Economic Development Institute workshop, "Internationalization of Financial Services." Singapore, August 8.

Nolle, D., and R. Seth. 1996. "Do Banks Follow Their Customers Abroad?" Research Paper 96-20. Federal Reserve Bank of New York.

Qian, Y. 1999. "Financial Services Liberalization and GATS: Analysis of the Commitments under the General Agreement on Trade in Services at the World Trade Organization." Washington: Asian Development Bank. Mimeo.

Sorsa, P. 1997. "The GATS Agreement on Financial Services—A Modest Start to Multilateral Liberalization." IMF Working Paper WP/97/55. Washington: International Monetary Fund.

Stiglitz, J. 2000. "Capital Market Liberalization, Economic Growth, and Instability." *World Development* 28 (6): 1075–86.

Terrell, H. S. 1986. "The Role of Foreign Banks in Domestic Banking Markets." In *Financial Policy and Reform in Pacific-Basin Countries*, edited by H. Cheng. Lexington Books.

World Bank. 2001. *Global Development Finance.* Washington.

World Trade Organization (WTO). 1997. "Opening Markets in Financial Services and the Role of GATS." *Special Studies.* Geneva.

PAUL MASSON $\qquad$ 6

Institutional Experiences in Emerging Markets: Summary of Comments

G21 F23
O16 G12

S ome useful information on institutional experiences in emerging markets can be drawn from the operations of the International Finance Corporation (IFC), Deutsche Bank, Goldman Sachs and Co., and America International Group (AIG).

International Finance Corporation

The IFC's mandate, says IFC director of the Global Financial Markets Group Cesare Calari, is to promote the development of the private sector through investments. IFC operates on a commercial basis. It is known mostly as a product financier, and historically that has been the bulk of its business. By far its largest line of business today is investment in financial services, which accounts for roughly one-third of the outstanding portfolio and nearly half of the new business. That means about $4 billion in outstanding investments, and about $1.6 billion or $1.7 billion a year in new investments.

IFC's growing involvement in financial services can be attributed to various factors. One of these is the widespread liberalization and privatization of financial services in countries until recently governed by heavily regulated, socialistic regimes. The boom in IFC's investment in financial services mirrors the growth in its involvement in private infrastructure, which is its second largest line of business. This sector has also experienced a degree of privatization and liberalization.

There are strategic reasons for IFC's involvement in financial services. One is that working through financial institutions makes it possible to reach down to small and medium-sized enterprises (SMEs), which have a major impact on job creation and social stability. The second reason, and probably the most important one, as a number of recent and not so recent financial crises have demonstrated, is that development cannot occur without a domestic financial system that works. Development cannot rely entirely on foreign capital transfers, nor can it be dependent on a highly distorted, inefficient, or corrupt banking system. Creating mechanisms for mobilizing and allocating financial savings is an important priority for IFC. Finally, since in most developing countries the financial sector has lagged behind other sectors of the economy, the opportunities for high economic and financial returns are greater. Thus IFC's returns from investing in financial services have been about 16–17 percent in dollar terms, somewhat higher than IFC's overall average.

In terms of concentration by lines of business, historically two segments have dominated IFC's portfolio. The first is private equity and venture capital, channeled through funds, partnerships, and other pooled vehicles. The second, actually the largest, is banking, which accounts for about one-half of the overall portfolio. A distant third is asset-based financing. Other lines of business such as housing, insurance and contractual savings, asset management, and securities firms are still behind, but they are growing.

Several trends are likely to shape IFC's involvement in the various subsectors. One important trend is the rise of a middle class in many emerging markets. As chapter 4 shows for insurance, when developing countries reach a certain stage of economic growth, financial services come into heavy demand. The rise of a middle class in countries ranging from Latin America to India, and even parts of Africa, is signaling a growing demand for various financial products. One important area is housing finance, particularly the development of secondary markets for mortgages. In recent years IFC has been involved in the creation of institutions that promote secondary mortgage markets, mainly in Korea, South Africa, Argentina, and Colombia, and it is now working on opportunities in Mexico, Brazil, Poland, Egypt, India, Bangladesh, and possibly China.

The second area of great promise is contractual savings, insurance, pension plan management, and asset management. Contractual savings and investment management will be boosted significantly by the pressures for pension reform resulting from the growth of the middle class and the urbanization-related breakdown of the extended family structure in many countries. Eventually, industrialized countries (the "North") will also put increasing pressure on emerging countries (the "South") to reform their domestic pension schemes because this is one of the few ways in which securities accumulated in retirement accounts in the North are going to be absorbed, in the absence of a growth in population in the northern countries. Pension reform may thus become part of the international political agenda, and this also will have implications for the way capital flows. Traditionally, it has flowed north to south. However, pension reform in Latin America means that capital is also starting to flow south to north and south to south because of the massive mobilization of pension plan assets in developing countries.

In insurance, IFC also sees opportunities in areas that are not life related, such as the health sector. Banking will continue to be an important line for the IFC, but the business is changing significantly, for a number of reasons. First, pressure is increasing to go down-market because the margins in the corporate banking business world are being squeezed, particularly for domestic banks in emerging markets. Second, more technology investment is needed to service the retail industry sector. And third, the banking business is experiencing more competition and increased risk. This mirrors trends in physical infrastructure, where companies develop a rating as public utilities, and telecoms and power generators are now becoming much more attuned to competition. As the risk increases, the returns are also likely to increase. In the past, the emphasis was on picking institutions that were managed soundly and that had strong financials, but in the future the trick will be to pick institutions that have the right strategy and the right market position.

In terms of regional focus, the IFC tends to go to those regions that have a better business environment. Right now, Latin America is easily IFC's largest region, with about 30 percent of the portfolio. Asia and Europe follow. Africa has traditionally been small, but it is growing very fast because of liberalization and privatization in financial services. Five or ten years down the road, Africa may possibly become the IFC's largest region.

IFC is a relatively passive investor and is not in the business of controlling or managing companies, rarely taking more than 25 or 30 percent of equity stakes. Because of that, IFC depends on the involvement of a strategic partner that can provide the management and the technology. Traditionally, its strategic partners have been financial institutions from countries of the Organization for Economic Cooperation and Development, mostly Europe and less so the United States, largely because American institutions have been more reluctant to work on a joint venture basis. The IFC is also doing more work with partners from other developing countries. Regional financial services groups are emerging, most notably in parts of Africa. The EcoBank and Bank of Africa offer such services.

Involvement in management is typically limited to participation in the Board of Directors, but corporate governance is taken quite seriously. This corporate governance is normally embodied in documents that are either the by-laws of the company or are contractual in nature.

As for exit strategies, where possible, IFC prefers to exit to a stock market listing. Normally, this situation allows the best returns and also is developmentally desirable because it spreads ownership.

Deutsche Bank

As Thomas Fischer, a member of the Board of Managing Directors, notes, Deutsche Bank's participation in the emerging markets is a long-standing one. Deutsche Bank was established in 1870, and at its inception the board decided to have four branches: in Bremen in North Germany, London, Yokohama, and Shanghai.

A strong influence on Deutsche Bank's business model in emerging markets dates back to its founding: the main purpose for its presence in emerging market countries in those days was to serve German industry with operations there. Emerging markets today play a substantial role in Deutsche Bank's profit and loss statements.

Its clients in Asia, for which Fischer is responsible at Deutsche Bank, include multinational corporations and large, local corporations. Deutsche Bank offers a fully integrated set of financial services in a targeted fashion. Of course, Deutsche Bank also caters to the financial institutions of the region, ranging from the major central banks for which Deutsche Bank is a major liquidity investment counterpart to large local banks. Deutsche Bank has also become a major supplier of restructuring advisory services in the region.

This is Deutsche Bank's current strategy in Asia; previously it was also involved in collateralized lending to smaller clients. As Michael Pomerleano and George Vojta pointed out in chapter 3, however, doing collateralized lending needs a lot of luck. Deutsche Bank had a good deal of luck for a long time, but then the tide turned and it lost a lot of money.

As a result, Deutsche Bank is now concentrating on what it is best at. These products include foreign exchange, money markets, repo, financial institutions services, over-the-counter derivatives, project finance, cash management, asset management, and to some degree, custody management. In other words, Deutsche Bank supplies products that need a global platform and that bring to the region something that it otherwise would not produce in its own right.

That is a key success factor. Good relations with the regulators are another, though like other major global firms Deutsche Bank has had a few problems with regulators. In Asia, in particular, it is important to be a law-abiding, good corporate citizen in order to be a partner in business. This is part of the business model and is critical to success.

To sum up, from the beginning the basic business model applied by Deutsche Bank, not only in Asia/Pacific but also in other regions, has been to cater to its clients. Later, Deutsche Bank added local business, taking deposits in local currency in order to match the funds. That went well until 1997, when the Asian crisis occurred, at which time Deutsche Bank had to protect the commercial lending franchise. At the same time, the integration of Bankers Trust added a global platform—investment banking, sales, and trading—to Deutsche Bank's commercial lending license and franchise, producing a superb combination. As a result, the firm no longer competes with the locals in what they are good at: local networking, origination, and distribution. Instead, Deutsche Bank concentrates on the global platforms and is very selective with its clients. It is confident that Asia (despite some downside risks) will once again become a major driving force in the world economy.

Goldman Sachs

The experience in emerging markets of Goldman Sachs, says Paolo Leme, its managing director of emerging markets economic research, has been very different from that of Deutsche Bank. In the past ten to fifteen years, the firm has become much more international. Since a few years ago, more than 50 percent of this investment bank's revenue has been coming from outside the United States. Certainly, this is not the case for other international commercial banks.

Unlike commercial banks that have been in Latin America, Asia, Eastern Europe, and Africa for decades, if not centuries, Goldman Sachs started in the emerging markets business in the early 1990s. And much more selectively. It was not saddled by commercial bank loans, which then became Brady bonds. It started as a very small, opportunistic trading shop. Since then Goldman Sachs has become one of the top five broker dealers and is very important in underwriting, particularly for the sovereigns in the dollar sector.

With the globalization of the financial industry, the need for a local presence has decreased rather than increased, particularly in the wake of technology advances and the integration of trading strategies. A great deal can be done virtually. Running a book from New York reduces the fixed cost and some of the variable costs of global presence, as well as some of the risk.

The emerging market clients of Goldman Sachs are primarily fund managers and funds—in both the developed and the developing world—in equities, fixed income, commodities (Goldman Sachs is a big player in metals, energy, and other commodity areas), and foreign exchange. Other important clients are sovereigns and corporates (in the underwriting business) and individuals (particularly through private client services).

Being New York-based, or Europe-based, or Asia-based, rather than having a local, emerging market presence, means missing many opportunities or important information useful to the proprietary trading business. At the same time, the lack of a local presence sometimes provides the advantage of not being involved in the local minutiae and thus being able to see the big picture. More and more, global variables are determining what happens in local markets. Thus selectivity sometimes is better.

On the other hand, not being local has the disadvantage of reducing the potential pool of clients and the potential expansion rate of the businesses. Consequently, Goldman Sachs has in a few cases chosen to have a local presence, sometimes just a local office (particularly in Asia and Latin America), sometimes a full-fledged bank with brokerage services, asset management, and commodities trading.

The firm applies three general criteria in deciding whether to establish a full-fledged, local investment bank. First, can the revenue stream be significantly enhanced? Given that Goldman Sachs is a public company, growth in revenue stream and earnings has become even more mandatory. Second, despite correlations across countries, there is still some capacity to diversify buckets of risk. Third, it makes sense to have a local arm that is able to absorb the global products. Returns to scale are very important, particularly for products where Goldman Sachs has an advantage, such as global intelligence and the distribution of higher value added products.

On balance, being global, as opposed to local, has numerous advantages. That is not surprising, given that many local brokerages and small investment banks have either been sold, acquired, or merged with international, global banks over the past ten years.

There are more specific criteria for going local with a full presence. A country needs a substantial market capitalization, satisfactory corporate governance practices, and moderate taxation. For example, a financial transactions tax, such as the one in Brazil, and now in Argentina, solves fiscal problems but causes intermediation to migrate to New York. The depth and the liquidity of the instruments in local markets are very important. A large, local market, as in Brazil, provides enormous scope for Goldman Sachs to do what it does best, which is derivatives, mortgages, and the like. Doing so is much harder out of New York. Hence a local presence is useful, though the existence of the Internet and electronic trading changes the trade-off. The regulatory framework and business practices are also important criteria. Although the rationale to expand locally exists, Goldman Sachs is much smaller and much more selective than its competitors. Nevertheless, the main potential for growth in emerging financial markets will come not from local presence but from international presence.

AIG

By contrast, AIG began as an emerging market company, notes Larry Mellinger, senior managing director. It was founded in Shanghai in 1919 as a life insurance company and moved to New York City in 1939. It became publicly listed in 1969. It is the largest international life insurance company, and the largest U.S. general insurance company, deriving about 40 percent of its earnings from life and 40 percent from general insurance. AIG is AAA-rated and is one of the largest market-capitalized companies in the world, with approximately $112 billion in assets under management. Private equity accounts for approximately $12 billion of the total. The longer liability contracts of life insurance lend themselves well to longer-term investments.

Private equity is a highly relevant subject for many emerging market countries, since the flow of foreign direct investment capital there sometimes exceeds the flows of portfolio capital, or even debt capital. Private equity capital tends to be of longer-term nature. It is "patient" capital. Private equity assets consist not only of private direct investments but also of hedge fund assets, real estate assets, and certain categories of mezzanine lending or investing. These include venture capital and leveraged buyouts.

AIG typically goes in as a minor participant figuring to invest for the long term and usually not taking a controlling interest. AIG expects to hold the investment for anywhere from three to seven years and then to exit through one of a number of vehicles: initial public offerings (IPOs), strategic buyers, or management buyouts. AIG sponsors private equity funds, contributing about 10 percent to their capital and inviting participation from large institutional investors and international companies.

The $12 billion private equity portfolio consists of twenty-eight funds sponsored by AIG. Twenty-two of them are in emerging markets, and the other six in the United States. Of the twenty-two emerging market funds, nine are in Asia, where AIG has deep roots (which include an extensive insurance network).

Six of these are in infrastructure: large, capital-intensive projects. AIG's first fund in Asia—the Asia Infrastructure Fund—was a $1 billion dollar fund invested throughout Southeast and East Asia. That was followed by a second AIG-sponsored Asia infrastructure fund, for $1.7 billion. Another group at AIG focuses on noninfrastructure, international investments—a more classic emerging markets group—with ten funds. Finally, there is a network of real estate funds in emerging markets.

The size of AIG and its fifteen or more years of experience in this area allow it to be very opportunistic and to take advantage of crisis situations. Participating in emerging markets is good business for AIG because globally it provides asset diversification, including sector diversification. Emerging markets provide a wealth of opportunities to add value to companies that need cash and technology to compete, to go global. This has traditionally been very profitable for AIG. Typically, AIG looks for annual average returns of 20–25 percent in its funds, unless the perceived risk is higher, in which case the goal would be perhaps 25–30 percent. In addition to making a nice return, it also attempts to grow a third-party asset business. The roots of AIG in its insurance network open up attractive investment opportunities in places such as China, India, Japan, even throughout Latin America, Africa, and Eastern Europe. Reputation and presence help, as does track record.

AIG usually considers four main factors in deciding to go ahead with an investment in a particular country. One is macroeconomic stability. Second, there has to be a sense of a pro-market orientation. Investors tend to avoid countries with extensive price controls and subsidies, or if they need to compete with parastatals. Third, the rule of law is critical to a commitment of private equity. Is there a respect for contracts? Is there a legal system to which one can appeal? Fourth, transparency is essential in the operation of government agencies and regulatory bodies. Is there a public register of all the steps that have to be taken when foreign investors apply for contracts? Of those four requirements—macrostability, a pro-market orientation, the rule of law, and transparency—any foreign direct investor is going to insist on at least two of them, should want three, and ideally would hope for all four.

Before going ahead with an investment, AIG looks at some other factors as well. First, local partners in transactions have to be strong, of high quality, and good character. They should have a track record that can be evaluated. Second, AIG typically needs a strategic operator to run the business because AIG does not get involved, generally speaking, in operating details. Third, AIG and other private equity investors do thorough due diligence, looking at tax and accounting records and everything that goes with them. AIG will run scenarios of what different assumptions do to the rate of return. Finally, AIG needs to find a way to maximize and add value, since it also wants to mobilize other capital, attract top-quality management, help in strategic planning, bring technology, and apply all those other best practices that make these investments truly outstanding.

AIG finds emerging markets an attractive space for long-term direct investment. For the countries concerned, its involvement brings various benefits because it has a direct and favorable impact on the capital account, providing a good source of long-term money. As a result, AIG contributes directly to the growth of jobs, technology, and exports.

PART **III**

What Foreign Institutions Do in Emerging Markets: Sector Report

DONALD G. SIMONSON

7

Foreign Bank Influence in the Czech Republic

P34   P33

G21   F23

For nine years after Czechoslovak communism ended in 1989, the Czechoslovakian and successor Czech governments tenaciously retained control of the republic's four large banks. The state used its control to direct lending to favored large industrial firms and to prevent the banks from coming under the control of foreign investors. Initially, the banking sector comprised four large banks. These were either hived off the old monobanking system, as in the cases of Ceska sporitelna (CS, the old savings bank), Ceskoslovenska obchodnibanka (CSOB, the old foreign trade bank), and Investicni y postovni banka (IPB, the combined investment bank and postal bank), or were created from assets of the old central bank, as in the case of Komercni banka (KB, the commercial or business bank). In 1991 Konsolidacni banka (KoB) was licensed as a state institution to acquire, administer, and amortize these banks' communist-era bad loans. The state recapitalized all four banks in 1991 by shifting bad loans to KoB and guaranteeing the loans under the state budget. In the subsequent early years of economic transformation, the state further recapitalized individual banks among the four, devoting special attention to KB.

The recapitalization measures in the early years of economic transition were forthright and enabled the Czech Republic to quickly acknowledge bad loans, clean them from bank balance sheets, and free the large banks to aggressively pursue state-directed lending. In ensuing years, however,

directed lending left a legacy of nonperforming assets at large banks, immo-
bilizing the banks and leading to the loss of Czech control. Foreign firms
came to dominate the banking sector as foreign strategic investors acquired
control of the large banks and organic foreign banking units continued
their growth from within. Including the pending privatization of KB, the
last large bank, before the end of 2001, foreigners are expected to control
nearly 90 percent of banking assets.

Banking Sector Nationalism

Legal and regulatory barriers were not a material factor in preventing foreign ownership of banks in the Czech Republic. The banking sector was
legally opened to foreign financial participation early in the Czech Republic's transition to a market economy. Licensing of foreign bank branches
began in February 1992 with the passage of the 1992 Act on Banks. The
new law permitted assessments of foreign branch license applications, if
anything, on less restrictive terms than the assessment of full banking license
applications by Czech nationals. The act made no essential distinction in
the requirements for bank license applications for groups led by Czech
nationals compared with foreign-owned groups.[1] Furthermore, it did not
limit foreign stakes in individual banks or in the foreign share of total banking sector assets.

While law and regulation were not barriers, politics was a consistent
deterrent. Members of the Czech Assembly and members of the government clearly resisted foreign participation in the large state-owned Czech
banks. Through 1996, the political motive of these bodies was to ensure
that the large banks were controlled domestically. Jonathan Stein reasons
that the state applied principles adopted in 1991, "according to which the
state would retain control of at least 40–50% of the basic capital, foreign
participation would be held to a 25% maximum, and no single foreign
investor would be permitted more than a 10% stake."[2]

The Czechoslovak and later the Czech government used voucher privatization in the early 1990s to shift state assets to private Czech ownership
and control. In explaining the Czech voucher privatization program several
years after its launching, then Prime Minister Vaclav Klaus asserted, "Where
no one has capital . . . and the goal is not to sell everything to foreigners,

1. Article 5 of the 1992 Act on Banks.
2. Stein (2000).

voucher privatization was the only possibility." The voucher program permitted only Czech citizens to participate. Especially in relation to large banks, the government seemed bent on maintaining domestic control. In the end, large minority shares in three of the four large banks were widely dispersed among investment funds and individual investors, enabling the state to retain controlling blocks of shares in each of them.[3] In this, the government remained true to the spirit of banking sector nationalism established with the founding of Czechoslovakia after the First World War.[4]

Through its control over the large banks, the government hoped to perpetuate numerous previous or current state-owned enterprises by inducing the banks to finance the continuation of their operations and their high levels of employment. In addition, the government depended upon the banks to assist in privatizing certain industrial firms. In numerous instances, the large banks supported privatization to Czech investors of major assets designated as sovereign and strategic, such as companies in the businesses of petrochemicals, electrical generation and distribution, coal, steel, and engineering. In lieu of nonexisting fresh external capital, Czech investors were given access to debt funding by the banks. In these so-called leveraged privatizations, the government effectively induced the banks to make large loans to Czech entrepreneurs, enabling the entrepreneurs to tender and acquire the firms.

The resulting growth of the large banks' assets was of dubious quality, but it did ensure that the banking sector would grow and remain highly concentrated for a few years. However, the poor quality of the growth assets in an environment of direct lending and underdeveloped banking supervision led to sharp deterioration in the financial health of the banks. In part owing to a policy of banking nationalism, the restructuring of much of Czech industry was delayed by a serious lack of financial and managerial capital. In the end, the large banks were immersed in state-directed support of select investors and of foundering old state enterprises and had no effective strategies for workout and rehabilitation.

Still, the official view that the banks should be controlled domestically persisted well into the 1990s. Significantly, in 1996, while the state continued to hold clear controlling positions in all of the large banks, Klaus

---

3. Shares of CSOB were not subject to voucher privatization because of this bank's unique involvement in foreign financial markets. The government feared that voucher privatization might alter CSOB's viability and have deleterious effects on the nation's monetary stability. In 1998 Czech government stakes were 65.7 percent in CSOB, 45 percent in CS, 36.3 percent in IPB, and 48.7 percent in KB.

4. Lacina (1990).

proclaimed massive wholesale privatization to be "practically over."[5] The implicit conclusion is that government policy emphasized large banks as sovereign assets with a mission too sensitive to entrust to foreign control.

A new government was elected in the summer of 1997 amid confusion over the future and possible privatization of the large banks. Delays in privatizing the banks provoked sharp criticism by the European Union.[6] Concerned over its goal of accession to the European Union early in the first decade of the 2000s, the new government took steps in December 1997 to push privatization of the large banks ahead on its agenda for the economy. The government's privatization order for the four largest banks in the country listed the following criteria, presumably in order of priority: sale price, strengthening of banks' capital, improving banks' efficiency, and maintaining banks' share of the Czech market. Ironically, what was perhaps the most urgent criterion—enlisting the large banks as agents in restructuring the real economy—did not receive mention.

Evolution of Foreign Dominance of the Banking Sector

Despite the government's bias in favor of Czech ownership, the banking sector has steadily shifted toward foreign dominance for more than a decade. There are three principal reasons for the shift. First, as noted, many years of state-directed lending in the large banks created large amounts of nonperforming loans. Figure 7-1 shows that, in recent years, nonperforming loans in the Czech banking system have far outdistanced those in the Polish and Hungarian systems. Credit flows to uses with high economic potential were stymied owing to the banks' preoccupation with bad loans. Ultimately, foreign financial and managerial capital was required to extract the large banks from this dilemma. Second, during 1992–94 a liberal bank license regime resulted in a flood of licenses to Czech-owned banks. Most of the banks receiving licenses proved to be nonviable and were put into conservatorships as bank supervision and regulation strengthened during 1995–97, leaving the field open to the expansion of foreign banking units. Third, the failure of small, Czech-owned banks and a too-big-to-fail policy favoring the large state-controlled banks undermined confidence in the banking sector and discouraged the further interest of Czech owners in establishing de novo banks.

5. Klaus (1996).
6. Most recently, see European Union (1998).

Figure 7-1. *Classified Credits/Gross Credits, 1995–2000*

Percent

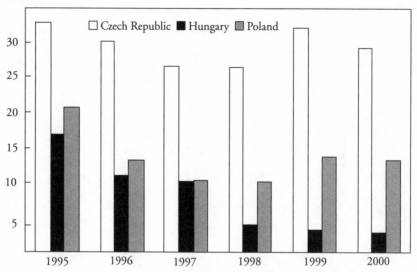

Source: Annual reports (various years), Czech National Bank, National Bank of Hungary, National Bank of Poland.

As long as the state continued to control the large banks, foreign owners were compelled to build a presence by starting up organic branches and newly licensed banks. With the privatization of IPB and CSOB in 1998, foreign banking participation began to reflect both buy *and* build entry. In the following year, foreign interests acquired CS. With these acquisitions and because the large banks accounted for most of the banking system, the magnitude of foreign participation jumped dramatically. By 2001, foreign financial firms held all of the large banks except KB.[7] It is expected that KB, the last large state-controlled commercial bank, will be privatized to a foreign strategic investor in late 2001. As detailed below, this final shift in large bank ownership will place nearly 90 percent of the Czech banking system in the hands of foreign entities.

FOREIGN BANKING UNITS. Figure 7-2 shows that the number of Czech-controlled banking units increased rapidly to thirty-four during 1991–94 and then, by 2001, plunged almost as quickly to twelve. Meanwhile, the number of foreign units grew steadily throughout the 1990s. The Czech

7. The large bank group was reduced from four to three with the collapse of IPB in June 2000 and its subsequent absorption by CSOB, finalized in 2001.

Figure 7-2. *Development of Banking Units: Czech vs. Foreign*[a]

Number of units

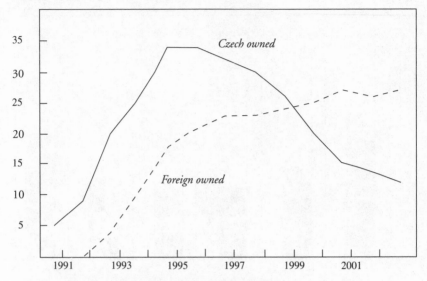

Source: Annual reports (various years), Czech National Bank.
a. Czech ownership includes state banks, banks with majority state ownership, and banks with majority ownership by Czech nationals. Foreign ownership includes banks with majority foreign ownership and branches of foreign banks.

banking sector in the first quarter of 2001 comprised forty banks. Of these, twenty-six were banking units with majority foreign participation. The foreign units included ten branches of foreign banks and three categories of proper banks: (1) two large banks privatized to foreign banks, (2) seven banks licensed to nonbank investors, and (3) seven banks licensed to foreign banks. With the exception of the large privatized banks, these totals represented foreign organic banking units. The identities of banking units in the above classifications are listed in the appendix to this chapter.

FOREIGN BANKING SHARES OF ASSETS. Table 7-1 shows the movement in asset shares by banking categories during the years 1994–2000. Through 1999, the Czech National Bank reported banking structure developments in six categories of banking entities: large banks, small banks, foreign banks, foreign bank branches, specialized banks, and banks under conservatorship. In table 7-1, foreign branches are combined with foreign banks to show organic foreign participation. The shares of organic banking assets with foreign participation have increased dramatically over the years. Without counting foreign participation owing to the recent shift in the control

Table 7-1. *Shares of Total Assets by Banking Group, 1994–2000*
Percent

Bank group	Shares of total banking sector assets[a]						
	12/94	12/95	12/96	12/97	12/98	12/99	12/00
Large banks	77.5	73.0	68.1	65.6	66.0	65.1	59.1
Small banks[b]	9.7	9.1	6.2	4.7	3.6	1.6	5.5[c]
Foreign banks, branches[d]	11.1	15.9	18.6	22.3	25.0	27.1	28.6[c]
Specialized banks	1.4	2.0	3.1	4.3	5.5	6.3	6.8[c]
Banks in conservatorship	0.3	0.0	4.0	3.1	0.0	0.0	0.0
Total banking sector	100.0	100.0	100.0	100.0	100.0	100.0	100.0

a. Totals exclude Konsolidacni banka.
b. Data for 2000 include medium-sized Czech units.
c. Estimates from CNB revised classification.
d. Foreign-controlled, "self-grown" banking units.

of large banks to foreign firms, the share of total assets accounted for by the organic foreign banks and foreign bank branches increased rapidly at the expense of both large and small banks that for the major part are Czech owned. The aggregate assets share of licensed organic foreign entities rose from 11.1 percent in 1994 to 28.6 percent in 2000.

The increase can be attributed in part to affirmative factors such as the foreign units' greater freedom to select assets using objective credit evaluation criteria, construct credit portfolios without a legacy of directed lending, offer broader product and service lines (greater scope), and to utilize more diverse sources of funding. The increase also reflects the negative effects of large nonperforming loans in large banks that eventually rendered them noncompetitive and kept them out of the hunt for new business. In addition, the large bank share declined dramatically in 2000 owing to the sloughing off to KoB of several large blocks of nonperforming loans in CS and KB.[8]

Two of the three large banks, CS and CSOB (including the good assets of IPB), have been privatized to foreign strategic investors. The addition of these banks to the totals of foreign participation increases foreign control to 71.3 percent of the banking sector. Finally, if the expected privatization of KB is included, foreign participation rises to 87.7 percent of the banking sector.

8. A large amount of bad loans from IPB will be shifted by CSOB to KoB during 2001.

Figure 7-3. *Shares of Net Credit, 2000*

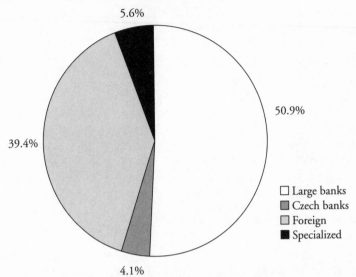

Source: Czech National Bank, basic indicators of the banking sector as of December 31, 2000, and author's estimation.

FOREIGN BANKING SHARES OF NET CREDIT. The shares of gross credit extended, amounting to CZK864 billion at the end of 2000, substantially concurred with the shares of total assets by banking unit category. However, the large bank share of *net* credit, defined here as gross credit less doubtful and loss loans, lagged well behind other banking categories. This definition omits deductions of substandard and watch loans typically used to define classified credits and therefore probably comes closer to true loan valuations. My estimates of net credit shares for large banks and other categories of banks in 2001 appear graphically in figure 7-3 and are based on several key premises. Shares of client deposits are treated later.

Estimates of net credit must reconcile a clash in the respective estimates by CNB and business media sources for doubtful and loss loans. CNB's reported sum of the banking sector's doubtful and loss credits at the end of 2000 was CZK115.3 billion, which underestimates these quantities. CNB's figures are composed of CZK26 billion doubtful and CZK89.3 billion loss loans. The total represents mostly bad loans held by the large banks.[9] However, business news media reports probably give a more accurate and current accounting of bad credit values. According to media reports, expected losses

9. Classified credits in 1996–2000, Czech National Bank.

on old IPB loans, to be recognized in 2001, will total CZK100 billion.[10] CS bad debts to be absorbed by KoB are in the neighborhood of at least CZK10 billion.[11] The media further reported that the remaining bad loans for KB, covered by state guarantees, are expected to total CZK20 billion.[12]

Together, then, this more recent information suggests that the three large banks alone account for loss loans of about CZK130 billion, far in excess of CNB's figure of CZK89.1 billion for loss loans in the entire banking sector at the end of 2000.[13] Assuming, conservatively, that large banks' share of banking system doubtful loans is proportionate to their share of gross credit, or 58.53 percent of CZK26 billion, yields CZK15.2 billion. Together with the above estimate for large bank loss loans, loss and doubtful credits for large banks then total CZK130 billion + CZK15.2 billion, or CZK145.2 billion.

Using these data, it is possible to estimate the large banks' true share of net credit. It is reasonable to estimate total banking sector doubtful and loss loans of CZK156 billion consisting of CZK130 billion large bank loss loans plus CZK26 billion doubtful loans for the entire banking sector. This total is far in excess of the CZK115.3 billion reported by CNB. From these data, total net credit (gross credit net of loss and doubtful loans) for the banking sector is CZK864 billion minus CZK156 billion, or CZK708 billion. According to CNB, gross credit extended by large banks is 58.53 percent of CZK864 billion, or CZK505.7 billion. Net credit by large banks then is CZK505.7 billion minus CZK145.2 billion, or CZK360.5 billion. The latter figure represents a 50.9 percent share of banking sector credit net of loss and doubtful loans, an amount that is significantly below large banks' total asset share of 59.1 percent. Net credit shares for other bank categories in figure 7-3 are estimated proportionately.

CLIENT DEPOSIT SHARES. By contrast, shares of client deposits at the end of 2000 significantly tilted toward the large banks. Shares of client deposits by categories of banks are illustrated in figure 7-4. The three large banks held a 69.4 percent share of client deposits (versus 50.9 percent of net credit and 59.1 percent of assets), owing largely to CS's dominant position. Foreign branches accounted for a very modest share of client deposits at 4.9 percent compared with their 12.1 percent share of assets.

---

10. "IPB Bill Will Be a Whopping Kc 90 Billion to 100 Billion," Reuters, March 5, 2001.
11. "Ceska Sporitelna: How Many Assets KoB Will Assume Is Not Yet Known," *Hospodarske noviny,* March 7, 2001.
12. "Komercni Banka Reduces Losses," *Prague Business Journal,* February 26, 2001.
13. Classified credits.

Figure 7-4. *Shares of Client Deposits, 2000*

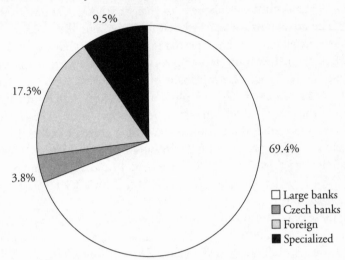

9.5%

17.3%

3.8%

69.4%

☐ Large banks
■ Czech banks
☐ Foreign
■ Specialized

Source: Czech National Bank, basic indicators of the banking sector as of December 31, 2000, and author's estimation.

Financial Flows: Interbank and Foreign Direct Investment

The noted allocation of client deposits sets up a crucial liquidity symbiosis in which large banks, led by CS, redirected large flows of interbank funding to foreign branches. The foreign branches alone accounted for one-third (December 2000) to more than one-half (September 2000) of interbank market demand compared with their 12.1 percent share of total banking assets. Overall, purchases of interbank funds accounted for 20 percent of all funding for the banking system.

Figure 7-5 shows the flows of client deposits, interbank funds, and net credit by banking group at the end of September 2000. The information pertaining to the interbank market indicates that large banks purchased 23 percent of available interbank funds while supplying 45 percent of the interbank market's funds for a net supply position of 22 percent. In contrast, foreign bank branches purchased 52 percent and supplied 27 percent of interbank funds for a net *purchased* position of 25 percent.[14] This pattern of funding reinforces the thesis that the large banks' level of credit production in relation to their funding resources has been compromised.

14. The data do not reveal whether interbank purchased funds are placed in the interbank market domestically or in sales to foreign institutions.

Figure 7-5. *Banking Sector Funding Patterns*

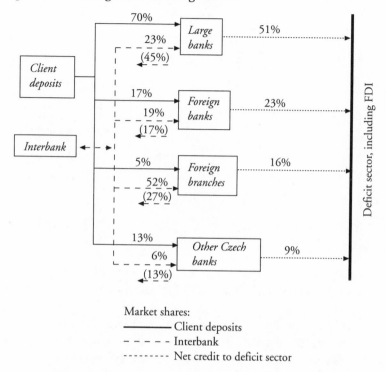

Market shares:
———————— Client deposits
– – – – – Interbank
-------- Net credit to deficit sector

Source: Czech National Bank, basic indicators of the banking sector as of December 31, 2000.

These banks have been preoccupied over the years with nonperforming loans and, owing to inadequate management capacity, have not sought nor served a meaningful number of credit clients that offer good commercial potential. The systemic funding pattern also highlights the fact that the net credit position of foreign branches is quite large in comparison with their small attraction of client deposits.

In a more fully developed financial system, the capital markets would make up for the blockage of credit flows from the large banks. Although a securities exchange has existed since 1993, it remains underdeveloped owing to a continuing lack of legislation and regulation and is not likely to be an effective channel for funds flows. The above evidence indicates that, in the absence of well-working capital markets, fund flows have been directed to foreign banking units. These flows have helped substitute for the incapacity of the large banks to provide needed credit flows for Czech enterprise. Between them, foreign bank branches and foreign banks proper, with 32

Figure 7-6. *Major Financial Flows Supporting Czech Republic FDI,*
1998–2000

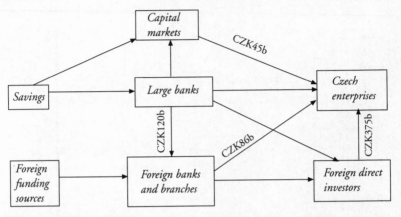

Source: Modified from Tuma (2000).

percent of banking sector assets, account for 22 percent of client deposits,
39 percent of net credit, and 71 percent of funds taken from the interbank
market.

In addition, foreign direct investors constitute a large source of funds to
Czech enterprises. In turn, the large banks provide an important part of the
funds available to foreign direct investors. The foreign investors bring the
ability to assess firms' future prospects, including repayment capacity, and
to acquire controlling stakes in Czech businesses, which ensures enforcement of loan terms. Zdenek Tuma, governor of the Czech national bank,
uses the Czech balance of payments accounts to develop rough estimates of
the fund flows attributable to foreign banking units and foreign direct
investors during 1998–2000 in by-passing the blockage of credit from the
large banks to Czech firms.[15] As shown in figure 7-6, foreign banking units
are important sources both of direct funding to Czech firms and of indirect
funding of firms through foreign direct investors.

Performance of the Banking Sector

Of the thirteen banking units that will remain under Czech control after
KB is privatized, only three offer reasonably broad commercial services and

15. Tuma (2000).

also have assets of more than CZK15 billion (US$387 million).[16] The other remaining entities are smaller or specialized, such as building societies. While perhaps providing valuable service to a limited clientele, Czech institutions in aggregate no longer constitute a significant force in the Czech financial system. This reality is not consistent with the goals implied in the early years of economic transformation of the banking hegemony when policymakers clung to their vision of significant Czech ownership and control, spurred by voucher privatization as the vehicle for shifting the state's productive assets to millions of citizens.

By 1997, with the coincident strengthening of bank supervision, rigorous capital requirements, and tough new accounting requirements for bad loans, it became clear that all but one of the large banks (the exception was CSOB) had very high levels of problem assets. As their losses mounted and their capital drained, the troubled banks had no alternative but to shut down new lending and stop growing, if not actually shrink. Rescues, in the form of shifting bad loans to KoB, the state economic cleanup bank, were used to recapitalize the banks to keep them going. The rescue efforts diverted the banks from pressing corporate clients to restructure and, rather, permitted the corporations to continue operations as usual. Thus scarce government funds were wasted. In addition, each rescue probably increased moral hazard as the large banks grew to expect periodic recapitalization by the state. Moreover, the banks' staffs were not sufficiently committed or trained to either monitor or restructure large corporate clients. The paralysis of the large banks, coupled with the closing of a cohort of smaller Czech banks, left the field wide open to foreign banks and branches.

The paralysis of the large banks and the attendant lack of economic vigor are revealed in data on the growth of gross credit in the Czech Republic compared with similar growth in Hungary and Poland since 1997. Figure 7-7 indicates that the growth rate of gross credit in the Czech Republic lagged well behind the growth in Hungary for two of the years and roughly matched Hungary in two years. Czech credit creation was far behind the dramatic credit growth shown for Poland in each year.

Foreign participation in the Czech banking sector promises vastly improved efficiency in directing credit flows to economic uses, wider product offerings, and higher levels of service. However, the first large bank privatization was not so promising. The piecemeal sale of state stakes in IPB to Nomura Europe Holding in 1998 shifted control to Nomura almost as

16. Ceska exportni banka, Ceskomoravska zarucni a rozvojova banka, and Unionbanka.

Figure 7-7. *Growth Rate of Gross Credit, 1997–2000*

Growth (percent)

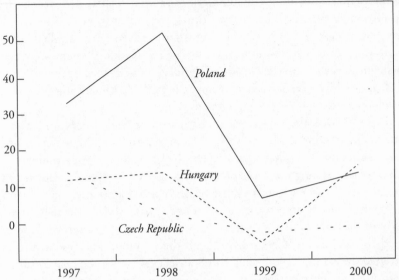

Sources: Annual reports (various years), Czech National Bank, National Bank of Hungary, and National Bank of Poland.

an afterthought. The new owner did not assert its role as strategic investor in the restructuring and management but was more attuned to acquiring the bank's investment company subsidiary with its strategic holdings in fields such as brewing, glass, paper, and insurance. Nomura placed the bank in the hands of managers who held a slightly smaller stake in the bank. With a balance sheet newly recapitalized by Nomura, the old management embarked on rapid but poorly selected loan growth, culminating in the bank's estimated 70 to 80 percent nonperforming to total loans by 2000.

The privatizations of CSOB in 1999 and CS in 2000 convey much greater promise. By exercising astute management principles during the years of the state's control, CSOB managed to insulate itself from most of the pressures of directed lending and to operate profitably with a comfortably small level of nonperforming loans. The bank obviously lacked capital to expand its products and services. When a controlling share of the bank was sold to Belgian banking and insurance operator KBC Group in June 1999, the bank's management was already prepared with a thoughtful business development model. With close support and investments by KBC, the bank has advanced plans for aggressive expansion in retail banking, exploited KBC's know-how in developing its investment banking business, and tapped into KBC's client relationships and international investor contacts. In addition, CSOB's greater management capacity, based on its parent's depth, enabled the bank to take over the good assets of recently failed IPB.

Before privatization, CS, the large savings bank, lacked capital for investment in product development and also lacked a strong retailed-minded staff. Austrian Erste Bank acquired CS in 2000 and hired a foreign manager with strong credentials in retail banking. With support from Erste Bank, CS is embarking on a high-stakes strategy involving massive investment in information technology. The bank is focusing on developing a unified client account. This product has enormous potential for servicing complete client financial needs, including new mortgage and credit card products and ATM services. The bank plans to convert a newly streamlined staff to a sales culture, "enabling" (instead of "training") the staff to serve customers and converting its branches into "sales centers." In addition, the bank will actively pursue fields of its parent's strengths, including securities brokerage and investment banking.

To date, large bank privatization has excluded control by Czechs. However, it has relied heavily on Czech participation in management. The first large bank privatization (IPB) encountered difficulties because the foreign investor abandoned strategic responsibility for the bank. Left in the care of inexperienced senior managers, some of whom also proved to be avaricious, the bank quickly ran aground. On the other hand, the CSOB and CS model of cooperation and shared responsibility between the foreign investor and Czech managers appears to be succeeding. Cooperation between foreign owners and Czech managers leverages the local understanding and intelligence of qualified Czech managers with the capital, experience, and technical know-how of international banks. The prospect appears to be a deepening and broadening of these two banks that would not be possible without this highly symbiotic cooperation.

Conclusion

For too long, the Czech government hoped that Czechs themselves would mobilize the capital and managerial know-how to drive the banking sector. In a word, it emphasized sovereignty over the large banks that once dominated all of Czech banking. The government's hopes led it to underestimate the importance of efficient finance to support restructuring of the nation's economy.

The government's holdout in privatizing the large banks to foreign strategic investors proved to be costly to the Czech economy. The financial system was denied the capital and expertise of foreign strategic investors to rehabilitate wayward borrowers and to facilitate the exit of nonviable borrowers. The banks were compelled to financially support their select, but often nonviable corporate clients and to withhold financial resources from more promising projects. As a consequence, the restructuring needed for economic growth was neglected. In no small measure, this was a factor in forcing the Czech economy to struggle with recession for too many years while the banking systems and economies of closely related former socialist states, such as Hungary and Poland, moved forward.

Directed lending soon resulted in the deterioration of three of the four large banks and paralyzed the banks' ability to generate economically viable credits for Czech enterprise. The banks themselves were denied the development that would have attended normal and healthy bank-client relationships. They could not realize their potential to develop the intensive client information required for effective production of credit and monitoring of clients' possibilities and progress. In this sense, the Czech Republic was fortunate to have the growing presence of organic foreign banking units that partly filled the credit vacuum left by its disabled banking hegemony. By starting from scratch, however, the foreign banking units were slow to develop the mass required to serve the needs of the many viable projects with economic merit that would have spelled economic success.

The delayed but inevitable privatization of the large banks to foreign institutions with strategic interest in the banks ought to have long-term positive returns. So far, the promise of the acquisitions of CSOB and CS stems from cooperation and synergies between foreign capital and expertise, on the one hand, and Czech managers' cultural understanding and intelligence, on the other.

A common feature of these so far successful banking marriages is the moderate size of the acquiring institutions.[17] To be sure, both are sufficiently deep in capital and technical know-how for the Czech environment. However, neither institution is so large and neither has sufficient depth that, even if they thought it necessary, they could summarily move

17. Both firms are concentrated in small countries: KBC in Belgium and Erste Bank in Austria. Both have some limited worldwide operations but are not ranked among the largest twenty or so international banks.

their own senior staff into the Czech affiliate's critical functions and replace the Czech senior managers. Such a move easily could be a detriment to smooth local operations.

One can only speculate, but had the acquirers been one of the largest five or ten international firms, the firm might have been tempted to supply many senior managers and attempt to replicate the product offerings and operating policies of a more anonymous and monolithic parent corporation. The result would not directly or discretely address the needs of a Czech environment.

Appendix

Bank Classifications, Czech Controlled vs. Foreign Controlled

Czech-controlled banking units
    State institution
        1. Konsolidacni banka
    Banks with dominant Czech control
        1. Komercni banka, a.s.
        2. Expandia banka, a.s.
        3. PLZENSKA BANKA, a.s.
        4. Prvni mestska banka, a.s.
        5. Union banka, a.s.
    Specialized banks with dominant Czech control
        1. Ceska exportni banka, a.s.
        2. Ceskamoravska hypotecni banka, a.s.
        3. Ceskamoravska zarucni a rozvojova banka, akciova spolecnost
        4. Ceskamoravska stavebni sporitelna, akciova spolecnost
        5. CS—stavebni sporitelna a.s.
        6. HYPO stavebni sporitelna a.s.
        7. Vseobecna stavebni sporitelna Komercni banky, a.s.
Foreign-controlled banking units
    Large banks privatized to foreign banks
        1. Ceska sporitelna, a.s. (includes Erste Bank Sparkassen (CR) a.s.)
        2. Ceskoslovenska obchodni banka, a.s.
    Banks originally licensed to nonbank foreign investors
        1. GE Capital Bank, a.s

2. IC Banka, a.s.

3. Interbanka, akciova spolecnost

4. J & T Banka, a.s.

5. Raiffeisenbank, a.s.

6. Zivnoestenska banka, a.s.

7. Wustenrot—stavebni sporitelna a.s.

Banks originally licensed to foreign banks

1. Bank Austria Creditanstalt Czech Republic a.s.

2. BNP–Dresdner Bank (CR), a.s.

3. Citibank, a.s.

4. CREDIT LYONNAIS BANK PRAHA, a.s.

5. HypoVereinsbank CZ a.s.

6. Volksbank CZ, a.s.

7. Raiffeisen stavebni sporitelna a.s.

Branches of foreign banks

1. ABN AMRO BANK, N. V.

2. COMMERZBANK Aktiengesellschaft, pobocka Praha

3. Deutsche Bank Aktiengesellschaft Filiale Prag, organizacni slozka

4. ING Bank N. V.

5. HSBC Bank plc–pobocka Praha

6. RAIFFEISENBANK IM STIFTLAND eG pobocka Cheb, odstepny zavod

7. SOCIETE GENERALE, pobocka Praha

8. Sparkasses Muhlviertel–West banka a.s. pobocka Ceske Budejovice

9. Vseobecna uverova banka, a.s. pobocka Praha

10. Waldviertier Sparkasse von 1842

References

European Union. 1998. *Report of the European Commission.* November 4.

Klaus, Vaclav. 1996. "A Czech Lesson for Europe." *World Link Magazine,* January/February.

Lacina, Vlastislav. 1990. *Formovani Ceskoslovenske ekonomiky, 1918–1923.* Prague: Academia.

Stein, Jonathan. 2000. "National vs. Rational Capitalism: The Privatization of Ceskaslovenska obchodnibanka (CSOB)." Internal document prepared for Ceskaslovenska obchodnibanka.

Tuma, Zdenek. 2000. "The Banking Sector and Its Regulation in the Czech Republic." Czech National Bank presentation. Paris, December.

JENNIFER S. CRYSTAL
B. GERARD DAGES
LINDA S. GOLDBERG

8

Does Foreign Ownership Contribute to Sounder Banks? The Latin American Experience

O ver the latter half of the 1990s, foreign banks significantly increased their ownership shares of emerging market banking systems. This trend reflects a range of factors, perhaps most notably the need for recapitalization of local banking sectors in the wake of crises, but also broader market trends of consolidation, integration, privatization, and liberalization. Increased foreign ownership of emerging market banking systems is particularly striking in Latin America and Eastern Europe, where foreign banks now account for 50 percent or more of system assets in a number of countries. These structural changes could portend significant implications for domestic financial intermediation.

Empirical analysis of the effects of broad foreign participation in emerging market banking systems is relatively limited, however, which in part reflects the recent timing of these developments. A number of recent studies focus on the systemic bank efficiency effects associated with the entry of foreign banks and the resulting increase in competition for domestic banking institutions. In the Latin American context, Martinez Peria and Schmukler conclude that foreign bank entry has been associated with both lowered profit margins and increased efficiency of local banks.[1]

---

1. Martinez Peria and Schmukler (1999). See related analyses by Burdisso, D'Amato, and Molinari (1998); Claessens, Demirguc-Kunt, and Huizinga (1998); and Clarke and others (1999).

A second line of analysis considers differences in lending patterns across domestically owned and foreign-owned banks operating within emerging markets. A study of Argentina and Mexico finds that private foreign banks and private domestic banks had similar lending activities in the 1990s, especially when financial condition was comparable.[2] Foreign banks tended to show stronger, less volatile loan growth during the period, potentially reflecting a more diversified funding base. The finding that foreign banks are relatively stable lenders to emerging markets is supported by a recent analysis of the behavior of international claims by individual U.S. banks.[3] These banks have not been particularly volatile lenders with respect to emerging markets. Indeed, the international claims of U.S. banks generally are considerably more sensitive to U.S. macroeconomic fundamentals than to emerging market fundamentals. Similar types of conclusions on lending are expressed by Peek and Rosengren and by Palmer, who find that foreign bank lending to Latin America was not characterized by cutting and running during recent crises in emerging markets, although cross-border claims declined relative to local claims.[4]

Whether broader strategic and operational differences exist across foreign and domestically owned banks in emerging markets remains an open issue. In this paper, we look for discernible differences between foreign and domestic banks in terms of financial condition and performance.[5] We focus on trends in Latin American banks in the late 1990s, a period characterized not only by substantial foreign presence, but also by cases of significant macroeconomic stress. Our approach is more of an analytical review of relative changes in bank condition than an evaluation of the impact of foreign bank entry on the condition of domestic banks.

After briefly reviewing trends in foreign bank ownership in Latin America, we undertake two related analyses using annual data for the mid-1990s through 2001. First, we examine a broad indicator of institutional strength, namely, Moody's Bank Financial Strength Ratings (BFSRs), for three categories of banks (foreign, private domestic, and government) in seven countries (Argentina, Brazil, Chile, Colombia, Mexico, Peru, and Venezuela). Second, we narrow the analysis to Chile, Colombia, and Argentina, using detailed data from individual bank balance sheets in order to more finely compare specific aspects of bank condition (that is, liquidity, asset quality,

2. Dages, Goldberg, and Kinney (2000).
3. Goldberg (2001).
4. Peek and Rosengren (2000); and Palmer (2000).
5. Banks are considered to be foreign if they are majority owned by foreign shareholders or if foreign shareholders exercise effective management control.

earnings, and capital adequacy) across types of banks during recent periods of financial stress. Our analysis focuses entirely on retail-oriented banks.

We conclude that the condition and performance of foreign banks are not systematically different from their privately owned domestic counterparts in the countries examined, although both are generally superior to government-owned entities. However, the broad measure of financial strength ratings does provide some evidence that local banks acquired by foreign entities fared marginally better than those institutions that remained under domestic control. Our more detailed evaluation of bank condition in three countries yields more interesting results. Foreign banks, particularly those with longer-standing in-country operations, had consistently stronger loan growth, on average, than private domestic banks. Foreign banks established through recent acquisitions undertook more defensive actions and posted the lowest loan and deposit growth rates. We observe more aggressive loan provisioning and higher loan recovery rates by foreign banks across-the-board. Their more proactive recognition of losses adversely affected foreign banks' profitability indicators, although risk-based capital ratios at foreign banks remain above those of private domestic banks. These tendencies may indicate that foreign banks are more willing to tolerate, or can better afford, lower returns in the near term for the sake of building longer-term institutional strength. Finally, foreign banks tended to maintain greater asset liquidity and relied less on deposit financing.

The lack of strong differences in foreign and private domestic bank condition may suggest that there is competitive space for both types of institutions. It may also reflect efforts in the three countries to improve supervision and regulation, promote increased consolidation, and progressively weed out the weakest players. Specific findings on foreign bank behavior, namely, stronger credit growth, more aggressive provisioning behavior, and higher loss-absorption capacity, suggest that foreign ownership can impart important stabilizing influences on domestic banking systems in emerging markets.

Trends in Foreign Bank Ownership in Latin America

Prior to the 1990s, very few foreign banks were present in Latin America, and foreign ownership shares of domestic financial systems were low, reflecting a generally closed regulatory environment for foreign investment in the sector. Domestic financial systems were fragmented, composed of a large

Figure 8-1. *Foreign Share of Latin American Banking System Assets,*
1995 and 2000

Percent

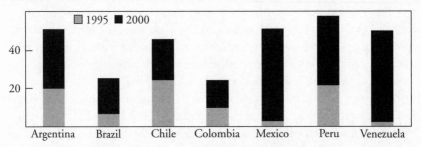

Source: Authors' calculations, based on statistical information from local bank regulators.

number of financial institutions (including a number of marginal players)
and a substantial state bank presence at the federal and regional levels.

Attitudes toward foreign participation in domestic financial sectors evidenced a dramatic shift following a series of banking crises in the mid-
1990s. The need for substantial recapitalization of a number of
institutions, as well as for structural consolidation and rationalization of
the state sector, led to significant liberalization of regulatory limitations on
foreign bank ownership. The sale of intervened institutions, privatizations
of state banks, and some recapitalization efforts of remaining banks triggered a substantial increase in the level of foreign bank ownership in
regional financial institutions.

Large-scale acquisitions began in 1995, when foreign banks acquired
controlling stakes in a number of the region's largest private banks, particularly those with a strong national or regional retail franchise. As a result,
the structure of bank ownership in Latin America changed dramatically
over the second half of the decade. Foreign banks now control majority
shares in nearly all of the larger Latin American financial systems, with the
important exceptions of Brazil and Colombia (see figure 8-1).[6]

This increasing foreign bank presence reduced both private and public
domestic ownership shares throughout the region. As shown in figure 8-2,
foreign entry largely displaced private domestic banks in Chile, Colombia,
Mexico, and Peru. In other countries where public sector banks have historically played a more significant role in the credit intermediation process,
such as in Brazil, foreign entry coincided with large-scale privatization

6. As shown by Peek and Rosengren (2000), data on local exposures of foreign banks understate
overall exposures due to the presence of direct cross-border lending.

Figure 8-2. *Change in Ownership Share of Banking Assets in Latin America, 1995–2000*

Percent of system assets held

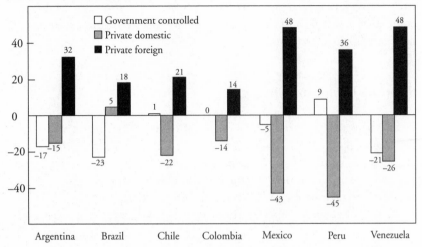

Source: Authors' calculations, based on statistical information from local bank regulators.

efforts. In countries like Argentina and Venezuela, foreign banks increased market share via both significant privatizations of state assets and the purchase of sizable domestic banks from private shareholders.

Liberalization of foreign entry and a renewed commitment to privatizing inefficient public sector banks were only two components of broader financial sector reforms undertaken in the region in the latter half of the 1990s. In a number of countries, these structural reforms were bolstered by the introduction of deposit insurance, the liquidation or consolidation of nonviable entities, and the dedication of substantial resources to strengthening supervisory oversight and the regulatory framework. A number of measures were implemented to enhance prudential supervision and regulation, including the establishment of higher capital requirements, more stringent loan classification and provisioning standards, and increased disclosure requirements.

In summary, regional financial systems experienced a dramatic transformation in the second half of the 1990s. The domestic banking environment underwent a marked consolidation and a significant change in the competitive landscape. Since many of these changes are relatively recent, the full effects of this transformation may not yet be evident. Moreover, recent episodes of weak macroeconomic conditions placed additional pressures on bank balance sheets, which limited lending activities and could constrain the observed differences between foreign and domestic banks. The initial strength of market participants and their capacity to respond to heightened competition will be important determinants of the future evolution of domestic financial systems.

Financial Institution Strength

Financial institution strength is usually thought of both in quantitative terms, namely, a bank's intrinsic financial condition as reflected in its capital, reserves, asset quality, earnings, and liquidity, and in qualitative terms, as evidenced in the underlying quality and effectiveness of bank management, internal controls, and risk management policies and practices. The soundness of financial institutions is founded on a strong balance sheet and strong management; significant deficiencies in either element generally suggest medium-term vulnerability.

Foreign ownership of domestic banks in emerging markets is generally argued to increase overall financial institution strength both quantitatively and qualitatively. Foreign banks are viewed as providing greater access to capital and liquidity and bolstering balance sheet strength. The knowledge, skill, and technology transfer that accompany foreign bank entry are expected to contribute to a stronger control and risk management environment. More broadly, foreign bank presence in emerging market financial systems is said to contribute to an improved financial system infrastructure by encouraging higher standards in auditing, accounting and disclosure, credit risk underwriting and reserving, and supervision.

However, the altered competitive environment may exert pressure on domestically owned banks.[7] If foreign banks cherry-pick the lower-risk clientele from the domestic banks, then the overall asset quality and earnings of domestic banks could decline. The implications for domestic bank financial strength presumably will depend on initial conditions, the overall regulatory environment, and the extent to which domestic banks take measures to retain competitiveness.

The intrinsic strength of a bank is usually evaluated based on a CAMEL framework, which consists of individual assessments of five core aspects of a bank's financial condition and performance: capital adequacy, asset qual-

7. Martinez Peria and Schmukler (1999).

ity, management, earnings, and liquidity. This framework is sometimes modified to include other aspects of a bank's condition or performance. The CAMELS framework, for example, which is employed by federal and state bank regulatory agencies in the United States, also evaluates a bank's sensitivity to market risk, while the CAMELOT framework includes individual components for assessing operational controls and technology.[8] Under such frameworks, individual components are typically evaluated on a rating scale. These individual ratings are then aggregated to arrive at a composite ranking of the institution which usually reflects differential emphasis on individual components and not a simple average. Table 8-1 provides an abbreviated summary of factors considered in a CAMEL analysis and the possible implication of foreign ownership for individual CAMEL components.

This section examines the data to determine whether domestic and foreign banks in Latin America exhibit significant differences on a number of indicators of bank balance sheet strength. We first analyze differences using ratings of institutional strength provided by Moody's and then assess possible differences following a CAMEL-based framework.

Quantitative Differences in the Financial Condition of Domestic and Foreign Banks in Latin America

One broad indicator of the soundness of a bank is its Moody's Bank Financial Strength Rating (BFSR). BFSRs reflect Moody's evaluation of the intrinsic financial strength of a bank on a scale of A to E, with A representing the highest rating, without regard for prospective parent or government support.[9] The exclusion of support is useful in that the BFSR better compares the basic health of domestic and foreign banks: it filters out possible support of domestic banks by the government or support of foreign banks by the parent. BFSRs are viewed as providing a relatively uniform metric over time.

One of the main limitations of BFSRs as a metric of soundness is their timeliness. The administrative process of assigning or revising ratings may cause a lag in adjusting ratings to reflect changes in underlying institutional condition. Additionally, BFSRs cover only a subset of banks in a given country, although they tend to include the largest institutions. Finally,

8. Related issues are covered in Barth, Caprio, and Levine (2001), along with a discussion of a new country-specific database on regulation and supervision of banks around the world.

9. Moody's defines the ratings categories as follows: A, exceptional; B, strong; C, good; D, adequate; and E, very weak. Banks are further distinguished by the assignment of pluses and minuses to their ratings.

Table 8-1. *CAMEL Ratings*

Component	Elements of review	Possible implications of foreign ownership
Capital adequacy	Compliance with regulatory standards; adequacy given nature/level of risk and future expansion plans; quality of bank capital	Improved access to and increased diversification of bank capital, leading to stronger and more stable capital levels
Asset quality	Creditworthiness of bank loans and investments; adequacy of credit policies and procedures; adequacy of loan loss reserve policies and levels; level of impaired assets relative to capital and reserves	Improved credit underwriting and administration, leading to lower nonperforming loan levels and higher reserve coverage of nonperforming loans
Management	Fitness and experience; adequacy of strategic and operating plans; risk management and control environment; succession planning	Secondment of management from head office, coupled with risk management and internal control practices closer to international norms, which generates better corporate governance
Earnings	Quantity and quality; diversification; sensitivity to market risk	Wider variety of products and services, stronger corporate governance, and potentially lower funding costs, leading to higher and more stable bank earnings
Liquidity	Adequacy of asset/liability management policies and procedures; appropriate level of asset and liability liquidity; diversification of funding sources; contingent funding plans	Foreign bank access to parent bank liquidity and international funding markets, together with the higher credit standing of the parent and more sophisticated balance sheet management techniques which leads to better liquidity management

Figure 8-3. *Share of Rated Banks by BFSR Value*

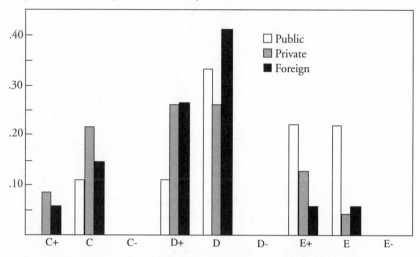

Source: Authors' calculations, based on Moody's rating data as of year-end 2000.

BFSRs only indicate the general health of an institution; they do not identify specific areas of strength or weakness, such as capital or asset quality.

We calculated the average asset-weighted BFSRs for seven Latin American countries, based on sixty-seven rated foreign and domestic banks. Between 1995 and 2001, the average ratings declined for four of the countries (Argentina, D+ to D; Colombia, C to D; Peru, C– to D; and Venezuela, D+ to D), improved for one country (Brazil, D to D+), and either fluctuated or remained unchanged for the other two countries (Mexico, D+ to D– to D; and Chile, C throughout). Historically, no Latin American bank has been rated higher than a C+ (considered by Moody's as good) largely as a result of broad environmental vulnerabilities, particularly in the underlying economies and legal and regulatory infrastructures. Figure 8-3 breaks out the current average BFSR ratings across ownership categories. Public bank ratings are clearly skewed toward the lower end of the rating scale, while private domestic and foreign banks have similar proportions of ratings in the D or higher range.

These data are useful for comparing changes in the ratings of foreign and domestic banks over time. The fact that a large number of rated banks (twenty-eight out of sixty-seven) were acquired by foreigners between 1995 and 2001 creates an opportunity to consider the evolution of the ratings of these banks, both in an absolute sense and relative to other banks at similar points in time. Since banks were acquired at different dates, we date the acquisition year as $T = 0$ and consider the rating changes observed within one, two, three, four, or five years after the acquisition event. We first analyze the path of actual changes in ratings in the aftermath of foreign acquisition of a domestic bank. We then generate a measure of relative ratings changes in which we adjust the ratings changes of a bank for country and year effects that influence all other banks within a country. For example, the relative ratings changes of an Argentine bank acquired in 1997 are the bank's actual rating changes in each year through 2000, minus an unweighted average of the ratings changes of all of those Argentine banks that were rated in 1997 and that can be considered a comparable cohort of institutions.

We compute these ratings paths for banks in each country, as well as an average across countries (unweighted by bank or country size) of the relative ratings changes of acquired banks. The main patterns of ratings results averaged across banks in all seven countries are captured by the cross-country summaries shown in figure 8-4. Each unit on the vertical axis represents a single ratings notch, for example, a move from D to D+ or from C- to C. The dots in the figures represent the average ratings change across all foreign-acquired banks at each of their post-acquisition years. The vertical dashes extending above and below these dots are the maximum and minimum ratings changes observed for any bank at the specified year after acquisition. The right-most entry in these figures, denoted cumulative, represents the average of total changes in ratings for acquired banks across their entire post-acquisition history.

The top panel of figure 8-4 shows that the actual ratings changes of acquired banks within one year of acquisition were either positive (and as high as three notches) or nonexistent. The average change in bank ratings in the first post-acquisition year is a small positive number, reflecting the fact that very few acquired banks had any immediate change in their ratings. Similarly, mean ratings changes were close to zero in all subsequent years, although isolated cases of acquired bank upgrades or downgrades are found in the second and third years after acquisition.[10] The cumulative entry shows the range of total ratings changes of the acquired banks in their entire post-acquisition histories. The basic lesson is that the ratings changes of domestic banks purchased by foreign banks were, more often than not, zero.

10. In Argentina, two of the acquired banks that were rated had downgrades, while the other four banks had no ratings changes in the period following acquisition. In Brazil, seven of the nine acquisitions (all since 1997) had no ratings changes, while the remaining two banks had upgrades of one and three grades, respectively. In Mexico, the three acquired banks all experienced upgrades within one year of acquisition.

Figure 8-4. *Average Absolute and Relative Changes in Moody's BFSRs of Foreign-Acquired Banks in Latin America*[a]

Average absolute changes in acquired bank BFSRs

Number of ratings notches

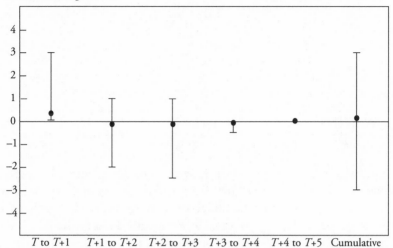

T to T+1   T+1 to T+2   T+2 to T+3   T+3 to T+4   T+4 to T+5   Cumulative

Average changes in acquired bank BFSRs relative to domestic bank BFSRs

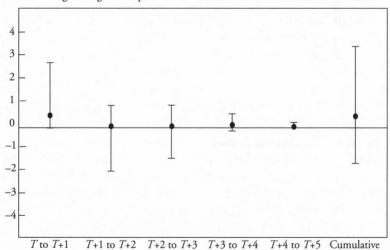

T to T+1   T+1 to T+2   T+2 to T+3   T+3 to T+4   T+4 to T+5   Cumulative

Source: Authors' calculations, based on Moody's ratings data.

a. Based on a total sample of sixty-seven rated banks. Each unit on the vertical axis represents a single rating notch (for example, from D to D+) and *T* is the year since acquisition. Dots indicate average rating changes for foreign-acquired banks; the lines above and below indicate the maximum and minimum rating changes observed in the sample. The cumulative entry is the average of summed rating changes for acquired banks over their post-acquisition history.

Table 8-2. *Cumulative BFSR Changes for Foreign-Acquired Banks*

Country	Actual changes	Foreign-acquired relative to all domestic banks	Foreign-acquired relative to domestic private banks
Argentina	−0.67	−0.33	−0.67
Brazil	0.44	0.63	0.66
Chile	1.00	1.61	1.71
Colombia	−3.00	−0.75	−1.00
Mexico	1.67	1.36	1.36
Peru	0.00	1.75	1.75
Venezuela	−0.25	0.38	0.38
All countries	0.15	0.56	0.50

Source: Authors' calculations, based on Moody's BFSR data.

The bottom panel of the figure shows that foreign-acquired banks performed modestly better than domestic banks, with most of the relative gains occurring soon after the initial acquisition. This overall difference between the results in the two panels arises because domestic banks tended to be downgraded while the foreign banks maintained more stable ratings. Across all countries, the cumulative difference in bank ratings was typically less than a single ratings notch. The magnitude of this relative improvement is similar for foreign bank ratings changes compared with only the private subset of domestic banks.

There were, of course, some differences in the ratings experiences of banks within individual countries. As shown in table 8-2, the relative ratings improvements of foreign banks were particularly strong in Peru, Chile, and Mexico, with small relative improvements for foreign banks in Brazil and Venezuela. The actual and relative ratings changes were negative for Argentina and Colombia, although these negative results may understate the relative gains of the foreign rated banks. Throughout our analysis foreign banks are being compared with the domestic banks that remained in operation (and were rated) in the latter half of the 1990s through 2000. Many of the weaker domestic banks were unrated and some closed or changed ownership status during this period, which biases the empirical results against foreign banks.

Bank Performance by CAMEL Components

This section analyzes the financial condition of foreign and domestic banks in more detail, using a CAMEL-based approach. We selected specific Latin

American countries based on three criteria: a sufficient mixture of foreign and domestically owned banks, a recent period of stress on the banking system, and data availability. Three countries and time frames satisfy these criteria, namely, Chile, Colombia, and Argentina in the post-1997 period.

For each country, we use publicly available, institution-specific data from supervisory authorities and Moody's Investors Service to calculate specific indicators of bank condition and performance across three broad categories of bank ownership: foreign, private domestic, and government. We also evaluate trends in these indicators across two subsets of foreign ownership: banks that were acquired by foreign shareholders relatively recently (since 1995) and foreign banks that have maintained significant local operations for a more extended period of time. We compare these foreign banks to the local banks that remained under domestic control. Throughout our analysis, results pertaining to foreign, private domestic, and government banks are exhibited in panel A of the tables, while the subsets of foreign ownership (recently acquired and longer standing) can be found in panel B.

Our analysis focuses on the twenty-five to thirty largest banks operating in each country, covering between 80 and 100 percent of banking system assets in the respective countries. Since we are primarily interested in evaluating commercial banks, we exclude from this sample institutions not actively engaged in the retail banking market (that is, those banks with deposits and loans representing less than 25 percent of assets); very small banks (defined as accounting for less than 1 percent of sample loans); and other financial institutions with unique charters and operational characteristics (such as credit cooperatives, national mortgage banks, consumer finance companies, and nonbanks).

We use unweighted averages within and across bank ownership categories to better evaluate the effects of foreign ownership at the institutional level. Results should therefore not be interpreted as precise indicators of the level or trend of the overall condition and performance of the banking sector. Moreover, bank financial results are prepared in accordance with local accounting and regulatory standards and are not necessarily comparable internationally or across the three countries. Individual banks or ownership types may also apply existing standards more or less rigorously.

For each country, we begin with an overview of the banking system and a description of the sample used for the analysis. We then outline sectoral trends in four categories: balance sheet structure and liquidity, asset quality, earnings, and capital adequacy. Finally, we sum up the country experience with an overall evaluation.

THE CHILEAN EXPERIENCE. Following a period of crisis in the early 1980s, the condition and performance of Chile's financial sector improved substantially on the back of enhanced regulatory and supervisory oversight, combined with sustained economic growth and relative stability. As a result, bank penetration is now the highest in Latin America—credit to the private sector represents almost 70 percent of GDP—and the sector is considered one of the soundest in the region. The effects of the crisis lingered well into the 1990s, however, particularly in the form of large dividend payments to the central bank to service bailout costs.[11]

The mid-1990s witnessed a period of escalating bank penetration, consolidation, and foreign entry. Real deposit and loan growth rates averaged above 10 percent annually, with banks increasingly focused on the consumer segment, where loan growth peaked at an annual rate above 30 percent in 1996. A series of mergers and acquisitions concentrated bank ownership, and the top five banks now control 60 percent of bank assets, compared with 45 percent in 1995.

Foreign banks have historically maintained more of a presence in Chile than in the rest of the region, controlling 25 percent of bank assets in 1995. Penetration accelerated in the late 1990s, however, with Spanish Banco Santander's purchase of fifth-largest Banco Osorno y La Union in 1996 and its subsequent acquisition of second-largest Banco Santiago from the Luksic group shortly after Santander's 1999 merger with Central Hispanoamericano. During this same time period, Banco BHIF was acquired by Spain's Banco Bilbao Vizcaya Argentaria (BBVA), and Banco Sud Americano was bought out by Canada's Scotiabank. These acquisitions, combined with organic growth, essentially doubled foreign participation in the Chilean financial sector between 1995 and 2000 to just under 50 percent. Roughly two-thirds of this foreign presence is attributable to Spanish banks and one-quarter to U.S. and Canadian institutions.

The Chilean economy began slowing in 1998 in response to the onset of the crisis in Asia (the destination of one-third of Chile's exports), historical lows for copper prices, and the adverse effects of El Niño on energy and agricultural sectors. A deterioration in global liquidity conditions following the Russian financial crisis and sharp domestic monetary tightening to support the peso further contributed to economic deceleration, with recession setting in by year-end 1998. These events adversely affected the operating environment and performance of Chile's banks. Although real GDP growth recovered in 2000, domestic demand and investment growth

11. Most of these debts have since been settled at substantial discounts to face value.

remain weak by historical standards, and banks have yet to evidence a recovery in credit activity. Below we evaluate the condition and performance of Chilean banks across ownership categories throughout this recent period.[12]

The Chilean banks that we evaluate account for virtually 100 percent of system assets. The number of foreign-controlled entities ranges from thirteen to fifteen, representing 21 to 48 percent of sample assets in any given year. Of these, up to ten (4.5 percent of system assets) are excluded because of business orientation or size. Of the remaining foreign banks in our sample, four (equivalent to almost 40 percent of sample assets) were acquired in 1995 or later and are thus considered to be recent acquisitions, and three (representing approximately 10 percent of sample assets) have maintained local operations for an extended period of time.

Among domestic banks, the number of privately owned institutions ranges from nine to eleven (38 to 64 percent of sample assets). In any given year, at most two institutions accounting for 0.6 percent of sample assets are excluded owing to business orientation or size. The Banco del Estado is the only government-owned bank operating in Chile. Over the sample period, this bank consistently ranked second in asset size, and its share of sample assets declined only slightly, from 15.2 to 13.6 percent. The Banco del Estado is largely excluded from the following analysis by virtue of its unique mission to provide financing to underserviced sectors.

We start the analysis with a review of balance sheet structure and liquidity. Foreign banks in Chile, on average, tend to rely less on deposits for funding, maintain a higher capital cushion, and dedicate a greater proportion of assets to lower-risk, liquid investments than do domestic banks (see table 8-3, panel A). Relative to privately held domestic banks, in particular, foreign banks dedicate significantly less of their balance sheet to lending activities. These behaviors may still be evolving, however. Foreign banks appear to have aggressively targeted growth in deposit market share, for example, as evidenced by an average annual growth rate of 31 percent over the sample period—significantly higher than private or public domestic banks.[13] Furthermore, foreign bank holdings of relatively lower-cost demand deposits are in line with those of their private domestic counterparts. Foreign banks also increased their loan portfolios marginally faster, on average, than domestic banks over the sample period, although sub-

12. The statistics discussed in this section are compiled using a variety of sources, including the Chilean banking superintendency and Moody's Investors Service (various years).
13. Average growth rates are in nominal terms and are adjusted for acquisition effects during the sample period.

Table 8-3. *Summary Balance Sheet Structure of Chilean Banks*
Percent of assets

| | Panel A: All banks by type of ownership[a] | | | Panel B: Private banks by type of ownership[b] | | |
| | Foreign- | Domestic | | Recently acquired | Existing | Domestic |
Item	owned	private	Government	foreign	foreign	private
Assets						
Liquid assets						
1997	34	24	40	19	38	26
2000	33	25	34	28	38	25
Loans						
1997	67	79	60	83	62	77
2000	61	73	59	67	54	73
Liabilities						
Total deposits						
1997	39	54	61	51	34	56
2000	45	53	55	45	44	53
Demand deposits						
1997	11	14	21	14	10	15
2000	14	14	18	14	14	14
Capital						
1997	11	6	6	7	12	6
2000	8	7	5	7	10	7
Loan and deposit trends						
Average annual loan growth[c]	14	12	13	3	29	15
Average annual deposit growth[c]	31	14	9	6	64	18
Loans/deposits						
1997	176	147	98	163	186	138
2000	137	139	108	148	122	139

Source: Authors' calculations, based on data from the Superintendencia de Bancos e Instituciones Financieras de Chile (SBIF).
a. Banks sorted by ownership status at year-end 1997 and 2000.
b. Historical data on banks sorted by ownership status as of year-end 2000.
c. 1997 through 2000, in percent.

stantially less than deposits, leading to enhanced liquidity. As a result of both acquisitions and organic growth, foreign banks' share of sample deposits and loans grew to just over 40 percent in 2000, from less than 20 percent in 1997.

Figure 8-5. *Average Loan Growth of Chilean Banks*

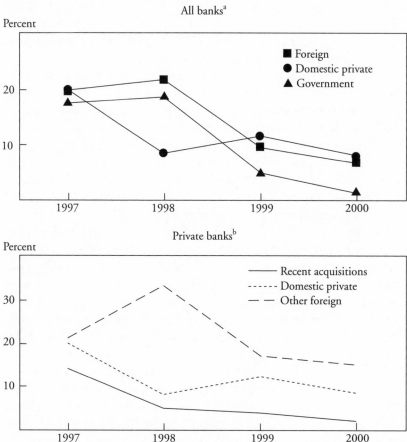

All banks[a]

Percent

Foreign
Domestic private
Government

Private banks[b]

Percent

Recent acquisitions
Domestic private
Other foreign

Source: Authors' calculations, based on data from the Superintendencia de Bancos e Instituciones Financieras de Chile (SBIF).

a. Banks sorted by ownership status at year-end 1997, 1998, 1999, and 2000.

b. Historical data on banks sorted by ownership status as of year-end 2000.

Over this time period, balance sheet structure and liquidity trends demonstrate important differences across banks recently acquired by foreign shareholders, foreign banks that have been operating in Chile for an extended period of time, and domestically owned banks. Banks acquired over the past five years had, on average, a much sharper shift in the asset mix away from loans and toward more liquid holdings (see table 8-3, panel B). At the same time, these acquired banks reduced their reliance on deposit-based financing, while other foreign banks with a long history in the

Chilean market sharply expanded deposit share. These distinct behaviors are clearly evident in figures 8-5 and 8-6, in which the average loan and deposit growth rates of recently acquired foreign banks contrast with much higher rates for longer-present foreign banks, as well as with the more moderate growth of private domestic entities.

These results are consistent with an inward management focus in the wake of large-scale acquisitions, as attention turns toward merger integration and absorption issues such as standardizing risk management and operating procedures, integrating technology platforms, and adapting management information systems. The runoff in loans as a proportion of average assets is similarly consistent with post-acquisition balance sheet cleansing. These findings also suggest that foreign banks that rely primarily on organic growth may feel the pressure to build market share and respond aggressively to industry consolidations.

Asset quality deteriorated over the sample period, as the stock of nonperforming loans more than doubled in nominal terms. However, nonperforming loans as a share of total loans remained broadly manageable at just under 2 percent of sample loans, on average.[14] Credit portfolio deterioration at private sector banks appears to have proceeded at a similar pace, regardless of bank ownership (see table 8-4). Grouping banks into peer groups with similar market orientation and penetration yields similar results; this suggests broad-based deterioration across borrowers.

However, institutions acquired by new foreign owners over the past five years had a somewhat stronger rate and level of asset quality deterioration. This may reflect either the purchase of banks of lesser health or a more proactive management of credit risks. Foreign banks with more established local operations maintained notably stronger asset quality ratios than private domestic banks during this economic downturn, which could reflect a more conservative loan orientation or credit risk management. The fact that these established foreign banks were also the most aggressive provisioners for potential loan losses over the sample period supports this argument. Both acquired and established foreign banks generally provisioned more heavily than their domestic counterparts. Perhaps in reflection of this activity, foreign banks—in particular more established foreign banks—outperformed their domestic peers in recovering losses. Over the sample

14. Chilean banks do not report as nonperforming the full balance of loans past-due, defined as at least ninety days delinquent on payment of principal or interest. Reported nonperforming loans include only the payments that are actually overdue, unless legal restitution has been initiated for the entire balance.

Figure 8-6. *Average Deposit Growth of Chilean Banks*

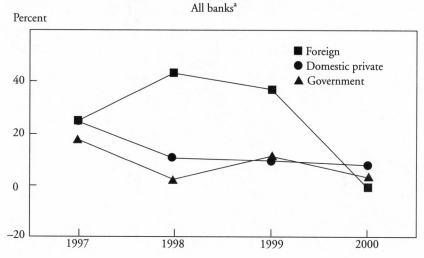

All banks[a]

Percent

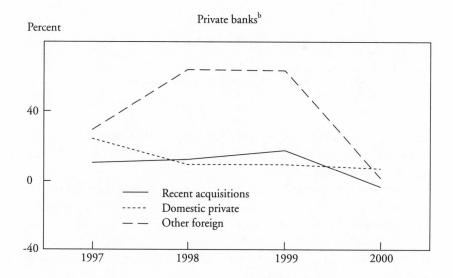

Private banks[b]

Percent

Source: Authors' calculations, based on data from the Superintendencia de Bancos e Instituciones Financieras de Chile (SBIF).

a. Banks sorted by ownership status at year-end 1997, 1998, 1999, and 2000.

b. Historical data on banks sorted by ownership status at year-end 2000.

Table 8-4. *Selected Average Asset Quality Indicators of Chilean Banks*
Percent of total loans, except as indicated

| | Panel A: All banks by type of ownership[a] | | | Panel B: Private banks by type of ownership[b] | | |
Item	Foreign-owned	Domestic private	Government	Recently acquired foreign	Existing foreign	Domestic private
Nonperforming loans						
1997	0.7	0.8	2.2	1.0	0.6	0.7
2000	1.9	2.0	1.3	2.3	1.5	2.0
Provisions						
1997	0.9	0.9	1.1	1.2	0.7	0.8
2000	1.9	1.4	1.1	1.6	2.3	1.4
Recoveries						
1997	0.2	0.2	0.6	0.3	0.1	0.2
2000	0.7	0.2	0.6	0.5	1.0	0.2
Loan loss reserves[c]						
1997	216	156	101	125	248	168
2000	181	192	159	126	254	192

Source: Authors' calculations, based on data from the Superintendencia de Bancos e Instituciones Financieras de Chile (SBIF).

a. Banks sorted by ownership status at year-end 1997 and 2000.

b. Historical data on banks sorted by ownership status as of year-end 2000.

c. Percent of nonperforming loans.

period, foreign banks as a group recovered 1.8 percent of average loans, with longer-standing foreign banks recovering 3.8 percent, while private domestic banks recovered 0.8 percent.

Banks across all ownership categories consistently maintained adequate reserves to cover potential losses embedded in reported nonperforming loans, although foreign banks with longer-standing operations clearly stand out. A stable reserve trend, on average, at recently acquired entities—despite rising provisioning activity—points to a relatively more aggressive approach to charging off problem loans.[15]

With regard to earnings, there is no clear trend in the overall profitability of either privately held domestic banks or foreign-controlled banks during the sample period. Both experienced downturns, with domestic banks

15. While we do not have institution-specific charge-off ratios for the sample set, a review of publicly released financial statements of a subset of the larger banks shows charge-offs as a proportion of average loans rising noticeably in the wake of foreign acquisitions.

Figure 8-7. *Return on Average Assets of Chilean Banks*

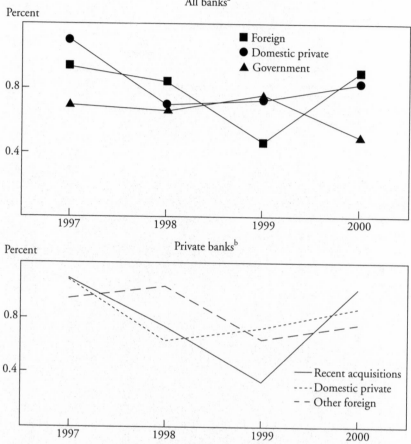

All banks[a]

Percent

Foreign
Domestic private
Government

0.8

0.4

1997   1998   1999   2000

Percent

Private banks[b]

0.8

0.4

—— Recent acquisitions
---- Domestic private
– – Other foreign

1997   1998   1999   2000

Source: Authors' calculations, based on data from the Superintendencia de Bancos e Instituciones Financieras de Chile (SBIF).

a. Banks sorted by ownership status at year-end 1997, 1998, 1999, and 2000.

b. Historical data on banks sorted by ownership status at year-end 2000.

more rapidly exhibiting the effects of a deterioration in operating conditions (see figure 8-7). Foreign bank profitability deteriorated more sharply than that of domestic banks from 1997 to 1999, but it then rebounded more quickly. This reflects higher provisioning expenses in the wake of acquisitions in 1998 and 1999 and possibly also a higher volume of market-related activities (evident in operating income and expense ratios; see table 8-5). Netting out these effects yields broadly similar operating income and expense ratios across banks.

Table 8-5. *Selected Average Profitability Indicators for Chilean Banks*

Percent of average assets

	Panel A: All banks by type of ownership[a]			Panel B: Private banks by type of ownership[b]		
Item	Foreign-owned	Domestic private	Government	Recently acquired foreign	Existing foreign	Domestic private
Income						
Net interest income						
1997	3.2	3.3	3.5	3.8	2.9	3.1
1998	3.1	3.5	4.1	3.8	2.7	3.5
1999	3.6	3.4	3.6	3.5	3.7	3.4
2000	3.7	3.7	3.6	3.5	4.0	3.7
Noninterest operating income						
1997	8.9	3.2	1.6	5.8	10.3	1.9
1998	9.9	4.4	2.3	7.5	13.5	2.6
1999	13.3	3.6	2.3	6.2	22.9	3.6
2000	14.2	4.3	2.3	10.3	19.4	4.3
Expense						
Provisions						
1997	0.7	0.7	0.7	1.0	0.5	0.6
1998	1.3	1.2	1.0	1.5	1.1	1.1
1999	1.9	1.5	0.8	1.8	2.1	1.5
2000	1.2	1.1	0.7	1.1	1.3	1.1
Noninterest operating expense						
1997	10.6	5.5	4.5	8.2	11.9	4.2
1998	10.6	6.4	4.9	9.4	13.5	4.6
1999	15.2	5.4	4.8	8.2	24.6	5.4
2000	16.1	6.0	4.5	12.0	21.6	6.0

Source: Authors' calculations, based on data from the Superintendencia de Bancos e Instituciones Financieras de Chile (SBIF).

a. Banks sorted by ownership status at year-end 1997, 1998, 1999, and 2000.

b. Historical data on banks sorted by ownership status at year-end 2000.

On average, banks that were recently acquired exhibited declining net interest margins, while those of longer-established foreign and domestic banks increased. This is consistent with the previously discussed loan and deposit growth trends. While all banks witnessed an increase in other operating revenues, the trend was particularly pronounced at foreign banks, although again, it was largely market driven. Net operating income exhibited broadly similar trends. All banks also recorded net efficiency gains over

Table 8-6. *Risk-Based Capital Ratios of Chilean Banks*
Percent of risk-weighted assets

Item	Panel A: All banks by type of ownership[a]			Panel B: Private banks by type of ownership[b]		
	Foreign-owned	Domestic private	Government	Recently acquired foreign	Existing foreign	Domestic private
Tier 1 capital						
1998	10.57	6.27	5.88	7.8	11.80	6.06
2000	9.31	6.67	5.79	7.39	11.90	6.67
Total capital						
1998	17.23	10.29	11.35	12.80	19.40	9.90
2000	15.41	11.14	12.70	13.20	18.40	11.14

Source: Superintendencia de Bancos e Instituciones Financieras Chile (SBIF).
a. Banks sorted by ownership status at year-end 1998 and 2000.
b. Historical data on banks sorted by ownership status as of year-end 2000.

the sample period, which were slightly but not significantly more pronounced at recently acquired banks.

Turning now to capital adequacy, foreign banks began the sample period with a higher ratio of capital to assets, and despite a moderate deterioration they remain broadly better capitalized than privately held domestic banks (see table 8-3, above). Stronger capital ratios are, however, concentrated in the foreign banks with a longer local presence. Recently acquired banks exhibit similar capital levels to domestic banks, suggesting either that ownership changes were not accompanied by significant recapitalization or that new capital was used to effect balance sheet cleansing.

A similar trend is evident in the evolution of risk-based capital ratios over the sample period (see table 8-6). In aggregate, foreign banks had sharply stronger, albeit decreasing, tier 1 and total risk-based capital ratios than domestic banks, which reflects their relatively lower-risk balance sheet structures. Again, stronger capital ratios were, on average, concentrated in those foreign banks that have been active in the local market for an extended period of time.

The disparity between foreign and domestic capital ratios may be explained, in part, by constraints on domestic banks' capital generation throughout the early 1990s, stemming from high dividend payout ratios on subordinated debt inherited from the crisis of the early 1980s. Domestic banks have since taken steps to boost capital adequacy levels to conform with 1997 banking reform legislation that, among other things, adopted the

8 percent risk-weighted capital standard advocated by the Basel Committee on Banking Supervision. As a result, privately owned domestic banks, on average, comfortably exceed minimum regulatory standards for capital adequacy.

Our overall assessment is that Chile's financial sector as a whole appears to have weathered the recent economic downturn relatively well, without clear-cut distinctions in quality or trend across ownership types. Domestic and foreign banks do exhibit important differences in operating behavior, however, which could point toward longer-term institutional trends. These differences are particularly pronounced when we evaluate condition and performance across banks that were recently acquired by foreign entities, foreign banks that have been active in the local market for an extended period of time, and private domestic banks.

Relative to domestic banks, foreign banks generally rely less on deposit-based financing (although foreign banks that are not absorbed by merger integration issues appear to be trying to change this); dedicate less of their balance sheet to lending; reduce deposit and loan growth less as macroeconomic conditions deteriorate; provision for potential loan losses (and possibly charge off bad loans) more aggressively, despite a similar degree of deterioration in nonperforming loan ratios; are more successful at recovering charged-off loans; maintain a deeper capital cushion; and appear more adept at diversifying revenue streams. However, foreign banks do not appear to be in substantially overall sounder condition than their domestic counterparts, which may reflect a supervisory framework geared toward the active monitoring of credit risks.

THE COLOMBIAN EXPERIENCE. As in the case of Chile, a banking crisis in the early 1980s triggered structural and regulatory reforms that significantly enhanced the condition and performance of the Colombian banking system.[16] Beginning in the early 1990s, Colombia implemented a number of measures to increase competition and efficiency in the financial sector as part of a broader program of economic liberalization and market reform. These measures included interest rate liberalization, a reduction in barriers to entry in Colombia's historically segmented financial system, the opening of the sector to majority ownership of banks by foreign financial institutions, and a reduction in financial intermediation taxes such as reserve requirements. These measures, coupled with strong domestic demand, contributed to rapid real credit growth of more than 20 percent

16. The statistics discussed in this section are compiled using a variety of sources, including the Colombian banking superintendency and Moody's Investors Service (various years).

a year from 1993 to 1995 and a decline in intermediation spreads attributable to heightened competition, in part reflecting increased foreign entry.

This period also witnessed substantial measures to enhance prudential regulation and supervision, including the adoption of Basel capital adequacy standards in 1994 and a range of measures to tighten requirements on loan loss provisioning, disclosure and consolidated reporting, and loan classification. Colombia's supervisory and regulatory regime is now considered one of the strongest in the region and is credited with fostering more prudent risk taking by private banks.

Notwithstanding these measures, the Colombian banking sector has faced significant difficulties in recent years. Restrictive monetary policy in defense of the currency in late 1998, a severe recession in 1999, significant declines in the real estate market, and local governments' debt-servicing problems all weighed on the sector's condition and performance. Such pressures were especially acute in the state-owned, savings and loan, and cooperative sectors, which together represent more than one-third of the financial system. Roughly fifty institutions were intervened, merged, or liquidated. These actions formed part of an overall program to contain the crisis; other measures involved recapitalizing the deposit insurance corporation, providing mortgage borrower relief, reforming the troubled cooperative sector, and recapitalizing the banking sector through direct grants to state-owned banks and soft financing to private banks. The costs of the overall rescue program have been estimated at more than 8 percent of GDP, before recoveries.[17]

The pressures were generally less intense for the top twenty-five banks in the sample (with the notable exceptions of the large state-owned banks) as a result of their better credit risk management and high initial capital levels. Still, even these banks initially had relatively low coverage ratios that needed to be bolstered through substantial provisions, leading in some cases to participation in the government support program.

Foreign banks have entered Colombia through a variety of routes, including the reacquisition of previously held majority ownership stakes (which were limited in the 1970s by joint venture requirements that were lifted in the early 1990s), de novo entry, and other acquisitions.[18] The largest transactions involved the acquisition of Banco Ganadero by BBVA in 1996 and of Banco Comercial Antioqueno by Banco Santander in 1997.

17. Swabey, Hernandez, and Edkins (2000).
18. See Barajas, Steiner, and Salazar (2000) for further discussion of the history of foreign bank ownership in Colombia and an assessment of the impact of foreign banks on the overall banking sector.

These acquisitions, together with organic growth by foreign banks, more than doubled the share of foreign ownership of system assets to approximately 24 percent. Roughly 60 percent of this foreign presence is attributable to Spanish banks and one-quarter to U.S. banks.

The share of sample assets under government ownership is similar to that of foreign banks (roughly 20 percent), and the Colombian authorities have committed to privatizing most institutions over the short term. In contrast to Chile and Argentina, overall concentration ratios, as measured by the share of banking system assets held by the top five banks, remained fairly steady between 1995 and 2000 (at approximately 45 percent), although the non-bank financial sector has undergone notable consolidation in recent years.

The larger Colombian banks that we evaluate account for 90 percent of banking system assets. The number of foreign banks is ten, or 25–28 percent of sample assets. Of these, up to four are excluded from the detailed analysis in any given year, either because they are not active in the retail banking market or because they are so small as to be irrelevant for a broad system discussion. These exclusions account for less than 3 percent of sample assets. Of the remaining six foreign banks (15 percent of sample assets), two are considered recent acquisitions (since 1996), and four have maintained local operations for an extended period of time (8 percent of sample assets).

The number of privately owned domestic banks ranges from eleven to twelve, or 53–55 percent of sample assets. In any given year, only one institution accounting for less than 1 percent of sample assets is excluded owing to business orientation or size. The analysis also covers several state-owned banks, which account for 18–19 percent of sample assets. In any given year, at most two state-owned banks are excluded, representing not more than 3 percent of sample assets.

As in the case of Chile, foreign banks generally rely less on deposits for funding, hold a relatively comparable share of lower-cost demand deposits to assets, and dedicate a greater proportion of their balance sheet to lower-risk, more liquid investments than do private domestic banks (see table 8-7). In contrast to Chile, however, foreign and private domestic banks operating in Colombia hold relatively comparable shares of loans, at least relative to total assets. Foreign banks also appear to generally have lower balance sheet liquidity than private domestic banks, as measured by loan-to-deposit ratios. Capital ratios are high at both private domestic and foreign banks, while they are significantly lower at state banks. Average loan growth in the period was slightly higher at foreign banks than at private

Table 8-7. *Summary Balance Sheet Structure of Colombian Banks*
Percent of assets

	Panel A: All banks by type of ownership[a]			Panel B: Private banks by type of ownership[b]		
Item	Foreign-owned	Domestic private	Government	Recently acquired foreign	Existing foreign	Domestic private
Assets						
Liquid assets						
1997	22	19	16	22	23	19
2000	25	22	31	37	19	22
Loans						
1997	64	63	64	64	66	63
2000	66	63	33	53	73	63
Liabilities						
Total deposits						
1997	55	59	59	56	57	59
2000	60	70	63	63	59	70
Demand deposits						
1997	16	12	17	18	15	12
2000	16	17	17	17	15	17
Capital						
1997	13	14	8	16	13	14
2000	10	12	5	10	11	12
Loan and deposit trends						
Average annual loan growth[c]	24	20	-1	9	32	20
Average annual deposit growth[c]	28	27	12	23	31	27
Loans/deposits						
1997	116	108	109	114	118	108
2000	108	88	53	84	123	88

Source: Authors' calculations, based on data from the Superintendencia Bancaria de Colombia.
a. Banks sorted by ownership status at year-end 1997 and 2000.
b. Historical data on banks sorted by ownership status as of year-end 2000.
c. 1997 through 2000, in percent.

domestic banks, while average deposit growth was comparable at both sets of institutions.

Foreign bank trends were quite different, however, between those banks that entered the market through recent acquisitions and those with exist-

Figure 8-8. *Average Loan Growth of Colombian Banks*

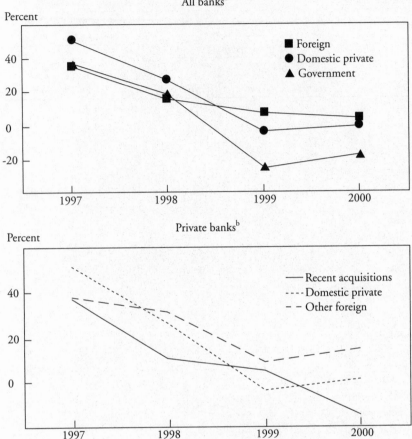

Source: Authors' calculations, based on data from the Superintendencia Bancaria de Colombia.
a. Banks sorted by ownership status at year-end 1997, 1998, 1999, and 2000.
b. Historical data on banks sorted by ownership status as of year-end 2000.

ing operations. Acquired banks demonstrate more defensive behavior, with sharply lower average loan growth, a declining share of loans in their asset mix, significant buildup in liquid assets, and improving loan-to-deposit ratios. These findings are consistent with the Chilean experience, and they suggest that acquired banks were more focused on consolidation than growth during the period. Capital levels also declined more sharply at acquired banks. Foreign banks with existing operations, however, were relatively more growth-oriented, exhibiting higher average loan growth than

Figure 8-9. *Average Deposit Growth of Colombian Banks*

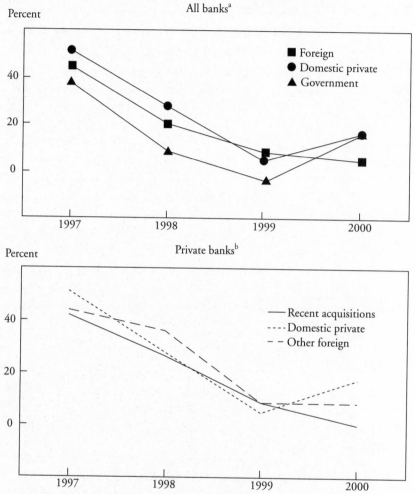

Percent

All banks[a]

■ Foreign
● Domestic private
▲ Government

Percent

Private banks[b]

—— Recent acquisitions
----Domestic private
– – Other foreign

Source: Authors' calculations, based on data from the Superintendencia Bancaria de Colombia.
a. Banks sorted by ownership status at year-end 1997, 1998, 1999, and 2000.
b. Historical data on banks sorted by ownership status as of year-end 2000.

either acquired banks or private domestic banks, as well as a slight deterioration in liquidity ratios.

Breaking out relative loan and deposit growth across the sample period shows these divergent responses more clearly, especially when considered in combination with the onset of difficult economic conditions (see figures 8-8 and 8-9). Foreign banks overall show less dramatic declines in loan growth

Table 8-8. *Selected Average Asset Quality Indicators of Colombian Banks*
Percent of total loans, except as indicated

	Panel A: All banks by type of ownership[a]			Panel B: Private banks by type of ownership[b]		
Item	Foreign- owned	Domestic private	Government	Recently acquired foreign	Existing foreign	Domestic private
Nonperforming loans						
1997	3.4	3.8	8.3	4.8	2.8	3.8
2000	4.8	6.6	9.7	4.7	4.8	6.6
Provisions						
1997	3.1	2.9	4.4	4.1	3.2	2.9
2000	4.8	4.5	6.4	7.8	3.4	4.5
Recoveries						
1998[c]	1.7	1.6	2.5	2.8	1.3	1.6
2000	4.1	3.3	1.8	5.3	3.5	3.3
Loan loss reserves[d]						
1997	84	60	39	79	98	60
2000	138	86	87	220	96	86

Source: Authors' calculations, based on data from the Superintendencia Bancaria de Colombia.
a. Banks sorted by ownership status at year-end 1997 and 2000.
b. Historical data on banks sorted by ownership status as of year-end 2000.
c. Comparable 1997 recoveries data not available.
d. Percent of nonperforming loans.

than do private domestic banks, although recently acquired banks show steep declines, on average. A notable distinction across banks is seen in 2000, when loan growth was negative at recently acquired banks, basically flat at domestic banks, and significantly positive at existing foreign banks, notwithstanding relatively stronger growth in deposits at private domestic banks.

As noted above, all institution types witnessed deterioration in asset quality over the period. As shown in table 8-8, nonperforming loan ratios rose across all types of banks, with more notable deterioration at state and private domestic banks and modest deterioration at foreign banks.[19] Both foreign and private domestic banks made aggressive provisions to address asset quality problems. Reserve coverage of nonperforming loans improved markedly over the period for both types of banks, although foreign banks showed the most dramatic increase: at year-end 2000 coverage was sub-

19. The ratios provided here for sample endpoints obscure the sharp rise in nonperforming loan ratios at state banks over the period. Average reported nonperforming loan ratios for state banks peaked at 23 percent, prior to recapitalization and clean-up of the sector.

stantially higher for foreign banks than for private domestic banks, at 138 percent versus 86 percent. Foreign banks also reported higher recoveries than private domestic banks over the 1998–2000 period (11 percent of loans versus 7 percent, respectively), which may indicate more aggressive and effective workout skills—or simply a higher average level of charge-offs. Limited availability of charge-off data precludes a more comprehensive discussion of asset quality trends, but more aggressive provisioning and recoveries at foreign banks are suggestive of more aggressive charge-off policies.

Table 8-8 identifies important differences in the performance of recently acquired and existing foreign banks. Acquired banks began the period with the highest average problem loan burden, and they made significantly higher provisions (and presumably charge-offs) to address problem loans. Although nonperforming loan ratios were basically unchanged over the period, reserve coverage improved dramatically to more than 200 percent. Existing foreign banks reported slightly higher provisions than private domestic banks over the period, maintaining higher reserve coverage and containing increases in bad loan ratios.[20]

With regard to earnings, the period of economic stress was generally marked by a deterioration in revenue streams, increasing provisions, and high noninterest expense, which contributed to declining and in some cases highly negative earnings as shown in figure 8-10. These findings are particularly true for state banks, but also for foreign banks.

A comparison of individual income statement items across private domestic and foreign banks suggests that foreign banks had weaker earnings across all major categories of revenues and expenses and were more negatively affected by the economic downturn (see table 8-9). On average, foreign banks show weaker interest margins and noninterest income, together with higher overhead and provisioning expenses. Acquired banks evidence the weakest results in terms of net interest margins, provisioning expense, and noninterest operating expense. Weaker interest income no doubt reflects the impact of higher relative problem loans, lower loan growth, and the significant buildup in liquid assets over the period, while higher noninterest operating expenses may reflect acquisition-related restructuring costs.

An analysis of capital adequacy reveals that the very high capital levels of both private domestic and foreign banks at the beginning of the period were important for maintaining financial institution soundness (see table 8-10, below). State bank capital levels, which on average turned negative in 1998,

---

20. The provisioning ratios provided here for sample endpoints do not fully represent average provision activity over the four-year period.

Figure 8-10. *Return on Average Assets of Colombian Banks*

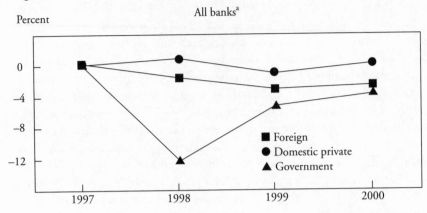

All banks[a]

Percent

■ Foreign
● Domestic private
▲ Government

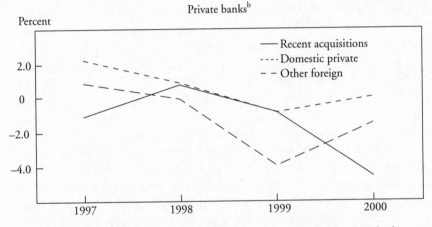

Private banks[b]

Percent

——— Recent acquisitions
- - - - Domestic private
– – Other foreign

Source: Authors' calculations, based on data from the Superintendencia Bancaria de Colombia.
a. Banks sorted by ownership status at year-end 1997, 1998, 1999, and 2000.
b. Historical data on banks sorted by ownership status as of year-end 2000.

benefited substantially from a large recapitalization in 1999, although capital levels declined further with subsequent losses. Capital injections during the period helped to maintain capital at robust levels for private and
foreign banks. However, foreign bank losses were larger, on average, than
those of domestic banks, and their capital ratios declined relatively more
over the period.

A review of risk-based capital ratios across the three ownership classes
portrays a somewhat different story, as shown in table 8-10. All entities

Table 8-9. *Selected Average Profitability Indicators for Colombian Banks*
Percent of average assets

Item	Panel A: All banks by type of ownership[a]			Panel B: Private banks by type of ownership[b]		
	Foreign-owned	Domestic private	Government	Recently acquired foreign	Existing foreign	Domestic private
Income						
Net interest income						
1997	6.7	6.9	6.9	7.1	7.6	6.9
1998	5.1	7.2	3.2	7.4	5.5	7.2
1999	5.0	5.2	2.2	4.7	5.2	5.2
2000	4.8	5.9	2.0	4.0	5.1	5.9
Noninterest operating income						
1997	...	...	...	...	...	...
1998	6.0	5.8	2.7	7.2	6.3	5.8
1999	6.6	5.3	4.7	7.1	6.3	5.3
2000	4.6	5.5	6.5	5.3	4.3	5.5
Expense						
Provisions						
1997	2.5	2.3	4.3	3.3	2.5	2.3
1998	2.6	2.6	5.8	3.5	2.0	2.6
1999	6.2	4.3	5.2	5.3	6.6	4.3
2000	3.6	3.5	3.1	5.4	2.7	3.5
Noninterest operating expense						
1997	...	...	...	...	...	...
1998	9.8	9.6	12.6	10.8	9.4	9.6
1999	9.7	8.2	7.5	10.1	9.5	8.2
2000	9.6	9.5	8.5	10.2	9.3	9.5

Source: Authors' calculations, based on data from the Superintendencia Bancaria de Colombia.
a. Banks sorted by ownership status at year-end 1997, 1998, 1999, and 2000.
b. Historical data on banks sorted by ownership status as of year-end 2000.

show notable improvement in risk-based ratios from 1997 to 2000, with foreign bank ratios exceeding those of private domestic banks at period-end. As in the case of Chile, this result most likely reflects lower risk levels at foreign banks, and it could suggest a more efficient use of capital by foreign banks. Acquired banks show the largest declines in leverage ratios, but they report higher risk-based ratios than private domestic and other foreign banks, attributable to the reorientation of the balance sheet toward more liquid, lower-risk investments.

Table 8-10. *Average Capital Ratios of Colombian Banks*
Percent of assets and risk-weighted assets, respectively

	Panel A: All banks by type of ownership[a]			Panel B: Private banks by type of ownership[b]		
Item	Foreign-owned	Domestic private	Government	Recently acquired foreign	Existing foreign	Domestic private
Capital/assets						
1997	13.18	14.18	7.88	15.60	13.20	14.18
2000	10.30	11.97	5.28	9.92	10.50	11.97
Total capital/risk-weighted assets						
1997	11.50	11.20	11.50	13.30	10.60	11.20
2000	12.70	12.10	14.30	13.90	12.10	12.10

Source: Superintendencia Bancaria de Colombia.
a. Banks sorted by ownership status at year-end 1997 and 2000.
b. Historical data on banks sorted by ownership status as of year-end 2001.

For the Colombian banking system as a whole, the period under review was clearly a challenging one as banks attempted to confront a worsening operating environment and weakening asset quality by implementing defensive measures to shore up loan loss reserves and capital and rein in new lending. With regard to discernible differences between foreign and domestic bank performance, we observe relatively similar trends. The key differences center primarily on foreign banks' higher average provisioning expense. This higher provisioning was an important factor behind significant losses at foreign banks, but it also led to substantially higher reserve coverage and lower levels of nonperforming loans. Losses eroded bank leverage ratios relatively more at foreign banks, but capital adequacy levels remained robust as a result of injections over the period and a move toward lower-risk investments. Notwithstanding these difficulties, foreign banks on the whole showed consistently higher average loan growth over the period.

These differences are magnified when one compares the relative condition and performance of acquired banks, existing foreign banks, and private domestic banks. Over the period, acquired banks appear mainly to have concentrated on cleansing their balance sheets, building liquidity, and curbing new lending. While existing foreign banks took efforts to limit the deterioration of asset quality and improve reserve coverage, these measures generated a less severe impact on loan growth, which was higher, on average, than at either acquired or private domestic banks.

THE ARGENTINE EXPERIENCE. Introduction of the Convertibility Plan in 1991 marked a turning point in Argentine financial history. It heralded profound monetary and fiscal reform, broad deregulation of domestic markets, privatization of government-owned entities, trade liberalization, elimination of capital controls, and, more generally, a macroeconomic environment conducive to foreign investment. Pegging the Argentine peso to the dollar also succeeded in stemming hyperinflationary pressures and helping restore economic growth relatively quickly. This contributed to significant financial deepening, with bank credit to the private sector almost doubling to just under 20 percent of GDP by the mid-1990s.

Beginning in early 1995, contagion from Mexico's Tequila Crisis severely tested the Argentine financial sector, sparking an outflow of almost 20 percent of system deposits. The transformation of the Argentine financial sector accelerated in the wake of the Tequila Crisis. Efforts undertaken to reestablish confidence in the banking sector included the introduction of deposit insurance, a renewed commitment to privatizing inefficient public sector banks, the liquidation and consolidation of nonviable entities, and the dedication of substantial resources to strengthening supervisory oversight and the regulatory framework. Within this context, foreign banks were permitted to play an important role in recapitalizing the Argentine banking system.

Very few foreign banks were present in Argentina prior to the 1990s, with U.S. institutions among the more active. The removal of restrictions on foreign direct investment and capital repatriation led to an increase in the number of foreign banks operating in Argentina, but they remained under 20 percent of system assets through 1995. Subsequent entry occurred mainly via the acquisition of existing operations, as foreign shareholders acquired controlling stakes in private institutions with a national or regional franchise, together with minority interests in a number of other financial institutions. By 1999, roughly half of banking sector assets were under foreign control. Roughly one-third of this foreign presence is currently controlled by U.S. and Canadian banks and two-thirds by European entities, half of which are Spanish banks.

Strong economic recovery in 1996 and 1997 was accompanied by a resurgence of deposit growth (averaging in excess of 20 percent a year) and a further deepening of bank credit to the private sector, which reached 24 percent of GDP by 1998. The broad-scale adoption of direct deposit salary payments further assisted bank penetration in the period. Growth prospects were adversely affected, however, when the Asian, Russian, and Brazilian financial crises, combined with domestic electoral uncertainties, triggered a tighter financing environment, volatile interest rates, and deteriorating terms of trade. Argentina's economy contracted 3.4 percent in 1999 and has yet to evidence a recovery.

Although the Argentine financial sector generally weathered this recent period of financial stress relatively well, deposit growth slowed markedly, credit to the private sector stagnated, and the quality of bank assets deteriorated. The following analysis evaluates the relative performance and condition of domestic and foreign banks from 1997 to 2000.[21]

The Argentine banks that we evaluate account for 80 to 85 percent of system assets over the sample period. The number of foreign-controlled entities ranges from fifteen to eighteen, representing 50 to 61 percent of sample assets in any given year. Of these, several were excluded from the detailed analysis either because they are not active in the retail banking market or because they are so small as to be irrelevant for a broad system discussion, such that their inclusion would inappropriately affect unweighted averages. In any given year, up to seven foreign-controlled banks, or 8 percent of system assets, were excluded under these criteria. Of the remaining foreign banks, seven are considered to be recent acquisitions (since 1995), equivalent to roughly 35 percent of sample assets, and five have longer-standing local operations, representing approximately 25 percent of sample assets.

Among domestic banks, the number of privately owned institutions ranges from one to three, or 11 to 14 percent of sample assets. All are considered to be retail oriented and of adequate size for inclusion in this analysis. Only one, which holds roughly 10 percent of sample assets, remained under private domestic ownership throughout the entire period. Government-controlled banks maintain a significant presence in Argentina, despite significant privatization following the Tequila Crisis. Up to six of these banks are included in our sample in any given year, representing 29 to 36 percent of sample assets. For purposes of this analysis, we have excluded from consideration two banks (roughly 4 percent of system assets) owing to size and business orientation.[22]

The balance sheet structure and liquidity of Argentine banks shows certain similarities with the Chilean and Colombian cases. Foreign banks in

21. The statistics discussed in this section are compiled using a variety of sources, including the Argentine central bank and Moody's Investors Service (various years).

22. In particular, the national mortgage bank was excluded from consideration because of its unique financing profile and credit orientation.

Table 8-11. *Summary Balance Sheet Structure of Argentine Banks*
Percent of assets

| Item | Panel A: All banks by type of ownership[a] | | | Panel B: Private banks by type of ownership[b] | | |
	Foreign-owned	Domestic private	Government	Recently acquired foreign	Existing foreign	Domestic private
Assets						
Liquid assets						
1997	32	36	35	34	29	38
2000	47	39	47	47	46	39
Loans						
1997	61	59	55	60	63	57
2000	52	55	51	51	53	55
Liabilities						
Total deposits						
1997	56	57	68	55	60	50
2000	54	57	76	55	53	57
Demand deposits						
1997	6	6	5	6	6	6
2000	4	4	4	4	5	4
Capital						
1997	9	9	8	9	8	10
2000	8	9	6	9	8	9
Loan and deposit trends						
Average annual loan growth[c]	22	15	4	12	36	15
Average annual deposit growth[c]	2	22	17	16	26	22
Loans/deposits						
1997	113	107	81	113	108	115
2000	96	97	69	93	102	97

Source: Authors' calculations, based on data from the Banco Central de la República Argentina.
a. Banks sorted by ownership status at year-end 1997 and 2000.
b. Historical data on banks sorted by ownership status as of year-end 2000.
c. 1997 through 2000, in percent.

Argentina, on average, dedicate a relatively larger proportion of their balance sheets to liquid assets than do private domestic banks (see table 8-11). In contrast to Chile and Colombia, however, the reliance on deposit-based financing of foreign banks in Argentina is broadly comparable to their private domestic peers. They also hold a similar proportion of assets in loans, and they even started the sample period with a higher loan-to-asset ratio, on average. This last point, which is consistent with the Colombian case, may reflect the relatively earlier timing of most major foreign acquisitions in Argentina and Colombia than in Chile. In Argentina, it may also reflect entry coincident with a strong economic recovery, correspondingly strong average deposit and loan growth, a higher volume of acquisitions, and a broader acquisition focus beyond just the top-tier institutions. As the macro environment deteriorated, foreign banks exhibited a sharper reduction in loans as a proportion of assets than did private domestic banks, combined with a much faster buildup of less risky, liquid investments (primarily government securities). These efforts contributed to lower loan-to-deposit ratios and enhanced liquidity, although foreign banks' average loan growth over the sample period still exceeded that of private and public domestic banks (see table 8-11).

Banks acquired since 1995, as well as other foreign banks present at least since the early 1990s, exhibit more similar balance sheet structures and trends than in the other two case studies, which may reflect the earlier large-scale entry into the Argentine market. At the same time, recently acquired banks maintained significantly lower average loan and deposit growth rates than their other private sector counterparts over the sample period, and they curtailed deposit taking and, in particular, new lending more quickly and sharply (figures 8-11 and 8-12). Growth trends also appear slower to recover at these banks, consistent with our findings in Chile and Colombia. Existing foreign banks reduced loan and deposit volumes more slowly than domestic counterparts as operating conditions deteriorated, however, and they reactivated new lending more quickly as the credit environment improved.

From 1997 to 2000, sample banks experienced a notable deterioration in asset quality, with the average stock of nonperforming loans rising to over 10 percent of gross loans. While Argentina's large public sector banks exhibited particularly weak asset quality indicators, private sector banks also reported a significant deterioration in credit quality over this time period (see table 8-12). In contrast to both Chile and Colombia, however, asset quality deterioration was concentrated in foreign banks, whereas their private domestic peers reported better nonperforming loan ratios by 2000. Foreign banks appear to have experienced either a more severe deterioration in credit quality or to have responded more quickly and aggressively in acknowledging potential losses. The combination of a deteriorating trend in the asset quality ratios of foreign banks and an improving outlook for pri-

Figure 8-11. *Average Loan Growth of Argentine Banks*

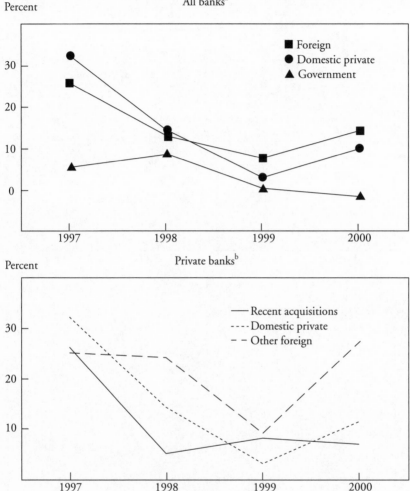

Source: Authors' calculations, based on data from the Banco Central de la República Argentina.
a. Banks sorted by ownership status at year-end 1997, 1998, 1999, and 2000.
b. Historical data on banks sorted by ownership status as of year-end 2000.

vate domestic banks—along with their shrinking number—suggests that relative credit quality trends were being driven to some extent by ongoing foreign acquisition of lesser-quality domestic banks.

As in both prior case studies, recently acquired foreign banks entered the sample period with higher nonperforming loan ratios than foreign banks with a longer-standing presence in the local market, which could reflect the

Figure 8-12. *Average Deposit Growth of Argentine Banks*

Percent

All banks[a]

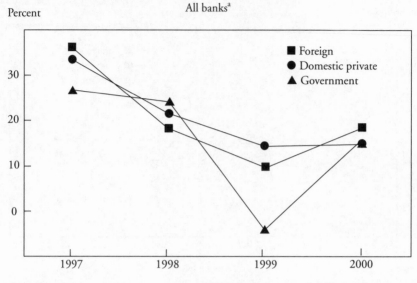

Private banks[b]

Percent

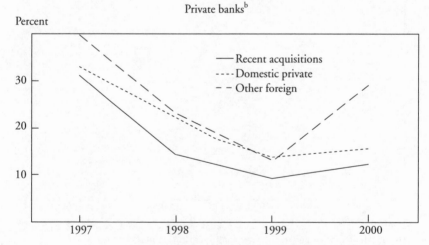

Source: Authors' calculations, based on data from the Banco Central de la República Argentina.
a. Banks sorted by ownership status at year-end 1997, 1998, 1999, and 2000.
b. Historical data on banks sorted by ownership status as of year-end 2000.

absorption of entities with less sound credit risk management practices. As in Chile, but not Colombia, asset quality indicators at these banks continued to deteriorate throughout the sample period, perhaps as a result of ongoing acquisitions (which were absent in Colombia). Longer-established

Table 8-12. *Selected Average Asset Quality Indicators of Argentine Banks*
Percent of total loans, except as indicated

Item	Panel A: All banks by type of ownership[a]			Panel B: Private banks by type of ownership[b]		
	Foreign-owned	Domestic private	Government	Recently acquired foreign	Existing foreign	Domestic private
Nonperforming loans						
1997	6.5	5.3	17.8	7.0	5.4	4.7
2000	8.7	3.5	18.5	8.7	8.7	3.5
Provisions						
1997	2.5	2.8	2.1	3.0	2.1	2.2
2000	3.8	2.6	2.2	3.8	3.8	2.6
Recoveries						
1997	0.2	0.2	0.2	0.3	0.1	...
2000	0.3	0.3	0.2	0.4	0.1	0.3
Loan loss reserves[c]						
1997	83	76	60	81	84	71
2000	78	77	57	84	69	77

Source: Authors' calculations, based on data from the Banco Central de la República Argentina.
a. Banks sorted by ownership status at year-end 1997 and 2000.
b. Historical data on banks sorted by ownership status as of year-end 2000.
c. Percent of nonperforming loans.

foreign banks also experienced a notable deterioration in asset quality as the macroeconomic environment deteriorated; the trend was all the more marked given their relatively stronger asset quality ratios at the onset of the sample period. This was also evident in Colombia, where more established foreign banks similarly concluded the sample period with nonperforming loan ratios that were comparable to acquisition banks.

Similar trends are evident in provisioning activity. Foreign-acquired banks entered the mid- to late 1990s with higher provisioning expenses relative to loans than their peers. These banks maintained higher loan loss provisions than domestic banks throughout the sample period, but they were matched by existing foreign banks at the end of the period. Despite this accelerated provisioning activity, flat to declining loan loss reserves at foreign banks suggest that the recognition of credit losses outpaced reserve buildup, which may be indicative of relatively more aggressive charge-off practices. As in the other case studies, foreign acquired banks entered the sample period with significantly higher recovery ratios, which they maintained or increased throughout the sample period. Across all four years, these banks recovered

Figure 8-13. *Return on Average Assets of Argentine Banks*

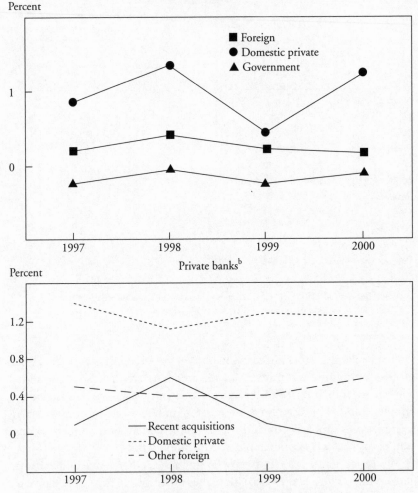

All banks[a]

Private banks[b]

Source: Authors' calculations, based on data from the Banco Central de la República Argentina.
a. Banks sorted by ownership status at year-end 1997, 1998, 1999, and 2000.
b. Historical data on banks sorted by ownership status as of year-end 2000.

1.1 percent of average loans, as compared with 0.2 percent by existing foreign banks and 0.5 percent by private domestic banks.

Foreign-controlled banks consistently generated weak returns over the sample period, and they significantly underperformed private domestic banks, although not state banks (see figure 8-13). This reflects somewhat

Table 8-13. *Selected Profitability Indicators for Argentine Banks*
Percent of average assets

Item	Panel A: All banks by type of ownership[a]			Panel B: Private banks by type of ownership[b]		
	Foreign-owned	Domestic private	Government	Recently acquired foreign	Existing foreign	Domestic private
Income						
Net interest income						
1997	4.6	5.2	3.6	4.8	4.6	4.7
1998	4.8	4.9	4.7	4.7	5.0	3.9
1999	4.6	4.7	2.6	4.1	5.8	4.1
2000	4.7	4.9	3.3	4.2	5.6	4.9
Noninterest operating income						
1997	2.5	2.5	2.6	2.5	2.7	2.1
1998	3.0	3.3	2.8	2.9	3.4	1.9
1999	2.7	3.4	2.3	2.4	3.7	2.5
2000	2.6	2.5	2.4	2.4	2.9	2.5
Expense						
Provisions						
1997	1.6	1.7	1.2	1.9	1.4	1.3
1998	1.6	1.2	1.5	1.6	1.6	0.7
1999	1.8	2.0	0.8	1.7	2.3	1.5
2000	2.0	1.5	1.0	2.0	2.1	1.5
Noninterest operating expense						
1997	5.5	5.2	6.0	5.4	5.7	4.3
1998	6.0	5.8	7.1	5.8	6.5	4.0
1999	5.5	5.7	4.6	5.0	6.6	4.6
2000	5.2	4.5	5.0	5.1	5.6	4.5

Source: Authors' calculations, based on data from the Banco Central de la República Argentina.
a. Banks sorted by ownership status at year-end 1997, 1998, 1999, and 2000.
b. Historical data on banks sorted by ownership status as of year-end 2000.

weaker net interest revenues and higher provisioning and operating expenses (see table 8-13).

As is evident in the second panel of the figure, all foreign banks, whether long present in the local market or recent entrants, performed poorly, on average, relative to the remaining large private bank under domestic control. As in Chile, recent acquisitions exhibited particularly weak performance as a result of heavy provisioning expenses and declining net interest margins (consistent with a pronounced retrenchment from credit activi-

Table 8-14. *Average Capital Ratios of Argentine Banks*
Percent of assets and risk-weighted assets, respectively

| Item | Panel A: All banks by type of ownership[a] | | | Panel B: Private banks by type of ownership[b] | | |
	Foreign-owned	Domestic private	Government	Recently acquired foreign	Existing foreign	Domestic private
Capital/assets						
1998	8.90	8.89	8.18	9.21	8.31	9.64
2000	8.31	9.00	6.04	8.54	7.91	9.01
Total capital/risk-weighted assets						
1998	17.12	17.75	...	17.99	15.90	17.19
2000	17.56	16.71	...	18.17	16.50	16.71

Source: Banco Central de la República Argentina.
a. Banks sorted by ownership status at year-end 1998 and 2000.
b. Historical data on banks sorted by ownership status as of year-end 2000.

ties). These banks also appear to have been relatively more successful than their longer-established peers in reducing operating expenses over the sample period, which might point to enhanced returns in the future. Consistent with credit and deposit growth patterns, longer-established foreign banks benefited from rising net interest flows and generated relatively strong operating revenues; this may reflect the absence of distracting merger issues. These banks also maintained relatively expensive cost structures, however.

In the area of capital adequacy, foreign banks in Argentina (as in Colombia) appear to have maintained capital-to-asset ratios that are comparable to, if slightly lower than, their privately held domestic counterparts (see table 8-14). Again, state banks notably underperformed in this regard. As in the other countries, foreign banks witnessed a moderate deterioration in total capital levels relative to the asset base over the sample period, probably as a result of heavier provisioning expenses, merger integration costs, and perhaps a different calculus in the efficient allocation of capital.

As in Colombia, but not Chile, foreign acquired banks entered the period with higher capital ratios than longer-standing foreign banks, which could reflect higher recapitalization needs to effect balance sheet cleansing. These banks also witnessed a sharper deterioration in capital levels as a proportion of assets throughout the sample period; this pattern is consistent with dampened earnings stemming from ongoing high provisioning and merger integration expenses. They remained above their longer-standing foreign counterparts, however.

As in the other two countries, foreign banks improved their risk-based capital ratios over the sample period, exceeding the levels maintained by domestic banks. This is consistent with the trend toward lower-risk asset holdings at these banks. It also suggests that foreign and domestic banks may differ in their ability to efficiently allocate capital.

Our overall assessment is that as in Chile, the Argentine financial sector as a whole weathered this economic downturn relatively well. Argentina differs from the other case studies, however, in the broader penetration of foreign banks, the winnowing presence of large, domestically owned banks, and the still-significant state bank presence. The most meaningful results are therefore derived from the evaluation of recent foreign entrants as compared with longer-established foreign players.

Overall, these banks exhibit broadly similar trends. As in Chile and Colombia, however, recently acquired banks retrenched from deposit and loan markets more quickly and more markedly than other local foreign players, and they reengaged more slowly. This may be due to the costs and energies associated with merger integration, in which case it may be a temporary short-run phenomenon as management carries out balance sheet cleansing and a reconciliation of risk-management and operational practices. This would be consistent with the higher nonperforming loan ratios reported by these banks and heavier provisioning expenses, all of which weighed on performance. However, healthier balance sheets and enhanced cost management may point to stronger, more sustainable returns in the longer term.

Conclusions

Our analysis shows that foreign and private domestic banks do not exhibit strong systematic differences in condition and performance over the sample period, although the broader BFSR analysis indicates some marginal relative improvement of the ratings of foreign-acquired banks compared to domestic banks over time. Across all measures, both foreign and private domestic banks exhibit clearly superior health relative to state banks. The case studies, however, indicate some noteworthy distinctions between foreign and private domestic banks with regard to balance sheet structure, loan growth, measures to address asset quality deterioration, and loss-absorption capacity.

In terms of balance sheet structure, foreign banks rely on deposit-based funding to a lesser extent than private domestic banks, which could reflect access to alternative funding sources or difficulty in attracting deposits away from entrenched local competitors. Foreign and private domestic banks have comparable shares of lower-cost demand deposits, however. Foreign banks maintain higher shares of liquid assets, perhaps as a result of a greater reliance on potentially more volatile nondeposit borrowings. Foreign banks also tend to maintain similar or lower loan shares and similar or weaker overall liquidity, as measured by loan-to-deposit ratios.

Across all three countries, foreign banks manifest consistently stronger average loan growth than private domestic banks. This is particularly true for existing foreign banks, which over the sample period show less reduction in credit growth, on average, with the onset of weakening economic conditions than private domestic banks, followed by stronger growth with macroeconomic improvement. The higher relative share of liquid assets maintained by foreign banks may support such a redeployment of assets. Recently acquired foreign banks undertook more defensive behavior: loan growth consistently ranked below that of established foreign banks and private domestic banks, and they experienced a more rapid buildup in liquid assets. This behavior is consistent with a greater initial focus on operational restructuring, balance sheet cleansing, and integration of local operations with the parent bank, rather than on market share expansion and growth.

With respect to trends in asset quality, our results are mixed in terms of differences in current levels and trends in nonperforming loan ratios across foreign and domestic banks. Ambiguous results may not be altogether surprising, however, given the traditional difficulties in evaluating bank asset quality by outside analysts, particularly in an emerging markets context: definitions of problem loans across countries often vary, and individual banks within a country may apply the same standard differently. Gaining a better understanding of differences in asset quality across ownership types would require the analysis of much more detailed data, which is beyond the scope of this review.

More concrete findings concern provisioning for bad loans. Foreign banks have higher loan provisioning expenses and comparable or higher reserve coverage of nonperforming loans relative to private domestic banks, which might suggest tighter credit review standards. Foreign banks also report higher average recoveries, reflecting higher provisions; this may be attributable to more aggressive or effective workout procedures—or simply higher average charge-offs. These observations characterize recently acquired banks in particular, which also have higher initial levels of problem loans and correspondingly higher provisioning and recoveries over the period. Overall, we conclude that foreign banks appear to take more aggressive actions in addressing asset quality deterioration.

In terms of earnings, foreign banks had similar or weaker overall profitability relative to domestic banks over the sample period. Foreign banks tend to have similar or weaker net interest margins. Noninterest income levels as a percent of total assets vary widely across the three countries, ranging from relatively high in Chile (and much above those of domestic banks), to relatively low in Argentina (but comparable to domestic bank levels).[23] Foreign banks also report comparable or higher noninterest expense.

Finally, with respect to loss-absorption capacity, foreign banks maintain higher risk-based capital ratios than private domestic banks across all three countries, notwithstanding similar or weaker profitability levels. This is particularly notable in cases in which foreign banks have suffered large losses, such as in Colombia. Higher risk-based ratios reflect foreign banks' relatively greater investment in liquid and lower-risk assets. Moreover, foreign banks' higher risk-based capital ratios, in light of generally lower capital-to-asset ratios in Argentina and Colombia, may point to potential differences between foreign and domestic banks in the efficient allocation of capital.

Given the wide range of relevant institutional and structural variables, the relatively short gestation period of significant foreign ownership, and the difficult macroeconomic conditions existent over the sample period, caution is warranted in generalizing our findings from the recent Latin American experience to the broader implications of foreign ownership for domestic financial stability. That said, some preliminary observations can be made.

First, the lack of strong differences in condition and performance between foreign and private domestic banks may suggest that there is space for strong domestic and foreign institutions to compete effectively in local banking markets.

---

23. This result may reflect the relatively greater development of Chilean financial markets, where foreign banks might be better able to exploit comparative advantages in such areas as trading, investment banking, and asset management.

Second, consistently stronger average loan growth by foreign banks supports similar recent findings that foreign banks do not necessarily cut and run during periods of economic difficulty in emerging markets. While recently acquired banks had lower loan growth, their focus on balance-sheet repair could potentially provide the foundation for future credit growth at a level more similar to that of longer-standing foreign banks.

Third, some of our case study findings challenge the cherry-picking critique that is often aimed at foreign banks. While existing foreign banks began the period with similar or lower average nonperforming loan ratios relative to private domestic banks, which is suggestive of cherry picking, their provisioning levels were relatively higher than those of the domestic institutions during the period. If relative provisioning reflects relative deterioration, it is hard to conclude that the portfolios of foreign banks consist of significantly more creditworthy borrowers than those of private domestic banks. Alternatively, if foreign banks do target low-risk clients, higher provisioning at foreign banks suggests that private domestic banks may be underprovided against potential loan losses.

Generally higher provisioning at foreign banks, particularly in the immediate aftermath of acquisitions, may suggest that foreign banks apply tighter credit review standards to their portfolios. Their comparable or higher reserve coverage of bad loans supports this conclusion. If this is the case, foreign bank participation may have broader positive efficiency implications, in that weaker credits are identified earlier and banks more quickly reallocate resources from weaker to stronger credits. A more qualitative review of foreign and domestic banks' credit review standards would be necessary to support this point.

Finally, foreign banks exhibited comparable or weaker earnings performance over the period, while maintaining higher risk-based capital ratios than their domestic counterparts. This finding points to a strong commitment to the local presence by head office, and it further undermines the cut-and-run critique.

Taken together, our findings that foreign banks have consistently stronger average credit growth, take more aggressive action to deal with asset quality deterioration, and possess the capacity and willingness to sacrifice short-term profitability for longer-term soundness suggest that foreign ownership may have quite positive implications for financial sector stability, development, and efficiency. Before extending these conclusions too far, however, more extensive analysis of these issues is clearly warranted. First, these ownership changes in Latin America remain relatively recent, and they have taken place during a rather inhospitable macroeconomic environment. The longer-term competitive dynamics of substantially increased foreign ownership will only become fully evident over time. Second, a fuller treatment of the structural and institutional differences across countries should inform this debate considerably. Third, our analysis is based on the average bank experience; a more explicit segregation of institutions by such variables as size, customer base, and national or regional scale would shed greater light on observed institutional differences. Fourth, this analysis is largely centered on quantitative rather than qualitative indicators of bank condition: a better understanding of qualitative differences in risk management and internal controls, particularly in the area of credit risk management, would also be informative. Finally, a more in-depth analysis of loan portfolio composition and asset quality trends would be useful to better gauge the issue of whether foreign and domestic banks systematically differ in their lending strategies and customer orientation.

References

Banco Central de la República Argentina. *Estadística Financieras* (various issues). Buenos Aires.

Baraja, Adolpho, Roberto Steiner, and Natalia Salazar. 2000. "The Impact of Liberalization and Foreign Investment in Colombia's Financial Sector." *Journal of Development Economics* 63(1): 157–96.

Barth, James, Gerard Caprio Jr., and Ross Levine. 2001. "The Regulation and Supervision of Banks around the World." Policy Research Working Paper 2588. Washington: World Bank.

Burdisso, Tamaro, Laura D'Amato, and Andrea Molinari. 1998. "The Bank Privatization Process in Argentina: Toward a More Efficient Banking System?" Unpublished paper. Banco Central de la República Argentina.

Claessens, Stijn, Asli Demirguc-Kunt, and Harry Huizinga. 1998. "How Does Foreign Entry Affect the Domestic Banking Market?" Policy Research Working Paper 1918. Washington: World Bank.

Clarke, George, and others. 1999. "On the Kindness of Strangers? The Impact of Foreign Entry on Domestic Banks in Argentina." Unpublished paper. Washington: World Bank.

Dages, B. Gerard, Linda Goldberg, and Daniel Kinney. 2000. "Foreign and Domestic Bank Participation in Emerging Markets: Lessons from Mexico and Argentina." Federal Reserve Bank of New York, *Economic Policy Review* 6(3): 17–36.

Goldberg, Linda. 2001. "When Is U.S. Bank Lending to Emerging Markets Volatile?" Working Paper 8137. Cambridge, Mass.: National Bureau of Economic Research.

Martinez Peria, Maria Soledad, and Sergio Schmukler. 1999. "Do Depositors Punish Banks for 'Bad' Behavior? Market Discipline in Argentina, Chile, and Mexico." Policy Research Working Paper 2058. Washington: World Bank.

Moody's Investors Service. 1995–2001. *Latin American Bank Financial Strength Ratings.*

———. Various issues. *Moody's Banking Statistical Supplements for Argentina, Chile, and Colombia.*

Palmer, David. 2000. "U.S. Bank Exposure to Emerging-Market Countries during Recent Financial Crises." *Federal Reserve Bulletin* (February): 81–96. Board of Governors of the Federal Reserve System.

Peek, Joe, and Eric Rosengren. 2000. "Implications of the Globalization of the Banking Sector: The Latin American Experience." *New England Economic Review* (September/October): 45–61.

Superintendencia Bancaria de Colombia. *Estadisticas Financieras* (various issues). Bogotá.

Superintendencia de Bancos e Instituciones Financieras de Chile. *Información Financiera* (various issues). Santiago.

Swabey, Rue, Felipe Hernandez, and Stephen Edkins. 2000. "Financial Sector Review: Intensive Care." *Latin American Equity Research* (May 10). Santander Investment Securities.

NICHOLAS R. LARDY

9

Foreign Financial Firms in Asia

Two years after the end of the Asian financial crisis, most of emerging Asia still faces the cost of restructuring impaired financial sectors. These costs will be substantial, ranging as high as 60 percent of gross domestic product in the case of Indonesia, according to the government's official estimate.[1] The Korean government injected 64,000 billion won (W) in 1998 to recapitalize troubled banks and protect depositors. Analysts initially thought this amount would be sufficient to deal with the financial sector problems revealed by the Asian financial crisis, but the bankruptcy of Daewoo and the emergence of problems at other large corporate borrowers made it clear that the clean-up was far from complete. By early 2001 total government outlays had reached W 160,000 billion.[2] As a result, public sector debt, including bank restructuring debt, jumped from only 14 percent of gross domestic product (GDP) at year-end 1996, before the onset of the Asian financial crisis, to an estimated 57 percent by year-end 2000.[3] Significant injections of government funds and carve-outs of bad loans by the Korean Asset Management Corporation have substantially reduced nonperforming loans in South Korean banks, but many banks are still taking provisions for new

1. JP Morgan, *Asian Financial Markets,* First Quarter 2000, January 28, 2000, p. 36.
2. Jane Fuller, "State Comes to the Rescue," *Financial Times, South Korea Survey,* October 19, 2000, p. V; Bear Stearns, *Korea: Limiting the Downturn in 2001,* February 7, 2001, pp. 5–6.
3. JP Morgan, *Asian Financial Markets,* Second Quarter 2000, April 28, 2000, p. 18; Bear Stearns, *Korea: Limiting the Downturn in 2001,* February 7, 2001, p. 7.

267

nonperforming loans that are absorbing a substantial share of their profits. Given the degree of bank exposure to Hynix Semiconductor (formerly Hyundai Electronics) and other corporations that are vulnerable to a slowdown in the United States and the world economy, government expenditures on financial restructuring are likely to continue to rise, pushing up the ratio of public sector debt to GDP still further.

In Thailand the government has provided less financial assistance to banks, but government debt, including the debt of state-owned enterprises and the Bank of Thailand, quadrupled compared with pre-crisis levels, reaching about 60 percent by year-end 2000.[4] Moreover, despite significant debt restructuring and the transfer of nonperforming loans to asset management companies, nonperforming loans remaining on the books still constituted 18 percent of the banks' total loans outstanding at year-end 2000.

It is widely believed that foreign financial institutions should play a significant role in the restructuring process. The Group of 22, for example, recommended in 1998 that "Foreign institutions and capital should be allowed to take part in the restructuring framework on the same conditions as domestic institutions, for instance when submitting bids for merger, assets or deposits."[5] Only a few months later, the Institute for International Finance argued that the strengthening of the financial systems in emerging markets "can be enhanced by... entry of foreign equity."[6]

Most governments in the region initially appeared to share this view, as they substantially eased long-standing legal restrictions on the foreign ownership of domestic banks. In Korea the banking law was revised to allow majority foreign stakes in domestic banks, including 100 percent foreign ownership. Thailand's rules were also revised. Indonesia raised the limit on foreign bank ownership to 99 percent. Even in Taiwan, which largely escaped the Asian financial crisis, the Banking Law was revised to raise the limit on foreign ownership from 5 percent to 50 percent and to create an escape clause that allows an even larger foreign ownership share in special cases. The objective is to allow foreign banks to play a significant role in a much needed bank consolidation.

4. JP Morgan, *Global Data Watch*, March 17, 2000, p. 71; April 21, 2000, p. 67; February 9, 2001, p. 12.

5. BIS (1998).

6. Institute of International Finance (1999).

The potential role of foreign financial firms is twofold: to inject capital and to provide sophisticated financial management skills. Whether their participation takes the form of wholly owned branch banks or their ownership role in domestic banks, foreign financial firms can provide substantial competitive pressure. Over time this will improve the performance of domestic banks.

China has attracted substantial attention from international financial institutions, because of both its much larger size relative to other Asian markets and the similarly precarious nature of its financial system. This paper examines the record to date on the role of foreign financial institutions in China and how the country's pending accession to the World Trade Organization might create new opportunities.

China

The magnitude of China's challenge in recapitalizing its banking system is roughly comparable to countries more directly affected by the Asian financial crisis. By year-end 2000, asset management companies, which were first established in 1998, had taken 1.4 trillion renminbi (RMB) in nonperforming loans off the books of various banks, with the bulk pertaining to the four largest state-owned banks. In addition, the government undertook a partial recapitalization in August 1998, injecting RMB 270 billion into these same four banks. The gross cost of dealing with the nonperforming loans to date has thus been RMB 1.67 trillion, or about 20 percent of GDP in 2000.

Asset management companies are authorized to dispose of these loans through auction, securitization, restructuring, or debt-equity swaps. It is difficult to anticipate the ultimate rate of recovery that the asset management companies will achieve because their strategy relies, in part, on swapping debt for equity, with the expectation that they will be able to resell the equity to the original borrowers in five to ten years. Recovery rates via this mechanism will not be known for some time. However, the low recovery rates on the assets sold to date suggest that the central government will have to provide massive budgetary funds to redeem most of the bonds issued to the state-owned banks in exchange for the loans that are being liquidated. The Huarong Asset Management Company, which is dealing with the nonperforming loans of China's largest state-owned bank, achieved a cash recovery rate of 26 percent on the loans sold through the end of 2000.[7] China Orient Asset Management Corporation had a much lower recovery rate of 6.9 percent on the RMB 18.8 billion in assets that it had disposed of by year-end 2000.[8] Given that the Huarong and Orient asset management companies are probably starting the liquidation process with their best assets, the ultimate average recovery rate will presumably be much, much lower than the ratios to date.

The capital injection and the large carve-out of bad debt are far from sufficient to deal with the weak balance sheets of the four largest state-owned banks. The governor of the People's Bank of China, China's central bank, revealed in his annual press conference in January 2001 that none of the four largest state-owned banks currently meets the 8 percent Basel capital adequacy standard. Moreover, although the reduction of nonperforming loans represented 10 percent of the total portfolios of these banks, Governor Dai acknowledged that the nonperforming loans remaining on the books of the four largest state-owned banks still account for 25 percent of their loan portfolios.[9] This implies that these four banks still have RMB 1.975 trillion in nonperforming loans on their books.[10] While one would hope that not all of this will have to be written off, it represents a potential liability to the government of an additional 22 percent of gross domestic product. Thus the total potential cost to the Chinese government of dealing with weak banks, assuming that the extension of new nonperforming loans can be avoided, is 45 percent of gross domestic product.

Even this estimate may be significantly downward biased for two reasons. First, Governor Dai's statement implies that about RMB 400 billion in nonperforming loans, an amount equal to 4 percent of gross domestic product emerged during the year 2000.[11] Thus the problem is not simply

7. Huarong was said to recover an additional RMB 215 million in physical assets. Since these assets were not sold, it is not clear how the valuation on these assets was made. See Li Gang, "Realizing Recovery of Value Is a Huge Change," *Jinrong shibao* (Financial News), January 17, 2001, p. 1.

8. "More Assets Disposed," *China Daily*, January 23, 2001, p. 3.

9. "Dai Xianglong Answers Foreign and Chinese Reporters' Questions," *Jinrong shibao* (Financial News), January 18, 2001, p. 1.

10. RMB 1.975 trillion equals 25 percent of the RMB 7.903 trillion that the four largest state-owned banks had outstanding at year-end 2000. People's Bank of China, *Quarterly Statistical Bulletin* 2001(1): 24.

11. Governor Dai said that the removal of RMB 1.4 trillion had reduced nonperforming loans from 35 to 25 percent. Of the RMB 1.4 trillion, all but RMB 100 billion, which were loans of the State Development Bank, came from the four largest state-owned commercial banks. About RMB 320 billion of the RMB 1.3 trillion was removed in 1999 and RMB 980 billion in 2000. Loans outstanding of the big four at year-end 1999 were RMB 7.19 trillion. Since 35 percent of this amount, or RMB 2.517 trillion, was nonperforming, the banks would have had about RMB 1.540 trillion in non-

one of absorbing the cost of nonperforming loans that already existed in 1998, when capital was injected and the asset management companies were created. New nonperforming loans continue to emerge, which suggests that the authorities face a flow problem rather than simply a stock problem.

Second, China generally uses a loan classification system based on the payment status of loans, rather than more forward-looking measures of the likelihood that borrowers will be able to service their loans. The central bank introduced a new loan classification system in 1998. The early evidence on the level of nonperforming loans as measured by these more realistic standards confirms what has long been suspected: Chinese data on nonperforming loans are understated. For example, the Bank of China is the first large state-owned bank to report its nonperforming loans based on the new, more forward-looking criteria. In 1999 its nonperforming loans were 14.86 percent on the old criteria but 39.34 percent on the new criteria.[12] The numbers that Governor Dai disclosed in early 2001 for the four large state-owned banks as a group appear to be based on the old loan classification system.[13] If so, the nonperforming loans of the four big banks as a group at year-end 2000 are actually likely to represent about 65 percent of their outstanding loans, or RMB 5.1 trillion, which is equivalent to about 60 percent of gross domestic product.[14] When the cost of the Ministry of Finance's previous injection of capital into the banks and the value of bonds issued by the asset management companies (and implicitly guaranteed by the Ministry) are included, the total potential cost of dealing with the weak balance sheets of these banks reaches more than 80 percent of GDP. Even this estimate makes no allowance for nonperforming loans in other parts of the banking system, which had outstanding loans of RMB 2.8 trillion at year-end 2000.[15]

---

performing loans remaining on their books after the transfer of RMB 980 billion to the asset management companies. At year-end 2000, however, these banks had RMB 1.975 trillion in nonperforming loans (see note 10). Adjusting for the approximately RMB 40 billion in loans the banks wrote off from their own reserves implies that RMB 400 billion in new nonperforming loans emerged in 2000.

12. Bank of China (2000, p. 57; 2001, p. 22).

13. The Bank of China's nonperforming loans at year-end 2000, measured on the new criteria, were 28.78 percent. Since the Bank of China is widely believed to have the highest quality loan portfolio of the four largest state-owned banks, it is very unlikely that the average nonperforming loan ratio for the group could be less than that for the Bank of China. It thus appears that Governor Dai's 25 percent figure is based on the old loan classification system.

14. This assumes that the 2.6:1 ratio of nonperforming loans measured in the new and old systems in the Bank of China is representative of the same ratio in the other three large state-owned banks.

15. People's Bank of China, *Quarterly Statistical Bulletin* 2001(1): 16 and 24.

Table 9-1. *Foreign Bank Assets in China, 1991–2000*
Billions of dollars

Year	Assets
1991	4.29
1992	5.53
1993	7.58
1994	11.84
1995	19.14
1996	29.92
1997	37.92
1998	34.18
1999	31.79
2000	34.43

Source: People's Bank of China, *Quarterly Statistical Bulletin* 1997(1): 46; 1998(1): 50; and 2001(1): 57.

Despite this evidence of considerable financial weakness, China agreed to open its financial sector as part of its negotiations to enter the World Trade Organization. This opening could prove to be at least as profound in the long run as the openings currently under way in Korea and Thailand. The agreement includes substantial liberalization of the Chinese market in banking, insurance, securities, fund management, and other financial services. Historically, China has either precluded or severely restricted the ability of foreign firms to compete with domestic firms in these areas.

These restrictions are most dramatically demonstrated in the case of banking. Although large numbers of foreign banks have operated in China for two decades, their role remains extremely limited. The Bank of Tokyo was the first foreign bank to receive a license to operate a representative office, which it opened in Beijing in 1979. The Nanyang Commercial Bank was the first to open a branch, in Shenzhen in July 1981. By 2000 154 foreign branch banks and an additional twenty-three foreign-funded and joint venture banks and finance companies were operating in China. As shown in table 9-1, the assets of these institutions grew rapidly but remained quite small, only $34.4 billion at year-end 2000.[16] Their loans in 2000 accounted for only 1.3 percent of loans outstanding from all financial institutions in China. While the number of foreign branch banks continued to grow in 1997, 1998, and 1999, outstanding loans by these institutions fell almost every month between April 1998 and September

16. All financial data given in dollars are in U.S. dollars unless otherwise specified.

2000, from a peak of $27.8 billion outstanding at the end of April 1998 to $18.3 billion at the end of the period.[17]

The modest role of foreign financial institutions in China is a consequence of both the perception of increasing country risk and the regulatory environment in which the institutions must operate. Lending to China by all foreign banks, mostly from locations outside of China, peaked at $90 billion at the end of the third quarter of 1997. Beginning in the fourth quarter of 1997, foreign bank lending to China fell continuously, reaching $63 billion at the end of the first half of 2000 (the most recent data available from the Bank for International Settlements).[18] This reduction appears to have had several causes. First, the Asian financial crisis led foreign banks to cut their lending throughout the region—even to China, which was not pulled into the contagion. Second, the closure of the Guangdong International Trust and Investment Company (GITIC) in the fall of 1998 and its formal bankruptcy in January 1999 was widely regarded as a watershed event for foreign banks, which had lent GITIC several billion dollars. GITIC was the investment arm of the provincial government in Guangdong, China's fastest growing and economically most successful province. By the late 1990s, for example, it was generating more than 40 percent of China's total exports. Foreign banks feared that if investments in that environment were not successful, they would suffer even greater losses on their lending to Chinese companies located in less favorable environments. Third, a growing number of other Chinese trust and investment companies failed to make timely payments of interest and principal to foreign banks. As foreign banks responded by cutting back their China exposure, foreign banks located in China, which lent only to foreign firms operating in the country, also cut back their lending, with a lag of about two quarters. The perception of China risk, it appears, extends even to foreign firms operating in China.

Longer term, the slow growth in the role of foreign banks and other financial institutions in China stems from the restrictive regulatory environment imposed by the People's Bank of China. A myriad of regulations restricts the role of foreign banks operating in China. Foreign banks are generally not allowed to offer local currency services or deal with Chinese clients, such that their operations are largely restricted to offering foreign currency banking services to foreign-invested companies, foreign embassies,

17. People's Bank of China, *Quarterly Statistical Bulletin* 1999(2): 50; 2000(4): 57.

18. Bank for International Settlements, "China's Total Liabilities to Foreign Reporting Banks" (www.bis.org [June 21, 2000, and February 7, 2001]).

and individual foreign citizens. The only exception is that the People's Bank has authorized a small number of foreign banks to provide domestic currency services in the Pudong district of Shanghai since early 1997 and in Shenzhen since August 1998. By the end of 1999, nineteen domestic currency licenses had been issued, but several regulations severely restrict the domestic currency activities of these foreign banks. First, with limited exceptions, foreign banks can provide such services only to wholly foreign-owned and joint venture firms, and not to Chinese companies or Chinese households.[19] This limits the market both directly, by narrowly defining the customer universe, and indirectly, since foreign banks lack local currency deposits from which to finance domestic currency lending to foreign clients. That constraint was eased somewhat in 1998 and 2000 when at first a few and then most foreign banks with a domestic currency license were authorized to borrow renminbi funds in the domestic interbank market. The cost of funds in this market, however, is significantly higher than the interest rates fixed by the central bank on savings deposits, the principal source of funds for domestic banks.[20] Thus foreign banks are at a distinct disadvantage in competing with domestic banks in the market for loans denominated in domestic currency. Second, foreign banks can conduct domestic currency transactions only with businesses based either within Pudong and Shenzhen or in provinces immediately adjacent to these jurisdictions. The existing domestic currency banking licenses of foreign banks are, in effect, only regional licenses, whereas their major competitors—the four large state-owned commercial banks—blanket the entire country with 145,000 banking offices.

The third, and less well known, constraint on the development of the domestic currency business of foreign banks is that the People's Bank limits their ratio of domestic currency liabilities to foreign currency liabilities to 50 percent.[21] This effectively limits the amount of domestic currency deposits that foreign banks can accept to half that of their foreign currency deposits. Once the 50 percent ratio is reached, the growth rate of foreign banks' domestic currency deposits is constrained by the rate of expansion of their foreign currency deposits. As long as this regulation is in effect, for-

19. The one exception is that since 1998 foreign banks have been allowed to participate with domestic banks in extending syndicated loans to Chinese firms.

20. For example, since mid-1999 the central bank has fixed the interest rate paid on three-month time deposits by Chinese banks at 1.98 percent. The average interest rate on the interbank market from June 1999 through September 2000 for ninety-day funds was 4.80 percent. For this particular maturity, domestic banks thus had a cost of funds about 280 basis points lower than foreign banks.

21. The limit was 35 percent prior to 1999.

eign banks will not be able to shift predominantly into domestic currency lending.

The domestic currency business of foreign banks in China remains minuscule as a result of these restrictions. At year-end 1999, the nineteen foreign banks authorized to extend domestic currency loans in Pudong had an outstanding loan balance of RMB 6.701 billion ($800 million), an amount equal to only 0.07 percent of the credit outstanding from all Chinese domestic financial institutions.[22] Foreign banks are extremely marginal players in renminbi lending.

The role of foreign banks in the much smaller market for foreign currency loans is considerably larger. At year-end 2000 foreign banks had $18.8 billion in outstanding foreign currency loans, which represented over one-fifth of all foreign currency loans extended by banks in China.[23]

The role of foreign financial institutions as investors in Chinese banks is even more limited than their role in domestic currency lending. Only three Chinese banks—Everbright Bank, Xiamen International Bank, and the Bank of Shanghai—have allowed any foreign equity investment to date. The Asian Development Bank (ADB) invested $10.4 million in 1991 to acquire a 10 percent stake in the Xiamen International Bank, a regional commercial bank operating in Fujian Province since 1985.[24] In January 1997, the ADB took a minority stake in the Everbright Bank, a national commercial bank established in 1992. Although the amount of its investment was small ($20 million), it made the ADB the bank's third-largest shareholder. In a similar transaction, the International Finance Corporation (IFC), the investment arm of the World Bank Group, invested $25 million to acquire a 5 percent stake in the Bank of Shanghai in 1999. Because these three domestic institutions are extremely small, it would be easy to dismiss the significance of these transactions. Everbright Bank in 1997 accounted for only 0.6 percent of assets of all Chinese financial institutions. In 1999

22. People's Bank of China (2000, pp. 39, 90).

23. Yang Shuang and Wang Baoqing, "Raise the Level of Central Bank Regulation and Supervision; Stress Paying Special Attention to the Work of Financial Supervision," *Jinrong shibao* (Financial News), January 16, 2001, pp. 1–2.

24. Chinese banking authorities classify Xiamen International Bank as a joint venture rather than as a domestic bank. The bank's only significant founding foreign partner, however, was Min Xin Holdings, the Hong Kong–listed arm of the Fujian International Trust and Investment Corporation (FITIC), a provincial government-owned company. FITIC was the second-largest initial domestic owner of the bank. Thus, legally speaking, the bank had a significant foreign owner, but as a practical matter it was initially a domestic bank. Apart from Min Xin Holdings, Xiamen International Bank was 25 percent foreign owned by the end of 1999: in addition to the 10 percent stake of the ADB, the Long-Term Credit Bank of Japan owned 10 percent, and the Sino Finance Group of the United States owned 5 percent. See "Xiamen International Bank," at www.xib.com (February 6, 2001).

the total assets of Hong Kong–based Xiamen International Bank were only H.K.$9 billion (U.S.$1.2 billion). Bank of Shanghai, which was formed through the merger of a number of credit cooperatives in China's largest municipality, is also quite small. At the time of the IFC investment, the bank's total assets were only RMB 60 billion ($7 billion), or about 0.5 percent of the assets of all Chinese financial institutions.

The role of foreign international financial institutions, however, is not limited to providing capital. The ADB launched a technical assistance program "to strengthen the Everbright Bank of China institutionally and operationally so as to provide a role model for the commercial banking sector in general."[25] The IFC also seeks to introduce enhanced business capability into the Bank of Shanghai. Moreover, the governance of both banks may be improved, since the foreign investor in each case is able to name a member of the board.

Foreign companies' access to China's domestic insurance market has been subject to similar limitations. Beginning in the early 1980s foreign insurance firms were allowed to establish representative offices, but as in the case of banks, these were not allowed to conduct any business. In 1992 the government issued the first license to a foreign firm, namely, the American International Assurance Company, Ltd., a unit of the American International Group (AIG). It initially was licensed to sell a single line of insurance (life insurance) in a single city (Shanghai). By the end of the decade China's regulatory authorities had issued only twenty-four licenses to fifteen foreign insurance companies from eight countries, authorizing them to sell a limited range of insurance products in only three cities—Guangzhou, Shanghai, and Shenzhen.[26] Moreover, firms licensed to sell life insurance are allowed to sell policies only to individuals; group sales are banned. Property and casualty insurers can sell policies only to foreign, not domestic, firms.

These restrictions significantly limit the role of foreign firms in the national insurance market. At year-end 1999 the assets of foreign insurance companies accounted for less than 2 percent of all insurance company assets, and in 1999 their total premium income was only RMB 1.8 billion ($217 million), or 1.3 percent of the total insurance premium income of RMB 139.2 billion ($16.8 billion).[27] The dominant firm in the market

25. Asian Development Bank (1996, p. 12).

26. In addition, there were four joint venture insurance firms. Szu Liang, "China's Insurance Sector Faces Tough Competition after WTO Accession," Zhongguo tongxun she (China News Agency), May 29, 2000, in Foreign Broadcast Information Service, *Daily Report: China*, May 29, 2000 (hereafter cited as FBIS-CHI-year-month, day).

27. "PRC to Relax Insurance Industry Investment Restrictions to Greet WTO Entry," *Ta Kung Pao*, October 5, 2000, in FBIS-CHI-2000-1005.

remained the People's Insurance Company of China (PICC), a position now held by the four specialized state-owned companies that were spun off from PICC in late 1998.[28]

Market Opening under the World Trade Organization

Under the terms of China's protocol for acceding to the World Trade Organization (WTO), China will ultimately be required to lift all of the existing restrictions on foreign banks. For example, the number of cities in which foreign banks can offer domestic currency services is scheduled to increase steadily until 2005, when all geographic restrictions will be lifted.[29] Most importantly, foreign banks will be able to conduct local currency business with Chinese corporations two years after entry and with Chinese households five years after entry, and they will enjoy full national treatment five years after accession. That means that the central bank will no longer be able to restrict the growth of the domestic currency business of foreign banks by limiting their ratio of domestic to foreign currency liabilities or by using any other nonprudential ratio to restrict their operations.

How rapidly might foreign banks be able to expand their presence in the market once China enters the World Trade Organization? At year-end 2000, 154 foreign branch banks were poised to expand their business in China as soon as China enters the WTO. An additional 430 foreign bank representative offices have been established in China, most with the expectation that they would soon become branch banks.[30] While these numbers suggest that foreign banks will expand their role dramatically after China enters the WTO, the reality is that foreign banks will have very little abil-

28. The PICC was reorganized along product lines in November 1998. The new companies are the China Reinsurance Company, the People's Life Insurance Company of China, the People's Insurance Company of China (focusing on property insurance), and the China Insurance Company (formerly Hong Kong PICC Ltd.), which operates in Hong Kong. Li Sin, "A Reshuffle in the Insurance Sector," *China Economic News*, vol. 20 (May 10, 1999), p. 6.

29. World Trade Organization, "Draft Report of the Working Party on the Accession of China to the WTO," July 18, 2000 (www.insidetrade.com [July 28, 2000]). This and other dates are those specified in the draft protocol, which appears to be based on the understanding that China would enter the WTO in 2000. As the accession schedule slides, China's date-specific commitments will be adjusted. Thus if China enters the World Trade Organization in 2001, the date for phasing out geographic restrictions on where foreign banks can offer domestic currency services would be 2006.

30. The regulator (namely, the People's Bank of China) requires foreign banks to operate a representative office for three years before they can apply for a branch license. People's Bank of China (2000, p. 99).

ity to increase their market share, at least in the first five years after China's WTO entry. One reason is the 50 percent limit on the ratio of domestic to foreign currency liabilities. Foreign banks in China have practically no domestic currency liabilities. If they were allowed to take domestic currency deposits starting in 2001, they could only have taken an amount equal to 50 percent of their total liabilities, which stood at $34.6 billion at year-end 2000.[31] Thus their total domestic currency deposits could have grown by RMB 143.6 billion, which in turn could be used to finance a substantial increase in domestic currency lending. That would give foreign banks domestic currency deposits equal to only 1.2 percent of the total deposits in the Chinese banking system at year-end 2000. The share of incremental deposits would be much higher, but not so great as to strongly reduce the inflow of deposits into the domestic banking system. In 2000 deposits in the financial system rose by RMB 1.5 trillion.[32] If foreign banks expanded to the maximum extent allowed by the 50 percent ratio regulation, the total assets of foreign banks would increase from about 1.5 percent of the assets of the financial system at year-end 2000 to about 2.2 percent.

In practice, foreign banks might not wish to expand their domestic currency deposits as rapidly as the above hypothetical calculation suggests. Given the assumption that foreign banks follow the prudential regulation limiting their loans to no more than 75 percent of deposits, they could increase their lending under the new regime by about RMB 110 billion, according to the calculation. All of the increased lending could be in domestic currency once the market for domestic currency banking services is liberalized. As already noted, total domestic currency lending of foreign banks was only RMB 6.7 billion at year-end 1999. It is quite unlikely that foreign banks would be able to increase their domestic currency lending sixteen-fold in a short period of time, simply because they might not be able to find a sufficient number of additional creditworthy borrowers. At year-end 1999 foreign bank lending was restricted entirely to foreign-owned and joint venture companies in China. These firms have the accounting records and other audited financial information required to satisfy the credit requirements of foreign banks, whereas many Chinese enterprises do not.

---

31. Yang Shuang and Wang Baoqing, "Raise the Level of Central Bank Regulation and Supervision; Stress Paying Special Attention to the Work of Financial Supervision," *Jinrong shibao* (Financial News), January 16, 2001, pp. 1–2.

32. Total deposits at year-end 2000 stood at RMB 12.38 trillion. Yang Shuang, "Steady Financial Circulation; Appropriate Money Supply," *Jinrong shibao* (Financial News), January 19, 2001, p. 1.

Thus once foreign banks are free to take domestic currency deposits and make domestic currency loans to Chinese firms, the scarcity of creditworthy domestic borrowers—not the rule that limits the buildup of domestic currency liabilities relative to foreign currency liabilities—will restrict the growth of their business, at least in the short run. Since foreign banks, like their domestic counterparts, have to pay interest on deposits, they will only be willing to take domestic currency deposits to the extent that they can be used to support interest-bearing loans. They will therefore limit the expansion of their domestic currency deposit-taking business if they are unable to identify a sufficient number of creditworthy borrowers. A few foreign banks may be able to overcome this constraint by focusing their domestic currency lending on the retail market. The market for home mortgages, for example, is just beginning to be established in China; a few foreign banks may be able to compete effectively in this rapidly growing market segment. Unless the mortgage and other consumer credit markets can be developed rapidly, however, commercial considerations may pose a greater constraint than regulations on the expansion of the role of foreign banks. Of course, Chinese firms will increasingly adopt accounting and other standards that will make them more attractive borrowers, which will allow foreign banks to expand their share of assets to the predicted 2.5 percent share.

Once that share is reached, the regulation limiting the ratio of domestic to foreign currency deposits to 50 percent will continue to restrict foreign banks' operations as long as it remains in place. Further growth of the market share of foreign banks will then depend on two factors: the relative growth rates of lending in domestic and foreign currency and the share of foreign currency lending controlled by foreign banks. If foreign currency lending expands at least as fast as domestic currency lending and if foreign banks expand their share of total foreign currency lending, then they will be able to scale up their share of domestic currency lending above 2.5 percent. This seems unlikely, however, at least in the short run, given that foreign currency lending by foreign banks has been shrinking for several years. At year-end 2000 foreign banks already accounted for more than a fifth of all foreign-currency lending. That was about the same share as at year-end 1997.

Five years after China enters the World Trade Organization foreign banks will be subject to national treatment and will thus be free to expand their domestic currency business without the restriction on the ratio of domestic to foreign currency liabilities. In the short and medium terms, the participation of foreign banks is likely to remain below that in other emerging markets in Asia, where their share of bank deposits at the end of the 1990s ranged from a high of 33 percent in Hong Kong to a low of 3 percent in Taiwan.[33] The role of foreign banks will probably remain so small that they will offer insufficient competitive pressure on domestic banks and thus not fulfill their potential as a catalyst in creating a modern commercial banking system.

Predicting the expansion of foreign insurance companies after China's accession to the World Trade Organization is more difficult than in the case of banks. Under the terms of its November 1999 bilateral WTO agreement with the United States, China agreed to phase out many of the restrictions that currently limit the expansion of foreign insurance companies. On accession, for example, China will license insurance companies only on prudential grounds; the numerical limitations that have long prevailed will be swept away.[34] Geographic restrictions will also be phased out over time. Two years after accession twelve additional cities—Beijing, Chengdu, Dalian, Chongqing, Shenzhen, Fuzhou, Suzhou, Xiamen, Ningbo, Shenyang, Wuhan, and Tianjin—will be opened to foreign insurance companies. China must lift all geographic restrictions on the operation of foreign firms in the insurance market three years after accession.

Some of the limitations on the scope of business of foreign insurance companies will gradually be phased out, as well. On accession, foreign insurance companies will be able to offer property and casualty insurance nationwide, and certain services, including reinsurance and international marine, aviation, and transport insurance, will be open to cross-border transactions, that is, contracted through offices outside of China. Foreign insurance companies will be able to offer health insurance within three years of accession and group policies, pensions, and annuities within five years.

In contrast to the liberalization of the banking sector, however, ownership restrictions in the insurance industry will not be fully lifted. On accession, foreign firms may have a 51 percent equity share of businesses that sell nonlife insurance. Wholly foreign-owned subsidiaries offering nonlife insurance may be established two years after China's accession. In life insurance a 50 percent ceiling on foreign ownership applies starting from the date of accession, but there is no provision for a further increase. Thus there will be no wholly foreign-owned companies offering life insurance products,

33. Goldman Sachs (1999).

34. Foreign insurance firms must meet three criteria in addition to the prudential criteria that are applied to licensing domestic insurance companies: they must have operated in a WTO member country for thirty years; they must have had a representative office in China for two consecutive years prior to applying for a license; and they must have global assets of more than $5 billion.

with one exception: namely, the American International Group, which has operated a wholly foreign-owned insurance company in Shanghai since 1992 and in Guangzhou since 1995. It will be allowed to continue to operate under a grandfather clause for trade in services, which was negotiated in the bilateral agreement between the United States and China and which will be built into China's protocol of accession. This provision states that the conditions of ownership, operation, and scope of activities of foreign service providers operating in China prior to its entry into the World Trade Organization will not be made more restrictive.

In addition, foreign insurance firms operating in joint ventures will be precluded from writing commercial insurance policies below a defined threshold determined by the annual premium. The limit has been set at $120,000 on accession and will then be reduced in steps to $50,000 over a three-year period.[35] This is substantially higher than the $10,000 threshold originally proposed by U.S. negotiators.

The continuation of ownership restrictions (for two years after accession in the case of nonlife insurance and indefinitely in the case of life insurance), limitations on the size of commercial risks they will be allowed to insure, and the complexities of the licensing and registering process make it difficult to anticipate how rapidly foreign insurance firms will be able to expand after China enters the World Trade Organization. In the final negotiations on China's WTO entry in 2001, China addressed the concerns of members of the working party with respect to the third of these problems by agreeing that licensing procedures would not act as a barrier to market access and that the process of registration for firms that received licenses would not extend beyond two months.[36] If these terms are implemented, foreign insurance companies probably will be able to gradually expand their share of the market, and within a few years they will probably exceed the market share they achieved in Japan over a period of several decades.

Foreign financial firms also expect to play a role in China's securities and fund management industries. China's WTO commitments in these areas, however, are less far-reaching than in either banking or insurance. Foreign ownership restrictions are more severe: foreign companies initially can own up to one-third of an asset management company, and this share rises to just 49 percent three years after accession. In securities operations,

35. "U.S., China Settle Outstanding Problems for WTO Accession," *Inside U.S. Trade*, vol. 19 (June 15, 2001), pp. 1, 21.

36. WTO Secretariat, "Draft Report of the Working Party," (WT/ACC/SPEC/CHN/1/Rev 7), Section VI: Policies Affecting Trade in Services, July 6, 2001 (www.insidetrade.com/public/2001.3226.2.pdf [July 16, 2001]).

foreign ownership is limited to one-third, with no provision for an increase in the limit. The scope of business is also restricted.[37] No geographic restrictions have been placed on the sale of securities, however. Foreign-invested securities and asset management firms may establish businesses in any location in China, immediately on accession.

In anticipation of China's entry into the World Trade Organization three foreign asset firms have formed alliances with Chinese securities firms. JP Morgan Fleming Asset Management, Schroders Investment Management, and Invesco have formed links with Hua'an Fund Management based in Shanghai, Huaxia Fund Management based in Beijing, and Penghua Fund Management based in Shenzhen, respectively. These technical cooperation and consulting relations are expected to be converted into true joint ventures shortly after China enters the WTO.

Foreign financial institutions regard China as a huge, underserved market. The financial sector is in an early stage of development, and the national savings rate has averaged almost 40 percent in recent years, most of which was generated in the household sector. Household savings in bank accounts expanded by a robust RMB 498 billion ($60 billion) in 2000 and at year-end stood at RMB 6.43 trillion ($775 billion), an amount equal to almost three-quarters of GDP. The only other major household financial asset is outsized holdings of currency, estimated to be RMB 1.0 trillion at year-end 2000.[38] Foreign banks have long believed that most of these funds could be used more effectively with the introduction of a modern payments system.

China's leadership has agreed to a significant opening of its financial sector and believes that competition from foreign banks can accelerate the development of a commercial credit culture in the domestic banking system. This potential is being weighed carefully against the risks associated with premature financial liberalization in the context of an admittedly weak state-owned banking system and a relatively new central bank with insufficient supervisory and regulatory experience. The large state-owned banks recognize the need to augment their capital. Their options, however, are quite limited. International equity markets will not be open to China's

37. These are discussed in detail in Lardy (forthcoming).

38. Currency in circulation at year-end 2000 was RMB 1.47 trillion, or 17 percent of GDP (Yang Shuang, "Steady Financial Circulation; Appropriate Money Supply," *Jinrong shibao* [Financial News], January 19, 2001, p. 1). If two-thirds of currency is held by households (the relevant share in the mid-1990s), then household currency holdings would be around RMB 1.0 trillion. Total currency in circulation relative to GDP is about eight times that in the United States, where payment systems are relatively well developed (Lardy, 1998, pp. 12–13, 132, 237).

largest state-owned banks until restructuring has proceeded further and the emergence of a commercial credit culture is clearly evident. The one possible exception is the Hong Kong branch of the Bank of China. This single branch has long been responsible for most of the bank's profits.[39] The other major state-owned banks plan to raise capital through domestic bond or equity listings, but prior to issuing stock they must clear the new hurdles imposed by the Ministry of Finance and the Chinese Securities Regulatory Commission. Any domestic listing by banks or other financial institutions, such as securities companies, must be preceded by a substantial increase in transparency. Banks will have to publicly disclose the magnitude of their nonperforming loans, as measured by the new forward-looking criteria that the central bank first introduced in 1998. To date only the Bank of China has disclosed this information.

One alternative that some banks are exploring for raising capital prior to cleaning up their portfolios and offering a public listing on domestic markets is the sale of subordinated debt on international markets. This approach, which has also been taken by several Korean banks, offers the prospect of meeting regulatory standards for capital adequacy in the short run while preparing for a future listing by cutting staff and increasing profitability. These banks would then be able to sell equity in the future at a much more favorable multiple of earnings.

The participation of foreign financial firms may thus encompass raising equity for the Hong Kong branch of the Bank of China or selling subordinated debt for a few banks. Unless China liberalizes its foreign financial sector more rapidly than required by its WTO commitments, however, the role of foreign financial institutions will remain relatively small, particularly in the banking sector. Their capital contribution is likely to be modest, given the various constraints analyzed above. Furthermore, the very small share of foreign banks in the domestic banking business will limit their role as a catalyst in encouraging the commercialization of the large domestic state-owned banks.

39. Overseas operations accounted for 61 percent of the bank's profits in 1997 (Bank of China, 1998). The vast bulk of these operations were undertaken by the Hong Kong branch, which is one of 1,844 branches the bank operated in 1997. The branch and its affiliated sister banks account for about one-fourth of all deposit taking and one-fourth of all lending activity in Hong Kong. See Lardy (1998, p. 210).

Korea and Thailand

Foreign banks began to play a substantially greater role in Korea and Thailand in 1998 and 1999 than they had historically. In early 1999 a group led by Goldman Sachs invested $500 million to acquire a 17 percent stake in Kookmin Bank, Korea's largest retail bank. Commerzbank invested W 200 billion to acquire one-third ownership in the Korean Exchange Bank, and Newbridge Capital invested W 500 billion ($417 million) in the fall of 1999 to acquire a majority stake in Korea First Bank.

In Thailand ABN AMRO acquired a 75 percent stake in the Bank of Asia, a medium-size bank, in September 1998. Standard Chartered acquired a small stake in Nakarnthon Bank in the summer of 1999, with a provision to increase its share to 80 percent over a five-year period. United Overseas Bank of Singapore purchased a 75 percent share of Radhanasin Bank, Thailand's smallest commercial bank. These early transactions in 1998 and 1999 generated a widespread expectation that foreign investors would buy up large parts of the banking sector in South Korea and Thailand, as banks that had been nationalized during the Asian financial crisis were restructured and sold off.

These expectations had not been realized by 2001, however. The proposed purchase of SeoulBank by the Hongkong and Shanghai Banking Corporation (HSBC) collapsed in the second half of 2000.[40] Moreover, the government's announced plan to sell its majority stakes in Chohung Bank and Hanvit Bank and its minority stakes in Korea First and Korea Exchange bank were abandoned in December 2000 in favor of injecting additional government funds and moving several of the institutions into a financial holding company. The prospect for sales of Korean banks to foreign financial institutions has thus diminished, at least in the short run. Similarly, the large transactions that were under negotiation for some time in Thailand collapsed in 2000. HSBC's $850 million investment to acquire a major stake in Bangkok Metropolitan Bank, a medium-size bank, fell through and Newbridge Capital's two bids to acquire Siam City Bank, one of Thailand's larger banks, were rejected. Finally, in early 2001, the newly elected Thai prime minister closed the door on any further sales of banks to international buyers.

The role of foreign financial institutions in contributing to the recovery and restructuring of the banking systems of the region is thus well below

40. The South Korean financial supervisory commission hired Deutsche Bank to restructure the bank, and it is possible that Deutsche could eventually acquire a controlling stake in SeoulBank.

initial expectations and substantially smaller than in parts of Latin America. In Mexico, for example, foreign banks controlled 45 percent of all banking assets by year-end 2000, just five years after the Mexican financial crisis. Foreign firms played a substantial role in providing capital, and the Mexican banking system now supports robust economic growth. In contrast, while Asia has experienced a V-shaped economic recovery, the failure to rehabilitate financial systems and the continued contraction of bank lending places the sustainability of the recovery in doubt. Moreover, governments in the region have incurred massive increases in domestic debt associated with protecting depositors from a loss of their savings.

If the injection of foreign capital via the acquisition of banks in Asia continues to be modest, investors will almost certainly shift their focus to the question of whether domestic fiscal resources are sufficient for financing the long-term restructuring of the banking systems. In Thailand, for example, "key debt ratios, under most scenarios, are not on a sustainable path."[41]

Finally, it remains to be seen whether the few banks that are now controlled by foreign institutions in these two countries can serve as a catalyst for a much needed broader reform of domestic banking systems. The refusal of the new foreign management of Korea First Bank to participate in the government-organized bailout of Hyundai and other large Korean corporations in January 2001 is a promising development. The risk, however, is that the share of bank assets controlled by foreign firms will remain so small that their catalytic role in the transformation to a commercial banking system will be marginal.

References

Asian Development Bank. 1996. *Report and Recommendation of the President to the Board of Directors on a Proposed Loan to the People's Republic of China for the Everbright Bank of China Project and a Proposed Equity Investment in the Everbright Bank of China.* Manila.
Bank of China. 1998. *Annual Report 1997.* Beijing.
———. 2000. *Annual Report 1999.* Beijing.
———. 2001. *Annual Report 2000.* Beijing.
Bear Stearns. 2001. *Korea: Limiting the Downturn in 2001.* New York (February 7).
BIS (Bank for International Settlements). 1998. *Report of the Working Group on Strengthening Financial Institutions.* Basel (October) (www.bis.org/publ/othp01.htm [July 11, 2001]).
Goldman Sachs. 1999. *China Banks: The Prize, WTO and the Opening of China's Banking Market to Foreign Banks.* Goldman Sachs Investment Research (December 14).

41. JP Morgan, *Global Data Watch,* February 9, 2001, p. 12.

Institute of International Finance. 1999. *Report of the Working Group on Financial Crises in Emerging Markets.* Washington (January).

Lardy, Nicholas R. 1998. *China's Unfinished Economic Revolution.* Brookings.

———. Forthcoming. *Integrating China in the Global Economy.* Brookings.

People's Bank of China. *Quarterly Statistical Bulletin* (several issues). Beijing.

———. 2000. *China Financial Outlook.* Beijing.

PART IV

Policies toward
Financial Sector FDI

EDWARD M. GRAHAM

10

Opening Banking to Foreign Competition

G21 G28

F23

As empirical studies have shown, foreign direct investment (FDI) typically brings host nations more than just macroeconomic benefits (meaning those that derive from the augmentation of national savings via an autonomously generated inward capital flow that produce faster rates of capital accumulation and hence faster economic growth than would otherwise be possible). The additional benefits tend to be associated with the transfer of technology or other "intangible assets" such as management skills, linkages to international networks to enable export possibilities that could not be realized in the absence of foreign direct investment, and the like.[1] But other, and perhaps underrated, benefits can accrue from more effective competition within the economy. These can be both static (mostly in the form of lower prices realized because monopoly rents are bid away by competition or greater market contestability) and dynamic.[2]

The author would like to thank Morris Goldstein and the editors of this volume, Robert Litan, Paul Masson, and Michael Pomerleano, for comments on an earlier draft.

1. See Dunning (1993) for a conceptual framework in which technology transfer occurs via foreign direct investment. It has been recognized for at least forty years that FDI is associated with technology transfer; the earliest empirical study yielding this result that I know of is Dunning (1958).

2. Thus at the microeconomic level, for example, it has been shown that not only are foreign-controlled activities typically more efficient with respect to a number of measures than locally controlled ones operating in the same sector, but that following entry by the foreign firm, locally controlled rivals often find their own performance improving by these same measures.

Together, these benefits can produce higher economic growth than would otherwise be achieved, as demonstrated by recent evidence from China.[3] Regions there that have received high amounts of foreign direct investment have experienced higher growth of gross domestic product (GDP) per capita than regions that have not received this investment, and it appears that the former regions might be converging to a higher equilibrium growth path than the latter regions.[4] Similarly, regions of China that have received large amounts of foreign direct investment since 1991 have experienced an acceleration of total factor productivity growth (which is an expected outcome if foreign direct investment brings with it technology transfer); regions that have not received this investment have not experienced such an acceleration.[5]

A growing body of evidence also suggests that the overall economic performance of a nation is a positive function of the state of development of its financial institutions, of which those in the banking sector are the most important in most nations. Countries with well-developed financial institutions in general, and well-developed banking sectors in particular, appear to experience more rapid rates of real per capita growth than do nations with less well-developed institutions.[6] It has also been shown that the level of financial intermediary development in a nation affects industry development unevenly, such that firms in sectors that are heavily dependent upon external finance do relatively better in nations with well-developed financial intermediaries than do firms in these same sectors in nations with less well-developed intermediaries.[7] The positive relationship between financial intermediary development and economic growth is not a result of simultaneity bias (there is no unknown third factor that creates both growth and well-developed financial intermediaries, such that the positive relationship between the latter two is not one in which the latter contributes to the former).[8] Two econometric procedures have been used to investigate why this positive relationship exists.[9] Controlling for a number of factors and sources of potential bias, one finds that the level of financial intermediary development does *not* significantly affect rates of private savings or

3. See, for example, Borzenstein, de Gregorio, and Lee (1998).

4. Dayal-Gulati and Husain (2000).

5. Graham and Wada (2001).

6. Levine and Zervos (1997). See also Levine's (1997) survey in which he concludes that the relationship between financial sector development and growth is positive and significant.

7. Rajan and Zingales (1998).

8. Levine, Loayza, and Beck (1999).

9. Beck, Levine, and Loayza (2000).

capital accumulation but does affect total factor productivity growth. This would seem to corroborate a circa 1911 observation by Joseph Schumpeter, who argued that financial intermediaries are important because they affect the *allocation* rather than the *amount* of savings.

The two observations—that FDI tends to improve efficiency and hence overall economic performance of an economy, especially per capita economic growth rates, and that a well-developed financial sector has much the same effect—would seem to imply that foreign direct investment in the financial sector would be especially welcome. After all, it would seem capable of providing a "double whammy" to the economy. Also important, evidence shows that there is a positive correlation between foreign ownership of banks and stability of the banking system.[10] Furthermore, contrary to widespread belief, the presence of foreign ownership seems to imply a lower vulnerability to a banking crisis in a country.[11]

Nevertheless, most nations have been reluctant to admit FDI in the banking or other financial sectors, especially without imposing a large number of restrictions or regulations on the entry and operations of foreign financial institutions that are discriminatory in nature, since they are not applied to similar domestically owned institutions.[12] Such discrimination is justified on various grounds, ranging from the purely political ("foreign ownership of domestic banks undermines national sovereignty") to the largely economic ("foreign banks cannot be counted upon to carry out national economic development goals"). Some would even argue that "a sound banking system is one in which banks earn some form of economic rent, and foreigners should not be allowed to capture that rent." Although

10. See, for example, Caprio and Honohan (2000); Diamond and Rangan (2000); and Goldberg, Dages, and Kinney (2000).

11. However, a distinction must be made between a nation opening the banking sector to foreign bank ownership and participation and opening its capital accounts, especially the short-term accounts, so that domestic banks (whether foreign or domestically owned) can borrow funds abroad more easily. The evidence would suggest that opening these accounts "too rapidly," that is, before appropriate prudential standards and sufficient supervisory capabilities are in place, might indeed make a country more vulnerable to a banking crisis after opening than before. Countries must therefore take certain steps to prepare themselves for capital account opening. However, this is a different issue from opening the banking sector to foreign ownership, which is discussed later in the chapter.

12. For purposes of this discussion, "FDI in the financial sector" is considered almost synonymous with "presence of foreign-owned institutions in the financial sector." If one wishes to split hairs, these two terms are not quite synonymous, because, for example, the entry of a branch of a foreign-owned bank into a nation's banking market may not, strictly speaking, set up a flow of foreign direct investment (the balance sheet of that branch might include no equity, which remains in the foreign parent, and FDI is by definition equity). Even so, some countries do consider interfirm loans to be FDI if the borrowing agent is located in a different nation from the lending agent, and hence these countries would consider any loan used to capitalize a local branch as FDI. Such nuances are not relevant here.

a case might be made for not letting foreigners capture rents, it remains doubtful that those rents are really necessary to maintain the health of this sector.

One main task of this chapter is to determine whether discriminatory restrictions on FDI in the financial sector in developing countries, especially on banking, make sense in the light of recent empirical research, which shows that FDI seems to promote efficiency and growth, that financial sector development does likewise, and that foreign ownership of banks is empirically associated with lower vulnerability to banking crises. The discussion begins with a brief survey of the kinds of restrictions that have been placed on foreign ownership of banks and whether they make sense. Next, some economic arguments are addressed regarding the need to restrict or regulate FDI in the financial or banking sector. The chapter concludes with a discussion of some policy issues. A particular concern here is the sequencing of policy changes required to liberalize FDI in the financial sector and yet avoid perverse outcomes.

Trends toward Liberalization

Some discriminatory restrictions on FDI in the financial sector exist in most countries, both developed and developing. Even where the participation of foreign-owned banks is not restricted, there are complaints of de facto discrimination (or, in some cases, lack of reciprocal treatment). The United States, for example, has enacted laws (the Stevenson-Reuss International Banking Act of 1978, the Foreign Bank Supervision Enhancement Act of 1994, and the Riegle-Neal Act of 1994) to ensure that foreign-owned banks do at least receive "national treatment" but cannot circumvent laws and policies that place restrictions on domestically owned counterparts. The European Union has complained that banking restrictions in the United States, even if applied on a national treatment basis, are such that European-controlled banks operating in the United States are more restricted than U.S.-controlled banks operating in Europe. (Some of these restrictions were eased, however, by the Riegle-Neal Act.) Japan provides de jure national treatment for foreign-controlled banks, but few such banks have had a major presence in Japan, at least until very recently, and regulation is said to have created a de facto bias in favor of locally owned incumbent banks. Arguably, the European Union maintains the most open banking sector in the world under the EU Commission's Second Bank

Directive of 1993, although some concerns remain about subtle discriminatory practices by individual member states.[13]

Restrictions on FDI in the financial sector tend to be most prevalent in nations where the government is heavily involved in the economy and uses banks and other financial institutions as instruments to implement its industrial policies. This has been the case in many developing nations. In recent years, however, a number of developing nations, especially in Latin America, have taken steps to open their banking sectors at least in part.[14] Argentina, for example, has begun to open as well as improve its banking system (the latter mostly by encouraging mergers and the consolidation of banks). Although Brazil's constitution has prohibited the establishment of either new branches or subsidiaries of foreign banks since 1988, this restriction has been more or less circumvented by a number of recent measures: for example, foreign banks are granted entry if this is needed to meet an obligation under an international agreement such as the Financial Services Agreement of the World Trade Organization (WTO), to meet a bilateral reciprocal agreement, or to safeguard national interest (a foreign takeover may be deemed necessary, for instance, for a troubled domestic bank). However, Brazil also tends to exact a "toll" for foreign bank entry, ranging from outright payments to the bank's willingness to accept assets of dubious quality where a foreign bank takes over a troubled domestic institution. Signs of change are also evident in Chile, which in 1997 passed a law both to liberalize regulations imposed on domestic banks and to formalize criteria for allowing new banks to enter the market. Other Latin American nations have also implemented liberalizing measures during the past ten years or so.

Outside of Latin America, liberalization has not been quite as pervasive. Although Korea moved to open its banking sector in 1998 by removing a previous prohibition on foreign banks establishing subsidiaries in Korea and by allowing foreign banks to participate in takeovers of domestic financial institutions, in practice obstacles remain. In particular, as a condition of takeover of domestic institutions, foreign banks have been asked to accept loan portfolios that they consider to be nonperforming but that the government does not recognize as such. Also, the nontransparent nature of financial accounting in Korea has proved an obstacle to foreign entry. Some foreign banks see prudential regulation in Korea, while applied on a

13. See U.S. Treasury (1998).
14. Ibid.

national treatment basis, as an entry barrier because this regulation in Korea differs substantially from regulation elsewhere.

Malaysia, by contrast, remains largely closed to new entry by foreign banks; no new licenses to allow such entry are currently being issued. The only means by which a foreign bank can enter the Malaysian market is via purchase of an existing institution, but then foreign ownership in a domestic banking institution is limited to 30 percent, so even this entry is necessarily in the form of a minority shareholder. New representative offices of foreign banks—arguably the lowest level of bank entry into a market, but also arguably not really an entry at all—are allowed in Malaysia, but even here no more than two personnel can be expatriates. However, a number of incumbent foreign banks have been licensed in the past to operate in Malaysia. They do so under discriminatory terms; for example, they cannot open new branches. Also, foreign-owned nonfinancial companies in Malaysia must source at least 60 percent of domestic credit requirements with domestically controlled financial institutions.

The Philippines has liberalized laws and policies pertaining to foreign banks since 1994, but these laws and policies remain quite restrictive and discriminatory. For example, a bank wishing to enter the Philippines de novo is required to be either among the top 150 banks in the world in terms of its net worth or in the top five in its home country. This requirement is meant to ensure that only the largest and soundest foreign banks enter the Philippine market but in practice might exclude smaller institutions that might be more innovative than large ones but nonetheless sound in terms of meeting prudential requirements. (The requirement also does not seem to preclude entry of a bank that is in fact in deep difficulty, if it is among the top five in its home country in terms of net worth: there are countries in which all the locally domiciled banks have a negative net worth!) Foreign banks can take over a 60 percent share in domestic banks, and consideration is being given to allowing 100 percent ownership.

In Singapore, entry of foreign banks is generally unrestricted if they wish to engage in offshore banking activities, but de facto and de jure restrictions exist on entry and operations of foreign-controlled banks in the domestic banking market. Thailand has liberalized its laws and policies toward foreign-owned banks in the wake of the Asian financial crisis, but barriers remain (for example, the number of expatriate managers in any institution is limited to six, and foreign-owned banks are required to keep some capital funds investments in certain low-yielding assets such as government bonds).

Table 10-1. *Changes in Banking Assets under Foreign Control in Selected Nations*[a]

Percent

Country	Banking assets under foreign control in December 1994	Banking assets under foreign control in December 1999
Czech Republic	5.8	49.3
Hungary	19.8	56.6
Poland	2.1	52.8
Turkey	2.7	1.7
Argentina	17.9	41.7
Brazil	8.4	16.8
Chile	16.3	53.6
Colombia	6.2	17.8
Mexico	1.0	18.8
Peru	12.3	33.4
Venezuela	16.3	41.9
Korea	0.8	4.3
Malaysia	6.8	11.5
Thailand	0.5	5.6

Source: International Monetary Fund.

a. Banking assets under foreign control = (assets of banks more than 50 percent foreign-owned)/(total banking assets).

In spite of all of these restrictions, the trend has been unmistakably toward the liberalization of foreign ownership of banking in many countries. As table 10-1 indicates, this liberalization has had marked effects. Most notably, the share of domestic banking assets has risen in a large number of countries in recent years. Furthermore, most of the nations mentioned above, including the Asian nations, are prepared to liberalize their banking sectors further.

All the same, some remain concerned about the potentially negative effects of this participation. Many fear that foreign ownership of banks will facilitate capital flight in periods of financial instability and thus perhaps contribute to such instability, or that an open financial sector will expose the country to risks of "contagion" (that is, the effects of a financial crisis in some other country will be transmitted to the domestic economy via the financial sector). Some also worry that greater foreign participation in the market, when coupled with large holdings of nonperforming loans, make it difficult for domestic institutions to compete with the foreign-owned ones. These fears were exacerbated in many cases by the Asian financial crisis of 1997–98 and its aftermath.

Such concerns are not without basis. Indeed, they are part of a larger concern, which is, as recent experience has shown, that financial sector reform (where the reform can include, but is not limited to, relaxation of barriers to entry by foreign institutions) can generate a host of problems. In most cases, the goals of reform have been to improve the functioning of the financial system, for example, to end implicit subsidies or taxes generated by the status quo, where such subsidies or taxes impede efficient intermediation of savings to investment. Such goals are laudable, of course, but implementing these goals can force financial institutions to take excessive risks. Thus the urgent task facing policymakers is to achieve the desired (and desirable) reform without simultaneously (and unwittingly) creating incentives that lead to perverse outcomes.

Does FDI in the Financial Sector Promote Efficiency?

Whether FDI in the financial sector promotes efficiency cannot be answered without first defining "efficiency" in this sector. Does it mean, for example, that financial institutions themselves are efficient, in the sense that, for any output, they minimize the input of resources, in other words, that they are cost-efficient? (This concept of efficiency is often termed "x-efficiency.") Or, does it mean that, given the volume of national savings that an economy generates, these institutions intermediate these savings into the best possible end uses, taking into account the risk characteristics of alternative end-use possibilities? In the first case, one is talking about the efficiency of individual financial institutions, but in the second it is about the efficiency of the entire financial system as it affects the performance of the economy. The two concepts of "efficiency" do not fully coincide, in that the latter might imply a different mix of financial services than is possible under the regulatory regime currently extant in a nation. This is so even if financial institutions are as x-efficient as the regulatory regime allows. The whole system might be inefficient because the regime itself is bad.

Fortunately, it is reasonable to assume that x-efficiency of institutions is positively related to efficiency of the system or, conversely, that x-inefficient institutions can create problems with respect to the efficiency of the system. To see why, suppose that widespread x-inefficiency within banks in a particular country has resulted from regulatory policies that have enabled the banks to operate as a cartel. The x-inefficiency can manifest itself either as high costs due to so-called organizational slack (basically, overstaffing) or as a lack of organizational capabilities that a bank operating in a more competitive market might see as essential to performing well or even competently in that environment (for example, risk assessment and management capabilities, monitoring capabilities, and the like). Suppose further that the cartel is able to exist because incumbent banks are protected by government regulation that effectively blocks entry by other banks. Also suppose that the continuance of this regulatory protection against competition is contingent (implicitly or explicitly) on the incumbent banks lending on favorable terms to politically favored borrowers, with the result that other potential borrowers who might have put the funds to better uses than the politically well-connected borrowers cannot get access to loans. In effect, then, the cartelization serves to promote the interests of politically well-connected persons or firms over the interests of the nation as a whole.

In this case, reformers might, for more reasons than simply reducing x-inefficiency, seek elimination of the banking cartel. Rather, such elimination might be necessary to achieve better allocation of savings toward investment in order to achieve both a higher growth rate of the economy and, over time, a more equitable distribution of income and wealth. In other words, attacking the source of x-inefficiency, notably the regulatory structure that blocks new entry of banks, is one means of attacking systematic inefficiency. The most straightforward way to do this is to deregulate so as to allow new entry into the banking sector, where the new entrants would not be bound by the old rules.

But, also, presumably, if new entry is sought as a remedy for systematic inefficiency, those new entrants that would be most sought are ones that are more x-efficient than the incumbent banks.[15] In fact, theoretical considerations would lead one to predict that any bank that has proved its ability to operate internationally must possess some form of x-efficiency that purely domestic rivals in foreign markets do not have. This is simply because a bank that operates in one country but seeks to operate in some other country must have some advantage if its entry is going to be successful; otherwise, it operates at an inherent disadvantage in relation to local rivals. For example, success in banking requires information; hence, all else being

15. It must be borne in mind that new entry might be desirable even if the new entrants are not significantly more x-efficient than the incumbents, if the new entrants were to shake up the old ways of doing things.

equal, a bank that has poor access to local market information would be expected to do poorly in comparison with rivals that have better access to information. But a new entrant into a banking market—especially a new entrant from another country—would in almost all circumstances have less access to relevant local information than an incumbent bank.[16] Also, a new bank entrant might have difficulty attracting deposits in order to create a deposit base on which to write new loans. This is because in ordinary circumstances incumbent banks will have reputation advantages over new entrant foreign banks, such that depositors will prefer to keep funds in the incumbents rather than move funds to what might be perceived as risky new banking institutions.[17] If the new entrant is to succeed against these expected advantages of incumbent banks, it must have an offsetting advantage, possibly in the form of higher x-efficiency.

However, this assumes that the foreign bank enters a national market in direct competition with local banks. In some cases, the foreign bank entry is not in direct competition, especially if it seeks to provide multinational firms based in the same home country as the bank with specific services not provided by local banks. In this event, the foreign bank might not actually possess a higher x-efficiency than local banks but might simply fill a niche that the local banks do not.

Suppose that lower x-efficiency in the incumbent banks, compared with at least some international banks, were to manifest itself in the form of the former banks not having developed the organizational skills required to assess properly business opportunities and the risks associated with these opportunities and to monitor the performance of borrowers. In this case, the reformer might be particularly inclined to encourage entry by banks that possessed these skills. Given that such skills are not available domestically, the reformer might be led to consider relaxing entry restrictions faced by foreign banks.

Thus one might ask whether the incumbent banks would be so damaged by the new entry that they could not survive or, perhaps worse, that they would behave perversely (for example, in a desperate effort to restore the value of equity diminished by new entry, they might invest in undertakings

16. This is indeed a main reason why an international bank often attempts to enter a new national market via acquisition rather than via de novo entry.

17. But, of course, this situation might be reversed if incumbent banks are widely known to be in difficulty such that local depositors fear that their deposits are at risk due to possible bankruptcy of these incumbent banks. In this case, a new entrant might actually hold an advantage in terms of ability to attract deposits. This would be especially so if the new entrant were an international bank with a strong reputation, such that this bank was known to local depositors even before its entry into the market.

that have a potentially high return but are very risky). This is a real issue, and there is substantial empirical evidence to suggest that in practice a switch from a less to a more competitive banking environment poses significant (but, presumably short-run) adjustment costs on the economy, resulting from incumbents having to reorganize themselves to perform effectively in the new environment. How a change in policy can still be achieved in light of this issue is discussed later in the chapter.

If new entry by more x-efficient banks is sought, it is reasonable to ask whether foreign banks typically are more x-efficient than domestically owned ones. As just noted, theoretical considerations suggest that this might be so, but not necessarily so, in the case of international banks, that is, those that have proved capable of operating outside their home countries. Because theoretical considerations do not fully resolve the issue, empirical evidence is of special relevance. Indeed a large amount of empirical research suggests that many banks, when attempting operations outside their home country, are typically more x-efficient than locally owned ones.[18] On this issue, it is difficult or even misleading to compare x-efficiencies of financial institutions on a cross-sectional basis across countries, for example, to determine whether banks in the United States tend to be more x-efficient than those in Germany. This is because the regulatory regimes in these two, or indeed any two, countries are different, and hence it is not out of the question for differences in measured performance of financial institutions to reflect more differences in these regimes than differences in innate x-efficiency.

For this reason, the most credible approach to examining empirically whether the financial institutions of one country are more x-efficient than those of another is to compare foreign-owned with domestic-owned institutions operating in the same country. A recent contribution following this approach is a study of the relative efficiencies of foreign versus domestically owned banks in five countries: France, Germany, Spain, the United Kingdom, and the United States.[19] In line with the theory of foreign direct investment, domestically owned banks would be expected to possess certain advantages, most notably intimate knowledge of local markets and regulatory conditions, not possessed by foreign-owned banks that, all else being equal, should enable the former to operate more efficiently than the latter. Compounding this is the fact that foreign-owned banks must be managed across national boundaries, and the transactional costs of doing so pre-

18. For an extensive review of the relevant literature, see Berger and others (2000).
19. Ibid.

sumably add to the costs and hence reduce the x-efficiency of this class of banks.

As suggested earlier, however, foreign-owned banks also might have offsetting advantages over domestically owned ones. Economies of scale or scope that come from international operations might account for these advantages.[20] Alternatively, a foreign-owned bank might possess certain advantages that accrue largely from operating in its country of origin; for example, if the banking sector in some particular country is exceptionally competitive, or is subject to particularly effective regulation, a bank domiciled in that country might develop exceptional firm-specific characteristics that will enable that same bank to operate more efficiently than competitors in other countries. (This would be consistent with the earlier assertion that the offsetting advantage of the international bank is greater x-efficiency than its local rivals.)

The alternative hypotheses can be summed up as follows: (1) domestically owned banks are generally more efficient than foreign-owned ones, indicating that "home field advantages" dominate advantages associated with globalization; (2) foreign-owned banks are generally more efficient than domestically owned ones, so that "global advantages" dominate over home field advantages; or (3) foreign-owned banks from certain countries of origin, but not others, are more efficient than either domestically owned banks or foreign-owned banks from countries other than these, so that "limited global advantages" (ones that derive from conditions specific to the home nation) dominate other sources of advantage.[21]

Two measures of x-efficiency show that hypothesis (1) dominates hypothesis (2) for all five countries. In other words, domestically owned banks in general tend to be more efficient than foreign-owned ones.[22] How-

20. Berger and others (2000) extensively review the literature bearing on whether banking institutions exhibit significant economies of scale or scope.

21. The "limited global advantage" hypothesis is virtually the same as the "OLI" framework of John Dunning for explaining foreign direct investment in general. Dunning hypothesizes that a firm becomes a direct investor when it possesses certain firm-specific "ownership" (O) advantages, usually deriving from home market operations, and is able to work these in the context of conditions found in another nation (he terms these "L-advantages" that are specific to the host nation, e.g., abundance of skilled labor) and where it is economically advantageous to do so internally within the firm rather than, say, granting licenses to local entrepreneurs in that country to work the O-advantages in their country (hence there are "I-advantages," those that accrue to internalization). See, for example, Dunning (1993, chap. 10).

22. For three of the host countries—France, Germany, and the United Kingdom—domestically owned banks tend to be more efficient by both measures used by Berger and others (2000) than foreign-owned banks. Some of the differences are small, however. For Spain and the United States, the results are mixed: foreign-owned banks are more efficient by one measure but not the other.

ever, hypothesis (3) dominates hypothesis (1): that is, foreign-owned banks from certain countries tend to be consistently more efficient than domestic banks in a number of host countries.[23] Specifically, banks from the United States tend to be more x-efficient by at least one measure than banks from other nations, whether in the United States itself or in the home country of the other banks. A similar but weaker result holds for German banks.

The subjects of the five-country study, it should be remembered, are all advanced industrial nations and presumably all have well developed banking sectors. Hence, in all likelihood, banks from all five tend to be at the high end of x-efficiency, especially in comparison with banks based in developing nations.[24] Nonetheless, banks that operate globally are not necessarily more x-efficient than ones that do not, as is clear from observations that at least some international banks serve mostly clients based in the home country of the bank that themselves operate globally (this seems to be true, for example, of Japanese banks). Rather, the five-country study shows that those banks that are forced by their home country environments to be x-efficient are able to transfer this efficiency to operations in countries other than their home countries.

Hence if a country wishes to attract foreign banks that are more x-efficient than local banks, it should take into account the home country of the foreign bank when choosing which banks are allowed to enter. Unless this criterion were applied in a nondiscriminatory fashion, however (say, through prudential tests that were blind to the nationality of a bank), it could run afoul of most-favored nation obligations under international agreements (the most relevant of these being the WTO Financial Services Agreement).[25] Although in cases where a nation's banking sector has performed poorly it is desirable to allow entry of banks that are more x-efficient than incumbent banks, there is much to be said simply for increasing the amount of competition in the banking market. In other words, it can be desirable to increase competition within this sector even if the new entrants that come into the sector are not significantly more x-efficient than incumbents. This is so even if it would be even more desirable that the new entrants indeed were significantly more x-efficient than incumbent banks.

---

23. The former result has been widely reported, whereas the latter is unique to Berger and others (2000).

24. On this point, see Claessens, Demirgüç-Kunt, and Huizinga (2000).

25. See Sauvé and Steinfatt's comments in chapter 12 of this volume.

The proposition that more competition is desirable for its own sake is supported by tests of the relationship between concentration in the banking sector and economic growth of manufacturing industries in forty-one countries and thirty-six manufacturing sector industrial categories.[26] These tests indicate that concentration (a proxy for lack of competition) has a "first-order" effect of depressing growth across all industries (that is, in general, the more concentrated the banking sector, the lower the growth of the combined output of all industries). However, there is an important caveat: banking concentration seems to affect growth across manufacturing industries heterogeneously. That is, the relationship between banking concentration and growth differs by industry. And, while banking concentration is negatively related to the growth of total output, concentration seems to be positively related to the growth of young firms that are particularly dependent upon external finance to achieve this growth; older and established firms can often finance growth via internally generated cash flow, but this is usually not so for younger firms.

This is thought to be so because, in an environment with few banks, banks are able to develop closer and longer-lasting relationships with young firms and thus are in a position to evaluate their growth potential better than in an environment with many banks. The reason for this is that "gentlemen's rules" tend to prevail where competition among banks is not intense, meaning that one bank does not try to take away customers of some other bank. If these understandings are observed, a bank knows that if it incurs those costs necessary to evaluate the prospects of young firms and, contingent upon a positive finding, supports the firm in its start-up phase, during which the firm might not be able to pay back the loans, the bank can nonetheless recover the investment as the firm grows and generates cash by continuing to lend to the firm at high rates of interest. In a more competitive environment, by contrast, a bank might be wary of undertaking such an investment on grounds that, if the firm is successful, other banks will bid for its business and undercut the lending rate that is necessary for the first bank to charge to recover the sunk costs associated with supporting the firm in its start-up period.

This last situation is essentially a "free-rider" problem. In a competitive banking market, banks will not commit to sunk costs because other banks might "free-ride" and make it improbable that those costs can be recovered. This problem can be circumvented by allowing banks to take equity positions in young start-up firms.[27] In fact, it has been shown that restricting

26. Cetorelli and Gambera (1999).
27. See Cetorelli and Gambera (1999).

commercial banking activity (for example, preventing banks from engaging in investment banking activity such as underwriting equity securities) is negatively associated with bank performance; thus it is arguable that banks should be allowed to take such positions.[28] Allowing banks to do so would correct the market failure created by the "free-riding" problem, whereas there seem to be no offsetting reasons not to allow banks to do so.

The market failure created by this free-rider problem does *not* warrant, in the absence of correction of this problem, that banking markets should be concentrated. Rather, the first-order effect of more competition is higher overall growth, and this effect dominates the ill effects of any market failure. Thus creating more competition in banking is desirable in its own right, as claimed earlier. Moreover, if the additional competition results from the entry of banks that are more x-efficient than the incumbents, this desirability is enhanced.

To illustrate, consider the effects of foreign bank entry on the domestic banking market in Argentina during the 1990s.[29] This case strongly suggests that (1) foreign bank entry creates benefits because new entrants have advantages, mostly in the form of greater x-efficiency, than domestic rivals; and (2) greater competition in this market is good in its own right. Foreign banks in Argentina have tended to concentrate their loan portfolios in the *manufacturing* sector, leaving consumer lending largely to domestic banks. Margins and profits of domestic banks whose loans are concentrated in the consumer lending sector in Argentina tend to be higher than those of domestic banks whose loans are concentrated in the industrial sector. This is largely because of the lack of competition in the former category and not because of greater efficiency of the former versus the latter.

Why Countries Regulate FDI in Banking Discriminatorily

Although foreign banks might be desirable from the point of view of national economic performance, governments worldwide remain reluctant to allow this entry, or at least are not likely to do so without imposing discriminatory regulations or conditions on foreign banks. This section explores reasons commonly given for this reluctance.[30]

28. See Barth and others (2001a). They control for other variables that might affect bank performance, for example, official supervisory procedures, capital regulations, regulations on competition, and "moral hazard engendered by deposit insurance schemes."

29. See Clarke and others (2000).

30. This section draws heavily on Hindley (2000).

The reason most often given for this reluctance is rooted in nationalism. A sovereign nation, many argue, cannot permit its banking sector to be under foreign control because banks play a key role in the national economy, intermediating national savings into national investment, and only nationals can be trusted to play this role. This is actually a statement of preference and does not establish a clear negative consequence of allowing such ownership.[31] Also, there is a clear and obvious fallacy in the statement: if the performance of the banking sector is critical to the performance of the economy of a nation, and if the overriding goal of the nation is to achieve robust economic performance, then the goal of the nation should be to have the best-functioning banking system possible. If this can be achieved by some degree of foreign control of banks operating in the nation, does it not make sense to allow such foreign control? Indeed, to test whether the people of a nation actually believe that foreign control of banks is or is not in their nation's interest, policymakers really should know how people would respond to a question such as "What is preferable, real annual growth of per capita GDP of 4 percent with at least some of our nation's banks under the control of foreigners, or real annual growth of per capita GDP of 2.5 percent, but with all of our nation's banks under the control of our own citizens?" The degree to which foreign ownership of banks was restricted might then be conditioned upon how much additional growth could be achieved by allowing the presence of foreign-owned banks, but balanced against how much growth the nation's citizens would be willing to forgo in order to prevent such foreign ownership.

In practice, of course (but unfortunately), no country determines its policy toward foreign ownership of banks in this manner. Instead, a range of arguments are made for and against such ownership. The most common of these arguments boil down to an infant industry argument or some variant of it. This argument, as applied to the banking sector in developing nations, is that domestic banks in these nations require protection from foreign competition for some limited time in order to allow them to mature. During this period, they can increase their efficiency by "learning by doing." Following this period of protection, they will have matured—that is, they will have increased their efficiency—to the point where they can

31. For example, the case has been made that foreign banks might facilitate capital flight during periods of crisis. But why? If, for example, a nation is (unwisely) defending an exchange rate pegged too high, do domestic banks tend to keep funds at home in local currency as a matter of patriotic duty when there are opportunities to send funds abroad and perhaps thus benefit from a devaluation that is seen as inevitable? Recent evidence would suggest that domestic banks do not tend to behave in this patriotic fashion, and, indeed, the case could be made that they should not do so.

compete effectively against foreign-owned banks, or so goes the claim. But, if exposed to this competition too soon, the foreign banks will annihilate the domestic ones by forcing huge losses on them. These losses occur because foreign banks are able to operate more efficiently than local banks and hence in order to meet foreign competition, the domestic banks must price loans and banking services below cost and incur losses by doing so.

The infant industry argument is, however, full of logical holes. To begin, suppose that this argument is correct at least in its assertion that, if allowed to mature, a local bank indeed will mature, so that over time it will transform itself from noncompetitive to competitive status in relation to its foreign rivals or potential rivals. But does this require that the local bank be granted temporary protection from these rivals? If the long-term prospects of the bank are such that it will indeed be competitive, and hence profitable, in an unprotected market but at the cost of short-run, temporary losses accumulated while the bank is learning how to compete, this situation is typical of many business start-ups, in developed as well as developing nations. Investors, if they can reasonably expect the future profits of a venture, appropriately discounted, to offset current losses such that the expected return on investment is positive, are willing to underwrite such a venture. Temporarily to protect such venture from competition, whether foreign or domestic, is in effect to tax the users of the products or services of the venture in order to subsidize these investors. The investors, for obvious reasons, are happy to accept such subsidies, but the subsidies are not required for the investors to participate in the venture.

A subsidy could, on the other hand, be warranted if the venture might be expected to create positive externalities, so that there is an expected positive social return on the venture but an expected negative private return (or, alternatively, the expected private return is positive but inadequate to compensate investors for the risks of the venture). A positive externality exists if benefits are created that are captured by neither the venture itself (or, more properly, the shareholders of the venture) nor the users of the venture's products or services. Rather, these benefits are captured by other, "external" agents in the economy. Such positive externalities can be created, for example, when a new technology is developed and commercialized by being diffused to parties other than the original developer.

If the positive externalities create a large enough "wedge" between the social and private returns to investment in the venture, some subsidy might be warranted to induce the investors to undertake a venture that they might otherwise forgo, in order that the externalities be created. However, no subsidy can exist without cost (any subsidy requires some tax in order to finance it, which sometimes may be implicit and hence nontransparent), and the main criterion for granting the subsidy therefore should be that the positive externalities have value greater than the true cost of the subsidy. What the subsidy does, then, is to tax the positive externalities so that funds are transferred from the general public (which benefits from the externalities even after the tax and hence in principle should be willing to pay the tax) to the investors in order to give the latter an expected return adequate to induce them to make the investment and where, in the absence of the subsidy, they are unwilling to invest.

In the case of banking, however, it is not clear that any positive externality arises from the creation of a domestically owned bank if the bank does not operate efficiently. Indeed, if the bank must be protected from competition because it is x-inefficient, the systematic efficiency of the financial sector would likely be impaired. In this case, it is arguable that the result of such protection is actually the creation of a *negative* externality, namely, that the growth prospects of the economy are reduced. Even if the premise of the infant industry argument is correct—that domestic banks that in their start-up phases are noncompetitive by virtue of their relative inefficiency with respect to foreign banks can mature into competitive institutions—it does *not* follow that these banks should be subsidized by being granted protection from competition from foreign banks.

If anything, the protection is more likely to inhibit the desired maturation of the start-ups than to foster it. The reason commonly given for protecting the "infants" is that, without protection, they cannot survive, let alone mature. But if they in fact are truly likely to mature, investors should be willing to incur start-up losses in order to achieve the positive returns that lie ahead. Furthermore, these investors would be expected to monitor the performance of their investments carefully and to take remedial steps if the required maturation does not proceed. By contrast, if banks are granted protection, they likely will become dependent on the implicit subsidy from which they may never wean themselves. This tendency will be reinforced because the investors will lose incentive to monitor their investments, because the return to their investment will be ensured even if the banks do not mature.[32]

32. Public ownership of the banks changes none of the above. In the case of such ownership, the state itself is the investor, and its behavior is not likely to be greatly different from that of a private investor. Thus in the telecommunications sector, it has been found empirically that introduction of competition is more important to achieving greater efficiency of state-owned service providers than is privatization (see Ergas 1997).

Indeed, it strains credibility to call incumbent banks in most developing nations "start-ups." Most such banks have been in existence now for several decades or longer. What does seem to be true is that, in spite of being chronological adults, many of these banks remain "infants" in terms of their development. As stressed in the previous section, an effective antidote to this arrested development is likely to be more competition, not more protection from it. However, it must also be acknowledged, nations that have introduced more competition and liberalized policy to allow admission of foreign banks have experienced some major problems. These are addressed in the next section.

Another argument for curtailing or limiting foreign ownership of banks in developing countries is that foreign banks will encourage perverse capital flows, particularly capital flight away from the country. A variant of this that gained particular cogency during the Asian financial crisis of 1997 was that foreign banks might facilitate large inflows of short-term capital into a nation during some period of euphoric expectations but, later, reevaluate their expectations downward and thence withdraw that capital hastily, precipitating severe balance of payments problems accompanied by a free fall of local currency. This then might send local institutions into tailspins from which they cannot easily recover. Such crises occurred in several Asian countries in 1997.[33]

What is not clear, however, is whether foreign ownership of domestic banking operations in the crisis countries has been to blame for this type of crisis or whether this ownership played much of a role at all. In the case of the 1997 crisis, foreign banks, before the crisis, had lent substantial sums to locally owned banks, but the lenders failed properly to evaluate and monitor their end uses. The local banks in several countries then made substantial loans to property developers and other end borrowers who invested funds in speculative ventures that in many cases either went bust or did not earn returns adequate to meet the servicing costs of the debt incurred to finance the ventures. The debacle that followed revealed many problems, including ones of public policy, notably, inadequate supervision and monitoring of banks by public authorities, too little capability of those banks that lent to speculative ventures to assess risk and monitor borrower performance, and perhaps too easy access of those banks to international finance permitted by recent policy reforms to open capital accounts. Also

33. For analytic treatments of major banking crises of recent years, see Goldstein (1998); Demirgüç-Kunt and Detragiache (1998); Goldstein, Kaminsky, and Reinhart (2000), who focus on early indicators that such a crisis is imminent.

revealed were significant deficiencies on the part of the international banks with respect to their own risk-assessment and monitoring capabilities. If locally owned banks were lending unwisely, international banks should have been able to ascertain this and not have funded this lending.

But, the key question is, does this have anything to do with foreign ownership of domestic banking operations? In fact, much of the problem was rooted in informational asymmetries (in particular, foreign banks did not have full information regarding the lending activities of local banks but rather depended upon the reputation of these local banks as a basis for lending to them; also, local banks themselves did not always have full information pertaining to the activities to which they were lending). Under these circumstances, it could be argued that local participation of foreign banks might have helped avert the crisis. This might have been the case if, say, the foreign banks had, through their local affiliates, access to better information regarding the creditworthiness of local borrowers and the ventures these borrowers were creating than the information they received through local banks.

This having been said, it follows that if a domestic financial system is in need of improvement, the import of foreign know-how by allowing the establishment of foreign banks is a means to achieve this.[34] However, it also follows, on the basis of the events of 1997, that the international financial system itself is in need of improvement. The point here is that one way of doing this as well is for developing nations to allow the establishment of foreign banks. This entry could serve to improve both the functioning of local credit markets and international markets.

To be sure, such action will not solve all or even the majority of problems revealed by the crisis. Perhaps the greatest single problem revealed in 1997 was the lack of transparency, especially at the level of the final borrower. More than anything, the Asian financial crisis was created because lenders (mostly banks) had advanced loans to activities that, had full information been available, the lenders might have avoided in the first place. In spite of the obvious lesson to be drawn from this experience, governments in the region have been slow to implement tougher requirements regarding financial transparency. A case in point is Korea. It now requires its large industrial groups, the *chaebol*, which are the major users of bank debt, to prepare and make public consolidated balance sheets and income statements. The main objective is to force these groups to reveal all liabilities and all losses. After much resistance on the part of these groups, the first such

34. Hindley (2000).

statements were released in July 2000, almost three years after the crisis first developed, and the statements in fact showed larger amounts of debt and a greater extent of loss-making activity on the part of many of the largest *chaebol* than had previously been admitted. Furthermore, the Korean government has treated the information contained in these statements almost as a state secret. Other nations hit by this crisis, such as Thailand, have been even more reluctant to implement meaningful requirements for transparency on the part of large borrowers.

As mentioned earlier, developing nations worry that foreign ownership will transmit financial "contagion" to their own system, since a foreign bank encountering problems in one country might then cut back on lending in other countries, in order to restore its capital-to-asset ratio to meet capital adequacy requirements or perhaps to meet margin calls or to adjust lending portfolios to reduce risk exposure. There is indeed evidence to indicate that this is a valid concern.[35] Of course, there can be other causes of "contagion," one being trade linkages.[36] For example, two clusters of countries might be subject to common lender effects. Suppose that one cluster borrows from Japan and another borrows heavily from the United States. Contagion via lending channels could explain regional contagion that has in fact occurred in each of these clusters.[37] Other transmission mechanisms include trade or common country-specific characteristics. An econometric comparison of financial linkages and trade linkages as transmission mechanisms in the Mexican crisis of 1995, the Thai (Asian) crisis of 1997, and the Russian crisis of 1999 demonstrates that financial linkages as measured by a broad measure of competition for bank funds do seem to account for the contagion, even when trade linkages are included in the specification.[38] Furthermore, the two types of linkages are highly correlated, which helps explain why financial linkages are not a robust explanator of contagion in some instances where trade linkages are included in the specification.

If contagion is a potential problem for the domestic banking sector, it can be addressed through diversification, by both the international banks and host countries. On one hand, a bank that operates in many countries and is not excessively dependent upon any one country for a large share of its total business is less likely to be forced to sell significant amounts of assets

35. See Kaminsky and Reinhart (2000); and van Rijckeghem and Weder (1999).
36. See Eichengreen, Rose, and Wyplosz (1996); and Glick and Rose (1999).
37. See Kaminsky and Reinhart (2000).
38. Van Rijckeghem and Weder (1999).

in one country to raise funds to deal with a crisis in some other country. Host countries, on the other hand, should strive to ensure that a large number of home nations of banks are represented in the foreign-owned banks that operate in their financial markets. This latter diversification is important because a local affiliate of a foreign bank might be forced to reduce lending activity locally in response to adverse conditions in the bank's home nation.[39] Even in diversified international banks, their overall portfolios are likely to be more dependent on assets held in the home country than in any other country, and if these home-nation assets become questionable, the bank might respond by cutting back on lending worldwide. Japanese banks, for example, retrenched worldwide in the 1990s in response to mounting nonperforming loans at home.[40] This may have magnified the contagion effects associated with the Asian crisis beginning in Thailand in 1997. Hence a country may not wish to have too large a share of the banking market held by banks from the same home country (as is the case in much of Latin America, where banks from Spain head the list of foreign-owned banks operating in several nations). The problem is relevant in both directions. For example, it might be bad for a Latin American country to rely too much on Spanish banks because they might transmit a crisis in Spain via the country's banks. Conversely, a crisis in Latin America, if too many loans of Spanish banks are held there, could spread to Spain.

Diversification by a host nation implies that when a country opens its banking sector to foreign bank participation, it should encourage banks from many countries, not simply one or two, to enter. This seems contrary to the notion expressed earlier that a country might wish to attract banks from certain home countries rather than others in order to benefit from superior x-efficiencies, which tend to be determined by a bank's home country. Recall, however, that more competition in banking is almost always preferred to less (as long as the country corrects for possible market failure caused by regulation, for example, by removing regulations prohibiting banks to invest in equities or otherwise to engage in broad financial intermediation activities). Furthermore, there is some benefit to international diversification of domestic banks that is by a home country.

Another argument marshaled against foreign ownership of banks is that, if domestically owned banks are saddled with nonperforming loans, the entry of foreign-owned banks will cause the domestic banks to be annihilated because the latter will be saddled with these loans while the former are

39. Caprio and Honohan (2000).
40. Peek and Rosengren (1997).

not. Given that nonperforming loans are a major problem in many developing nations, this is a common concern.

An immediate problem with this argument is that, if nonperforming loans are prevalent in a nation, and if the banking system is closed to entry by new competitors, the "good" borrowers—those who are able to pay servicing charges on their debt—will, in effect, via the banks subsidizing "bad" borrowers, be those who cannot meet these servicing charges. An equivalent statement is that "good" borrowers are subject to an implicit tax in the form of higher charges than would be necessary were there no nonperforming loans (or at least if these loans were to be in a range that healthy banks in a competitive environment would consider normal). This subsidy/tax scheme is made possible by the entry restriction.

This situation is of concern to any nation for two reasons. First, at the margin, the higher costs of debt service will cause some borrowers to fall over the line from "good" to "bad" (that is, these borrowers might be able to service debt were interest charges lower, but high interest charges jeopardize their viability and hence their ability to pay back the loans). Thus unresolved nonperforming loans that force banks to increase debt-service charges on loans that are not nonperforming has the perverse effect of creating more nonperforming loans. Second, and more important (and more perverse), national savings under this situation are being used to support nonviable activities, at the cost of not having those savings available to finance viable ones.

Furthermore, the situation is open-ended: the subsidy to the banks to offset losses from nonperforming loans is, in effect, granted with no condition attached that the nonperforming loans be resolved. There might be, in fact, some logic to granting subsidies to allow nonperforming loans to be resolved, for example, to enable workers employed in nonviable activities to exit those activities and to move into other activities offering better long-term prospects. However, a situation where banks simply continue to carry nonperforming loans and cover the resulting losses by charging high rates to good borrowers provides no incentive to resolve the problem. This creates a major social cost because, in colorful terms, activities that are economic "zombies" siphon off resources from more vital activities, leaving them stunted by malnourishment if not starved. If the problem is pervasive, the whole economy stagnates.

The solution, simply put, is to resolve the problem of the nonperforming loans. If necessary, public money must be spent to this end, though governments must ensure that this money does not merely allow the problem to continue to fester. Governments seem hesitant to tackle nonperforming loans, mostly because this requires hard steps: enterprises that have no realistic prospect of meeting debt-servicing requirements (and indeed typically require continuing infusion of funds to survive) must be shut down and their assets sold for partial recovery of funds owed. Those enterprises that, by contrast, might have some prospect of meeting debt-servicing requirements but must restructure themselves to do so must be forced to produce and implement plans to turn themselves around. Alas, in most cases, the required restructuring involves the shedding of excess labor. In either case—shutting down nonviable activities or restructuring ones that can be viable but are not so at the present time—the effect in the short term is increased unemployment, which is political anathema. But, as noted earlier, to keep these enterprises alive but on "artificial life support" would over time condemn much of the nation's population to lower and lower standards of living. Even so, given the choice between short-term pain and even greater suffering stretched out over the long term, most politicians will avoid the former even if the latter is sure to happen.

Governments often insist that nonperforming loans in the incumbent domestically owned banks must be resolved before foreign banks can be allowed to enter the domestic financial sector but then fail to take steps necessary to resolve the loans. This subjects the economy to a negative "double whammy": the nonperforming loans themselves, for reasons just noted, create a drag on growth, while a financial sector that is less efficient than it could be creates an additional drag on this growth. This situation is so perverse that it almost defies imagination. It is almost akin to a patient refusing to undergo an operation to rid himself or herself of a malignancy on grounds that the operation will be painful. In fact, the operation is necessary to prevent loss of life.

An additional fear is that foreign-owned banks in the domestic sector will be able to "cream-skim," that is, draw away the "good" business from incumbent local banks, leaving only unprofitable activities to these banks. If this is a real possibility, then incumbent banks must in fact be engaged in unprofitable activities (such as government-forced "policy lending" to nonviable enterprises that cannot meet debt-servicing charges on normal commercial terms).[41] Banking reform should encourage banks to either get rid of such activities or, if possible, to restructure so as to be profitable (for example, by forcing nonperforming borrowers to restructure themselves so that they can meet their debt-servicing requirements). The threat created

41. See Hindley (2000).

by the entry of foreign-owned banks might even persuade local banks to undertake these reforms, so the case can be made that foreign entry could help resolve such problems and bring about meaningful reform.

Getting to There from Here

To reiterate, FDI in a nation's banking sector is likely to improve overall efficiency of that sector, both by enhancing competition and by allowing the skills held by foreign institutions (leading to greater x-efficiency of these institutions) to permeate the sector. These are not independent events: forced to compete with foreigners, domestic banks have much greater incentive to learn and adopt "best practices" than if sheltered from this competition. Greater efficiency is desirable for more than its own sake. Given the key role banking plays in intermediate savings to investment, greater efficiency is likely to lead to greater overall economic growth. Although many countries are still cool to FDI, their opposition can be questioned on both logical and empirical grounds.

Other countries have looked at FDI more favorably. Many of these took steps to reduce entry barriers to foreign banks during the 1990s. However, as already noted, problems that culminated in the Asian financial crisis of 1997–98 have caused at least some nations to rein in the pace of liberalization.[42] They did so mainly out of fear that the entry of foreign banks could decimate the domestic banks weakened by the crisis. As I argue shortly, one reason for the crisis was bad sequencing with respect to capital account liberalization, and this had little to do with bank sector liberalization, which, had it been conducted properly, might have actually helped avert the crisis. Given the outcome of this bad sequencing, however, much liberalization has been postponed. Therefore what policymakers in these nations want to know more than anything is how to achieve the benefits of liberalization while avoiding, or at least minimizing, the perverse results that might, in light of current circumstances, come with it.

Thus the main problem many developing nations face with regard to liberalizing their policies toward foreign bank entry is that local incumbent banks are already close to bankruptcy. They fear that further liberalization might throw weak local banks to the wolves, imposing substantial (and politically unacceptable) adjustment costs on the economy even if foreign banks are able to step in to fill the void.[43] These costs derive from loss of

42. See Dobson and Jacquet (1998); and Dobson and Hufbauer (2001).
43. See Cargill and Parker (2001).

"franchise value" of incumbent banks and the perverse incentives created by this loss of value.

It is important to remember that most of the problems of domestically owned banks have not been created by foreign ownership of banks per se. Rather, as just noted, they have resulted from poor decisions regarding sequencing of capital account opening, which in turn weakened local banks, leaving them unable to adjust readily to foreign entry. For example, the case is strong that the Korean government erred in the mid-1990s by opening short-term capital accounts while leaving long-term accounts (foreign direct investment in particular) by and large closed. This sequencing was done largely for political reasons, and against the advice of many economists. In particular, Korea at that time sought to join the Organization for Economic Cooperation and Development (OECD), but a requirement of membership was that capital accounts be opened. The large Korean industrial groups (the *chaebol*) and the domestic banks that lent to these groups welcomed the prospect of short-term capital account opening, because both sets of institutions sought to increase borrowings from abroad. (In doing so, they apparently forgot some important lessons that should have been learned by Korea during the late 1970s and early 1980s.) But both groups resisted direct investment liberalization because they were concerned about the consequences of increased competition from greenfield entry by foreign institutions and (possibly) foreign takeovers of domestic institutions. Most of all, they were worried that they would not be able to cope well with increased effective competition, even though this competition would have been quite good for the Korean economy.

Thus in its negotiations with OECD the Korean government offered immediate short-term account opening but deferred on opening long-term accounts. The ultimate result was a rash of borrowing that led to both a mismatch of term structure of foreign liabilities against the assets financed by these liabilities and, in some cases, plainly bad investment decisions.[44] The eagerness to borrow abroad was doubtlessly exacerbated by a moral hazard problem created by the perception that the *chaebol* were "too big to fail." That is, if any of these groups or their main creditor banks were to get into a situation where they could not pay back funds owed to foreigners, many believed that the Korean government would stand behind their debts. To add to the problem, banking regulation and supervision in Korea had not been implemented at the level required of a modern economy.

44. See Krueger and Yoo (2001).

This failure was, to a large degree, a result of rapid growth in Korea during the 1970s and early 1980s under industrial policies largely conceived by government planners that left the financial sector underdeveloped in relation to the rest of the economy. During the industrial policy period, banks played little role other than to fund activities favored by the government. Then in the late 1980s, when the Korean government went out of the "industrial policy" business, it failed to lay a proper groundwork needed for a well-functioning financial sector to emerge. In particular, prudential regulation and supervision of banks was not fully undertaken.

The crisis in Korea erupted when it became clear that a large percentage of the loans made by Korean banks were nonperforming and, as a result, foreign lenders would not roll over the short-term loans that had been extended to Korean banks. Furthermore, a large percentage of these loans had been extended by banks domiciled in Japan, which themselves were in trouble at home and were reducing loans in all of their markets (thus Korea arguably suffered some contagion from Japan). The Korean government did not have sufficient foreign exchange reserves to back up the Korean banks, and the crisis ensued.

The key point in this regard is that these adverse events all happened *before* moves were taken to liberalize the Korean banking sector. Foreign bank entry did not create the problems that emerged in 1997; the blame lies largely with the government's decision to open short-term accounts before effective prudential supervision and monitoring capabilities were in place. Had foreign banks entered Korea before the crisis, their presence might well have forced more prudent lending or, at least, had foreign banks had on-the-ground experience in Korea, these banks might not have extended short-term credit that was to be used for imprudent lending. This might indeed have helped avert the crisis.

Instead, domestic banks in Korea and other countries have been left in a weakened state, and this does pose problems with respect to opening the banking sector to foreign ownership. This is not to say that the problem of weak domestic banks exists in all developing countries. In countries where nonperforming loans are not problematic to any great degree, the danger that foreign bank entry will destroy the franchise value of existing banks is remote. Furthermore, empirical evidence does not suggest that foreign entry places undue stress on healthy local banks.[45] There is no reason to expect foreign participation in such countries to create especially adverse effects on the economy, although some transitory adjustment costs would

45. See Claessens and others (2000); Goldberg and others (2000).

be incurred. These costs would be manageable, however, and the benefits of the opening would be expected to be greater than the costs.

Yet another possible problem is that developing countries might not wish foreigners to share rents that might be present in the banking sector. An even bigger problem is that there are rents in the first place, which are themselves indicative of inefficiencies in the banking sector. Countries where such rents are present would be wise to increase the level of effective competition in the banking sector so that the rents are bid away. This implies banking sector deregulation to allow incumbent banks to enter new lines of business in which they might have advantages over the new foreign-owned entrants, so that domestic banks are better prepared to meet the challenges posed by competition from foreign banks.[46] As already noted, such deregulation brings benefits in its own right, mostly in the form of greater systematic efficiency of the banking sector. The main reason why countries should choose to deregulate is to capture those benefits. That deregulation can create new opportunities for incumbent banks to offset the loss of business that might occur as the result of foreign entry is an extra benefit of this deregulation. If countries worry that foreign banks will capture rents even during the adjustment phase, they might wish to sequence deregulation so as to allow a widening of the types of activities in which domestic banks are allowed to participate *before* allowing new entry by foreign banks. But they must do so on a firm schedule that makes clear this entry will be allowed at some time in the proximate future.

On the other hand, a rapid opening to foreign ownership could create significant adjustment costs where the banking sector does have deep prior problems. In such cases, the prospect of foreign entry could worsen the plight of weak incumbent banks and could lead them to lose their franchise value. To begin with, depositors might switch from these banks to what they perceive as stronger foreign banks. Second, incentives deepen for incumbent bank owners or managers to take large risks. Indeed, the main reason that banks need to maintain some threshold of franchise value is to remove incentives for excess risk taking.[47] Such incentives become problematic whenever a bank is approaching bankruptcy. The foreign entry could very well drive local banks in this direction.

46. Thus, for example, in China the incumbent banks might be able to move into mortgage writing, in part because private ownership of housing is now allowed there and is becoming more prevalent.

47. One main reason that banking regulatory regimes restrict new bank entry is to create franchise value, and hence induce prudent behavior on the part of existing banks by enabling these banks to earn some rent on their banking activity. The problem with this line of reasoning is that the entry restrictions are often excessive or overzealously enforced.

The main underlying reasons for this problem are x-inefficiency of local banks and accumulation of nonperforming loans. The two are not unrelated, of course. Banks accumulate nonperforming loans in part because they do not properly evaluate risk and do not properly monitor the uses to which borrowed funds are put. Both of these failings qualify as sources of x-inefficiency. One goal served by foreign bank entry, as discussed earlier, is to improve the x-efficiency of its banking institutions. But if past accumulations of nonperforming loans exist, this goal might not be achieved, and bank managers may be motivated to act perversely when the sector is opened to foreign entry, especially if no offsetting measures are taken.

Even if an effort is made to resolve nonperforming loans, as suggested earlier, what should come first, attention to the nonperforming loans, to prevent the perverse incentives from growing, or a quick opening of the sector, to keep the nonperforming loans from festering, but taking measures to offset the perverse incentive problem? Thus far most countries have taken the first route, but without making much headway in resolving the nonperforming loans. This slow progress and the lack of new competition in the banking sector can only undermine the growth potential of the economy. Furthermore, because resolution of loans almost surely does require capital infusion into the troubled banks, either from bank shareholders or the government, blocking foreign entry into the banking sector also blocks access to one potential source of capital infusion and places the entire burden on domestic residents.[48]

One way out of the bind would be to enlist foreign bank participation in resolving the nonperforming loans. To achieve this, governments could allow foreign investors to take over incumbent banks on the condition that they absorb and resolve nonperforming loans held by the local bank, while blocking de novo entry by foreign banks. Foreign banks entering the domestic realm must therefore help resolve the problem and not compete on unequal terms with domestic banks, as would be the case if the latter held large portfolios of nonperforming loans but the former started with a completely clean slate. As recent experience suggests, few foreign investors are likely to agree to these terms. Hence the condition that foreign investors must absorb fully the portfolios of nonperforming loans might be softened so as to create positive incentives for them to engage in such takeover.

48. One possibility, albeit a largely untried one, is for a country to sell nonperforming loans directly to foreign investors, as China is doing. In May 2001, China announced that it would sell bad loans owed by state-owned enterprises to foreigners; details of how it plans to do this and, in particular, what discounts will be offered, are not available at the time of this writing. See "China Set to Lure Foreign Investors to Bad-Loan Sale," *Financial Times*, May 10, 2001, p. 1.

One approach taken by Korea, for example, has been to encourage foreign takeover of at least some local banks (in 1998, all banks in Korea were in effect nationalized), and one such takeover has actually occurred (First Korea Bank by Newbridge) on the condition that the foreign owners work to resolve nonperforming loans, but with a positive incentive: the bank has been assured that if loans inherited by it that were classified as performing prove to be nonperforming, these loans can be sold to the government, albeit at a discount. The bank has reason not to sell these loans to the government, because if the borrowing firm can be restructured so that the loan becomes performing, no discount must be taken. But if loans that were inherited at face value prove to be nonperforming, then at least some of the value of these loans can be recovered by the bank. With their risks capped in this manner, the new owners have significant potential on the "upside" and limited risk on the "downside."

The advantage these terms offer to the country concerned is that they open the door to foreign knowledge and experience in restructuring firms whose debts have become nonperforming, especially where this knowledge and experience is lacking in locally owned banks.[49] Thus, under foreign control, the bank might be able to recover value from nonperforming loans where, in the absence of such control, the loans have no value. The foreign investor receives two incentives to take over the local bank: first, the opportunity to recover value from nonperforming loans, and, second, some insurance against loans it inherits at face value proving to have no value at all. For this type of scheme to work, however, advantage must accrue to both parties, the nation and the foreign investor. For there to be value to the nation, there must be a reasonable expectation that the bank, under foreign control, can turn around at least some nonperforming loans. But, for there to be value to the foreign investor, the expected value of the investment must be positive. For both these values to be positive, declared nonperforming loans inherited by the new owner must be priced correctly (that is, sufficiently below face value so that the foreign investor expects to earn a positive return on the portfolio but not so low as to invite accusations of a "fire sale"). It would serve a country well to have expertise available to determine the appropriate price at which to sell any given portfolio of domestic banking assets, where these are subject to risk.

One objection to such a proposal might be the reductio ad absurdum argument, namely, that it might allow all domestic banks to fall under for-

49. Is this approach working? Interviews conducted by this author in Korea in December 2000 suggested that it is too early to tell.

eign control. In practice, this does not seem to happen (indeed, in those countries where such takeover is now encouraged, the problem seems to be not loss of the entire banking system to foreigners but, rather, too few foreign banks willing to take over ailing domestic banks). Nonetheless, to allay fears of a complete foreign takeover, it would seem reasonable for governments to take measures to place an upper limit on the total banking assets that can come under foreign control.

In addition, governments need to take steps to ensure that those practices that led these loans to accumulate in the first place are not repeated. Entry of foreign banks that have the expertise to evaluate and manage risk is, as stressed earlier, one such step. Another would be to deregulate banks, in the sense of ending restrictions on the scope of assets that banks might hold and financial activities in which banks may participate. This would improve, rather than weaken, bank stability. Another necessary step is to strengthen national government capabilities to supervise and monitor bank activities to ensure that prudential standards conform to international best practice, especially in regard to transparency. Indeed, governments should not even attempt to "deregulate" until this strengthening is achieved, especially if they wish to assure the people that they are able to provide adequate supervision and monitoring of foreign bank activity.[50]

How, then, is it possible to resolve nonperforming loans and implement more effective prudential supervision without delaying needed deregulation or the admission of foreign banks? For one thing, governments could move quickly to pass laws to permit deregulation and the opening to foreign bank participation (where, as noted, these might include ceilings on the total banking assets that can come under foreign control), but to allow a reasonable period of time to elapse before these laws come into full force. The key is for the government to make a credible commitment to make the deregulation and market opening happen on schedule. In particular, as is widely noted in the literature on market contestability, the near certainty that market opening will happen will give domestic banks ample incentive to get their house in order, but they can do so only if the government has

---

50. There might be something to be said for the approach of the Philippines, which allows entry by foreign banks only if they meet preestablished criteria. Nevertheless, these criteria, as actually employed by the Philippines (see U.S. Treasury, 1998; and my discussion above), are somewhat too restricted (because they might exclude some quite qualified potential investors). Such criteria also have the potential to run afoul of international obligations (such as national treatment commitments under the Financial Services Agreement of the WTO). Furthermore, if national prudential standards are properly implemented, special criteria beyond meeting these standards are not necessary (and, if these standards are implemented in a nondiscriminatory fashion, they will not be inconsistent with any international obligation).

in place a credible scheme to resolve nonperforming loans. After all, as Samuel Johnson once observed, "when a man is to be hanged in a fortnight, it concentrates his mind wonderfully."

Even so, the question looms large as to whether governments should take measures to soften the impact of foreign bank entry upon domestic banks when this entry does occur. Figuring importantly in this matter is the role of deposit insurance. The well-intended goal of deposit insurance is to guarantee that depositors, small retail (individual or household) depositors in particular, do not lose their assets in the event of bank failure. Underlying this goal is the desire to create stability in the banking system, most notably by removing incentives for these depositors to liquidate their accounts if they fear bank failure (and, by doing so, perhaps precipitate the very failure that they fear might happen). But, in the case of actual (or imminent) foreign bank entry, deposit insurance can also serve to eliminate or at least significantly reduce the incentive for depositors to switch from domestic banks to foreign ones.

The problem is that deposit insurance can itself create an incentive for bank owners (or managers) to take undue risks, adding to the incentive to take undue risks that foreign entry itself can create. The risk derives from the fact that depositors whose deposits are fully insured have reduced (or no) incentive to monitor the banks' lending activities, such that bank managers in their lending decisions must take into account the possibility that undue risk taking might be punished via withdrawal of deposits. Some incentive to take risks thus is always created by deposit insurance, but the risk becomes acute if a bank faces a bankruptcy risk created by nonperforming loans. If bank managers or owners perceive that they are at risk of losing their capital (or, in the case of managers, they perceive that they are at risk of losing their jobs), they can be tempted to gamble on high-risk, high-reward investment opportunities without feeling that they have a responsibility to protect the interests of depositors. If the opportunity fails to pan out, the depositors are protected from loss. This asymmetry leads to a classic "moral hazard" problem, wherein managers in effect gamble with other people's money in a nontransparent way (if the deposit insurance is publicly financed, these "other people" are the taxpayers, and "nontransparent" implies that the gamble is taken without the knowledge or consent of these taxpayers).

Ideally, this moral hazard problem could be self-resolving if banks were charged an insurance premium for deposit insurance that fully reflected the risk of the bank's asset portfolios.[51] If so, owners and managers would find that the expected costs of gambles were reflected in higher prices for the insurance, so that a disincentive would be created against taking the gamble in the first place. However, evidence suggests that the price of deposit insurance as paid by banks rarely reflects the true cost of this insurance in cases where large risks have been taken.[52] Rather, some element of subsidy is typically implicit in the insurance.

If anything, bank deposit insurance schemes are likely to increase the likelihood of a banking crisis in countries with weak institutions but not in countries with strong institutions. Indeed, even controlling for effective bank regulation and supervision, such schemes seem to contribute to the likelihood of crisis in countries with weak institutions.[53] These schemes appear not to work in fostering stability in the banking system. Moreover, they tend to produce results that are the opposite of what is intended *if* the banks are weak to begin with. Where banking systems are weak, public provision of deposit insurance inhibits financial sector development rather than stimulates it, possibly because depositors recognize that the costs of the insurance are unrestrained and hence actually avoid the domestic banking system in order to avoid eventually being forced to pay for these costs.[54]

On the other hand, deposit insurance does not seem to lead to perverse results if banking institutions are strong. Also, as a pragmatic matter, political considerations might make it difficult to eliminate deposit insurance: politicians who propose complete abolition of deposit insurance might not survive the next election. And, as noted, deposit insurance does surely provide some reassurance that, if foreign bank entry is permitted in a nation where domestic banks do have problems with large portfolios of nonperforming loans, domestic depositors will not switch en masse from the domestic to the foreign banks

Rather than eliminating deposit insurance, the best course might be to remove the moral hazard and the resultant perverse incentives that the existence of such insurance can create in those countries where domestic banks are weak. One straightforward way to do this would be to enforce limits on deposit insurance, such that small depositors are insured but large depositors are not, or at least that there are caps on the liability of the

51. See Calomaris (1992, 1999).
52. See Caprio and Honohan (2000).
53. Demirgüç-Kunt and Detragiache (2000). See also Barth and others (2001b).
54. Cull, Senbet, and Sorge (2000).

insurer to any one depositor. Large depositors presumably have the resources to monitor bank performance and thus determine which banks are risky places in which to place deposits and which are not. The critical point is to cover small depositors, not small deposits: if the latter are insured, then large depositors will have an incentive simply to create multiple accounts. One way to do this would be to impose a maximum total for which the deposit insurance agency would be liable to any depositor, irrespective of where or how that depositor splits up the sums that are under deposit. Another possibility would be to encourage banks to issue subordinated debt (or bonds) as part of their overall capitalization.[55] Subordinated debt or bondholders would not be subject to deposit insurance and hence would have a strong incentive to play a monitoring function. Such holders would normally be large institutional investors and would have the capacity to play this role.

Beyond this, the main thing is to improve the strength of domestic banking institutions. If governments do underwrite deposit insurance, they themselves must be prepared to play the role of monitoring agents to ensure that banks do not engage in casino-like behavior. This requires above all else that public officials who administer banking regulations and deposit insurance are competent to regulate and that they themselves are accountable if things go badly awry. But essential elements must also be in place to enable these officials to do the job properly.

The most important of these elements is transparency and the powers of deterrence and correction. At a minimum, officials must have timely and accurate information with respect to what banks in fact are doing. Countries might follow the example of Chile in this regard. Inspectors from the office of the Superintendent of Banks and Financial Institutions make regular evaluations of the riskiness of assets held by Chilean banks, including estimates of losses that might be expected to incur, and they monitor the likely impact of any nonprovisioned loss on the solvency of the bank.[56] Furthermore, the superintendent publishes information on the banks at quarterly intervals. Such disclosures could be very useful on a wider scale, especially if comparable information could be published from one country to another. Two other countries that have already begun to supply similar information are the United States and New Zealand.

---

55. This has been advocated by Goldstein and Turner (1996), among others. They note that current Bank for International Settlements regulations actually discourage this by placing a cap on the amount of subordinated debt or bonds that a bank can issue as a percentage of total capital.

56. Ibid.

With respect to a bank supervisor's powers of deterrence and correction, perhaps the most far-reaching scheme put forth thus far is what is known as "structured early intervention and resolution" (SEIR).[57] Much of this proposal was incorporated in the U.S. Federal Deposit Insurance Corporation Improvement Act of 1991, itself motivated by certain moral hazard issues that were revealed in the U.S. savings and loan crisis of the late 1980s. The idea of SEIR is to structure the response of bank supervisors to an emerging bank crisis so as to mimic the response of bondholders. To do this, SEIR sets up a gradated response to the deterioration of bank capital, creating what are in effect "tripwires" that set off specific regulatory responses when they are triggered. Some of these responses are mandatory and others are left to the discretion of the regulators. Thus, for example, if a bank's capital were to fall below a certain "tripwire" level, regulators must require that the bank suspend dividends and management fees, restrict further asset growth, restrict deposit interest rates, restrict the pay of officers, and require that a recapitalization plan be prepared by the bank's management; other measures such as an order to recapitalize could be taken. If these measures fail to stop the erosion of the bank's capital, still other measures would at some point become mandatory, such as suspension of payment on subordinated debt, and recapitalization would now have to be ordered (if not ordered earlier under discretionary power). If the deterioration of the bank still continued and the final tripwire were crossed, the mandatory response of the authorities would be to close the bank before the market value of the bank's capital became negative.

In addition to the largely "negative" provisions of SEIR that are triggered in the event of an emerging crisis, governments could take "positive" steps. For example, they could encourage banks to undertake more forward provisioning for loan loss by allowing them to take tax deductions for loan loss provisions in excess of those typically now allowed.[58] Banks might be allowed to make loss provisions (and to take deductions for these) on the basis of projected loan losses as revealed by credit-risk models that measure longer-term risks; such losses typically are greater than those indicated by currently nonperforming loans.[59]

---

57. This was first put forward by Benston and Kaufman (1988). See also Goldstein and Turner (1996).

58. See Dobson and Hufbauer (2001).

59. Tax deductions are generally allowed only for loan loss provisions to cover currently declared nonperforming loans. But, as noted in ibid., both bank managers and regulators are reluctant to classify a loan, even if problematic, as "nonperforming." One consequence is that, when banking crises do erupt, loan-loss provisions have historically been far short of what would be adequate to protect bank solvency.

In sum, to make deposit insurance work properly, especially to make certain that this insurance plays a constructive role in opening the banking sector to foreign participation, governments must have in place both effective regulatory frameworks and accountable and competent institutions to monitor bank compliance with regulations. Equally important, they must take appropriate action when banks are not in compliance. But, as stressed throughout this chapter, such institutions are necessary for the banking system to function effectively in any case (even if deposit insurance does not exist). Their existence is simply necessary for this sector to play its all-important role properly.

References

Barth, James R., Gerard Caprio, and Ross Levine. 2001a. "Bank Regulation and Supervision: What Works and What Doesn't." Washington: Research Department, World Bank. Mimeo.

———. 2001b. "Banking Systems around the Globe: Do Regulation and Ownership Affect Performance and Stability?" In *Prudential Regulation and Supervision: What Works and What Doesn't?* edited by Frederic Mishkin. Cambridge, Mass.: National Bureau of Economic Research.

Beck, Thorsten, Ross Levine, and Norman Loayza. 2000. "Finance and the Sources of Growth." *Journal of Financial Economics* 58 (1–2): 261–300.

Benston, George, and George Kaufman. 1988. "Regulating Bank Safety and Performance." In *Restructuring Banking and Financial Services in America*, edited by W. Haraf and R. Kushmeider. Washington: American Enterprise Institute.

Berger, Allen N., Robert DeYoung, Hesna Genay, and Gregory F. Udell. 2000. "Globalization of Financial Institutions: Evidence from Cross-Border Banking Performance." In *Brookings-Wharton Papers on Financial Services.* Vol. 3.

Borzenstein, E., J. de Gregorio, and J. W. Lee. 1998. "How Does Foreign Investment Affect Growth?" *Journal of International Economics* 45(1): 115–35.

Calomaris, Charles W. 1992. "Getting the Incentives Right in the Current Deposit Insurance System: Successes from the Pre-FDIC Era." In *The Reform of Federal Deposit Insurance: Disciplining the Government and Protecting Taxpayers*, edited by James R. Barth and R. Dan Braumbaugh. Harper Business.

———. 1999. *The Postmodern Banking Safety Net: Lessons from Developed and Developing Economies.* Washington: American Enterprise Institute.

Caprio, Gerard, and Patrick Honohan. 2000. *Finance for Growth: Policy Choices in a Volatile World.* Washington: World Bank.

Cargill, Thomas F., and Elliott Parker. 2001. "Asian Finance and the Role of Bankruptcy." Department of Economics Working Paper. University of Nevada at Reno.

Cetorelli, Nicola, and Michele Gambera. 1999. "Banking Market Structure, Financial Dependence, and Growth: International Evidence from Industry Data." Federal Reserve Bank of Chicago. Mimeo.

Claessens, Stijn, Asli Demirgüç-Kunt, and Harry Huizinga. 2000. "How Does Foreign Entry Affect the Domestic Banking Market?" In *The Internationalization of Financial Services: Issues and Lessons for Developing Countries*, edited by Stijn Claessens and Marion Jansen. Dordrecht, The Netherlands: Kluwer Academic.

Clarke, George, Robert Cull, Laura D'Amato, and Andrea Mollinari. 1999. "The Effect of Foreign Entry on Argentina's Banking Sector." In *The Internationalization of Financial Services: Issues and Lessons for Developing Countries,* edited by Stijn Claessens and Marion Jansen. Dordrecht, The Netherlands: Kluwer Academic.

Cull, Robert, Lemma Senbet, and Marco Sorge. 2000. "Deposit Insurance and Financial Development." Washington: Research Department, World Bank. Mimeo.

Dayal-Gulati, Anuradha, and Aasim M. Husain. 2000. "Centripetal Forces in China's Economic Take-off." Working Paper WP/00/06. Washington: International Monetary Fund.

Demirgüç-Kunt, Asli, and Enrica Detragiache. 2000. "Does Deposit Insurance Increase Banking System Stability? An Empirical Investigation." Policy Research Working Paper 2247. Washington: World Bank.

———. 1998. "The Determinants of Banking Crises in Developing and Developed Countries." *International Monetary Fund Staff Papers* 45(1): 81–109.

Diamond, Douglas, and Raghuram Rangan. 2000. "Banks, Short Term Debt, and Financial Crisis: Theory, Policy Implications, and Applications." Working Paper 7764. Cambridge, Mass.: National Bureau of Economic Research.

Dobson, Wendy, and Gary C. Hufbauer. 2001. *World Capital Markets: Challenge to the G-10.* Washington: Institute for International Economics.

Dobson, Wendy, and Pierre Jacquet. 1998. *Financial Services Liberalization in the WTO.* Washington: Institute for International Economics.

Dunning, John H. 1958. *American Investment in British Manufacturing Industry.* London: George Allen and Unwin.

———. 1993. *Multinational Corporations and the Global Economy.* Wokingham, U.K.: Addison Wesley.

Eichengreen, Barry, Andrew Rose, and Charles Wyplosz. 1996. "Contagious Currency Crises." *Scandinavian Economic Review* 98 (4): 463–84.

Ergas, Henry. 1997. "International Trade in Telecommunication Services: An Economics Perspective." In *Unfinished Business: Telecommunications after the Uruguay Round,* edited by G. C. Hufbauer and E. Wada. Washington: Institute for International Economics.

Glick, Reuven, and Andrew Rose. 1999. "Contagion and Trade: Why Are Currency Crises Regional?" *Journal of International Money and Finance* 18(4): 603–17.

Goldberg, Linda B., Gerard Dages, and Daniel Kinney. 2000. "Foreign and Domestic Bank Participation: Lessons from Argentina and Mexico." Federal Reserve Bank of New York, *Economic Policy Review* (September): 7–36.

Goldstein, Morris. 1998. *The Asian Financial Crisis: Causes, Cures, and Systematic Implications.* Washington: Institute for International Economics.

Goldstein, Morris, Graciela Kaminsky, and Carmen M. Reinhart. 2000. *Assessing Financial Vulnerability: An Early Warning System for Emerging Markets.* Washington: Institute for International Economics.

Goldstein, Morris, and Philip Turner. 1996. "Banking Crises in Emerging Economies: Origins and Policy Options." Economics Papers 46. Basle, Switzerland: Bank for International Settlements.

Graham, Edward M., and Erika Wada. 2001. "Foreign Direct Investment in China: Effects on Growth and Economic Performance." Working Paper 01-3. Washington: Institute for International Economics.

Hindley, Brian. 2000. "Internationalization of Financial Services: A Trade-Policy Perspective." In *The Internationalization of Financial Services: Issues and Lessons for Developing Countries,* edited by Stijn Claessens and Marion Jansen. Dordrecht, The Netherlands: Kluwer Academic.

Kaminsky, Graciela, and Carmen Reinhart. 2000. "On Crises, Contagion, and Confusion." *Journal of International Economics* 51 (1): 145–68.

Krueger, Anne O., and Jungho Yoo. 2001. "Chaebol Capitalism and the Currency-Financial Crisis in Korea." Working paper, available at: http://www.columbia.edu/~drd28/Findlay_Conference.htm.

Levine, Ross. 1997. "Financial Development and Economic Growth: Views and Agenda." *Journal of Economic Literature* 35(2): 688–726.

Levine, Ross, Norman Loayza, and Thorsten Beck. 1999. "Financial Intermediation and Growth: Causality and Causes." *Journal of Monetary Economics* 46 (1): 31–77.

Levine, Ross, and Sara Zervos. 1998. "Stock Markets, Banks, and Economic Growth." *American Economic Review* 88 (3): 537–58.

Peek, Joe, and Eric S. Rosengren. 1997. "The International Transmission of Financial Shocks: The Case of Japan." *American Economic Review* 87 (4): 495–505.

Rajan, Raghuram G., and Luigi Zingales. 1998. "Financial Dependence and Growth." *American Economic Review* 88(3): 559–86.

U.S. Department of the Treasury. 1998. *National Treatment Study.* Government Printing Office.

Van Rijckeghem, Caroline, and Beatrice Weder. 1999. "Sources of Contagion: Finance or Trade?" Working Paper 99/143. Washington: International Monetary Fund.

BENN STEIL 11

Borderless Trading and Developing Securities Markets

(selected Countries)

G21 G15 G12 G18 O16

The past decade has been one of enormous change in the securities trading industry. Automation of trading systems, led by the continental European exchanges and U.S. "electronic communications networks" (or ECNs), has led to significant declines in trading costs, massive increases in turnover, internationalization of trading and settlement system operations, and major reforms in exchange governance. Yet the policy advice given to developing country governments looking to create or expand securitized finance in their markets has been largely unaffected by these developments. This is unfortunate, as developing countries now have the opportunity to leapfrog the evolving infrastructure of the mature markets and to define the global efficient frontier in trading technology, exchange governance, investor access, and market structure regulation. This chapter analyzes the technological and economic forces driving change in the securities trading industry and examines the implications for developing markets.

I am grateful to Charles Vuylsteke and Bob Litan for very helpful comments on an earlier draft of this chapter.

The Role of Securitized Finance

There is a broad and disparate literature on the relative importance and desirability of loan-based and securitized (equity and bond) financing in the development of enterprises and national economies. In the developed economies, studies of "bank-centered" and "market-centered" finance have tended to contrast Japan and Germany, on the one hand, with the United States and United Kingdom, on the other. The conclusions of these analyses appear to be highly correlated with economic cycles. Studies published during the late 1980s and early 1990s, when economic growth was higher in Japan and Germany than in the United States and United Kingdom, have tended to praise banking.[1] Studies published since the mid-1990s, when relative growth rates were reversed, have tended to accord a more favorable role to markets.[2] The Asian debt crisis of the late 1990s also precipitated a substantial literature highlighting the role of either developing country equity markets or banking systems in creating or fueling the crisis.

Broadly, market finance has been alleged to involve the following drawbacks:

—Markets allow large, rapid, and destabilizing reversals of foreign equity flows.

—Investors tend to "herd," driving asset prices up or down to levels that cannot be justified on the basis of economic fundamentals.

—The volatility inherent to markets leads to capital misallocation and damages long-term wealth creation.

—Markets encourage "short-termism" in corporate behavior, leading to underinvestment.

—Markets facilitate takeover threats, which further discourage long-term investment.

—Fragmented ownership leads to poor corporate governance and insufficient monitoring of management.

These propositions are, to varying degrees, controversial, and the empirical evidence supporting them ranges from minimal to mixed.

Economies dominated by bank-based debt financing, on the other hand, have been held to suffer a different set of drawbacks:

—Lending fuels booms and exacerbates downturns.

—Lending tends to be influenced by political interference.

1. See, for example, Porter (1992); and, very notably, Singh (1993).
2. See, for example, Davis and Steil (2001).

—Lending results in a higher fluctuation in the borrower's consumption than equity finance.

—Banking crises frequently trigger exchange rate crises.

—Adverse selection and moral hazard problems encourage credit rationing.

—The absence of takeover threats discourages management discipline and accountability.

—Banks attract state guarantees, which distort risk bearing and necessitate large-scale public bailouts.

Support for these propositions is, quite naturally, also mixed, although the combination of developed- and developing-market banking crises over the past fifteen years has certainly increased the influence of those alleging systematic problems in bank-centered financial systems.

Rather than attempt to identify an optimal balance among forms of financing, I emphasize two observations that are highly relevant to the development of effective financial sectors. The first is that the development of securities markets must be considered important in ensuring adequate financing for growing enterprises and in promoting domestic investment and wealth creation. Among the benefits they bring, the following are perhaps the most salient:

—They increase the economy-wide mobility of productive resources.

—They represent a highly efficient mechanism for channeling local savings to investments.

—They allow efficient reallocation of financial risks.

—They dramatically increase the scope for foreign financing.

—They complement, rather than substitute for, the development of the banking sector.[3]

—Empirically, equity investments in developing countries appear to offer more attractive risk-return profiles than debt.[4]

—Countries with more liquid stock markets enjoy faster growth rates of real per capita gross domestic product (GDP) over subsequent decades.[5]

—Stock markets are critical to the development of venture equity financing, as they provide an essential exit mechanism for venture capitalists, who are therefore able continuously to reallocate their capital toward promising new enterprises.

3. See, for example, Demirgürç-Kunt and Maksimovic (1996); and Garcia and Liu (1999).
4. See, for example, Buiter, Lago, and Rey (1999).
5. See, for example, Levine and Zervos (1996); and Rousseau and Wachtel (2000).

The second observation is that government efforts to suppress the development of securitized financing or to control too rigidly the institutional structure under which it develops are likely to have significant unintended consequences. Companies seeking to raise capital do not react passively to the financial structures favored by their governments or government-backed financial institutions.

Bank dominance in Japan, for example, has been sustained through regulation and cartel practice but has been fiercely resisted in the corporate sector when cheaper sources of financing have been uncovered. Restrictions on corporate bond issuance successfully discouraged Japanese companies from issuing any domestic straight bonds in 1989 and 1990, yet could not prevent them from issuing 2.9 trillion yen worth in the eurobond markets those same years.[6] The investors in these bonds were overwhelmingly Japanese; the eurobond markets were merely a vehicle for regulatory arbitrage. Far from reinforcing the role of bank financing in Japan, government support for the sector only served to slow the adaptation of the major Japanese banks to an irreversible shift toward securitized corporate finance. In Germany, banks have been able to discourage the expansion of equity finance via their proxy voting rights (acquired from shareholders depositing their shares for safekeeping) and consequent ability to place representatives on corporate supervisory boards.[7] Yet the competitive pressures to find cheaper sources of financing did not abate and led many German (and other European) high-tech start-ups to establish facilities in the United States and list on Nasdaq. Belatedly, this led to a crash program to build Nasdaq-styled small cap markets throughout the continent in an effort to forestall further emigration of local start-ups.

While endorsing the efforts of governments in poorer countries to facilitate the development of domestic securities markets, I argue against the grain of much of the policy literature in developmental economics and advocate a highly circumscribed role for government in the actual creation and management of exchanges and related trading institutions (such as central securities depositories, or CSDs). Instead, governments should focus on the establishment of a legal and regulatory framework that would encourage existing purveyors and operators of trading infrastructure outside the country to offer services locally. This would serve to facilitate the domestic market's integration into a burgeoning *international* marketplace for equity transaction services, enabling both rapid absorption of the most

6. See Steil (1995).
7. See Edwards and Fischer (1994).

successful trading and settlement technology and lower capital costs for growing local enterprises. I begin the discussion by examining the impact of trading automation on the governance and strategic positioning of exchanges in the advanced economies and then move on to draw out the implications for countries that are considering how best to expand domestic access to both local and foreign equity capital.

Technology and Exchange Governance

The traditional model of an exchange as a locally organized mutual association is a remnant of the era before trading system automation. As trading required visual and verbal interaction, exchanges were necessarily designated physical locations where traders would meet at fixed times. Access to the exchange had to be rationed to prevent overcrowding and, when single-price periodic call auctions were prevalent, to ensure that simultaneous full participation was physically feasible.

As trading "systems" were simply rules governing the conduct of transactions, exchanges were naturally run by the traders themselves as cooperatives. Access was generally rationed through a combination of substantial initial and annual membership fees, in order to ensure self-selection by high-volume users. Nonmembers naturally wished to benefit from the network externalities of concentrated trading activity (commonly referred to as "liquidity"), and therefore paid members to represent their buy and sell orders on the exchange floor. This is how exchange members came to be intermediaries ("brokers") for investor transactions.

The economics of automated auction trading are radically different. The placement and matching of buy and sell orders can now be done on computer systems, access to which is inherently constrained neither by the location nor the numbers of desired access points. In a fully competitive "market for electronic markets," the traditional concept of membership becomes economically untenable. As the marginal cost of adding a new member to a trading network declines toward zero, it becomes infeasible for an exchange to impose a fixed access cost, or "membership fee." Rather, only transaction-based (that is, variable-cost) charging is sustainable. The transactors on such electronic networks, therefore, come to look much more like what are normally considered "clients" or "customers" of a firm than "members" of an association. And since an electronic auction system is a valuable proprietary product, not costlessly replicable by traders, it is feasible for the owner to operate it, and sell access to it, as a normal for-profit commercial enterprise. This contrasts with a traditional exchange floor, whose value derives wholly from the physical presence of traders. A private operator could offer traders nothing more than access to commercial real estate.

The fact that an automated exchange can be operated as a commercial enterprise, unlike a traditional floor-based exchange, does not in itself make a case for a corporate rather than mutual governance structure. However, such a case emerges naturally from an analysis of the incentive structures under which a mutualized and corporate exchange operates. Exchange members are the conduits to the trading system, and they thereby derive profits from intermediating nonmember transactions. They can therefore be expected to resist both technological and institutional innovations that serve to reduce demand for their intermediation services, even where such innovations would increase the economic value of the exchange itself. If the members are actually *owners* of the exchange, they will logically exercise their powers to block disintermediation where the resulting decline in brokerage profits would not at least be offset by their share in the increase in exchange value.

Since a major economic benefit of automated auction trading is the elimination of the need for trade intermediation, mutualized exchanges can be expected both to have difficulties introducing such systems and, once introduced, allowing their full potential to be exploited by nonmember investors. Both of these effects can be well documented. The largest U.K.-based market-makers on the London Stock Exchange fought to block the adoption of electronic auction trading in the mid-1990s. New York Stock Exchange (NYSE) specialist firms have long fought against automated matching of investor orders and display of their limit order books to the trading floor and the wider public. Nasdaq market-makers blocked the incorporation of price-time priority in Nasdaq's trading system upgrade (SuperMontage), successfully arguing that customers should be allowed to trade with them even if they were not posting the best price, or the earliest best price (they could simply match the best posted price). Nonmember-based commercial trading system operators, on the other hand, have always chosen both to operate automated auction structures and to do so without any intermediation requirement (except for retail orders, for which such operators have traditionally not wished to manage the credit risk function).

What are the costs to investors and listed companies of exchanges continuing to operate as broker-dealer cooperatives? Recent empirical evidence makes this very clear: significantly higher trading costs (and therefore lower returns) to investors, and higher capital costs to listed companies. Domowitz and Steil (2001) estimate total trading costs to be 28–33 percent higher through NYSE and Nasdaq traditional broker members than through nonintermediated for-profit trading system operators (now commonly referred to as ECNs).[8] They estimate that European trading fees alone would fall a massive 70 percent if the European exchanges were to move to an ECN governance model: eliminating membership and allowing direct investor access. Historically, mutualized exchanges have sought to fix commissions and prevent price competition.[9] For-profit nonmember-based trading system operators, on the other hand, have the opposite incentive: to mitigate access costs to their system imposed by intermediaries. In developing markets, facilitating the emergence of commercial rather than mutualized trading operations should, importantly, result in lower capital costs to domestic listed companies. Domowitz and Steil demonstrated that distintermediating trading reduced trading costs and that trading cost reductions in turn reduced the cost of raising equity capital. The halving of total trading costs that they document in the United States between 1996 and 1998 resulted in an 8 percent decline in equity capital costs to S&P 500 companies. The authors further estimated that the elimination of mandatory broker intermediation at the European exchanges would result in at least a 7.8 percent savings to European blue-chip companies.

Demutualization

Stockholm was the first stock exchange in the world to demutualize, doing so in 1993. The initiative came on the back of major competitive inroads into Swedish equity trading made by London's SEAQ-International between 1987 and 1990, a period in which Stockholm's turnover declined by a third and its market share of global reported Swedish equity turnover dropped as low as 40 percent.

Half of the shares in the new Stockholm corporate structure were retained by the members, and half were allocated to listed companies. The shares became freely tradable in 1994, and in 1998 they were listed on the exchange itself. Following the demutualization, the exchange became the first in Europe to offer remote cross-border membership (1995) and direct electronic access for institutional investors (1996), although trades must still

8. Domowitz and Steil (2001).

9. For example, Banner (1998) notes that from the NYSE's founding "the Board organized brokers into a classic cartel with respect to brokerage commissions" (p. 266).

Table 11-1. *Exchange Demutualizations*

Exchange	Year
Completed demutualizations	
Stockholm Stock Exchange	1993
Helsinki Stock Exchange	1995
Copenhagen Stock Exchange	1996
Amsterdam Exchanges	1997
Borsa Italiana	1997
Australian Stock Exchange	1998
Iceland Stock Exchange	1999
Athens Stock Exchange	1999
Stock Exchange of Singapore	1999
SIMEX	1999
LIFFE	1999
Toronto Stock Exchange	2000
Sydney Futures Exchange	2000
Chicago Mercantile Exchange	2000
New York Mercantile Exchange	2000
London Stock Exchange	2000
Deutsche Börse	2001

Agreements or board proposals for demutualizations and public offerings in 2001

Chicago Board of Trade	Chicago Board Options Exchange
Euronext	Hong Kong Stock Exchange
International Petroleum Exchange	London Metal Exchange
Nasdaq	Nymex
Oslo Stock Exchange	PCX Equities
Sydney Futures Exchange	

be notionally executed via a sponsoring member. Local Swedish members resisted both of these initiatives but could not block them given their minority interest.[10] The new nonmember owners, in contrast, had an unambiguous incentive to support these measures. The exchange as a commercial enterprise appeared to have performed well following the demutualization. Turnover quadrupled in the first two years of demutualized operation, and the exchange's share price rose nearly sevenfold.[11]

The Stockholm model has since been widely emulated by other automated exchanges. Table 11-1 documents demutualizations. The biggest

10. Anecdotal evidence from exchange officials suggests that smaller local members did, in fact, suffer financially from a diversion of foreign order flow to the new, larger remote intermediaries.

11. The exchange itself credits part of the increase in turnover to the removal of a 1 percent transaction tax at the end of 1991, according to Rydén (1995).

difference among them has been in the initial allocation of shares. Helsinki and Copenhagen, for example, applied a 60-40 share split between members and listed companies. Amsterdam allocated 50 percent to members and auctioned off 50 percent to both listed companies and institutional investors. Australia allocated all shares to the members but listed them on the exchange itself the day following the demutualization.

Member-based exchanges are demutualizing in order to approximate better the incentive structure of a public company with a diversified shareholder base. In contrast, trading system operators in the United States and United Kingdom which have entered the market with automated auction products have avoided the mutual structure entirely. U.S. operators such as Instinet, POSIT, B-Trade, and Archipelago are formally regulated as brokers but sell order-matching services on a transaction fee basis directly to institutional investor-clients.

Forces for International Exchange Consolidation

Every exchange in Western and Central Europe is now using the same basic architecture for its primary trading platform: the continuous electronic auction market, where matching buy and sell orders are automatically executed by computer. As more and more of the trading firms dominating these exchanges are major international banks and are increasingly trading cross-border (particularly from London), member-firm allegiances to national exchanges are naturally dying away, and issues related to reducing pan-European trading costs are coming to the fore. The banks must pay membership fees to each national exchange and bear significant internal access costs for each of the trading system and settlement linkages they maintain. The launch of the euro has accelerated the shift from country-based portfolio management to international sector-based investment, yet cross-border settlement costs in Europe are generally upward of ten times domestic settlement costs. The international banks are therefore bringing increasing pressure to bear on the exchanges and CSDs to consolidate their systems, and in some cases to merge their organizations outright.

The trend toward the internationalization of exchanges is clear. Table 11-2 documents agreements to link automated exchanges that were launched between 1997 and July 2001. These are classified into four broad categories: strategic alliances and joint ventures, common access systems, common trading systems, and mergers. Given the size of this list, it is

Table 11-2. *Automated Exchange Mergers and Alliances, 1997–2001*

Merger or alliance	Status
Exchange mergers	
AEX: Amsterdam Stock Exchange and European Options Exchange	I
HEX: Helsinki Stock Exchange and SOM	I
BEX: Brussels Stock Exchange and BELFOX	I
OM Stockholm Exchange: Stockholm Stock Exchange and OM	I
Wiener Börse and ÖTOB	I
Paris Bourse and Monep	I
Paris Bourse and MATIF	I
Borsa Italiana and MIF	I
Eurex: DTB and SOFFEX	I
NYBOT: Coffee, Sugar & Cocoa Exchange and NY Cotton Exchange	I
Singapore Exchange: Stock Exchange of Singapore and SIMEX	I
Euronext: Paris, Amsterdam, Brussels, and Lisbon exchanges	I
virt-x: Tradepoint and Swiss Exchange (blue-chip equities)	I
HEX and Tallinn Stock Exchange	A
Hong Kong Stock Exchange and Hong Kong Futures Exchange	A
Bovespa (Brazil) and BVRJ	A
Archipelago ECN and PCX equities	A
International Petroleum Exchange and Intercontinental Exchange	A
Chicago Board of Trade and Chicago Board Options Exchange	N
MATIF and MEFF	N
Alberta Stock Exchange and Vancouver Stock Exchange	N
BVLP (Lisbon) and Oporto Derivatives Exchange	N
Eurex Bonds and EuroMTS	N
Australian Stock Exchange and New Zealand Stock Exchange	N
Common trading system	
Oslo Stock Exchange and OM (derivatives)	I
FUTOP (Denmark) and OM (derivatives)	I
Norex: OM Stockholm Exchange and Copenhagen Stock Exchange	I
Deutsche Börse, Wiener Börse, and The Irish Exchange	I
Eurex and HEX	I
Chicago Board of Trade and Eurex	I
NEWEX (Central and Eastern European equities): Deutsche Börse and Wiener Börse	I
Norex and Oslo, Reykjavik, Riga, and Vilnius exchanges	A
International Petroleum Exchange and Nord Pool	A

Table 11-2. *Continued*

Merger or alliance	Status
Common trading system (cont.)	
Globex Alliance: Chicago Mercantile Exchange, MATIF, MEFF RV,	
Singapore, Montreal, and BM&F (Brazil)	A
ParisBourse and Australian Derivatives Exchanges	A
Euronext and Bourse de Luxembourg	A
Common access system	
MATIF and MEFF RV	I
Chicago Mercantile Exchange and LIFFE	I
Euro-Globex Alliance: MATIF, MEFF RV, and MIF	A
SWIFT-FIX access protocol: Amsterdam, Brussels, Frankfurt, London,	
Madrid, Milan, Paris, and Zurich	A
Strategic alliance/joint venture	
Benelux exchanges	I
Globex: Chicago Mercantile Exchange and MATIF	I
Cantor Financial Futures Exchange: Cantor Fitzgerald and	
New York Board of Trade	I
MITS: London Metal Exchange and MG	I
OM Gruppen and NGX	I
Nasdaq Japan: Nasdaq and Osaka Securities Exchange	I
Nasdaq and Hong Kong Stock Exchange	I
Chicago Board Brokerage: Chicago Board of Trade and Prebon Yamane	I
Nasdaq and Australian Stock Exchange	A
NYMEX-SIMEX	A
ParisBourse, Swiss Exchange, Borsa Italiana, and Lisbon Stock Exchange	A
London Stock Exchange and Buenos Aires Stock Exchange	A
Nord Pool and Leipzig Power Exchange	A
Australian Stock Exchange and Singapore Exchange	A
GEM: Amsterdam, Australia, Bovespa (Brazil), Brussels, Hong Kong,	
Mexico, New York, Paris, Tokyo, and Toronto exchanges	A
Chicago Mercantile Exchange and Cantor Fitzgerald	N
International Petroleum Exchange and NYMEX	N
Eurex and NYMEX	N
Chicago Board Options Exchange and Osaka Securities Exchange	N
LIFFE and Boston Stock Exchange (options trading)	N

I = implemented; A = agreed; N = being negotiated.

particularly notable that these types of consolidation initiatives were relatively few and far between prior to 1997.

An example of the strategic alliance strategy is that implemented by the Chicago Mercantile Exchange (CME) and MATIF. The CME has adopted the MATIF NSC-VF trading technology as the basis for its own electronic trading system, and MATIF has adopted the CME's clearing system.

A deeper form of alliance is exemplified by the creation of a common electronic system to access multiple exchange systems, a strategy agreed by eight European stock exchanges, but subsequently abandoned.[12] It is important for developing countries to take note of the fact that the evidence to date suggests that common access systems are generally far more complex and costly than anticipated when first widely proposed in the late 1990s. Few of them have been successfully implemented, which indicates that linking a national system to foreign systems is simply not a cheap and easy alternative to systems consolidation.

The Norex alliance between OM Stockholm Exchange and the Copenhagen Stock Exchange goes a step further, producing a single trading system, based on the Stockholm SAXESS technology, to trade both Swedish and Danish stocks. Although the exchanges remain separate legal entities, members of one are offered free membership in the other. The Oslo, Reykjavik, Riga, and Vilnius exchanges are expected to join the common trading system beginning in 2001. The CBOT and Eurex have implemented a similar strategy, deepening an earlier one based on the model of a common access system.

The most notable example of a fully consummated exchange merger during this period is Eurex, which combined Deutsche Börse's DTB derivatives arm with the Swiss Exchange's SOFFEX derivatives arm into a single corporate entity, utilizing a common trading system. The Euronext merger of the Paris, Amsterdam, Brussels, and Lisbon exchanges has, at the time of writing, not yet consolidated equity or derivative trading platforms. The virt-x exchange is a product of the Swiss Exchange taking a 38.9 percent equity stake in London-based Tradepoint. virt-x transfers Tradepoint's pan-European blue-chip equity trading to the Swiss SWX system in June 2001, with the Swiss Exchange legally migrating all of its Swiss blue-chip order flow to the new entity.

---

12. London, Frankfurt, Paris, Amsterdam, Zurich, Milan, Madrid, and Brussels.

Developing Securities Markets in the Age of Automated Trading

As in other areas of the economy where technological innovation has wrought revolutionary changes in products and services, such as mobile communications, developing countries actually benefit from not having to adapt or replace inferior legacy systems. As can be seen from the European and, particularly, American experience, the transformation of exchange technology and governance structure can be a complex, time-consuming, and costly process. Developing countries with no legacy of a government-controlled or mutualized exchange—or no legacy with strong political or economic vested interests to protect it—are in a position to facilitate the rapid emergence of the most efficient institutional and technological infra-structure for trading. The key decisions that need to be made are discussed next.

Exchange Governance

The development of commercial, for-profit trading system operators should be considered a priority. Mutualized exchanges entrench intermediary con-trol of market development and are less able to innovate and react to the demands of investors and issuers.

Should developing countries perhaps see the creation of a national mutu-alized exchange as a preliminary step to eventual liberalization of market structure rules and demutualization of the exchange? There are dangers in this phased approach.

Building obligatory broker-intermediation into the trading structure encourages the growth of questionable business practices between brokers and institutional investors that can result in excessive investment costs for domestic fundholders and forestall later progress toward nonintermediated trading. Specifically, brokers have learned to package non-trade-execution activities (such as research, computer systems, and access to initial public offerings) into institutional trading commissions, allowing institutions to use client assets to pay for services that they would otherwise have to pay for themselves (or pass on to clients transparently through the manage-ment fee). Otherwise known as soft commissions or bundled commissions, this practice is widespread in the United States, which explains why weighted average agency commission rates fell only 10 percent from 1994 to 1998, from 6.1¢ per share to 5.5¢ per share,[13] even though trading vol-

13. Greenwich Associates (1999).

umes climbed fourfold over this same period.[14] This compares with non-intermediated electronic trading commissions of 0.25 to 2¢ per share currently prevailing in the U.S. market. Studies further indicate that paying higher institutional commissions does not result in lower implicit execution costs: in fact, there appears to be a positive correlation between the two.[15]

In short, the ability of brokers both to apply their strategic control over the exchange and to exploit payment monitoring problems in the fund manager–fundholder relationship can impose significant transition costs when moving from a mutualized national exchange structure to a structure based on competitive nonintermediated trading system operators. Developing countries should therefore consider seriously adopting the competitive operator model as early as possible in the development of their capital markets.

Build versus Buy

Around the world, most notably in Europe, the 1990s were a decade of enormous wasted investment in redundant trading and settlement systems. Despite the fact that virtually every trading system implemented in Europe during these years applied the same market architecture (the continuous electronic auction), almost every exchange decided to build its own proprietary version. Within a few years, most were making plans to abandon their investments and to adopt another exchange's system in response to pressure from the major international trading houses to begin consolidating platforms. Deutsche Börse and the London Stock Exchange each paid Andersen Consulting over $100 million to build separate systems applying identical architectures, but on incompatible hardware platforms. This proved to be the biggest barrier to the successful completion of their proposed alliance in 1998 and merger in 2000.

In less politically sensitive sectors of the economy, the build-versus-buy decision is a straightforward matter of cost-benefit analysis. The exchange business should be no different. With few exceptions, fledgling exchanges should find it most cost-effective to buy, lease, or pay for access to trading and settlement systems already in operation elsewhere. Once built, the cost

14. The value of shares traded in the United States rose from $3.56 trillion in 1994 to $13.15 trillion in 1998 (Securities Industry Association, 1999).

15. See Berkowitz, Logue, and Noser (1988), who adjust for trade difficulty. The findings of Domowitz and Steil (1999), which compared execution costs between "traditional" brokers and execution-only electronic trading service providers, are consistent. Keim and Madhavan (1997) find a positive correlation coefficient between explicit and implicit costs of 0.14 for sells and 0.07 for buys.

of adapting such systems to new products is almost always minimal compared with the cost of creating a new system. The owners of systems in use in the largest markets further have a powerful commercial incentive continuously to improve their functionality and robustness, thereby insuring exchanges contracting their services against the risks of obsolescence.

Ownership

Even more fundamental than the build-versus-buy decision is the question of whether a domestically *owned* exchange must operate the trading infrastructure. In fact, if no foreign trading and settlement system operators are interested in competing for such business, the government needs seriously to reevaluate whether the existing political or legal framework is even capable of nurturing a successful equity market.

Given the extent of the literature highlighting the importance of stock markets as an element of a country's financial infrastructure, it may appear strange to suggest that there is no need for governments actually to "create" them, or to ensure that ownership of exchanges remains local. However, computers and telecommunications technology are also widely seen as vital to economic development, yet few if any political leaders would maintain that their countries must design and produce laptops and cell phones in order to develop. If the local market demand exists, and the local resources are available to purchase them, there will be ready and enthusiastic suppliers from around the globe. If neither is there, however, public investment to create a domestic securities industry will only serve to destroy scarce economic resources.

As illustrated by Domowitz and Steil, investors and issuing companies suffer significant economic costs from inefficient trading structures and excess intermediation.[16] Developing countries must therefore avoid the temptation to use exchange building as an employment scheme for excess civil servants, bankers, and aspiring local technologists.

It is important to recognize that the structure of a genuinely efficient exchange will look the same whether the ownership is local or foreign. As in other industries, the nationality of ownership should not have a determinant effect on the optimal level of local management and staffing. But foreign ownership is likely to be able to exploit excess systems capacity abroad, thereby yielding significant operating cost savings locally. In the future, it is highly likely that local exchanges will, as a matter of course, have

16. Domowitz and Steil (1999, 2001).

a trading system supplier in one country and a settlement supplier in another, and those suppliers may themselves have computer operations in third countries. Thus, in terms of technological infrastructure, the local exchange may have responsibility for nothing more than maintaining the local network servers. Its primary responsibilities are likely to focus on relations with client traders and infrastructure suppliers.

Remote Foreign Access

I will not revisit here the debate over the costs and benefits of foreign portfolio investment flows. I need only emphasize that if foreign participation in local equity trading is to be accommodated, it is not in the interests of foreign investors, local investors, or local listed companies for such trading to have to be facilitated through physical local offices of foreign banks, or intermediated by local financial institutions. These merely add to the cost of market access: Domowitz and Steil found that every 10 percent decline in trading costs yields an 8 percent increase in U.S. and European blue-chip trading volume.[17] Remote foreign "membership" should therefore be actively encouraged as a means of increasing market liquidity, reducing trading costs, and reducing the cost of equity capital to local listed companies. Importantly, the higher turnover it facilitates should also boost the profitability of the local exchange, helping it to increase investment in trading infrastructure and expansion of its product range (into areas such as index derivatives).

Dealing with Illiquidity and Volatility

Shares in most companies listed in developing markets tend to be thinly traded and are therefore more volatile than shares listed in developed markets. This often gives rise to political concerns, yet the issues are best managed by commercial organizations with a clear incentive to attract investor confidence and participation.

Developing-country monopoly exchanges have a tendency to reproduce exchange models used in developed countries with little regard for cost or applicability. For example, periodic call auctions for developing-market stocks can mitigate the problems associated with illiquidity, but very few developing-country exchanges use them. Call auctions concentrate orders for matching at discrete points in time—typically, one to three times a day. All matched orders change hands at the same price (that is, there is no bid-

17. Domowitz and Steil (2001).

ask spread), a feature that is apt to bring credibility to the market in countries where the public is accustomed to "insiders" routinely getting a better deal in commercial transactions.

When I asked the head of trading at one such exchange why they were using an internally designed continuous trading system rather than a call auction, his response was telling. He first remarked that the large exchanges were using the same sort of system used by his exchange, implying that this in itself was justification for their decision. He then put a question back to me: "If we did it your way, what would our brokers do?" The answer, as he realized, is "virtually nothing" (except underwrite the investor's credit risk), which is precisely the reason why developing-country exchanges are better off operating as demutualized commercial organizations. Brokers are not necessary in simple call auctions, which is why broker-controlled exchanges rarely use them.

One young exchange that did begin with a call-auction-based market is the Warsaw Stock Exchange. (Re-)established in 1991, the exchange began trading with only one call auction per stock per week. It only moved to a daily call auction in 1994, after sufficient trading volumes had been established. Continuous trading for the most liquid stocks was not added until 1996. As of the start of 2001, 102 of the 225 stocks listed (45 percent) are traded continuously, with opening and closing calls; 34 (15 percent) trade in an opening and closing call; and 89 (40 percent) trade only in an opening call. Half of the exchange's trading volume (in money terms) is still accounted for by the call auctions, indicating their clear attractiveness to Polish equity investors. Warsaw uses the state-of-the-art ParisBourse NSC continuous trading system, indicating that the success of the call auctions would be difficult to interpret as a failure of the continuous trading infrastructure. Two-thirds of the exchange's market capitalization is owned by Polish investors, which is also a sign of success for a developing-market exchange that is open to foreign investors.

Designation and Regulation of Exchange Functions

In developed countries, exchanges typically perform functions wholly unrelated to the actual trading of securities and indeed are frequently required by national law to perform such functions. The most significant one is "listing" the company shares to be traded on the exchange.

Listing is fundamentally a quality control function, designed to ensure that companies admitted to a given segment of the market (for example, large cap or small cap) meet disclosure requirements appropriate to their size and age. Its role in the equity markets is comparable to that of "ratings" in the bond market, even if the mechanisms of being listed and rated are very different. But just as bond rating agencies have a strong incentive to rate bonds more accurately than their competitors, listing agencies should have strong incentives to set listing requirements for publicly traded companies neither too high nor too low. If disclosure requirements are excessive for the size and age of the companies wishing to be publicly traded, then the agency will unnecessarily sacrifice listing revenues. If they are set too low, however, investors are more likely to be harmed by unexpected events, like profit warnings. Investors will therefore shun such stocks, and the agency's reputation and pricing power in the listings market will suffer.

It is an unfortunate historical legacy, however, that in much of the world governments have treated listing as a self-regulatory function to be performed by the monopoly national exchange. As a matter of logic and history, however, listing should never have been considered an obligation that needed to be imposed on exchanges. The board of the NYSE began imposing formal listing standards in 1856 and did so wholly of its own accord and in consideration of its own interests. The main reasons for the development of such standards would appear to have been the protection of members trading on their own account and the incentive to listing provided to companies from the public signal of financial soundness and stability.[18] This incentive is reflected in the fact that exchanges typically extract a significant proportion of their annual revenues from listing activities (36 percent on the NYSE in 1999).

Whereas listing is clearly a valuable market function, there is no logical reason why trading system operators should necessarily be the ones to carry it out. It could just as easily be performed by accounting firms or rating agencies, and done on a competitive basis. Competition for listing standards should help both to drive down listing costs and to discover the optimal listing standards for companies with different characteristics.

Any assumption that listing standards will always be set too low if established on a purely commercial basis is clearly faulty. A recent example illustrating this comes from Germany's Neuer Markt, a small cap market operated by Deutsche Börse. Having concluded that a 70 percent year-on-year decline in its listed share prices needed to be at least partially ascribed to a lack of investor confidence in company disclosure—following a string of profit warnings, insider dealing investigations, and insolvencies—the

18. Banner (1998).

exchange implemented new rules to mandate more comprehensive and standardized company reports and revelation of directors' share dealings. Offenders were made subject to new punitive actions and publication of their offenses on the Internet. These actions were taken wholly on the basis of the exchange's evaluation of its commercial self-interest.

The implications for developing-country equity markets are clear: listing should be a competitive business, fully open to nonexchanges. Exchanges should be permitted to trade any stock listed in the country, whether or not they are the listing agency for that stock. The government may wish to establish minimum base standards for companies to be publicly traded in the country (as in the United States and United Kingdom), but these standards should be kept at a low and general level in order to encourage private sector competition for the establishment of quality standards (which are inherently unknowable in advance). Once again, there is no reason why foreign firms should not be allowed to compete for local listing business. If they are successful, this will mean that local investors have confidence in their standards and are therefore more willing to invest locally than if the standards were less rigorously set.

Post-Trade Systems

Exchanges require settlement systems linked to central bank payments systems. There are different ownership models for CSDs around the world. The most fundamental distinctions are whether the CSD is owned by an exchange or is self-standing, and whether self-standing CSDs are private or government-owned organizations.

In the euro zone, a process of CSD consolidation that has just begun is having the effect of expanding cross-border private CSD activities. The merger of Cedel and Deutsche Börse Clearing to create Clearstream was the first such major event. Given the enormous economies of scale and network externalities in CSD operation, it is important for developing country governments and exchanges to consider how these can be exploited. This requires that they not reflexively rely on CSDs built or owned by trading system operators, whether domestic or foreign, but rather that they actively seek out cost-minimizing combinations of compatible trading and settlement systems. Vertically integrated structures for trading, clearing, and settlement have been popular among European exchanges but are increasingly being called into question now that regional consolidation is accepted as a business imperative. Perceived benefits from building proprietary interlocking trading and post-trade systems must be weighed against potential costs in rapid obsolescence and inflexibility.

CSDs may for the foreseeable future have to be linked to the national payment system controlled by the central bank (the development of commercial bank money may obviate this need), but this does not require that they be domestically owned or operated. Furthermore, the technical regulations applied to CSD operations can have a significant impact on the efficiency of those operations. It is therefore important that governments not import such regulations from abroad without regard for whether they have been optimally adapted to the cross-border electronic trading environment that is currently emerging. For example, the long-standing requirement for central registration of individual investor accounts within the national CSD has hampered the efforts of the Scandinavian exchanges and CSDs fully to integrate their markets and to reduce cross-border trading costs among them. Such rules were implemented well before the advent of electronic trading but now represent a barrier to the development of more efficient cross-border private sector solutions.

A Blueprint for Developing a Modern Securities Trading Infrastructure

For developing countries with no exchange or poorly functioning ones, the base requirements for fostering securitized investment are political stability, monetary stability, and enforceable and transferable property rights. If these are not well established, governments should not devote scarce public resources to exchange building. Dormant or, much worse, corrupt securities markets are a poor symbol of a government's commitment to the development of a market economy. In economies that have developed to the point where basic commercial banking activities are widespread, however, there is much that governments can and should do to put fledgling exchange operations on the global efficient frontier.

Corporate Disclosure and Governance

The ability to trade shares cheaply and efficiently will mean little if the companies issuing the shares are not subject to some base level of enforceable standards for disclosure and governance. There are significant differences among developed market accounting and corporate governance standards, but it is beyond the scope of this discussion to attempt to identify the components of an optimal regime. Fortunately, it is not critical to do so. The choice between International Accounting Standards (IAS) or U.S. Generally Accepted Accounting Principles (GAAP), for example, will hardly be determinant in the drive to create a successful local equity culture, but the ability to enforce disclosure according to some base "adequate" standard (for example, as defined by the International Finance Corporation) is very likely to be. Levine and Zervos found that countries with at least "adequate" accounting standards had a higher level of stock market development than those that did not, but that moving from adequate standards to IAS did not correlate with a further increase in market development.[19] The same held for investor protection laws. Whereas regulatory fragmentation can itself represent a significant cost of doing business across borders, however, governments should craft regulations with an eye to maintaining compatibility with EU and U.S. standards.

Privatization Program

The privatization of state enterprises is a powerful tool for assisting the growth of securitized finance. Distributing shares widely throughout the populace is the most rapid means of creating public companies, enfranchising citizens in the development of the economy, and kick-starting fledgling exchanges.

Functional Regulation and Competition

Governments should establish a legal and regulatory structure for exchange operations that is based on the *functions* to be carried out in the market, rather than on the *institution* of an exchange as such. This will allow companies to offer trading, listing, CSD, or other ancillary services, but not require them to be offered together by the same institution. It will also allow companies to compete to provide any or all of these services. As the trading system and CSD businesses feature powerful network externalities, such competition may be *potential* rather than actual, but it should still be effective. Despite growing concern among European exchanges and regulators over ECNs and trading fragmentation, European share trading is actually more concentrated than it has been at any time over the past fifteen

19. Levine and Zervos (1998).

years (since the launch of London's SEAQ International). Yet the very *threat* of new competitors combined with cross-border mergers and takeovers has spurred an unprecedented efficiency drive across the continent.

To ensure that potential competition is real rather than just a legal fiction, the authorities should seriously consider barring a trading system operator from owning a controlling stake in a CSD. A dominant trading system operator can use ownership of the CSD to prevent potential competitors from gaining access to it and thereby effectively block them from trading the same securities. It is highly unlikely that Tradepoint (now virt-x) could ever have gotten off the ground in the United Kingdom had the London Stock Exchange owned Crest, the U.K. CSD. This issue is not a theoretical one for developing countries: it is, in fact, at the root of an ongoing dispute between two Nigerian exchanges.

Encouraging Foreign Participation

The world already has far more functionally identical trading systems and CSDs than it needs. A government that does not actively attempt to exploit this overcapacity in fostering the growth of a local equity market is doing a great disservice to its citizens and its domestic enterprises. If the cost of investing in the local market is not competitive internationally, local individual savers and collective investment schemes will invest in shares traded in more efficient markets. Foreign trading system and CSD operators should therefore be actively encouraged to provide services locally, whether in collaboration with local institutions or on their own. Economies of scale and network externalities in trading system operation, combined with strong commercial incentives for major market system operators continuously to modernize their platforms, should make foreign outsourcing a highly efficient alternative to local systems development. If foreign interest is not forthcoming, therefore, it is imperative for the local authorities to identify any impediments to foreign participation and their options for mitigating them.

Technological Infrastructure and Public Investment

A modern telecommunications infrastructure is important for taking full advantage of the latest trading and settlement technology: in particular, to eliminate distance costs and facilitate the widest possible network of direct market participants. Public financing of such communications infrastructure, or parts of it, may be necessary to attract foreign investment into the establishment of the trading infrastructure. However, governments should not target public investment into projects that operate as direct subsidies for the proprietary operations of any particular exchange or trading service operator.[20] Such operators have a strong financial interest in pleading for special treatment as a "national institution," but any such designation is bound to thwart competition and misdirect the allocation of private financial resources. As it is the primary role of securities markets to promote the efficient allocation of financial resources, the institutions composing such markets need themselves to confront the full exigencies of market forces.

References

Banner, Stuart. 1998. *Anglo-American Securities Regulation: Cultural and Political Roots, 1690–1860.* Cambridge University Press.

Berkowitz, Stephen A., Dennis E. Logue, and Eugene A. Noser. 1988. "The Total Cost of Transportation on the NYSE." *Journal of Finance* 43: 97–112.

Buiter, Willem H., Ricardo Lago, and Hélène Rey. 1999. "Financing Transition: Investing in Enterprises during Macroeconomic Transition." In *Financial Sector Transformation: Lessons from Economies in Transition,* edited by Mario I. Blejer and Marko Škreb. Cambridge University Press.

Davis, E. Philip, and Benn Steil. 2001. *Institutional Investors.* Cambridge, Mass.: MIT Press.

Demirgüç-Kunt, Asli, and Ross Levine. 1996. "Stock Market Development and Financial Intermediaries: Stylized Facts." *World Bank Economic Review* 10 (2): 291–321.

Domowitz, Ian, and Benn Steil. 1999. "Automation, Trading Costs, and the Structure of the Securities Trading Industry." Brookings-Wharton Papers on Financial Services.

———. 2001. "Innovation in Equity Trading Systems: The Impact on Transactions Costs and Cost of Capital." In *Technological Innovation and Economic Performance,* edited by Benn Steil, David Victor, and Richard Nelson. Princeton University Press.

Edwards, Jeremy, and Klaus Fischer. 1994. *Banks, Finance and Investment in Germany.* Cambridge University Press.

Garcia, Valeriano F., and Lin Liu. 1999. "Macroeconomic Determinants of Stock Market Development." *Journal of Applied Economics* 2 (1): 29–59.

Greenwich Associates. 1999. "Advances and Anomalies in 'Nontraditional' Trading." A Report to Institutional Investors in the United States. Greenwich, Conn.

Keim, Donald, and Ananth Madhavan. 1997. "Transactions Costs and Investment Style: An Inter-Exchange Analysis of Institutional Equity Trades." *Journal of Financial Economics* 46 (December): 265–92.

---

20. An example of such subsidies is building space. Exchanges are frequently established in palace-like structures at taxpayer expense, which is no more justifiable economically than handing such facilities to the city sewer operator.

Levine, Ross, and Sara Zervos. 1996. "Stock Market Development and Long-Run Growth." *World Bank Economic Review* 10 (2): 323–39.

———. 1998. "Capital Control Liberalization and Stock Market Development." *World Development* 26 (7): 1169–83.

Porter, Michael E. 1992. "Capital Choices: Changing the Way America Invests in Industry." Council on Competitiveness. Washington.

Rousseau, Peter L., and Paul Wachtel. 2000. "Equity Markets and Growth: Cross-Country Evidence on Timing and Outcomes, 1980–1995." *Journal of Banking and Finance* 24: 1993–57.

Rydén, Bengt. 1995. "The Reform of the Stockholm Stock Exchange." Stockholm Stock Exchange, November.

Securities Industry Association. 1999. *Securities Industry Fact Book*. New York.

Singh, Ajit. 1993. "The Stock-Market and Economic Development: Should Developing Countries Encourage Stock-Markets?" *UNCTAD Review 1993*.

Steil, Benn. 1995. "Illusions of Liberalization: Securities Regulation in Japan and the EC." Special Paper Series. Royal Institute of International Affairs. London.

PIERRE SAUVÉ
KARSTEN STEINFATT

12

Financial Services and the WTO: What Next?

The Financial Services Agreement (FSA) concluded in December 1997 under the auspices of the World Trade Organization's (WTO) General Agreement on Trade in Services (GATS) represented one of the hallmark achievements of the Uruguay Round. Thanks to GATS and the FSA, there is now considerable awareness that financial services are key inputs in the production of all that a nation produces, brings to market, and trades in, whether goods, ideas, and services. Simply put, financial services are the central nervous system of the body economic.[1] There is, similarly, a much greater recognition that the ability of efficient providers of financial services to deploy their competitive skills in foreign markets and contest prevailing rents is crucial for their clients' growth and commercial success in those markets. That success, in turn, serves the employment, innovation, growth, and development prospects—to say nothing of consumer welfare—of host countries.[2]

This improved understanding of the role of financial services providers has lent support to continued efforts worldwide at fostering competition-friendly domestic regulatory reform in the sector, amidst considerably

We are grateful to Julian Arkell, Stefano Bertasi, Claudio Borio, Gavin Bingham, Charles Freeland, Pierre Jacquet, Yoshiiro Kawai, Kate Langdon, Robert E. Litan, Donald J. Mathieson, Aaditya Mattoo, Julia Nielson, Johanne Prévost, Joel P. Trachtman, and Phillip Turner for helpful discussions.

1. Crockett (2000).
2. Levine (1996); and Jacquet (1997).

heightened capital mobility and occasionally severe financial market turmoil. Much of that reform has been undertaken voluntarily on a unilateral
basis, while some has been achieved pursuant to conditionality packages
designed by the Bretton Woods organizations. An important challenge in
the ongoing negotiations at the WTO is to secure such liberalization
through commitments under GATS.[3]

The need for such forward momentum took on added systemic significance following the collapse of the third WTO ministerial meeting in Seattle in 1999, and the rising chorus of globaphobic sentiments directed
toward the continued pursuit of services trade and investment liberalization.
Governments and the private sector must today mount a more spirited
defense of the strong case for sustaining liberalization's forward movement
in a sector of considerable economywide importance. Although the initial
set of services negotiations elicited little by way of public scrutiny (or even
much interest beyond fairly narrow business, government, and academic
circles), the current negotiations have drawn a loud and concerted attack by
various pressure groups, especially within the member countries of the
Organization for Economic Cooperation and Development (OECD).
These groups allege that GATS will all at once force governments to privatize essential services, will further erode domestic regulatory sovereignty,
and will oblige member states to pry open service sectors to predatory foreign multinational companies.[4] Such arguments have demonstrable political traction even when they are patently false, grossly exaggerated, or
deliberately misconstrued. Proponents of the benefits of multilateral trade
diplomacy must therefore engage in the debate forcefully to counteract
their influence. Failing to do so could hold back or even reverse progress in
opening financial markets, a process which many civil society groups see
(wrongly once more) as tantamount to lifting all barriers on capital movements. These risks are likely to be amplified if WTO members are unable
to launch a new, broader round of multilateral negotiations at the upcom-
ing Qatar ministerial meeting, given the narrowness of the current negotiating mandate on agriculture and services.

An important distinguishing feature of the FSA relates to the degree of
support and the political legitimacy it generated through a shared sense of
transatlantic purpose and commitment on the part of the financial services
industry itself. The sector was truly unique in that respect, and there is lit-

---

3. Sauvé and Gillespie (2000).
4. Frances Williams, "WTO Foresees Tough Talks on Opening up of Services Provision," *Financial Times,* March 16, 2001; and WTO (2001d).

tle doubt within the trade policy community that financial sector support in the European Union and the United States was a determining force in concluding the FSA.[5] The strength of those ties has not diminished since the FSA's conclusion. The industry's resolve and strategic focus is rather striking when compared with other segments of the business community.

Properly marshaling that sense of direction is a key to the success of the current negotiations and to agreement on a broader negotiating agenda in Qatar. Equally important is accessing the public and private channels of cooperation that underpin the broadly shared vision found in Canada, the European Union, Japan, and the United States (the so-called Quad countries). Doing so would do much to intensify the overall dynamic of liberalization within the WTO system as a whole and ensure that GATS remains an efficient means of overseeing the growing integration of national economies in an orderly, predictable, fair, and transparent manner.

Owing to the protracted nature of negotiations in the sector and to the implementation difficulties encountered by a number of WTO members, the GATS rules governing the financial sector only entered into effect on March 1, 1999, some twelve years after the launch of the Uruguay Round.[6] Consequently, the FSA was a mere nine months old when negotiations resumed on January 1, 2000, as scheduled under the Uruguay Round's so-called built-in agenda. Negotiations have yet to begin in earnest, however, as key players have only recently put forward their respective market access agendas. The coming negotiations will present many new challenges for the financial services community. The post–Uruguay Round negotiating agenda on financial services will, in all likelihood, be a highly differentiated one, encompassing countries at different levels of development, alternative modes of supply (cross-border trade versus establishment-related trade), competing business models (e-finance versus traditional channels), and specific market segments (banking versus securities versus insurance). The agenda must also take into account new players whose increasing ability to contest and capture the rents of traditional financial institutions is fast eroding the neat lines of demarcation that used to prevail in the market.

<hr />

5. Freeman (1997); and Moore (2000).

6. Seven countries—Brazil, the Philippines, Poland, Uruguay, Bolivia, the Dominican Republic, and Jamaica—have yet to accept the GATS Fifth Protocol establishing the FSA. Of these, all are currently engaged in domestic implementation processes of varying length and complexity, on which they make regular reports to the GATS Committee on Financial Services. The Fifth Protocol was reopened briefly in December 2000 to allow Kenya and Nigeria to sign the FSA. See Sauvé and Gillespie (2000) for a description of the FSA's complex negotiating history.

This essay addresses two central questions. First, what financial sector harvest can the GATS 2000 round realistically be expected to generate? And second, what can be done to enhance the quality and size of the achievements? To answer these questions, the essay considers the key market access issues that negotiators will likely confront in the coming talks. It then depicts and contrasts the liberalization and rulemaking challenges arising within the OECD area and in the developing world. The paper concludes with a discussion of a number of political economy issues that will influence the substantive outcome of negotiations in the financial services sector.

The essay comes to a threefold conclusion. First, although the FSA provides a solid foundation on which to pursue negotiations on trade and investment in financial services, much remains to be done to achieve increased market contestability. This is true both in developed countries, particularly with regard to cross-border transactions at the retail level, and in developing countries, where unilateral policy decisions have frequently established a degree of financial market openness that far exceeds what is currently reflected in legally bound WTO commitments. Second, important differences between developed and developing countries regarding the substantive nature of the negotiating agenda in financial services, combined with the limited export interests of most developing countries in the sector, will lessen the scope for intrasectoral bargaining. Accordingly, the financial industry in OECD countries (the main *demandeurs* in WTO talks) has an important stake in the launching a broad-based round of multilateral negotiations. Third, the important early progress that has been made in developing, promoting, implementing, and monitoring compliance with international standards for financial market supervision in the wake of recent financial market turmoil forms a strong complement to WTO-anchored attempts at advancing and securing the liberalization of financial markets. Any progress in regulatory and prudential convergence, whether coordinated through or pursued outside the WTO framework (as it currently is and should remain), will do much to enhance prospects for a greater overall degree of global competition in financial markets.

A Traditional Contestability Agenda in Financial Services

The liberalization of trade in services, in particular financial services, cannot be achieved by relying solely on the negotiated removal of border measures and the general multilateral principles on which the liberalization of trade in goods is based.[7] The barriers to trade in financial services are diverse and virtually always embedded in domestic regulatory practices. Such regulation may not be primarily concerned with the goals of free trade and competition, but may rather seek to promote certain social or noneconomic objectives. In the case of financial services, regulation is typically directed to limiting systemic risk, for example, by preserving the solvency of financial service providers or protecting depositors. Consequently, many measures that either directly or inadvertently pose barriers to trade in financial services cannot simply be eliminated or reduced.

As this opening section illustrates, however, many countries maintain a myriad of trade- and investment-impeding measures that might be easily amenable to negotiated reductions or to some of the traditional trade disciplines found in GATS, especially nondiscrimination principles. This is particularly the case among developing economies. Given that the dividing line between such restrictions and those with a more fundamental or systemic prudential component can at times become blurred, barriers to trade and investment in financial services might best be understood as lying along a continuum. At one extreme lie various market entry restrictions that simply bar foreign entry or limit the level of contestability by restricting the number of market entrants. At the other extreme are prudential regulations (typically of a nondiscriminatory nature) with an incidental effect on financial services trade—and often a disproportionate incidence on foreign service suppliers. Scattered in between are post-market entry measures affecting the operating conditions of financial institutions in foreign markets.

A traditional contestability agenda in financial services, as defined in this essay, would rely on negotiated reductions and nondiscrimination principles to address market entry and certain postestablishment barriers. Regarding other types of nondiscriminatory regulations, such an agenda would aim to strengthen disciplines on transparency and increase the level of regulatory convergence across borders through harmonization, recognition, and the adoption of international standards.

The first category of barriers that a traditional contestability agenda would seek to address consists of measures that act as barriers to market entry, including barriers to the cross-border supply of financial services. It also encompasses barriers to foreign entry, that is, restrictions that inhibit foreign service providers from establishing a commercial presence in a host-country market. Such restrictions typically include limits in the following four areas:

7. Trebilcock and Howse (1999).

—The number of service suppliers. This type of restriction is usually applied through numerical quotas or economic needs tests for licenses, as well as moratoria or freezes on new licenses. The national context for such restrictions may include a nationalized domestic financial sector or a supplier that holds a monopoly or acts as an exclusive provider.

—Foreign equity participation. These measures specify the maximum share of equity in domestic financial institutions that foreign service suppliers can own.

—The type of legal entity or joint venture through which a service can be supplied. This type of restriction, which is one of the most commonly used mechanisms in emerging markets, delimits how a foreign financial institution may operate in the domestic market. For example, the rules of participation may specify only a representative office, a separately capitalized and locally incorporated subsidiary, or mandatory partnership with the government.

—The ability of residents to purchase financial services in another territory.

The second category of barriers addressed by a traditional contestability agenda consists of measures that affect the operating conditions of foreign service providers once they have established a commercial presence in the host country. Examples include limits on the total number of services operations or the total quantity of service output; the geographical range of operations; the type of services that can be provided; the number and type of natural persons to be employed in a particular sector; the value of transactions or assets being managed; and restrictions on the ownership of land or real estate. The application of taxes and subsidies (including indirect subsidies flowing from regulations that artificially reduce the cost of capital to domestic firms) may also affect the operating conditions of foreign service providers.[8]

An important element in this category of barriers concerns the issue of grandfathering the acquired rights of established operators. This issue assumed considerable importance in the final days of negotiations leading to the FSA, and it came close to derailing its conclusion. A grandfather clause protects existing investments (and investors) from commitments by

8. The Association of German Banks (2001) cites the interesting case of how public guarantees provided to the country's savings banks and their central institutions, the Landesbanken, allow such banks to fund themselves relatively cheaply on the capital market, thereby giving them a competitive edge over their domestic and foreign competitors. Competition is further distorted by the fact that in many federal states, public housing agency funds have been transferred to Landesbanken at below-market interest rates. Following a complaint filed by the European Banking Federation, the European Union is now examining the lawfulness of public guarantees under European law on state aid.

the host country in the context of a negotiation that could adversely affect such investments' existing operating conditions.

Table 12A-1 (in appendix A) provides country-specific examples of the types of measures covered by a traditional contestability agenda for each of the three core financial services subsectors, namely, banking, securities, and insurance.[9] The bulk of measures affecting market entry are quantitative in nature and amenable to negotiated, progressive liberalization. Under GATS, the principal means for liberalizing such measures is contained in Article XVI (Market Access), which prohibits the use of most of the market-entry barriers described above in sectors in which countries agree to undertake specific commitments. Alternatively, the Understanding on Commitments in Financial Services, which is annexed to the FSA, offers a means for countries to voluntarily subscribe to a higher degree of liberalization in the sector. Articles 5 and 6 of the Understanding provide for the right of establishment, which would result in substantial liberalization of market-entry restrictions in those countries that decide to schedule specific commitments in accordance with this instrument. Articles 3 and 4 would have a similar liberalizing effect, since they require that subscribing countries allow foreign financial service providers to supply certain services on a cross-border basis and also allow residents to purchase these services abroad.

The liberalization of barriers belonging to the postestablishment category of a traditional contestability agenda is significantly more complex than the liberalization of barriers to market entry. Postestablishment barriers encompass not only measures imposed on foreign services or service providers in a discriminatory fashion, but also nondiscriminatory measures that may impede trade in financial services. While discriminatory measures fall within the scope of Article XVII (National Treatment) of GATS or Article C.1 of the Understanding on Commitments in Financial Services, nondiscriminatory measures are not caught by the national treatment discipline of either instrument. Furthering trade and investment liberalization in heavily regulated sectors like banking, securities, and insurance must therefore be based on negotiating approaches that seek to balance two potentially competing objectives: ensuring that regulation (often shading into prudential regulation) is not used to limit competition from abroad and ensuring that freer trade in financial services does not undermine the prudential objectives pursued by such regulation.

9. These lists are not intended to provide a comprehensive inventory of barriers to trade in financial services, but rather they seek to highlight the most common measures affecting trade in each of the three core subsectors of financial services.

Two approaches have been suggested to help reconcile this twofold objective. First, in the context of work proceeding under Article VI on domestic regulation, GATS members have drawn attention to the notion of necessity and the circumstances under which domestic regulatory measures may depart from the requirement that they be the least trade restrictive possible and not needlessly burdensome.[10] Work in this area has raised acute sensitivities within regulatory circles and civil society. Many financial regulators feel that viewing regulation through a necessity prism could undermine the sound public policy rationales that underpin such regulation. To the extent that regulation, including that taken on prudential grounds (and despite the prudential carve-out found in the Annex to the FSA), remains subject to multilateral dispute settlement provisions in cases of demonstrable protectionist capture, the political costs of developing more highly codified disciplines on the issue of necessity may well outweigh any putative economic benefits.[11]

A second, and significantly more consensual, approach toward reconciling the twofold objective described above consists of designing measures to support greater regulatory transparency. The primary purpose of such measures would be to shed light on the way in which existing regulations in the financial services (and other) sectors are developed, adopted, and enforced; mechanisms would include prior notification procedures in domestic rulemaking.[12] The rationale behind such a proposal is simple and powerful: measures that are designed on the basis of broad consultations with all potential stakeholders, including foreign firms, are likely to command greater legitimacy—and hence more readily meet any implicit necessity requirements. Chances are, moreover, that measures developed and implemented through a fully transparent process are less likely, on balance, to be challenged by trading partners through dispute settlement procedures.

10. WTO Members are obliged under GATS Article VI:5 to ensure that domestic regulation is based on objective and transparent criteria, is no more burdensome than necessary, and in the case of licensing procedures, does not in itself restrict the supply of the service. The procedure for determining whether a member is in conformity with this obligation takes into account the international standards of relevant international organizations, if applied by the member. The WTO Working Party on Domestic Regulation is discussing the issue of developing regulatory disciplines as mandated under GATS Article VI:4. Such disciplines would apply to those sectors and subsectors in which members have scheduled liberalization commitments. To date, the WTO has made no attempt to develop disciplines that would apply to prudential regulation in financial services. A proposal to clarify the scope of prudential measures was recently rejected by the WTO Committee on Trade in Financial Services (Kawai, 2001).

11. This argument is seemingly strengthened by the fact that no trade disputes have been lodged so far under GATS in the field of financial services.

12. OECD (2001b).

While increased transparency with respect to nondiscriminatory regulatory measures can prove to be a powerful instrument in promoting domestic regulatory reform, it might not be sufficient, in itself, to achieve greater market openness in the sphere of financial services. A stronger commitment to transparency may, however, serve as a springboard for initiatives that aim to minimize the impact of nondiscriminatory regulation in financial services trade. In particular, such initiatives, which include the development of rules on harmonization and mutual recognition, may help speed the adoption and diffusion of best regulatory practices and international standards. The adoption of such standards across countries is likely, in turn, to reduce the scope for commercial conflict by lessening incentives for regulatory arbitrage. In this sense, the far-reaching degree of voluntary, nonbinding regulatory convergence in prudential supervisory practices that is currently taking place in various international fora is fully compatible with—and strongly complements—efforts at progressive, legally bound, financial market opening in the WTO.

The specific elements of a traditional contestability agenda in financial services that will be at the core of the ongoing GATS 2000 negotiations can be deduced from the various proposals that have been submitted to the GATS Council. Six WTO members—Australia, Canada, the European Union, Japan, Norway, and the United States—have tabled proposals that directly address financial services (see table 12A-2 in appendix A for a summary). A priority area for all six appears to be mode 3 of GATS, which deals with commercial presence or establishment-related trade in services. Indeed, the proposals demonstrate a broad consensus on the need to further liberalize quantitative measures impairing investment in the three financial services subsectors (banking, securities, and insurance). The measures most often mentioned in this regard include constraints on foreign ownership, foreign equity participation, the legal form of establishment, and the number of service suppliers.

The different financial services proposals are somewhat less uniform with regard to the remaining GATS modes of services delivery. Only half of the proposals underscore the need to reduce restrictions on the ability of residents or firms from one territory to purchase services in another territory (GATS mode 2). With respect to cross-border trade (mode 1), some WTO members have identified specific subsectors within banking and insurance that they consider ripe for liberalization, rather than calling for across-the-board commitments as in the case of mode 3 and, to a certain extent, mode 2. For example, the European Union and the United States, with strong backing from the International Chamber of Commerce (ICC), propose the elimination of barriers that impede cross-border trade in financial information and advisory services; marine, aviation, and transport (so-called MAT) insurance; reinsurance and retrocession; and services auxiliary to the provision of insurance, such as consultancy, risk assessment, and claim settlement services. Norway wishes to see cross-border trade in maritime shipping insurance included in the services negotiations, while Australia and Canada do not identify any specific subsectors as candidates for cross-border liberalization. Finally, all proposals except that of Norway refer to the fourth mode of services delivery. Together, they cover a wide array of issues related to the temporary entry of natural persons, including the temporary movement of intracorporate transferees and contractual service suppliers, nationality and residency requirements for executives and employees, and the reduction of limits on the number of foreign employees.

Given that postestablishment barriers to trade in financial services are highly pervasive in developed and developing countries alike, it should come as no surprise that a majority of countries' GATS 2000 proposals devote significant attention to this type of barrier. The sheer number of postestablishment barriers listed in the proposals reflects not only their pervasive nature, but also the numerous forms that these mostly regulatory barriers can take. The diverse items that countries would like to discuss during the ongoing services round include restrictions on the number and type of products that can be offered by foreign firms in domestic markets (Australia); nondiscriminatory membership in self-regulatory bodies and in stock, securities, and futures exchanges (the European Union); nondiscriminatory tax treatment (Japan); and licensing procedures (the United States).

The six WTO members demonstrate consensus on the important role of transparency in reducing the trade effects of postestablishment regulatory barriers. All the proposals suggest putting transparency on the negotiating table, usually with a view to refining and deepening current disciplines.

A Two-by-Two Negotiating Proposal

A useful way of focusing cooperative efforts in the financial services area at both the governmental and private sector levels is to distinguish the twin challenges of liberalization and rulemaking as they concern OECD and developing countries. While both groups of countries face work on each front, the nature of that work, the technical difficulties it entails, the regu-

Table 12-1. *Negotiating Challenges of the GATS 2000 Round in Financial Services*

Challenge	OECD countries	Developing countries
Rule-making challenges	Address the regulatory challenges of e-finance	Improve domestic prudential standards and supervisory capacities before liberalizing financial services
	Establish regulatory dialogue among trade and finance regulators in a WTO setting	Experiment with safeguards provisions specific to financial services
	Enshrine a right of nonestablishment in the Understanding on Commitments in Financial Services	Bind the regulatory status quo
	Show a readiness to experiment with a safeguards clause specific to financial services	Promote greater coherence between World Bank, IMF, and FSAP surveillance of regulatory regimes, WTO negotiations, and TPRM surveillance
	Consider scope for open, plurilateral recognition agreements in areas of greater regulatory convergence or lesser regulatory burden	
Liberalization challenges	Predominant focus on e-finance (mode 1: cross-border trade; mode 2: consumption abroad)	Predominant focus on commercial presence (mode 3)
		Secure a higher overall level of bound liberalization through the Understanding on Commitments in Financial Services
		Phase-in liberalization, with appropriate transition periods and pre-commitments to future liberalization
		Focus on competition and market entry rather than ownership

latory challenges it raises, and the political calculus to which it gives rise are all noticeably different. Establishing a clear, explicit hierarchy of negotiating priorities early on will be important in addressing these challenges, as will the skilful deployment of diplomatic and advocacy efforts in countries that question the wisdom, relevance, and price tag (in terms of concessions in areas of priority export interest) of forward trade and investment liberalization in the financial sector. Table 12-1 depicts this contrasted negotiating agenda in a simple two-by-two matrix, which is elaborated in the discussion below.

Negotiating Challenges in OECD Countries

For OECD member countries, by far the greatest challenge of the coming round will be to adapt the FSA (and GATS) to the unfolding landscape of e-commerce and the possibilities it opens up for the genuine liberalization of cross-border trade in financial services. The FSA largely predated the advent of e-finance; some measure of catching up is a first-order priority if the FSA is to retain its nascent credibility. The e-finance agenda carries both rulemaking and liberalization dimensions that OECD countries must productively explore.

RULEMAKING CHALLENGES. The most pressing challenge in the area of rulemaking will be that of fostering acceptance and cooperation (sometimes called buy-in) on the part of financial regulators. Without their participation, it is difficult to see how a commercially meaningful set of liberalization commitments on cross-border trade in financial services might emerge from the GATS 2000 negotiations (particularly at the retail end of the market where much of the GATS talks will likely concentrate). The intensity and historical antecedents of regulatory cooperation across the Atlantic, together with the resulting level of mutual trust and understanding that such cooperation affords, means that both governments and private sector firms in the United States and the European Union are uniquely placed to assume a leadership role in this area.

Unlike most developing and transition economies, OECD countries generally bound the regulatory status quo in the financial sector under the FSA, and they displayed considerable regulatory caution with regard to committments on cross-border trade in financial products. As a result, commitments under GATS modes 1 and 2 (cross-border supply of services and consumption abroad) were far less common and more narrowly drawn than were liberalization commitments scheduled for trade through a commercial presence (mode 3). Most OECD countries used the Understanding on Financial Services Commitments as the basis for scheduling commitments in the sector, although the relevant obligations cover only a very limited range of insurance activities and auxiliary and advisory services—and even then, mostly on the demand side (consumption abroad) rather than on the supply side.

Winning over the regulatory community is easily preached. Doing so in practice is quite another matter. A strong push from the private sector, which has most to gain from such market opening, will likely prove instrumental in this regard. Leaders in the world's financial community must encourage regulatory officials to launch a process of regulatory cooperation that aims to strike a sensible balance between legitimate prudential concerns, on the one hand, and the promotion of greater doses of effective market access, on the other.

Financial regulators in OECD countries are still very much in the initial stages of discovery in this area. Most countries have only just begun to address the domestic regulatory implications of the e-finance revolution, let alone their international ramifications. While efforts to come to grips with the multifaceted implications of e-finance for approaches to regulation and prudential supervision have only recently been initiated in various international forums, important avenues for deepened regulatory cooperation have already been identified (see appendix B). In the main, such work does not involve the WTO directly, whose raison d'être is not to proclaim financial market regulations or to second-guess the decisions, recommendations, norms, and best practices that flow from the ongoing dialogue among supervisory authorities in matters of e-finance. Still, there is a need for continued, deeper dialogue between the trade policy and financial regulation communities, as their core mandates are mutually supportive and strongly complementary.

The second major rulemaking challenge is promoting regulatory dialogue. Institutionalizing closer regulatory contacts between the relevant supervisory committees of the Bank for International Settlements (BIS), the International Organization of Securities Commissions (IOSCO), the International Association of Insurance Supervisors (IAIS), trade officials, and officials responsible for developing global standards in the fields of accounting, auditing, and data privacy is key to ensuring that commitments to open up cross-border trade in financial services are underpinned by the proper set of practices and disciplines on matters of regulatory cooperation, recognition, and prudential supervision.

An important objective of GATS 2000 should thus be to set up the institutional machinery conducive to a healthy regulatory dialogue on these issues in a trade policy setting. The GATS Committee on Financial Services should create a subcommittee dedicated to this work. Stakeholders should be under no illusion that the regulatory journey ahead will be easy or lead to quick fixes. The great difficulties that members of the European Union have recently experienced in pushing financial market integration forward is a sobering reminder of the slow pace at which international regulatory cooperation often proceeds.[13] Experience shows that determined prodding

---

13. Paul Mentré, "Union Européenne: Difficile harmonisation des services financiers," *Le Figaro*, March 24, 2001, p. 8.

and leadership on the part of the business sector can help encourage greater cooperation on the part of regulators and improve mutual understanding between the trade and financial policy communities.

A third rulemaking challenge for OECD countries concerns the scope for enshrining a right of nonestablishment, subject to positive (or voluntary) undertakings. That is, wherever practicable, governments should refrain from mandating the establishment of a commercial presence in the host-country market as a prerequisite for the delivery of a service. This new GATS discipline could be effected through a modification of the Understanding on Commitments in Financial Services. Such an approach was successfully pursued in the services chapter of the North American Free Trade Agreement (NAFTA), and it would be a natural complement to, or even an essential ingredient of, a stronger push on cross-border trade in financial services. It would also help focus the attention of regulators on the need to satisfy legitimate prudential concerns through means that are the least trade restrictive possible. Such channels may not always exist. Evidence indicates that a so-called click-and-mortar approach to retail e-finance, which requires some degree of physical proximity to a targeted customer base, may be an important means of overcoming consumers' reluctance to engage in pure cross-border transactions. Still, the key is to determine what may be practicable in this area.

Finally, the fourth rulemaking challenge concerns the controversial area of emergency safeguards, whose alleged liberalizing virtues (and countervailing insurance-policy features) have hitherto been championed mostly by developing countries. The community of financial regulators is likely to agree, on prudential grounds, with many of the arguments that are commonly voiced in favor of designing GATS-specific safeguard measures. Should this prove to be the case in the coming round when attention turns to cross-border issues, the financial community may prove instrumental in seeking workable solutions to negotiations that have lingered inconclusively for close to seven years.

LIBERALIZATION CHALLENGES. As noted above, the key liberalization challenge for OECD countries in the coming round will be to determine the scope for greater commitments in the area of cross-border trade in financial products. This is where the greatest restrictions to trade in financial services are currently found, particularly at the retail level, although the nature of the constraints may be more prudential than overtly discriminatory.

Candidates for speedier progress in the financial area include those areas in which regulatory convergence across countries has been greatest to date (such as wholesale banking; nonlife insurance, such as maritime, aviation, and travel insurance; and reinsurance) or in which the regulatory burden is relatively light (for example, information and financial advisory services). These areas also hold potential for supporting efforts at setting in motion a process of mutual recognition (foreseen under Article 7 of GATS as well as under Article 3 of the Annex on Financial Services).

Negotiating Challenges in Developing Countries

As with OECD countries, developing countries are likely to face a combination of rulemaking and liberalization challenges in the financial sector during the current GATS talks. They will probably not be offensive players in the next round of financial services negotiations, however, for several reasons, including the prevailing nature of financial regulation in emerging markets; the widespread (if slightly disingenuous and inaccurate) belief that the recent financial market turmoil may have been caused by trade and investment liberalization in the sector; the need to enhance the soundness of domestic financial markets and improve the quality of prudential oversight and financial supervision; and the absence of significant export interests in the sector in most developing countries.

RULEMAKING CHALLENGES. The first major rulemaking challenge for developing countries involves strengthening domestic standards of prudential supervision. Financial markets cannot be relied on to function satisfactorily without sound regulation and effective supervision. History shows that they are vulnerable to periodic excesses. The existence of actual or implied guarantees from governments can dull prudential incentives. The resulting instability is even more troubling in a world in which capital markets are increasingly integrated. Contagion can spread financial difficulties from country to country, and the costs can be severe: the direct costs of resolving financial crises have exceeded 10 percent of GDP in more than fifteen countries over the past two decades.[14] The indirect costs and their attendant social consequences have been even greater.

Given the financial turmoil that a number of developing countries have experienced since the conclusion of the FSA, it may be expected that some countries will place a higher priority on improving regulatory oversight systems than on deepening market liberalization. Other countries will likely find scope for speeding up domestic reform efforts by remedying structural

14. Crockett (2000); and Kaminsky and Reinhart (1995).

weaknesses in bank balance sheets, which will entail greater financial market consolidation and a further openness toward outside capital.

OECD countries must show patience as developing countries navigate such policy cross-currents. Developing countries will need proper technical assistance to enhance their systems of prudential supervision, as well as encouragement to phase-in liberalization over appropriate transition periods. While a proper sequencing of reform holds the key to a sustainable liberalization path, the presence of foreign financial firms can contribute to raising prudential standards and improving the measurement of risk, which leads to a more efficient allocation of resources.[15] Securing precommitments to future liberalization may also be useful for ensuring that the needed strengthening of prudential supervision not become an excuse for covert trade and investment protectionism in the sector.[16]

Financial regulators play a key role in efforts to strengthen the functioning of the international financial system. They are drawing up the basic rules that should enable institutions and markets to function more stably and efficiently, and they are implementing internationally agreed rules in their national jurisdictions. It is hard to overstate the importance of this activity: while far removed from the world of multilateral trade bargaining, it is nonetheless strongly conducive to securing increased market openness.

At the international level, financial regulators have responded by setting up groupings such as the Basel Committee on Banking Supervision, the International Association of Insurance Supervisors (IAIS), the International Organization of Securities Commissions (IOSCO), the International Accounting Standards Council (IASC), and the International Association of Actuaries (IAA).[17] All of these organizations are involved in codifying principles of best practice, promoting their adoption worldwide, and monitoring compliance with such standards. Another key development in this regard was the creation of the Financial Stability Forum (FSF) in 1999, which for the first time brings together in one body the principal national and international authorities concerned with financial stability. The Compendium of Standards advocated by the FSF provides a common reference for the various economic and financial standards that are internationally accepted as relevant to sound, stable, and well-functioning financial sys-

15. Claessens and Glaessner (1998).

16. Mattoo (1998).

17. The Basel Committee, the IAIS, and IOSCO are also involved in cross-sectoral cooperation within a Joint Forum, which features annual meetings with supervisory officials from the developing world to discuss issues arising from the proliferation of financial conglomerates that span the banking, insurance, and securities industries.

tems.[18] The FSF has been described as providing an overarching framework for the international effort to strengthen financial systems.[19] Another key element in this improved international architecture of prudential supervision and regulatory cooperation stems from the joint activities of the International Monetary Fund and the World Bank, which have recently developed an organizing framework for assessing the observance of standards and relevant policies. In particular, the joint Financial Sector Assessment Program (FSAP), which might be described as the financial sector's equivalent of the WTO's Trade Policy Review Mechanism (TPRM), aims at assessing financial sector vulnerabilities and identifying developmental priorities, including an assessment of financial sector standards.[20] Another joint project is the experimental Reports on the Observance of Standards and Codes (ROSCs), which provide a vehicle for assembling summary assessments of standards across a range of areas, including financial sector standards assessed in the context of the FSAP and standards for data dissemination, fiscal transparency, and, in the future, corporate governance and accounting.[21] Taken together, these various initiatives depict a remarkable scene of rapidly expanding (if still far from complete) multilateral cooperation that is achieving de facto international harmonization through consensus building on core principles, model approaches to rulemaking, and best practices.[22] Measures are indeed becoming internationally harmonized even though formal recognition agreements are not being negotiated.[23]

Exploring the scope for overcoming differences and promoting greater coherence between the WTO negotiating process and the insights flowing from the above efforts at monitoring prudential standards could be particularly useful in promoting the progressive lock-in of domestic reform efforts. Such efforts will also remind trade policy officials (and the business

18. The compendium highlights twelve standards designated as deserving priority implementation, with an additional fifty-four considered relevant (Arkell, 2000–01). The twelve core standards are grouped under three broad headings: (1) macroeconomic fundamentals, which encompasses monetary and financial transparency, fiscal policy transparency, and data dissemination; (2) institutional and market infrastructure, namely, insolvency, corporate governance, accounting, auditing, payment and settlement, and market integrity; and (3) financial regulation and supervision, including banking supervision, securities regulation, and insurance supervision.

19. Crockett (2000).

20. The FSAP is a collaborative effort involving a range of national agencies and standard-setting bodies.

21. Financial Stability Forum (2000).

22. Litan and Santomero (2000).

23. Arkell (2000–01).

interests that lie behind their negotiating requests) of the need for careful sequencing in market opening.

The second rulemaking challenge is experimenting with emergency safeguards. Developing countries will almost certainly link OECD country demands for further market opening to the development of a GATS-specific emergency safeguards measure (ESM), with a view to mitigating, under conditions of multilateral surveillance and nondiscrimination, any potentially adverse (and unforeseen) effects arising from the liberalization process. The financial services industry seems particularly well suited for such experimentation, given the critical need to maintain orderly conditions of competition in the sector and promote the safety and soundness of financial systems.[24] It also happens to be the sector that members of the Association of Southeast Asian Nations (ASEAN)—the key proponents of a GATS ESM—have consistently identified as justifying the need for emergency safeguard provisions.

Negotiating efforts could thus be directed to adopting, either in the GATS framework per se or in countries' schedules of committments provisions similar to those that govern the progressive liberalization of Mexico's financial markets under NAFTA. Under the terms of the latter agreement, Mexico is allowed to impose market share caps if the negotiated foreign ownership thresholds of 25 percent for banks and 30 percent for securities firms are reached before 2004. Mexico may only have recourse to such market share limitations once during the 2000–04 period and may only impose them for a three-year period. Under no circumstances may such measures be maintained after 2007.[25] It bears noting that Mexico has not made use of such provisions even as the aggregate share of foreign participation in its financial system has increased noticeably since 1994.[26] After experimenting with such measures in the financial sector, GATS members could decide to extend the logic of the approach to other sectors or indeed to develop a generic safeguards instrument.

Finally, the third rulemaking challenge for developing countries is binding the regulatory status quo. One pragmatic means of advancing a traditional contestability agenda in financial services revolves around securing the regulatory status quo, particularly in emerging markets.[27] Currently, some countries exhibit large differences between the level and quality of bound services commitments lodged under GATS and the actual openness

24. Sauvé (2001).
25. Sauvé and Gonzalez-Hermosillo (1993).
26. The latter stood at about 19 percent in December 1999 (IMF, 2000).
27. Sauvé and Wilkie (2000).

afforded by their domestic regulatory regimes. The wedge between countries' GATS commitments and their current regulatory practices is particularly conspicuous in the area of financial services.

A preliminary assessment of the commitments of ten emerging markets under the Financial Services Agreement in December 1997 revealed that "save for actual advances in the field of insurance services, [the Financial Services Agreement] barely goes beyond binding the status quo."[28] A study by the U.S. Department of the Treasury of the principal barriers facing U.S. banks and securities firms in foreign markets in mid-1998 also found that several countries bound their commitments under the GATS at levels below their regulatory status quo. India, for example, bound foreign equity participation in financial services companies at 51 percent, whereas in practice, the government approves up to 100 percent foreign equity.[29] The Philippines bound foreign equity participation in underwriting and financial leasing services at 51 and 40 percent, respectively, while the law already allows for foreign ownership of up to 60 percent in these two areas. Hong Kong, Indonesia, and Korea also made commitments below the national status quo in both banking and securities. Examples of countries that made commitments at the level of their regulatory status quo in one or both of these industries include Argentina, the Czech Republic, Hungary, Malaysia, Singapore, Thailand (in banking only), and Venezuela. Actual practice today is, in all probability, even further removed from countries' financial services commitments, given that much liberalization has been undertaken since 1997 both in the context of IMF-brokered adjustment lending programs and through unilateral domestic reform efforts.[30]

There is thus considerable scope for binding the regulatory status quo in emerging markets under GATS and for raising the overall level of liberalization in financial services trade worldwide. Doing so, however, will require institutional alternatives that alter the costs and benefits associated with binding services and investment regimes at less than the regulatory status quo. One possibility is to close the loophole that currently allows countries to replicate in services trade a form of mercantilism long practiced in tariff negotiations. Accordingly, GATS members could seek agreement on a new framework obligation that would prospectively compel them to lock in the

---

28. Dobson and Jacquet (1998).

29. U.S. Department of the Treasury (1998).

30. For example, Korea failed to incorporate all of its OECD accession commitments into its GATS schedules. One such exclusion was the commitment to raise foreign portfolio investment in listed companies from 23 percent to 100 percent by the end of 2000 (Mattoo, 1998, p. 20).

status quo in all sectors, subsectors, and modes of delivery in which they voluntarily agree to schedule liberalization commitments. Another option is to develop a NAFTA-like ratchet provision, whereby any liberalization measure—whether unilaterally decreed, negotiated in a bilateral or regional setting, or achieved between two multilateral negotiating rounds—is automatically reflected and bound in countries' GATS schedules.

Industry groups have suggested that GATS schedules should also lock in any liberalization induced by IMF or World Bank conditionality programs occurring between WTO negotiating rounds. In the WTO, however, liberalization proceeds on the basis of a broad political consensus. Thus while the liberalization induced under conditions of financial duress has been significant in recent years, any cross-conditionality with the WTO would raise serious (and largely legitimate) objections on the part of developing countries. The political legitimacy and sustainability of such reforms might thus be weakened as a result.

At present, WTO members seem to feel that the benefits they derive from binding at less than the status quo outweigh the costs. The primary benefit is presumably negotiating leverage, as in the case of goods trade. The costs, however, can be significant with regard to trade in services. Such a stance on the part of developing countries (particularly smaller ones) may well deter foreign investment by maintaining needless regulatory uncertainty.

A possible solution might lie in the design of an institutional alternative that encourages countries to narrow and eventually eliminate the mercantilistic incentive to maintain a large wedge, while at the same time providing countries with some means of engaging in the give-and-take of multilateral negotiations. For example, the WTO might grant some form of liberalizing credits to countries willing to bind the status quo or to narrow the gap between current domestic regulatory arrangements and their GATS commitments.[31] Countries receiving such credits would then decide whether to apply them toward negotiations in the area for which they were obtained or toward negotiations in another WTO sphere. Such a mechanism would offer incentives for countries to link their unilateral liberalization efforts (including, in some cases, liberalization pursuant to IMF or

31. The issue of how to treat autonomous liberalization measures already promises to be one of the thorniest issues confronting negotiators as they enter the market access bargaining phase of the GATS 2000 talks. In agreeing on the modalities that will govern market access negotiations under GATS, WTO members recently decided that "based on multilaterally agreed criteria, account shall be taken and credit shall be given in the negotiations for autonomous liberalization undertaken by Members since previous negotiations. Members shall endeavor to develop such criteria prior to the start of negotiation of specific commitments" (WTO, 2001e).

World Bank adjustment programs) with multilateral disciplines. It would also alleviate some of the problems derived from the compartmentalization of WTO negotiations described above. Countries that are unwilling to bind their commitments at the same level as their regulatory status quo would be entirely free to continue doing so; they would simply forgo the opportunity of receiving credits.

The costs and technical complexity of implementing such an institutional alternative are admittedly nonnegligible. A credit-based mechanism would indeed require agreement by all WTO members on how to credibly measure the commercial value of liberalization and regulatory reform efforts across very diverse sectors and institutional settings. Such an endeavor might be relatively simple for sectors in which barriers primarily take the form of border measures, but it might prove exceedingly difficult for sectors such as financial services, in which barriers to trade and investment arise almost exclusively behind the border.[32]

LIBERALIZATION CHALLENGES. Developing countries face four major challenges with regard to liberalization. With the exception of countries with highly developed financial centers and a high degree of Internet penetration (such as Hong Kong, China; and Singapore), developing countries are unlikely on the whole to focus on the liberalization of cross-border trade in financial services and e-finance, despite the clear welfare gains that domestic users can derive from such services and the fact that e-finance activity is indeed picking up in a number of emerging markets. Rather, the first liberalization challenge to face developing countries in the coming round will likely encompass the more traditional contestability agenda described earlier in this essay, which consists of repealing barriers to entry and establishment and reducing discriminatory postestablishment barriers to operation in foreign financial markets. Priority will therefore be given to mode 3 of GATS dealing with commercial presence and investment, as well as to a broad set of commitments relating to national treatment (Article XVII) and market access (Article XVI).

The second liberalization challenge is achieving a higher overall level of bound liberalization. The first round of financial services negotiations yielded fairly modest liberalization in the developing world. While the FSA saw 105 WTO members initiate legally bound commitments in the sector

32. The design of a credit-based system would also need to establish the procedure whereby countries are granted credits: should it be an automatic procedure administered by, say, the WTO Secretariat, or should credit be granted only after consensus among all WTO members has been reached?

(the second largest number after tourism services), few developing countries undertook broad commitments across all financial market segments. They showed greatest regulatory precaution with regard to cross-border trade (modes 1 and 2 of GATS), as did developed countries, and instead focused primarily on commitments on mode 3 (establishment-related trade). A few developing countries—notably India, Malaysia and the Philippines—made use of the FSA to establish precommitments to future liberalization, but most opted to codify the regulatory status quo prevailing when the agreement was concluded. As noted earlier, following the logic of mercantilistic negotiating techniques long employed in goods trade, many developing countries lodged bound commitments at a level well below the regulatory status quo.

To date, no developing country has opened domestic financial markets on the basis of the provisions contained in the Understanding on Commitments in Financial Services, which allows WTO members to voluntarily subscribe to a higher level of bound liberalization in the sector.[33] In part this reflects the collective reluctance to use an instrument brokered outside the formal GATS negotiating context by the Group of Ten countries in the early stages of the Uruguay Round. Although GATS does not specify the degree of liberalization to which a WTO member should commit itself, promoting the use of the Understanding on Commitments in Financial Services among developing countries could result in a more coherent set of GATS commitments in the sector while also raising the overall level of bound liberalization.

The third challenge involves the related processes of phasing in liberalization at an appropriate pace and securing precommitments to financial market opening. The GATS 2000 negotiations offer developing countries a good opportunity to anchor ongoing policy reforms firmly in their country schedules, so as to impart greater permanency to domestic regulatory

---

33. The Understanding on Commitments in Financial Services consists of a predetermined set of commitments, from which exceptions remain possible, covering the following issues: the scheduling of monopoly rights and a best endeavors commitment for their elimination; most-favored-nation and national treatment in public procurement of financial services; cross-border provision of MAT insurance, reinsurance, and retrocession, as well as services auxiliary to insurance; the transfer of financial information, financial data processing, and other auxiliary financial services, excluding intermediation; the right to purchase abroad a wide range of financial services (basically excluding direct insurance); the right of establishment and expansion of a commercial presence; permission for established suppliers to offer new financial services; permission for the entry of certain personnel of established suppliers, including senior managers and specialists, subject to certain conditions; and standstill on certain nondiscriminatory measures.

reform. The ongoing negotiations also provide developing countries with an opportunity to exploit the considerable flexibility that is built into GATS with regard to liberalization matters, namely, by promoting the gradual, orderly opening of their financial markets. Equally important is the possibility of using GATS to forge precommitments to future market opening. With few exceptions, developing countries did not make use of the signaling properties of GATS and the FSA by announcing future market opening initiatives. Encouraging more countries to do so in the GATS 2000 round should be high on the negotiating agenda, as it would allow developing countries to pursue a sequenced approach that combines progressive market opening with a strengthening of domestic regulatory and prudential standards.

Finally, the fourth major challenge for developing countries going into the GATS 2000 round is to be clear on the economywide implications of the liberalization path that they voluntarily undertake in a GATS context. The first round of negotiations, both in financial services and elsewhere, saw a clear bias in commitments toward the promotion (and often the entrenchment) of the market position of existing domestic and foreign suppliers, rather than the advancement of new entrants. The literature on regulatory reform suggests, however, that protecting the privileged status of incumbent suppliers is not the most economically rational policy to follow. Larger welfare gains arise from an increase in competition than from a simple change of ownership, whether through the privatization of public enterprises, the transfer of domestic firms to foreign ownership, or a relaxation of restrictions on foreign equity participation in domestic firms—however much the latter course of action may be desirable given prevailing restrictions in many emerging markets.[34]

The maintenance of undue restrictions on new entry into domestic service markets is increasingly difficult to justify in the face of growing awareness of the enabling characteristics of key service industries such as finance and the mounting empirical evidence on the benefits of competition and regulatory reform in service industries.[35] The debate over entry versus ownership takes on specific characteristics in finance, since foreign entry, as well as incentives for increased market concentration, may be greatest in periods of financial market instability. Such developments may, in turn, call for heightening competition policy activism in the sector.[36]

34. Mattoo (1999).
35. OECD (2001b).
36. IMF (2000).

Political Economy Considerations

The above discussion identified the structure and contents of a possible negotiating agenda on financial services at the WTO. Important questions remain, however, concerning the extent to which such an agenda can be usefully pursued in a multilateral setting. The traditional contestability agenda described in the essay is primarily directed at emerging countries, where most of the market-entry barriers and measures affecting the operating conditions of foreign financial service providers are found. Such an agenda contrasts quite significantly with that arising in much of the OECD area, where the core concerns are the nascent landscape of e-finance and the degree to which GATS can be harnessed to deepen cross-border liberalization of financial services. This area was left largely untapped in the FSA's first incarnation, with the exception of the very limited undertakings of OECD countries in the Understanding on Commitments on Financial Services.

The fact that the traditional contestability agenda is of greater relevance to developing countries may well limit the scope for WTO-brokered market opening. The room for reciprocal exchange, which has served as the basis for successful multilateral trade negotiations in the goods area over the past fifty years, is undoubtedly constrained in the presence of a decidedly one-way negotiating agenda.

Developing countries often feel that they alone make market opening concessions in the financial services sector. For many such countries, access to the financial markets of industrial countries is not an immediate priority.[37] The distinct possibility that a number of emerging markets could develop a comparative advantage in some financial services subsectors in the future is unlikely to change the current state of affairs in the ongoing negotiations.

The tendency for GATS negotiations to proceed along sectoral lines exacerbates the problem of the limited scope for reciprocity in a traditional contestability agenda. The compartmentalization of multilateral negotiations, coupled with the fact that financial services negotiations are typically led by finance rather than trade officials, poses additional constraints on the ability of countries to make credible offers of reciprocity.[38]

Despite its many drawbacks, however, the multilateral trading system remains uniquely positioned to promote and lock in better access to and

37. Dobson and Jacquet (1998).
38. Freeman (1997).

presence in financial services markets around the globe. The main thrust behind greater financial sector liberalization in recent years has largely come from unilateral initiatives. Even if plagued with pitfalls, domestic financial reform has been shown to have a strong positive effect on economic growth and development, including in the OECD area.

The pace of unilateral financial reform will probably accelerate in the coming years, as emerging markets increasingly tap into foreign savings to finance their development needs, deepen their capital markets, and accelerate financial innovation to serve the needs of corporate borrowers and households. The multilateral trading system in general, and GATS in particular, can make a significant contribution toward opening financial markets. It can, under conditions of considerably heightened regulatory transparency, solidify and legitimate reform efforts undertaken unilaterally or in various regional configurations, and it can give countries the opportunity to exploit the trading system's signaling properties by announcing precommitments to future market opening.[39]

There remains, finally, the battle of convincing developing countries that they can achieve sustained improvements in growth and development prospects by making greater use of GATS as a means of anchoring past regulatory reforms and signaling future reforms.

Many developing countries face the political challenge of overcoming domestic resistance to the notion that becoming a more efficient importer of financial services can usefully serve the national interest. The financial industry must therefore stress, in mantra-like fashion, the strong economywide case to be made for a greater (albeit progressive) degree of trade and investment liberalization in the financial sector. This task is all the more important now that the very notion of market openness has come under stinging criticism, as have the institutions through which liberalization is most efficiently pursued and achieved. By assuming this key role, the industry can renew the proud tradition of leadership and foresight it established almost two decades ago in helping launch the GATS journey.[40]

39. Mattoo (1998).
40. Moore (2000).

Appendix A: Supplementaries

Table 12A-1. *Selected Barriers to Trade in Financial Services, by Country*

Type of barrier	Banking	Securities	Insurance
Limit on number of service suppliers	**Brazil:** approval of foreign entry or expansion on a case-by-case basis; since 1999, foreign banks can only enter the Brazilian market by acquiring one of the state-owned banks being privatized	**Brazil:** approval of foreign entry or expansion on a case-by-case basis	**Brazil:** private insurers cannot enter the market until the Reinsurance Institute is privatized
	Chile: licensing of foreign financial service providers subject to economic needs and national interest tests	**China:** foreign firms cannot provide services in underwriting or engage in trading in domestic stocks or bonds	**Russia:** foreign insurance companies are not allowed to sell life insurance
	China: Bank of China enjoys a monopoly on forward foreign exchange contracts		
	India: foreign bank branches and representative offices permitted on the basis of reciprocity and the country's perceived need for financial services; minimum of twelve new licenses for foreign bank branches issued per year		
	Malaysia: freeze on licenses for banks (foreign and local)		
	Pakistan: foreign banks restricted to twenty-five branches		

	Philippines: freeze on licenses for new bank branches; foreign banks permitted to open six offices each Thailand: foreign banks limited to three branches Venezuela: licensing of financial services firms subject to economic needs test		
Ceiling on foreign equity participation	Philippines: 60 percent foreign ownership of new and existing local subsidiaries	Malaysia: 70 percent foreign ownership in fund management companies providing services to foreigners and local investors; 49 percent foreign ownership in stockbroking companies; 30 percent in unit trusts Philippines: 60 percent foreign ownership in securities underwriting, factoring, and financial leasing Thailand: foreign firms are allowed to own majority shares (that is, greater than 49 percent) of Thai securities firms only on a case-by-case basis Pakistan: foreign brokers may join one of the country's three stock exchanges only as part of a joint venture with a domestic firm	Ghana: 60 percent foreign ownership in the entire insurance sector India: foreign equity in domestic insurance companies limited to 26 percent of paid-up capital Malaysia: 51 percent foreign ownership in locally incorporated insurance companies Pakistan: 51 percent foreign ownership in the life and general insurance sectors
Choice of legal structure	Malaysia: foreign banks must operate as locally controlled subsidiaries		Malaysia: foreign insurance companies are required to incorporate locally Romania: foreign insurance companies are required to establish a joint venture with a domestic partner

Table 12A-1. *Continued*

Postestablishment measure		
Argentina: lending limits for bank branches are based on local paid-in capital, not parent bank capital	**India**: holdings by single foreign institutional investors (such as pension funds, mutual funds, and investment trusts) are limited to 10 percent of issued capital in individual firms	**Chinese Taipei**: insurance companies' premium rates and policy clauses are subject to regulatory approval
China: foreign banks can only take local currency deposits from, and make loans to, registered foreign investors	**Indonesia**: multifinance companies with foreign partners are required to deposit 100 percent more paid-in capital than domestically owned multifinance companies	**Pakistan**: capital investments by foreign firms in the life and general insurance sectors cannot be repatriated
Colombia: use of foreign personnel in the financial services sector limited to administrators, legal representatives, and technicians		**Philippines**: coverage for government-funded projects and public and private build-operate-transfer (BOT) projects can only be provided by the government insurance system
Costa Rica: to provide certain services, banks are required to lend between 10 and 17 percent of their short-term assets to state-owned commercial banks or to open branches in rural areas of the country		
Korea: a certain share of banks' loan portfolios (foreign and domestic) must be allocated to companies other than the top four chaebol; introduction of new financial products is subject to approval		
Russia: at least three-quarters of the employees and half of the management board of a foreign bank must be Russian nationals		
Pakistan: foreign banks cannot lend more than a specified amount to state-owned corporations		
Philippines: foreigners cannot participate in rural banking		
Thailand: foreign banks can only locate one branch in Bangkok; expatriate management personnel are limited to six professionals in full branches		

Source: U.S. Trade Representative (2001).

Table 12A-2. *GATS 2000: Summary of Negotiating Proposals in Financial Services*

Category of request	Banking (including securities)	Insurance
Reduction of scope of monopoly rights		**Japan**, International Chamber of Commerce
Cross-border trade (ability of nonresident firms to supply services)	**Australia** **Canada** **European Union**: financial information, auxiliary services (excluding intermediation) **United States**: financial information advisory services **International Chamber of Commerce**: especially trading and financial information	**Australia** **Canada** **European Union**: MAT insurance (including intermediation), reinsurance and retrocession, auxiliary services **Norway**: maritime shipping insurance **United States**: MAT insurance, reinsurance and retrocession, insurance intermediation, auxiliary services **International Chamber of Commerce**: MAT insurance, large construction risks, credit insurance, reinsurance, intermediation
Consumption abroad (ability of residents and firms to purchase services in another territory)	**Canada, European Union, United States, International Chamber of Commerce**	**Canada** **European Union**: excluding direct insurance **Norway**: maritime shipping insurance **United States** **International Chamber of Commerce**: MAT insurance, reinsurance, tourist insurance
Commercial presence (choice of legal structure and equity participation, reduction of quantitative limitations on number of service suppliers, expansion of commercial presence, grandfathering)	**Australia, Canada, European Union, Japan, Norway, United States, International Chamber of Commerce**	**Australia, Canada, European Union, Japan, Norway, United States, International Chamber of Commerce**

Table 12A-2. *Continued*

Temporary entry of natural persons	**Australia**: transfer and employment of company personnel **Canada** **European Union**: including temporary movement of intra-corporate transferees and contractual service suppliers **Japan**: nationality and residency requirements for executives and employees; reduction of limits on number of foreign employees **United States** **International Chamber of Commerce**: definitions of key business personnel; common terms for intra-company transfers; provision for short-term movement of key business personnel
Postestablishment barriers	**Australia**: reduction of restrictions on number and type of products foreign firms can offer in domestic markets **European Union**: nondiscriminatory access to payment systems and funding and refinancing facilities; nondiscriminatory membership in self-regulatory bodies, stock/securities/futures exchange or market, clearing agency **Japan**: nondiscriminatory tax treatment **United States**: improved cross-sectoral and finance-specific disciplines pertaining to the development, adoption and application or enforcement of regulations (including licensing procedures) **International Chamber of Commerce**: nondiscriminatory enforcement of regulation (especially capital and reporting requirements); reliance on home-country supervision for legally-dependent branches of foreign firms; elimination of obstacles to repatriate earnings; elimination of restrictions on foreign exchange; reduction of restrictions on number and type of products offered by foreign firms; reduction of requirements to invest minimum percentage in specific categories of assets; adoption of accounting and auditing standards based on recognized "best policy" standards; nondiscriminatory treatment of foreign insurance firms by state-owned enterprises
Additional disciplines on transparency	**Australia** (especially licensing criteria) **Canada**: clarification of transparency disciplines specific to the financial sector **European Union** **Japan** **United States**: transparency in the development and application of regulations (including public accessibility to regulations and proposals, as well as opportunity for public comment) **International Chamber of Commerce**: transparency in regulation, particularly licensing criteria (including public accessibility to regulations and opportunity for public comment); disciplines to prevent arbitrary actions and sudden changes in regulatory environment
Elimination of most-favored-nation exceptions	**European Union, Japan, Norway**

Table 12A-2. *Continued*

Negotiating modalities and scheduling of commitments	**Canada:** model schedules, request-offer, use of Financial Services Annex (FSA) classification in scheduling
	European Union: scheduling on the basis of the Understanding
	Japan: scheduling on the basis of the Understanding
	Norway: use of FSA classification in scheduling
	United States: use of FSA classification in scheduling

Sources: International Chamber of Commerce (2000a, 2000b); World Trade Organization, (2000a, 2000b, 2000c, 2001a, 2001b, 2001c).

Appendix B: The Emerging Landscape of Electronic Finance

Technological advances are leading to major changes in the global financial landscape. To date such changes have been felt most strongly within the OECD area. While financial institutions have communicated with each other and with their major corporate clients via electronic networks for decades, the advent of open network architectures has enabled them to broaden their activities to reach smaller enterprises and households, as well. One of the main attractions of e-finance for both entrenched financial institutions and new entrants is the long-term scope for cutting costs in the retail supply of financial services. Developments in e-finance have been largely demand driven to date, with new entrants bidding for market shares and entrenched institutions attempting to defend their client bases in areas in which consumers have shown a particularly strong willingness to purchase financial services online. The state of development of e-finance therefore differs sharply across segments of the financial sector. Clients are particularly interested in the online supply of financial services that are relatively simple, take place frequently, and, if possible, are offered at a discounted price. This palette of demand factors has been most readily satisfied by the securities sector, notably, but not exclusively, as regards discount brokering. The online delivery of a range of banking-related services, such as current accounts, bill payment, and credit cards, has also gained importance in a number of countries. Financial services that are complicated, infrequently traded, or based on lengthy contractual relationships—such as insurance contracts and mortgage loans—are rarely traded online. Institutions in these sectors have, however, begun moving parts of their value chains onto the Internet, including services such as price discovery and loan application.[41]

Small and medium-sized enterprises in the most Internet-advanced economies have embraced online finance as an efficient means of conducting a major part of their financial transactions, such as adjusting their positions vis-à-vis banks, asset managers, insurers, and pension funds in real time. The uptake of e-finance among households has generally been slower and more divergent across countries and market segments. The main differentiating factor is clearly the degree of Internet penetration. Differences in the structure of financial intermediation among member countries has also led to different patterns of e-finance, notably a high penetration of online equity trading in North America and a high penetration of online banking in northern Europe.

The supply of e-finance services on a purely cross-border basis has so far been limited, except, to a certain extent, for securities services. Even in the absence of formal legal or regulatory restrictions, such as within the European Economic Area, banks have generally been unwilling to solicit clients on a purely cross-border basis. The preferred strategy for expansion in other jurisdictions remains the acquisition or establishment of a small commercial presence (the so-called click-and-mortar business model).

Cross-border trade has been held back by both demand and supply factors. On the demand side, most customers continue to demand proximity and an established relationship of trust with their preferred financial institutions.[42] Also, differences among national tax systems can complicate attempts to purchase (or sell) financial products across borders. The most immediate obstacle to further development of e-finance is that most households consider that the Internet is not a safe and reliable place to do business. Part of this problem will no doubt be overcome as e-finance institutions gain experience and households get used to the new medium. Other developments could help establish trust, notably in fields such as authentication and digital signatures. Most OECD countries, for example, have either recently put in place legislation that establishes legally binding digital signatures or plan to do so shortly. In addition to acting as a confidence-building measure, this will enable e-finance institutions to offer online fulfillment in areas requiring formal contracts, such as insurance and mortgages.

41. OECD (2001a).
42. Basel Committee on Banking Supervision (2000).

On the supply side, differences in regulatory approaches are an important factor restraining would-be suppliers. Such problems are especially acute in a cross-border setting, where technical obstacles (such as the lack of unified execution, clearance, and settlement systems) co-exist with legal and regulatory impediments. In most jurisdictions, cross-border electronic financial services do not fall neatly under the existing regulatory regime designed for traditional brick-and-mortar financial services providers, with well-designed functional and geographical borders. Cross-border e-finance providers must therefore cope with multiple sets of regulations. Financial regulation and supervision has at times been accused of holding back the development of cross-border e-finance. In some jurisdictions and areas of business, online transactions are likely to be hampered by the reluctance of financial regulators to accept electronic contracts. The cross-border selling of financial services (especially to supposedly unsophisticated clients) is severely restricted in many jurisdictions, whether in the form of e-finance or through traditional channels. Even where cross-border finance is allowed in principle, foreign providers remain subject to national consumer protection rules, as well as to national conduct-of-business rules if business is seen as being located in the host jurisdiction. A special problem relates to solicitation, which is not permitted in certain jurisdictions. Defining what constitutes solicitation in the Internet environment is not a straightforward task, and nascent efforts at regulatory co-operation across countries have yet to come up with a universally accepted definition. Financial institutions share a strong common interest in effective, even-handed regulation of e-finance. In particular, the potential for unsupervised institutions to offer financially related services in competition with traditional, regulated institutions could run the risk of creating an uneven playing field.

Various policy options are being considered in regulatory circles to help secure compliance with regulatory and supervisory requirements while allowing the continued growth of e-finance. Such options include the following: regulatory harmonization in a multilateral context, so as to provide a coherent international legal framework for cross-border e-finance; seal-of-approval labels for service providers operating from countries that meet certain international best practices in e-finance; mutual recognition of regulatory regimes in the field of e-finance on a bilateral, regional, or multilateral basis; bilateral, regional, or multilateral regulatory cooperation through the use of memorandums of understanding (MOUs) or other mechanisms such as joint surveillance and inspection arrangements; and the promotion of greater transparency and clarity in national regulatory regimes through increased use of guidance notes, publication of safe-harbor provisions, strengthened disclosure requirements, the issuing of no-action letters, and the like.

Technological developments will further change the face of e-finance. In addition to the continued use of personal computers, alternative future delivery technologies will include mobile phones and interactive television (iTV). Views differ on the relative importance and commercial promise of such new distribution channels. Interactive television offers undeniable promise, not least because it is likely to be available to a larger number of households than internet-connected personal computers. Not surprisingly, several large financial institutions have recently entered strategic alliances with telecom companies, with a view to developing iTV platforms. The advent of telecommunication service technologies such as the wireless application protocol (WAP) has already made it technically possible to surf the Internet on a handheld device, and the future allocation of third-generation UMTS licenses will boost the availability of this channel. Mobile phones, like iTVs, are available to a larger group of people than Internet-connected personal computers; they also have the obvious advantage of mobility.

The global reach of e-finance has the potential to change the competitive dynamics in various jurisdictions and among different groups of players in financial markets. Together with the general trend toward greater consolidation in financial industries, cross-border e-finance will likely have a major impact on competition and market structure issues. Increases in the use of e-finance could lead, for instance, to a breakdown of the value chain in parts of the financial sector. This process has arguably already started in the field of online brokerage, with specialized entities unbundling traditional brokerage services. Enabling online clients to access all their accounts from one single portal has the potential to lead to a complete commoditization of financial services, at least in principle. Such developments will pose new and potentially complex challenges for regulators in pursuing their core objectives of protecting consumers and promoting the soundness of financial systems. The inherently borderless nature of the rapidly developing e-finance landscape requires active cooperation on the part of financial market supervisors around the world in sharing information on common risks and facilitating the development of sound risk management and other assorted best regulatory practices. Reasonable prudential standards should provide for safe, sound conduct without inhibiting innovation and competition that will benefit the financial industry as well as the customers it serves.

References

Arkell, Julian. 2000–01. "Financial Services and the WTO Negotiation—Issues Raised at the Sixteenth Progres Seminar, Geneva, Switzerland (September 14–15, 2000)." In *Progres—Geneva Association Information Newsletter* 32 (December-January): 5–12.

Association of German Banks. 2001. "Liberalization of Banking Services in the WTO." Berlin (January).

Basel Committee on Banking Supervision. 2000. *Electronic Banking Group Initiatives and White Papers.* Basel: Basel Committee on Banking Supervision and Bank for International Settlements (BIS).

Claessens, Stijn, and Tom Glaessner. 1998. "Internationalization of Financial Services in Asia." Policy Research Working Paper 1911. Washington: World Bank.

Crockett, Andrew. 2000. "Insurance and Financial Stability: What Is the Nexus?" Keynote address to the Seventh Annual Conference of the International Association of Insurance Supervisors. October 10, Cape Town, South Africa.

Dobson, Wendy, and Pierre Jacquet. 1998. *Financial Services Liberalization in the WTO.* Washington: Institute for International Economics.

Financial Stability Forum. 2000. "Report of the Follow-up Group on Incentives to Foster Implementation of Standards." Basel.

Freeman, Harry. 1997. "A Pioneer's View of Financial Services Negotiations in the World Trade Organization: Sixteen Years of Work for Something or Nothing?" In *Papers from the Twelfth PROGRES Seminar,* vol. 2: *Services and Insurance in the International Scene.* Etudes et Dossiers 204. Geneva: Association Internationale pour l'Etude de l'Economie de l'Assurance.

International Chamber of Commerce. 2000a. "Policy Statement: The Liberalization of Trade in Insurance Services." Document 113-2/16 Rev. 2 (May 25). Paris.

————. 2000b. "Policy Statement: The Liberalization of Trade in Insurance Services." Document 113/70 Rev. 6 (December 18). Paris.

IMF (International Monetary Fund). 2000. *International Capital Markets: Developments, Prospects and Key Policy Issues.* World Economic and Financial Surveys, by a staff team led by Donald J. Mathieson and Garry J. Schinasi. Washington.

Jacquet, Pierre. 1997. "Internationalization of Financial Services and Growth: A Preliminary Survey." Paris: Institut Français des Relations Internationales. Mimeographed.

Kaminsky, Graciela, and Carmen Reinhart. 1995. "The Twin Crises: Causes of Banking and Balance of Payments Problems." Washington: International Monetary Fund and Board of Governors of the Federal Reserve System. Mimeographed.

Kawai, Yoshiiro. 2001. "IAIS and Liberalization in Insurance Services." Speech delivered at the European Services Forum. January 11, Brussels.

Levine, Ross. 1996. "Foreign Banks, Financial Development and Economic Growth." In *International Financial Markets: Harmonization versus Competition,* edited by Claude E. Barfield. Washington: American Enterprise Institute Press.

Litan, Robert E., and Anthony M. Santomero. 2000. "The Need for a New Financial Architecture." *International Economy* 14(6): 14–17.

Matoo, Aaditya. 1998. "Financial Services and the WTO: Liberalization in the Developing and Transition Economies." Working Paper TISD-98-03. Geneva: World Trade Organization.

———. 1999. "Developing Countries in a New Round of GATS Negotiations: From a Defensive to a Pro-Active Role." Paper prepared for the Conference on Developing Countries in a Millennium Round, World Trade Organization and World Bank. September 20–22, Geneva.

Moore, Mike. 2000. "Financial Services and the WTO." Speech delivered at the Bank for International Settlements. September 11, Basel.

OECD (Organization for Economic Cooperation and Development). 2001a. "Electronic Finance: Current Trends and Future Prospects." Paris. Mimeographed.

———. 2001b. *Trade in Services: Transparency in Domestic Regulation—Prior Consultation.* Paris. Also available at www.oecd.org/ech.

Sauvé, Pierre. 2001. "Completing the GATS Framework: Addressing Uruguay Round Leftovers." Washington: World Bank. Mimeographed.

Sauvé, Pierre, and James Gillespie. 2000. "Financial Services and the GATS 2000 Round." In *Brookings-Wharton Papers on Financial Services 2000,* edited by Robert E. Litan and Anthony M. Santomero. Washington: Wharton School of Business and Brookings.

Sauvé, Pierre, and Brenda Gonzalez-Hermosillo. 1993. "Implications of the NAFTA for Canadian Financial Institutions." *C.D. Howe Institute Commentary* 44 (April).

Sauvé, Pierre, and Christopher Wilkie. 2000. "Investment Liberalization in GATS." In *GATS 2000: New Dimensions in Services Trade Liberalization,* edited by Pierre Sauvé and Robert Stern. Washington: Harvard University Center for Business and Government and Brookings.

Trebilcock, Michael J., and Robert Howse. 1999. *The Regulation of International Trade.* Routledge.

U.S. Department of the Treasury. 1998. "National Treatment Study: 1998 Report on Foreign Treatment of U.S. Financial Institutions."

U.S. Trade Representative. 2001. "National Trade Estimate Report on Foreign Trade Barriers." White House.

WTO (World Trade Organization). 2000a. *Communication from Japan: The Negotiations on Trade in Services.* Geneva (December 22).

———. 2000b. *Communication from the European Communities and Their Member States: GATS 2000: Financial Services.* Geneva (December 22).

———. 2000c. *Communication from the United States: Financial Services.* Geneva (December 18).

———. 2001a. *Communication from Australia: Negotiating Proposal for Financial Services.* Geneva (March 28).

———. 2001b. *Communication from Canada: Initial Negotiating Proposal on Financial Services.* Geneva (March 14).

———. 2001c. *Communication from Norway: The Negotiations on Trade in Services.* Geneva (March 21).

———. 2001d. *General Agreement on Trade in Services: Facts and Fiction.* Geneva.

———. 2001e. "WTO Services Talks Press Ahead: Members Adopt Negotiating Guidelines at Special Session, 28–30 March." Press Release 217. Geneva.

PART V

Moving into the Future: Potential for Financial Sector E-Commerce

PHILIP TURNER 13

E-Finance and
Financial Stability

A nyone writing about e-finance must beware of being carried away by
fashion. Even in advanced countries, consumer acceptance of online
retail financial services is still relatively limited. Some of the expectations
held only a few years ago have not materialized. So it is not surprising that
the conventional wisdom among most practitioners in the developing world
is that new information technology is not at present likely to impinge much
on the development of the financial industry in most emerging economies.
In particular, the low level of penetration means that the Internet is not considered as much of a threat to traditional banks as in industrial countries.
There is some truth to this: as an *immediate* issue, e-finance is probably not
at the top of the agenda for many developing countries, where policymakers have more pressing issues to consider.

Nevertheless, this view is almost certainly too complacent about
medium-term developments. The new information technology is capable
of transforming the transmission and processing of information, which is
after all the very essence of the banking business. Moreover, no financial system is an island unto itself. The issues that are beginning to confront finan-

This chapter draws heavily on Sato, Hawkins, and Berentsen (2001). Setsuya Sato has been an
inexhaustible font of information on e-finance questions. In addition, I have had the benefit of very
helpful discussions with colleagues in Basel, notably Marc Hollanders, Jochen Metzger (FSF), and
Jean-Philippe Svoronos, as well as Helen Allen of the Bank of England. The opinions expressed are mine
and not necessarily those of the BIS.

cial institutions and regulators in the advanced economies will before long preoccupy their counterparts in the emerging markets. The World Bank has done much valuable work in laying out the issues clearly, and indicating the issues that arise for developing countries.[1]

This chapter is organized as follows. The first section outlines three elements that seem important in any assessment of the impact of the Internet on the financial system. The second section summarizes the likely implications for banks, and the following section focuses on four key risks that seem to arise from these developments. A final section considers some issues that arise for regulators.

Three General Observations

Three general observations need to be made at the outset. One is that the Internet promises a revolution, not just one more development in the progress of automation. Second, the exact nature of future changes and their impact on the financial system are quite uncertain. Such uncertainty has several implications for firms and for policymakers. Third, the financial system's need for deep infrastructural support is likely to be even greater with the Internet than before. This has major implications for the developing world.

The Revolution of the Internet

The Internet, allied with the other innovations made possible by information technology advances, has the potential to revolutionize the financial industry. In all likelihood, it will prove to be much more than just another incremental change in the ways of doing business. Earlier progress in information technology had the effect of making it progressively cheaper to process information (facilitating the development of new financial instruments) and to transmit information (which make it less and less feasible to isolate domestic financial markets from global forces). The continued decline in the cost of computing and processing power can be expected to accentuate these well-established trends.

The spread of the Internet promises an even more radical change. In the pre-Internet era, the electronic technologies employed by the financial services sector were generally based on proprietary networks and standards

1. See, in particular, Claessens, Glaessner, and Klingebiel (2000).

Table 13-1. *Banking Costs per Transaction*
U.S. dollars

Service	BAH	GSBCG
Physical branch	1.07	1.06
Phone	0.54	0.55
ATM	0.27	0.32
PC-based dial-up	0.02	0.14
Internet	0.01	0.02

Sources: Booz, Allen & Hamilton (BAH) "Booz Allen's Worldwide Survey Revealed a Huge Reception Gap between Japanese and American/European Banks Regarding Internet Banking," 1997 (www.bah.com/press/jbankstudy.html); Goldman Sachs & Boston Consulting Group (GSBCG) cited in graph in Claessens and others (2000).

with *restricted access*. The Internet, however, relies on *open networks* and standards. This shift from closed to open systems is crucial for at least three reasons. One is that it allows vastly cheaper and easier direct access by consumers. By contrast, earlier technological changes affected primarily the professionals who operate in wholesale markets. Some indications of the relative costs of different delivery mechanisms are given in table 13-1. Second, it also introduces a whole new dimension to international trade in financial services that will be much harder for governments to control. Finally, new business models will become viable and some older ones will become uneconomic, leading to major changes in the financial structure.

However, the view that the Internet is likely to be revolutionary in its impact does not mean that financial systems everywhere are going to be transformed overnight. Access to personal computers and to the Internet varies enormously between countries (table 13-2 gives some comparative measures). Within many developing countries, use of the Internet will remain the privilege of the elite for many years.

Nor does it mean there will not be reversals as firms swept along with "irrational Internet exuberance" are forced to retrench. The last couple of years have witnessed an enormous swing in sentiment toward e-commerce from almost frenzied overoptimism to much greater realism, and even pessimism. A huge number of companies were created and many since died without generating any profit. That the financial industry so far has been largely spared this cycle of entrepreneurial creation and destruction is partly thanks to the prudential limits on entry into the banking business through licensing rules.

Table 13-2. *Banking and the Internet*

Country	Percentage of bank customers using online banking (late 1999)	Internet users as a percentage of population (1999)	Personal computers per thousands of persons (1999)	Internet hosts per thousands of persons (July 2000)
China		1	12	0
India	11	0	3	0
Russia		2	37	2
Hong Kong	5	36	298	18
Singapore	5	24	437	39
Indonesia	0	0	9	0
Korea	13	23	182	10
Malaysia	<1	7	69	3
Philippines	<1	1	17	0
Thailand	1	1	23	1
Argentina	3	2	49	5
Brazil	5	2	36	4
Chile	10	5	67	3
Colombia	<5	2	34	1
Mexico	3	2	44	5
Peru		2	36	0
Venezuela		2	42	1
Czech Republic	1	7	107	13
Hungary	6	6	75	13
Poland	1	5	62	7
Israel	<10	13	246	26
Saudi Arabia	<1	1	57	0
South Africa		4	55	4
Memo items				
Finland	20	41	360	136
Sweden	31	41	451	70
United Kingdom	6	21	303	35
Germany	12	18	297	23

Sources: BIS questionnaire; Claessens and others (2000, 2001); *Economist*, September 23, 2000; World Bank, *World Development Indicators 2001,* table 5.10.

Uncertainty about the Nature of Change

The second major general point is that the precise nature of developments in an Internet-based financial system is almost impossible to predict. It is difficult to know which technologies will work best, how customers will respond, how aggressive foreign financial firms will be, and so on. The fast pace of developments means that there is considerable uncertainty about which parts of the financial system will feel the greatest stress. How quickly institutions will have to adapt to changes remains uncertain. From what we have learned so far, the adoption of online delivery seems to differ across sectors, mainly reflecting the complexity and time-sensitivity of the product or service. For instance, the advantage of real-time transactions is clear in the case of securities and foreign exchange dealing, but less evident for mortgages or the sale of insurance products.

Uncertainty about the nature of the prospective changes has some major implications for both the private and the public sector. The *private sector* would be prudent to maintain a questioning attitude about specific information technology (IT) developments. It is wise to recall examples of earlier overestimation of demand for technical products such as smart cards. Although many electronic purse pilot schemes are still in place, the customer resistance they have encountered has turned initial euphoria into, at best, cautious optimism. Another example would be pure Internet banks, which have had only limited success so far.

In making IT investment decisions, firms need to balance two conflicting considerations. On the one hand, technology is constantly changing and prospective returns on new technology may be undermined by still newer technology. Moreover, technological progress may lower barriers to entry so that the prospective rents to be earned by innovating can be quickly driven down by competition. This means that expected future returns need to be heavily discounted. On the other hand, so-called network effects may create "first-mover" advantages that encourage market players to adopt quickly the latest technology, without awaiting a full evaluation of costs and benefits. The difficulties that many telecommunications, media, and technology companies have experienced in recent months seems to weigh the balance more heavily in the direction of caution. Attempting to be ahead of the pack in introducing the newest technology may not bring long-term profits to the leading companies because other companies follow. Decisions will be difficult because none of these considerations is easy to quantify.

The *public sector* faces a dilemma too. On the one hand, the authorities cannot predict the future shape of the financial industry. This argues against regulatory actions that risk stifling the process of innovation. On the other hand, there is a danger of new unregulated developments going too far, too quickly. It may then be more difficult to introduce prudent guidelines: once out of the bottle, the genie may be difficult to put back. Balancing these two concerns is not easy. In principle, the public sector should be "technology-neutral," neither favoring nor hindering particular technical approaches. "Technology-neutral" has rightly been the guiding principle of some recent legislation (such as the U.K. Electronic Communications Act, 2000, which gave legal status to digital signatures). But what this means in practice is not always easy to define. It is often said that many European countries favor limiting e-finance to regulated institutions. The United States, on the other hand, tends to favor a more hands-off approach in dealing with the types of institutions that deliver financial products and types of delivery channels used. Yet U.S. supervisors have been strong advocates of the systematic on-site inspection of unregulated service providers. (The issue of whether or how to supervise technology providers is difficult and is considered further later in the chapter.)

Need for Deep Infrastructure Support

The third general remark is that sound financial system development using Internet technology will be even more dependent on the existence of a solid supporting infrastructure. The cone in figure 13-1 illustrates a conceptual e-finance structure, with six basic layers:

—*Online products*, the financial services and products being exchanged online.

—*Intermediaries*, the entities that produce financial services and products or deliver them.

—*Exchanges and trading systems*, the market coordination environment within which buyers meet sellers and negotiate over prices.

—*Clearing and settlements systems*, a mechanism to send, execute, and settle orders (including payments).

—*Legal and regulatory framework*, a nexus of rules governing rights and obligations of parties to transactions and supervisory framework, a set of mechanisms ensuring the implementation of the legal and regulatory framework.

Figure 13-1. *E-Finance's Six-Layer Structure*

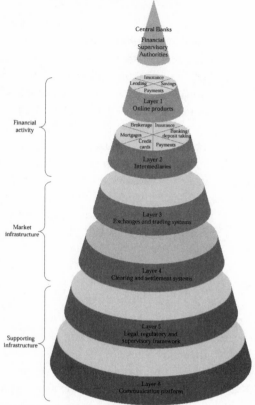

Source: Sato and others (2001).

—*A communication platform*, carrying messages about prices, quantities, service, or product characteristics.

Developing the infrastructure will provide a very demanding policy agenda for many emerging market countries. Although this chapter focuses mainly on the implications for regulation or supervisors, it bears stressing that legal questions have assumed central importance. A fundamental issue is whose courts have jurisdiction and whose laws apply to an institution offering virtual services, or to a transaction concluded over the Internet. *Jurisdictional predictability*, if not certainty, is critical in allowing the participants to consummate electronic financial transactions without undue concern over the legal risks, the means of enforcement, and the rules of dispute resolution. If the fear (founded or not) of breaching some law prevents agents from using the full potential of the Internet, then some inefficiency is created.

Some countries are developing new sets of principles and concepts to address these questions, covering both banking/payment services and securities businesses.[2] One with particular relevance for supervision is the concept of "targeting." Language, graphics, and software of a specific website could be used as a basis for judging whether a website is targeted to a particular jurisdiction and whether the service provider in question is aware that contracts may be subject to its rules. While most of the issues raised by e-finance do not significantly differ from classical conflict of law questions addressed by cross-border finance, some are new. This is particularly true in the case where the geographical location of the parties concluding a contract over the Internet cannot be determined. The resolution of the jurisdictional uncertainties in cyberspace may therefore require reconciliation of a wide variety of factors and national interests.

Implications for Banks

Of the many possible implications for banks, three of the most important are probably: the increased entry of nonfinancial institutions into the banking industry, significant change in the underlying business model of banking, and greater financial sector consolidation, both among domestic firms and across borders. Each of these developments poses new challenges and dilemmas for regulators.

Increased Entry of Nonfinancial Firms

The Internet is likely to blur still further the distinction between banks and other information-intensive enterprises. The trend to de-couple the creation of financial products from their distribution is being intensified. Firms now find it easier to retail products they have not themselves produced. Though it remains an open question how much further this integration of financial activities will progress, the boundaries between banks, brokers, and insurers are likely to be further eroded. One force behind this is increasing consumer demand for personalized asset management services, which is pushing banks to respond with products that cross financial boundaries. These "hybrid financial services" are nothing new, but the advent of tech-

2. American Bar Association (2000); Vartanian (2000).

nologies such as fixed and mobile Internet as well as digital TV promises to transform both their design and their delivery.

Perhaps the key factor that acts as a limitation on this progress is the importance of the public trust for any financial institution, especially for banking. Indeed, the difficulties in securing public acceptance explain why pure Internet banks have not been very successful to date. It has become clear that a good brand name and a large portfolio of clients serve as two potent barriers to entry into the banking business. One recent survey showed that even the most promising demographic groups—such as young, educated, wealthy, active consumers of financial services—are unlikely to switch to technology firms for financial products. A "brand premium" is probably the best protector of established banks against pure Internet banks. The fact that some banks that started as pure Internet operations have opened physical branches as "relationship enhancers," or acquired ATM networks for the consumers' cash withdrawal and deposit convenience, illustrates the continuing importance of physical presence. The implication is that the choice is not that of "clicks-versus-bricks": it may be clicks and bricks that will have the ultimate advantage.

There is, however, an important wrinkle on this argument that could have major implications for regulators. It is that the need to inspire the trust of the public does not necessarily favor existing banks because firms that have built up consumer trust and achieved a high degree of name recognition in other lines of business (for example, Siemens, Sony, General Electric) may also command confidence. While hardly unique to e-finance, the increasing reliance on untested and sophisticated technology implies a greater need to have a brand name that the public knows and trusts to deliver high-tech services reliably. It may lead to new forms of conglomerate that bring together financial and nonfinancial companies.

The most serious challenge to the banking industry probably comes from the entry of telecommunication companies that already possess the necessary IT skills, exercise command over an important delivery channel, and have built an extensive customer base. This probably explains why banks in the industrial world have been so interested in alliances or joint ventures with telecom companies. For emerging markets, this trend can be expected to give added impetus to policies designed to make local telecom companies more competitive, including privatization and deregulation.

A major challenge for bank supervisors that arises from this is deciding how far to explore and monitor the business activities of such conglomerates (or of allied companies). This poses a difficult dilemma of

principle. Typically, banks both are regulated and benefit from a public
sector safety net. Indeed the existence of a public sector safety net is one
argument for regulation. But does this mean that the expansion of the
scope of regulation or oversight to nonbank firms or lines of business
would create the presumption that such firms would also benefit from the
safety net? Most authorities would—and should—be reluctant to give
any impression that they were willing to extend the safety net at present
available to banks. In addition, several practical issues would arise from
any extension of the scope of supervision. One is the feasibility of adapting supervisory techniques that are traditionally used in licensing new
entry (such as fit and proper tests; the clarification of business plans;
policies on mergers and acquisitions) to different types of business.
Another is that the very meaning of concepts such as consolidated supervision would become more problematic in the context of overseeing nonbank activities.

Change in the Business Model of Banking

E-finance has the potential to create new and radically different business
models for banking. This change is in many ways the most difficult to analyze. In the current model, a bank makes use of private information it has
gathered about its customers in evaluating and pricing credit risk. By transforming information gathering and by altering the way communication is
handled, the Internet will make several new models possible.

One example of such a new business model that has attracted much
attention is that of the so-called aggregators, firms that offer customers
one-stop shopping for financial and nonfinancial products offered by a
multiple of suppliers. By monitoring the transaction patterns of their customers, such firms are uniquely placed to observe individual consumption
patterns and obtain information on the financial profile of an individual.
Such information can in turn be used to directly market financial products,
assess credit risk, and pursue other activities. This poses various threats to
banks. Banks may lose their direct links and delivery channels to reach customers. At the same time, banks fear being held responsible for the mis-
handling of confidential customer data by the aggregator.

In a move to counter attempts by nonfinancial players to enter the banking market, banks could capitalize on their brand name and the trust they
enjoy with the public by expanding into services like certification, digital
signatures, and secure communication. An important issue in that context

is evenhandedness in the official treatment of financial and nonfinancial firms. Supervisors are usually reluctant to allow banks to expand into nonfinancial commercial business. But how can and should they react to traffic in the opposite direction?

Greater Consolidation in the Financial Industry

Several elements of e-finance may in effect stimulate financial consolidation, both nationally and across borders. One argument is that the Internet will tend to drive down operating costs in relation to the fixed costs of maintaining the computing capacity needed to sustain Internet-based financial transactions. This could give rise to much greater potential for economies of scale. A second argument is that large client lists made available through consolidation can increase the profitability of the provision of a broad range of different financial products. Third, name recognition also favors big players.

Although these arguments have much force, fully fledged consolidation is not inevitable as strategic alliances could in principle achieve the same goal of saving costs without requiring a full merger. The merger of back-office functions is one obvious case in point. Several banks have indeed begun to cooperate in this way. This possibility may help the authorities in improving the trade-off between reaping economies of scale and the usual drawbacks of increased concentration in the banking industry (reduced competition, greater moral hazard risks arising from too-big-to-fail perceptions, and so on).

E-banking will probably intensify cross-border consolidation because it allows foreign institutions to expand at minimum cost and maximum flexibility. How easy will this be to resist? In many jurisdictions, foreign banks can offer e-finance only if they have a physical presence in a country. Host supervisors can see advantages to such restrictions in ensuring they retain the capacity to conduct on-site examinations and, perhaps, in ensuring they have assets within their jurisdiction that can be seized if the bank runs into difficulties. But such restrictions are not likely to keep out the big international banks. Such banks could establish a minimum physical presence but use their formidable IT resources to reach much more widely.

Because the resources devoted to foreign e-banking business (staff, computing resources, and so on) can more easily be centralized, the output of banking services can be readily switched from one foreign market to another. It is therefore much easier to retrench quickly from a virtual offering than a branch-based one. If it is easier to retrench, there will be less hesitation about entering.

Key Risks

Regulators and supervisors worldwide need first of all to identify the key risks that such developments entail. A good deal of work is under way in national and supervisory agencies considering how a bank's risk management processes need to be adapted to meet the different challenges of e-finance.[3] The identification of risks is actually quite difficult. Deciding which have key practical relevance now, and which do not, is also hard. There is a paucity of reliable information even about the current situation, let alone good estimates about future growth. While e-broking, some types of e-banking, and some e-trading have spread much more rapidly than earlier predicted, e-money developments have failed to meet earlier expectations of growth. Perhaps it is human nature to exaggerate a little with the importance of new trends. Moreover, what will be a major risk or preoccupation in one country will not necessarily be one in another country where the degree or nature of Internet penetration, for example, is much different. (This has implications for the harmonization of regulatory approaches, as explained shortly).

At the risk of some oversimplification, however, four classes of risk can be identified. The first is the risk of *business miscalculation*, which is always much greater in conditions of profound technological change. Two characteristics of recent innovation may have accentuated this risk. One is that much Internet-related activity has been driven by the hope of long-term profits and the acceptance of high initial costs. The absence of a simple short-term profit test, given limited near-term revenue, makes it very difficult for companies to assess whether their strategy is working. That mistakes can be made is quite evident from the volatility of high-tech stocks and the failure of many high-profile ventures. This means that it can take time before banks recognize that some of their strategies have been mistaken. A second characteristic is the very short time that elapses for many e-finance innovations between conception and production. Much faster innovation may leave little time for conducting pilot projects.

3. For a good example of the development of very specific guidelines, see Banque de France (2000). See also Hong Kong Monetary Authority (2000); and Basel Committee on Banking Supervision (2000, 2001), which is playing a key coordinating role in this work.

The second risk is *operational*, resulting from reliance on a complex technology that bank employees do not completely master. Such complexity means that core processing operations are increasingly outsourced. Banks have on occasions found themselves temporarily unable to complete certain key operations (such as providing up-to-date balances or records of transactions for customers, preparing end-of-period accounts, and ensuring debits and credits are made in time) because of IT problems. Often the resolution of such problems depends on the intervention of individuals or firms based in other companies, sometimes in other countries. This raises a fundamental question: how far, and by what mechanisms, should a bank's management oversee the operations of service providers? The arrangements between a financial institution and a whole chain of service providers—a main contractor with multiple subcontractors providing the various different elements of the IT architecture—have become increasingly complex, creating novel oversight problems. A recent report by the Basel Committee on Banking Supervision suggests that the comfort from outsourcing may be illusory.[4] A related concern is that the concentration of service providers to a relatively small group of vendors would amplify the magnitude of the problem if several banks are using the same system.

The third risk arises from *uncertainty as to the location of the counterparty* in e-finance transactions. Even the question "Where is the headquarters of an e-finance firm?" cannot always be answered easily. Another question is whether location is physical or legal. This obviously greatly complicates the question of defining the home and host supervisor, which is essential for cooperation between different supervisory jurisdictions. The danger of "regulatory arbitrage" could well be significantly increased as financial firms shift their national headquarters to laxer supervisory jurisdictions.

The fourth is *systemic risk*. Because financial institutions use similar software programs, there is a risk that many large institutions could be hit simultaneously. This was the worry about the possible 2000 year bug. A simultaneous problem is a potential systemic nightmare. Computer systems are vulnerable to hackers, even very young ones. So far incidents appear to have been relatively minor and contained. In some cases, however, financial institutions in major countries have hidden or minimized attacks on them in the interests of maintaining public confidence. Supervisors need to be alert to this and ensure that firms make complete and accurate (even if confidential) reports of significant episodes of security failures. Risks may well increase as platforms become more open. For instance, inadequate

4. Basel Committee for Banking Supervision (2000).

segregation between internal systems for retail and large-value payments may allow a breach of the lighter security net around a lower value system (such as a bank's retail website) to allow entry to a high-value system where major damage could be done. Banks in emerging markets and their supervisors may need help from their counterparts in the major countries in dealing with such risks.

A second element with potential systemic implications is that the deeper involvement of greater numbers of new and different firms—including nonfinancial firms—in financial markets may make it much more difficult to monitor the links between the various actors and assess the risks to which they are exposed. As the links between financial and nonfinancial institutions become more pervasive, the sources of possible systemic threats are likely to become harder to identify.

Important work addressing these risks is being undertaken by the Electronic Banking Group of the Basel Committee on Banking Supervision. This group has recently enunciated fourteen key principles for the risk management of e-banking. These principles, designed to serve as guidance to promote safe and sound e-banking rules, are reproduced in the appendix to this chapter. Because the risk profile of each institution is different, the exact approach to be followed will depend on the scale of e-banking operations, the nature of risks present and the ability of the particular institution to manage such risks.

Some Issues for Regulators

I have argued that the Internet is likely to have profound implications for the financial system and, therefore, for the structure and operation of prudential regulation. Yet one of the great ironies of the Internet is that, although it has vastly expanded the availability of information, there are very few reliable data on e-finance itself. The statistics produced by market analysts are generally piecemeal, based on different definitions and assumptions, and are sometimes biased toward optimism. People need to think about designing some internationally consistent way of collecting data about this rapidly developing area. Work is under way at the Organization for Economic Cooperation and Development (OECD) on this topic. A prerequisite for work on data is the development of a clearer conceptual framework for e-finance than exists at present. Nevertheless, the general lines of development that have been sketched out in this chapter do suggest several issues for regulators. Five of these issues merit top priority.

Flexibility of Regulation

Because change in an "Internet-rich" (not necessarily entirely Internet-dependent) financial system is rapid, unpredictable, and (literally) intangible, an approach relying on detailed regulations and prescription is not likely to work. However, this does not mean an absence of regulations. In particular, licensing rules for banks will remain crucial in maintaining high standards in the financial system and building public confidence. But it does mean that the old regulatory mind-set is no longer appropriate. There is a need for guidance, not rules. Different contexts require different responses. There will have to be greater emphasis on operational and reputational risk.

Greater reliance will have to be placed on disclosure. In the past, regulators could protect consumers by simply defining which financial products could be offered in their jurisdiction, and which not. Consumers can now get the financial products they want without the blessing of the regulator. The rule becomes: caveat emptor. For this to work, disclosure requirements need to be raised to a much higher standard and become more common internationally. In addition, rating agencies will inevitably have a greater role in helping the nonspecialist digest ever-more-complex information. Technology of course facilitates the generation of such information but does not by itself guarantee digestion. Finally, e-finance will raise many additional complexities. For example, the question of "What is a bank?" becomes even more difficult to answer. Moreover, the answer could well differ from one supervisory jurisdiction to another. The good news is that advanced technology permits more effective monitoring of the complex issues that technology has created.

Monitoring Service Providers

Even large banks in major countries have come to depend more and more on external service providers. This is a major break from the past, when banks typically built and managed their own proprietary networks and processing operations. This does not of course relieve banks of their responsibility for the integrity of their operations, and this will imply monitoring their outsourced operations carefully. It is perhaps realistic to expect major banks to exercise effective and continuous oversight on these providers. In some countries (for example, Australia), banks are represented on the Board of Directors of their service providers to facilitate such oversight. It is also realistic to expect U.S. regulators to keep a close watch on them (assuming they are able to hire enough staff with the necessary technical expertise). But is it realistic to expect small or medium-sized banks in emerging markets (or their supervisors) to exercise such oversight? This raises the issue of the mechanisms by which such banks can assure themselves of the reliability of their service provider. In practice, many small banks may feel that using a service provider of major banks gives them enough reassurance. But it may not.

An important subsidiary question concerns the nature of contingency planning in the event of a failure of a service provider. Without such planning, there is a risk that any discontinuity in the computing services supplied could lead to a disruption in the operations of the bank. One potentially troubling feature is that increased reliance on a small number of service providers may be creating a new type of concentration risk in the financial system. This could prove problematic, particularly in a crisis.

Containing Settlement Risks

The Internet has increased operational risk. Accidental system failures in, or deliberate attacks on, financial institutions could disrupt the entire settlement and clearing system in which they participate. The information technology infrastructure supporting the settlement of financial market transactions must therefore be entirely reliable. This will require investment in normally redundant back-up capacity to guarantee the safe and orderly operation of banking and financial systems at all times. This is essential to ensure public trust.

Security is critical to allow customers to do financial transactions online. It is important that a "virtually closed" network be built supported by robust technology such as cryptology and digital signature. Progress here has been relatively slow to date. Digital signatures have not taken hold as rapidly as once thought (perhaps because it takes time for new technology to be accepted by the public). As long as online payments are cleared and settled through the existing clearing and settlement infrastructure that complies with "best practice," such as the core principles recently published by the

Committee on Payment and Settlement Systems, the development of e-finance should have only a limited impact on payment system risks.[5]

Indeed, by stimulating the development of more efficient and robust back-office operations, e-finance could actually make settlement safer. "Straight-through" processing will reduce not only operational risks—by minimizing errors caused by human intervention—but also settlement risks by shortening the settlement cycle. However, this will be so only to the extent that systems work reliably. One question is whether the growing concentration of some service providers could itself create problems for payment and settlement systems.

Coordination Issues

The development of the Internet is likely to pose coordination problems for financial regulators even in single jurisdictions because it will further blur the distinctions between different financial sectors as well as products. This will make banks less "special," increasing the need to be aware of linkages across sectors, particularly between banks, insurance companies, and securities companies. This implies a greater need for consultation and coordination among regulators in different sectors. Because depositors are less familiar with e-banks and know deposits can be withdrawn faster, e-banks may be more susceptible to a sudden flight of deposits than traditional banks. The challenges for banks, supervisors, and central banks will remain the same, but the nature of cyberspace may leave them far less time for crisis management and resolution. As just mentioned, as banks become less special, new questions will be raised about various safety nets the authorities provide only for banks (access to central bank finance, deposit guarantees, and so forth). One view is that banks should, as they become less special, be offered less protection.

The challenges for international coordination are even more formidable. A bank that develops an online service no longer chooses which country to service in a way a traditional bank would have done. The bank will reach every country with Internet access, whether intentionally or not. Who should supervise such banks? The supervisory authorities in the world have to face the fact that the traditional home-host understandings about cross-border supervision developed for the physical world are not likely to work

5. Bank for International Settlements (2001).

as well in the virtual world. Responses differ significantly. Some supervisors impose no specific requirements on banks operating virtually in their jurisdiction; others impose requirements if they find evidence that banking services are specifically targeted at their residents. This creates an important degree of legal uncertainty for banks, which may find they unintentionally fail to comply with local regulations. One obstacle to resolving such problems is that countries differ considerably in how far e-finance has developed. This means that potential worries that seem important for one country will preoccupy other countries much less. It will therefore be difficult for countries to agree on the harmonization of regulatory approaches. In such circumstances, the challenge is to devise practical cooperative arrangements that actually work.

The Financial Stability Forum, which brings together national regulatory authorities and international standard setters, has a special role to play in this effort of cross-sector cooperation and coordination.[6] The forum has already prepared a mapping of e-finance issues and international groups working on them. A contact group that comprises chairpersons of the various e-finance working groups of the standard-setting bodies and Basel-based committees has now been established to examine areas where enhanced cross-sector cooperation and coordination on e-finance issues would be beneficial. In time, it may be necessary to extend and formalize the current network of contacts.

Competitive Position of Local Banks

There are at least two points of view about this issue. One camp argues that the Internet will both widen the performance gap between local banks and their foreign competitors (usually much larger and more sophisticated banks) and facilitate foreign bank entry into local markets. The public in many countries may have more confidence in well-known foreign banks than in local banks. The penetration of foreign banks is in any case increasing, and the Internet will probably reinforce this trend. A supporting argument is that even as local banks become more geared to the Internet they will be led to transfer (often labor-intensive) processing operations abroad. In short, an increasing proportion of the value added generated by banking could, according to these lines of argument, disappear abroad.

---

6. More information about the Financial Stability Forum is available at its website: www.fsforum.org.

The second camp has a more optimistic vision: that new technology will help banks in emerging markets to advance much more rapidly from a rudimentary to a fairly advanced stage of development of risk management and other commercial banking functions. Such potential "skipping" of financial development stages would not have been possible in the past, when information processing was not readily available. In addition, computing skills are much cheaper and sometimes better in developing countries than in some industrial countries. And the population is often younger and so find it easier to embrace the Internet. The example of India, where some international banks have placed parts of their back-office operations, comes to mind. Another example is Brazil, where very rapid inflation forced the leading banks to computerize their operations much faster than some European banks.[7]

Moreover, the rapid catch-up phase could be facilitated by the impetus given by the Internet to financial market development. In many developing countries, wholesale markets hardly exist. Such markets could be much easier to establish via the Internet. Local wholesale markets would help local banks manage liquidity and other risks.

There is an enormous potential in major developing countries for rapid development of commercial banking functions offered by alternative delivery channels such as ATMs, debit cards, and telephone, Internet, and electronic banking. Brazil's Banco Itaú, for instance, reports that 1.2 of its 7 million customers now use Internet banking. Despite the still low level of usage of such channels (with the exception of ATMs, which are now very widespread), the vast majority of banks in the emerging economies see such channels as a must for their industry. Banks fighting for some important part of the retail market believe that they have to offer such services as an essential marketing tool, although the true demand for them has so far been limited in most countries. Given the economies of scale involved, banks in many emerging economies are under pressure to merge or build alliances with domestic or foreign-owned banks and technology companies to share the costs and exploit the benefits of the development of new IT applications. As international competition in the provision of financial services intensifies, rather fundamental questions arise about the implications of the doctrine of comparative advantage for developing countries that lack the infrastructure or the size to sustain a competitive financial industry.

7. Pomerleano and Vojta in chapter 3 of this volume suggest that back-office operations tend to be concentrated in certain regional operation centers, as in the case of Singapore.

Conclusion

The Internet revolution is just beginning to affect the financial industry. There is much to learn about the process that is under way. Financial firms worldwide, including those in developing countries, need to follow closely how developments related to the Internet are likely to affect their business operations. Nor is it ever too soon to start thinking about the risks that could arise as Internet-based intermediation spreads more widely. Some of these risks are new; others represent the intensification of well-known risks.

The Internet will probably reinforce the competitive pressures that financial institutions in the developing world already feel from major financial firms in the developed countries. Nevertheless, the new technology is likely to create new opportunities. Those institutions and countries that frame policies with their eyes wide open to these developments will do best.

Appendix: Principles for Risk Management of Electronic Banking

1. The Board of Directors and senior management should establish effective management oversight over the risks associated with e-banking activities, including the establishment of specific accountability, policies, and controls to manage these risks.

2. The Board of Directors and senior management should review and approve the key aspects of the bank's security control process.

3. The Board of Directors and senior management should establish a comprehensive and ongoing process of due diligence and oversight for managing the bank's outsourcing relationships and other third-party dependencies supporting e-banking.

4. Banks should take appropriate measures to authenticate the identity and authorization of customers with whom it conducts business over the Internet.

5. Banks should use transaction authentication methods that promote nonrepudiation and establish accountability for e-banking transactions.

6. Banks should ensure that appropriate measures are in place to promote adequate segregation of duties within e-banking systems, databases, and applications.

7. Banks should ensure that proper authorization controls and access privileges are in place for e-banking systems, databases, and applications.

8. Banks should ensure that appropriate measures are in place to protect the data integrity of e-banking transactions, records, and information.

9. Banks should ensure that clear audit trails exist for all e-banking transactions.

10. Banks should take appropriate measures to preserve the confidentiality of key e-banking information. Measures taken to preserve confidentiality should be commensurate with the sensitivity of the information being transmitted or stored in databases.

11. Banks should ensure that adequate information is provided on their websites to allow potential customers to make an informed conclusion about the bank's identity and regulatory status of the bank before entering into e-banking transactions.

12. Banks should take appropriate measures to ensure adherence to customer privacy requirements applicable to the jurisdictions to which the bank is providing e-banking products and services.

13. Banks should have effective capacity, business continuity, and contingency planning processes to help ensure the availability of e-banking systems and services.

14. Banks should develop appropriate incident response plans to manage, contain, and minimize problems arising from unexpected events, including internal and external attacks, that may hamper the provision of e-banking systems and services.

References

American Bar Association. 2000. *Achieving Legal and Business Order in Cyberspace: A Report on Global Jurisdiction Issues Created by the Internet.* Jurisdiction in Cyberspace Project. July.

Bank for International Settlements, Committee on Payment and Settlement Systems. 2001. *Core Principles for Systemically Important Payment Systems.* Available from www.bis.org.

Banque de France. 2000. *Internet: The Traditional Consequences.* Available from www.banque-france.fr.

Basel Committee on Banking Supervision. 2000. *Electronic Banking Group Initiatives and White Papers.* October. Available from www.bis.org.

———. 2001. *Principles for Risk Management of Electronic Banking.* March. Available from www.bis.org.

Claessens, Stijn, Thomas Glaessner, and Daniela Klingebiel. 2000. "Electronic Finance: Reshaping the Financial Landscape around the World." Financial Sector Discussion Paper 4. Washington: World Bank.

———. 2001. "E-Finance in Emerging Markets: Is Leap-Frogging Possible?" Financial Sector Discussion Paper 7. Washington: World Bank.

Hong Kong Monetary Authority. 2000: "Guideline on the Authorisation of Virtual Banks." *HKMA Quarterly Bulletin* 23 (May): 46–51.

Sato, Setsuya, John Hawkins, and Aleksander Berentsen. 2001. "E-Finance: Recent Developments and Policy Implications." In *Tracking a Transformation: E-Commerce and the Terms of Competition in Industries.* Brookings. Forthcoming.

Vartanian, T. P. 2000. "A Global Approach to the Laws of Jurisdiction in Cyberspace." Testimony to the Subcommittee on Courts and Intellectual Property of the Committee on the Judiciary, U.S. House of Representatives, June 2.

TOM GLAESSNER
ED HOROWITZ
ROBERT LEDIG
ED RITCHSER

14

E-Commerce Issues and Challenges for Emerging Markets

The future of e-commerce in emerging markets is bright, but also clouded by a number of legal and technological uncertainties. To some extent, the uncertainties can be resolved by examining the course of e-commerce in the developed countries, where it was launched and has been so successful. But in other respects, countries and societies in the developing world will have to find their own ways of using e-commerce to afford consumers and businesses the benefits of lower cost and added convenience that the Internet is now bringing to the developed world. In this closing chapter, four knowledgeable experts on e-commerce offer their views of some of the issues and challenges that confront emerging markets on this important subject.

Tom Glaessner

To be successful in e-commerce, any country must have an effective communications infrastructure, security privacy infrastructure, contract enforcement, and good corporate governance. Many countries in the developing world do not yet meet all these conditions.

Data on the extent of e-commerce in developing countries generally are not available and even in the developed world are spotty. Governments must step up their efforts to collect such data. Counting Internet "hits" or the numbers of online accounts is not enough. They need to establish a consistent methodology for measuring such concepts as Internet penetration and electronic provision of different financial services.

What data do exist show that Internet penetration is increasing and the e-business environment is improving, while economic integration and migration of capital is growing and moving from developing to developed countries. Connectivity growth rates are often very rapid for emerging markets, as shown by the Economist Intelligence Unit (EIU) index. Data on Africa remain poor, although the fragmentary evidence from that continent suggests the growing importance there of mobile phones.

Meanwhile, the flows of investment capital to emerging markets continue, increasing rapidly during the 1990s. The overall trading in American Depository Receipts (ADRs) now exceeds U.S.$1 trillion. The huge migration of capital offshore has led to co-integration, meaning that many types of stock price indexes are highly correlated. This pattern suggests that it may be more important for investors to diversify across economic sectors than across countries.

In the countries where Internet penetration is highest, such as Norway and Sweden, online banking is showing strong growth. Data for online banking in most other countries are very inconsistent. But because the definition of the customer base varies from country to country, the numbers are difficult to interpret. In Turkey, for example, banks generally have not been performing well, and the numbers for online banking vary widely across banks.

A fairly careful examination of the penetration of e-banking and e-brokerage in a sample of countries suggests somewhat surprisingly that developed and developing countries differ very little in these areas. A contributing factor may be that in this sample Hong Kong and Singapore, where Internet penetration is relatively high, were classified as developing countries. We also found that e-brokerage is narrowing the net interest margin significantly in both developed and developing countries.

Looking ahead, the growth of e-commerce in the developing world is likely to depend heavily on the regulatory framework for telecommunication as well as the broader business environment. In particular, security on the Internet—which is related to privacy, authentication, and the enforcement of contracts—will be more important than laws governing the financial sector or market structure. Privatization of telecommunications companies also remains important, as is the licensing of new telecommunications firms. To ensure workable competition, the new firms must be allowed to interconnect with incumbent monopolies, at reasonable rates. Chile and Peru have experimented with specialized funds that auction off the rights to subsidies to develop telecommunication services in low-income and rural areas, and policies of this sort might also be appropriate.

As for Internet security, governments must step in to define standards and to determine whether certification authorities should be public or private. Governments must also set appropriate penalties for securities infractions. Our survey work suggests that present penalties are not stiff enough compared with those for other forms of theft. Another aspect of improving security is working to improve authentication. South Africa uses biometrics to identify people and give them access to a unique e-mail account.

Improving information and privacy standards is related to security. Privacy policies must ensure four things: notice to the consumer, choice, access, and security. The United States generally has a self-regulatory approach to information and privacy standards, although the Congress recently imposed some privacy rules for financial information held by most types of financial institutions. The European Union appears to have even tougher requirements, and (at this writing) it is still at odds with the United States on this subject. Risk management for consumers, investors, and institutions also is a top priority. Our survey of twenty-seven developed and developing countries suggested that increased sharing of both positive and negative credit information could improve risk management. Cooperation between the public and private sectors would contribute to this objective. Internet disclosures about timing and the release of information, online order routing, and investment advice and all complex areas that must be addressed in the area of investment protection are already available, and all improve risk management.

As e-finance grows, governments must reassess their approach to financial regulation and supervision. There will need to be more emphasis on functional as opposed to institution-based regulation, to competition policy in the provision of financial services, and to the development of key information, legal, and technology infrastructure. More broadly, there may be less need for direct government intervention altogether, and the government will increasingly have to act as an enabler via what it does to create a conducive environment for e-finance.

Ed Horowitz

In today's business environment, commerce requires the movement of money (configuring it in the right currency as one travels across borders). But it also defines the "know-your-customer" environment. That environment and its rules are very stringent. They are placed on banks and financial institutions by governments, and the strictness of the rules means it is easy to get into trouble with regulators and legislators. The complexity of the challenge increases in a global environment, especially as financial institutions enter nonfinancial activities.

Financial institutions use people-based organizations to contact each individual involved in a transaction. Cross-border transactions require similar relationships. Trust between financial institutions preserves the integrity of transactions. This network of relationships allows financial organizations to know the individuals they are serving.

There are similar rules in the consumer world, but many more transactions, in smaller amounts, are involved than in the case of commercial dealers. The large numbers of consumer transactions require a secure payment system, which has led to the development of credit cards. Because credit card transactions are completed between institutions, there is no need for all institutions to know each of the customers involved.

Banks have taken the "know-your-customer rule" they use in the corporate environment and transferred it to the consumer realm. As a result, banks impose relatively strict requirements on individuals who set up credit or debit accounts. Then there are rules established by cooperatives that facilitate certification and authentication of customers in physical environments. Those rules rely on the merchant to certify identity. Moving away from a physical environment to a phone or mail-order environment stretched these rules, and as a result fraud increased. Institutions and merchants responded by using the time delay between the placement and fulfillment of orders to check out the authenticity of consumers and their ability to make payment.

The Internet adds considerable complexity to the payments environment because now each computer becomes the source or destination of a transaction. Both buyers and sellers must be able to certify and authenticate each other in order to decide whether to conduct business. Also both must be connected to a payment system in which the know-your-customer rule still applies. In my view, the industry is still struggling with this. Fraud is high. Only about 5 percent of those with access to the Internet conduct financial transactions, and of those 5 percent, 70 percent abort their transactions. The increase in "endpoints" complicates billing. Eavesdropping and theft of electronic information are a problem. But Internet-based commerce and payment are inevitable.

Looking ahead, we must establish international rules of authentication and certification. Those rules must respect the current know-your-customer environment. Local banks, telecommunications companies, and technology firms all must be involved in developing the rules. Agreements between telecoms and banks can provide the requisite know-the-customer link and rely on existing relationships between cross-border financial institutions. The process requires connecting a person to a private code and to a web address or phone number, then connecting that system to an account with funds. There are companies that have the security technology to support such a system. Telecom companies could easily extend their relationships with customers to include the provision of electronic wallets.

The importance of capital has recently been underscored by Hernando De Soto, in his book, *The Mystery of Capital: Why Capitalism Triumphs in the West and Fails Everywhere Else*. De Soto writes,

> Imagine a country where nobody can identify who owns what, addresses cannot be easily verified, people cannot be made to pay their debts, resources cannot conveniently be turned into money, ownership cannot be divided into shares, description of assets are not standardized and cannot easily be compared, and the rules that govern property vary from neighborhood to neighborhood or even from street to street. You've just put yourself in the life of a developing country or a former Communist nation. More precisely, you've imagined life for 80 percent of its population.

What is lacking in developing countries is a method of connecting people's assets with a system in which they can conduct legally enforceable transactions based on property rights. I suggest the World Bank take advantage of technology to establish a micro-lending experiment in the most impoverished nations of the world in order to unleash the value of property. The Bank could design a five- to ten-year experiment, involving micro-lending experts, sociologists, anthropologists, and teachers. By teaching people about how to conduct commerce beyond their existing physical space, we can educate a new generation about how they can make more transactions and improve upon their current economic situations. This is my challenge to the World Bank.

Robert Ledig

The Internet creates global geographic reach. Websites are simultaneously and instantaneously accessible to Iowa farms and the Falkland Islands in ways that television and printed media are not. This high visibility in both directions has important implications for globalization as it dramatically increases opportunities for interaction between developed and developing countries.

The Internet also makes activities more visible. Financial service providers in developed countries that deal with wealthy clients in developing countries now have a new and possibly more effective way to service them via the Internet. But doing that may make service providers' operations more visible and subject them to the jurisdictions of the developing countries in new ways.

Firms have two options when dealing with clients in other countries. They can position themselves outside the country and serve the client from without, which raises jurisdictional issues about whether they are obligated to comply with the law of the countries of their customers. Or they can set up shop within the countries they want to serve. The Internet makes it far easier to pursue the first option.

Developed countries may believe that developing countries offer a base for objectionable activities. Developed country clients may be serviced in developing countries in ways to which the developed countries are opposed, but those activities could create wealth in developing countries. This tension is increasing as firms in the developing world are now much better able to contact and service clients in developed countries.

Jurisdiction is key in Internet regulation, and levels and methods of regulation vary greatly across developed and developing countries and between jurisdictions, so that the same service may be performed differently and be subject to different regulations and protections in developing countries. Two types of jurisdiction affect Internet commerce. Adjudicative jurisdiction means a court or plaintiff in a country has the right to bring a defendant into court and enforce orders and judgments against him or her. Prescriptive jurisdiction gives a court the power to apply its laws to an individual's conduct, superseding other laws.

The United States is clearly the leader in adjudicative jurisdiction. The Zippo lighter case in 1997 demonstrated that if a company sells online and knows it is selling to consumers in New Mexico (for example), then a New Mexico court may attempt to assert jurisdiction over the company. This means website operators need to think about things such as choice of forum and choice of law when constructing websites. Companies or institutions can choose which jurisdiction's laws to abide by when writing their terms and conditions, but this choice may not be enforceable, particularly in a consumer context. Companies that do business online can protect themselves by issuing targeted disclaimers making clear that they will not deal with clients in certain jurisdictions and that they screen for such clients.

Companies doing business online also have a challenge in dealing with prescriptive jurisdiction: they may be forced to deal with multiple jurisdictions and laws they do not even know about. Firms now avoid this situation by having country-specific sites that deal with the laws of each country, but this can be complicated because many activities that are appropriate in one country are not legal elsewhere. One example is comparative advertising, which is taken for granted in the United States but is illegal in the European Union.

Another example where the assertion of jurisdiction has become controversial is the finding by a French court that the U.S. English Yahoo site was violating French law by allowing Nazi memorabilia to be available for auction on the site. The French courts required Yahoo to screen all French residents from being able to see the site, or the parts of the site that were objectionable, or else be subject to a fine of $13,000 per day. Yahoo responded by going to court in California seeking a ruling that the French determination was unenforceable in the United States on First Amendment grounds. The company argued that the U.S. Constitution protects Yahoo's right to place anything it wants on its site so long as it does not violate the law in this country. This would preclude the extraterritorial application of French law to the United States. At this writing, the case is pending in federal District Court. Interestingly, Germany considered taking action against Yahoo earlier this year but decided the company was not responsible because it serves only as an auctioneer. In light of these cases, Americans should keep in mind that if the United States wants to assert jurisdiction over companies doing business outside their border, the same thing can happen when other countries do the same to them.

Consider the recent situation in which the Idaho Department of Financial Institutions became aware that a number of Idaho citizens were doing business with an Internet bank based abroad that was widely believed to have ties to organized crime. The Idaho agency accused the bank of not being chartered in Idaho, not being a national bank, and not being insured by the Federal Deposit Insurance Corporation (FDIC). But many state-chartered banks in the United States would also be guilty of not being chartered in Idaho and not being national banks, and Idaho has no law requiring banks to be FDIC-insured. The bank in question eventually folded and the money disappeared, but the Idaho matter nonetheless highlights the dangers of selective prosecution when it comes to online operations.

There are limits to what website managers can feasibly do to protect themselves against different jurisdictions asserting authority. California's code requires businesses serving residents of California to put specific disclosures on their web page dealing with California customers. While this option may work under some circumstances, it is clearly not feasible for global corporations that serve customers from many countries. There are 190 countries in the United Nations, and many more local jurisdictions, and writing disclosures for each, in the appropriate language, quickly becomes a monumental task.

The jurisdictional land grab also is complicated by the fact that the activities most likely to attract prosecutorial attention—online gambling and pornography—are widely condemned on moral grounds in many countries. Judges and regulators seem to react differently, or to set higher standards, when it comes to these kinds of activities. There is a well-known matter in which a case was brought in New York against a company incorporated there that had a subsidiary in Antigua. This subsidiary had a valid casino license from Antigua and offered gambling services on the Internet. At the same time, the New York parent was engaged in illegal securities offerings. The court chose to ignore corporate separateness in order to go after the Internet gambling on the basis that some of its customers of the Antigua subsidiary were from New York, this despite the fact that the Antigua website had a screening mechanism that denied access to users who revealed they were from New York. The court nonetheless overlooked this defense mechanism, finding it was ineffective. The principle that emerges from this case seems to be that, at least in the gambling context, Internet companies are subject to all the jurisdictions in which their customers do business.

Another example of how jurisdiction is applied differently in cases of gambling is a case that was the subject of a feature story on the popular U.S. television show, *60 Minutes*. Three men went to a Caribbean nation and launched a sports gambling site. They were indicted by the Southern District of New York for violations of the Wire Act, a federal law that may prohibit Internet sports betting. One man returned to the United States and was tried and convicted and faces five years in prison, while the other two did not return and remain free in Antigua.

Congress has made some efforts to limit Internet gambling, including the introduction of H.R. 556, the Unlawful Internet Gambling Funding Prohibition Act. Congress, however, does not want to monitor individuals' gambling activity itself, so this bill would make it illegal only for gambling institutions to accept electronic funds transfers originated from the United States.

In sum, the Internet has opened up whole new and controversial areas of the law. One of the most vexing is deciding which jurisdiction's law applies in any given situation. It will be fascinating to see how this develops over time. There is a real danger that if all websites are subject to the laws of all jurisdictions, international Internet commerce could be significantly disrupted, or at the very least, its rate of growth significantly slowed.

Ed Ritscher

I will try to address the question of how technology has affected the business aspect of e-finance. I work for Unisys Corporation, which is a technology provider to the financial services industry. My background, however, is in banking.

E-business affects all parts of the financial industry, especially the banking industry. In particular, the Internet has changed the roles of payment and credit, while creating an added level of liquidity in the capital markets.

As Ed Horowitz discussed, a key question about the Internet is whether a business (or a customer) knows who is on the other side of the transaction. It is inherently more difficult to trust others on the Net because one is not in physical contact with them. One technological solution to the problem of trust is Public Key Infrastructure, or PKI, which enables users to certify other parties. But beyond trust, online businesses must also create customized experiences for specific customers in order to attract them to their sites.

Just as it more difficult for companies to know their customers online, so, too, is it more difficult to know who the competition is. Online customers now deal with many companies, and every bank's customer is now someone else's as well. Financial institutions must be able to turn what may be transitory customer experiences on the Net into long-term relationships. Institutions face other challenges as well. They need to figure out how to protect or create brand equity online. They also must determine which pricing mechanisms work best: auctions or various forms of price discrimination.

The business model has changed too. It is very hard to build revenue and sustain it online. There is a saying that sales is vanity, profit is sanity, and cash flow is reality. Dot coms are generally in the vanity stage. Many have created sales but they have not created consistent cash flow.

Some have questioned whether there is an economic role for middlemen on the Net. I believe there is, but a different sort from what can be seen in the physical world. On the Net, the key middlemen are "aggregators," who compile information from various sources on a single site. Aggregators will play an important role in electronic bill presentment and bill payment. Financial brokers, who understand the whole relationship a customer may have with a financial institution, are also aggregators of a type.

Financial institutions are also facing a new sort of competition on the Net. The traditional banking franchise has changed as telecom companies become payment companies and business-to-business exchanges have enough financial liquidity to fund and create credit finance in the place of the bank. These developments raise the issue of whether telecoms are disenfranchisers or partners. In many situations, they make the best partners because they provide transaction volume.

E-finance is a moving target, a changing business environment, and, at the same time, an immature market. It is also quite costly, although necessary, for financial institutions to engage in e-finance: usually an investment of six or seven figures. Moreover, doing business online requires institutions to cannibalize their old ways of doing business, while requiring the full-time commitment of senior management.

There is still much to do on the payments side of business. The current banking system is not well equipped to handle e-payments. In order to protect their payment franchises, financial institutions must reengineer their payment systems. In a B2B exchange, for example, payments have to be linked to customers' supply chains. E-finance payments systems must also be able to handle trade finance. Today, a letter of credit is probably the most expensive financial instrument in the marketplace. Several electronic initiatives now under way—one by SWIFT and another in Europe—are attempting to develop a virtual letter of credit, which has potential large cost savings. PKI can help solve the authentication problems associated with these transactions. The key to PKI, however, is cost. At the same time, well-funded B2B exchanges can supply their own trade credit and in the process disenfranchise financial institutions. As a result, financial institutions may have to build new franchises with management, online brokerage, and Internet banking service.

E-finance will be relevant to emerging markets, if for no other reason than that is where the big growth in population and incomes is likely to be in the future. Financial institutions need to be ready to serve those markets, and doing so electronically may be the most efficient way of doing so.

Contributors

Jennifer S. Crystal
Federal Reserve Bank of New York

B. Gerard Dages
Federal Reserve Bank of New York

Attila Emam
Securities Commission, Malaysia

Tom Glaessner
World Bank

Linda S. Goldberg
Federal Reserve Bank of New York

Edward M. Graham
Institute for International Economics

Ed Horowitz
EdsLink, LLC

Nicholas R. Lardy
Brookings Institution

Robert Ledig
Fried, Frank, Harris, Shriver, and Jacobson

Robert E. Litan
Brookings Institution

Paul Masson
International Monetary Fund

Donald J. Mathieson
International Monetary Fund

Michael Pomerleano
World Bank

Ed Ritchser
Unisys Corporation

Jorge Roldós
International Monetary Fund

Pierre Sauvé
*Organization for Economic
  Cooperation and Development*

Donald G. Simonson
Asian Development Bank

Ranjit Ajit Singh
Securities Commission, Malaysia

Harold D. Skipper Jr.
Georgia State University

Benn Steil
Council on Foreign Relations

Karsten Steinfatt
Organization of American States

Kar Mei Tang
Securities Commission, Malaysia

Philip Turner
Bank for International Settlements

George J. Vojta
Financial Services Forum

Index